In a historical moment characterized by many crises and
this rich and provocative volume helps our understanding ....s or repression
of progressive protests. Covering a broad range of cases (from the roman republic
to Black Lives Matter and from independentists in Catalonia to Indigenous peoples
in Latin America), the research convincingly shows the vicious circles developing
between the undercriminalization of the violation of the powerful and the over-
criminalization of dissent. An important reading for critical criminologists as well as
for social movement scholars and activists.

Donatella della Porta
Professor and Dean of the Faculty of Political and Social Sciences
Scuola normale superiore Firenze Italy

This book is an outstanding example of the kind of insurgent scholarship we need
in our troubled times. A breathtaking tour de force through the history, the present,
and the futures of social movements on a global scale, Valeria Vegh Weis's Activism
through the Language of Criminality is a must-read for activists, scholars and anyone engaged in the struggle to end the police state.

Alessandro de Giorgi
Professor at the Department of Justice Studies,
San José State University
Editor in Chief of Punishment & Society
Editorial Board Member of Social Justice

This impressive collection of empirical and theoretical interventions show that as
much as policing is a tool to manage unique local challenges to state authority,
there are also remarkable global continuities. Throughout much of the world, police
have become the primary tool for managing social movements erupting out of the
contradictions of neoliberal austerity through a process of criminalizing dissent. This
process is rooted not in the rule of law, but instead in a "state of exception" in which
the perpetuation of state-backed regimes of exploitation trump legal frameworks
and liberal democratic processes. In the end, this volume forces us to question the
fundamental legitimacy of political policing and the political economic arrange-
ments they enable.

Alex S. Vitale
Author of The End of Policing

At a time in which a global police state is in the making, this is a most opportune
book. It must be read by all democrats because democracy is precisely what is at risk.

Boaventura de Sousa Santos
Author of Toward a New Legal Common Sense, Cambridge,
3rd edition 2020

The criminalization of activism, political dissidence and even the criminalization of the exercise of certain professions itself is more and more extensive in various areas of the world. When this work is published I do not even know how the criminal proceedings initiated against me by prison unions will be found for my denunciation of torture in prisons in Catalonia. Teachers, activists, musicians, graffiti artists, poets ... there is no specific profile. Criminalization increases in a similar proportion to the loss of rights and guarantees. But, for that reason, the (collective) struggle is more necessary than ever. As Walter Benjamin pointed out forever, "let us know how to organize pessimism".

Iñaki Rivera Beiras
Professor at the University of Barcelona
Director of the Observatory of the Penal
System and Human Rights

This is a fascinating collection that provides a great deal of valuable empirical information and rich theoretical insights about the ways in which protest and dissent can become criminalized. The case materials cover a broad geographic range and include both contemporary and historical protests. The editor's introduction provides a valuable framework for understanding both the under-criminalization of actions by the state, state agents and powerful elites that harm people and the over-criminalization of actions by the oppressed to survive and resist harm.

Pamela Oliver
Professor Emerita of Sociology at the University of Wisconsin

This is a much required work in contemporary times when neoliberal authoritarianism is involved in redefining the idea of 'democracy' itself. It shows one of the many ways in which neoliberal capitalism tries to exercise control of state over its citizens towards an unchallenged hegemonic ideological order. This dissent is no longer limited to only those who want to overthrow the state but even those who seek reforms that may impact interests of capital in specific ways. This work will go a long way as a reference material for anyone researching on democracy and modern nation state.

Ravi Kumar
Associate Professor at the Department of Sociology,
South Asian University

This book makes a significant contribution to debates in the arena of social movements. It tells us responsible thinking (inside and outside the university) is treated as criminal and repressive brutality against such thinking is endorsed as legitimate activity. This is not a recent phenomenon. It has criminalized society and, has messed up social institutions, public spaces and everyday life. For the activists, it draws attention to the need for perseverance over several generations to make people at large see the creative significance of saying 'no' as a mode of opening up diverse ways seeing and living in this world.

Savyasaachi
Professor at the Department of Sociology,
Jamia Millia Islamia

It would be impossible to over-emphasize the temporal significance of this book. As we enter an era of intensified criminalization of activism and dissent, bolstered by the impacts of the globalized policing of the Covid pandemic and further enabled by a proliferation of Artificial Intelligence, there could not be a better time to reflect on histories of criminalization and the importance of sustained activism in the face of violence and repression. In this edited volume, Valeria Vegh Weis has drawn together an exemplary collection of interdisciplinary scholar-activists focusing on such issues. Concept, theory and action are combined with issues of historic and contemporary significance – from environmental harm to the Nuremberg Trials to Black Lives Matter; India to Catalonia and Latin America, the breadth and depth of this book is astounding. It is essential reading for anyone interested in social control and the criminalization of activism and dissent.

Victoria Canning
Senior Lecturer in Criminology at University of Bristol
Co-coordinator of the European Group for the Study of
Deviance and Social Control
Associate Director of Oxford Border Criminologies

CRIMINALIZATION OF ACTIVISM

Criminalization of Activism draws on a multiplicity of perspectives and case studies from the Global South and the Global North to show how protest has been subject to processes of criminalization over time.

Contributors include scholars and activists from different disciplinary backgrounds, with a balance between authors from the Global North and the Global South. An introduction frames the topic within critical criminology, while also highlighting the possible disciplinary approaches and definitions of criminalization of resistance/activism. The editor also investigates the particularities of the current times in comparison to dynamics of criminalization in prior stages of capitalism. Bringing together a range of criminalization themes into a single volume, compromising historical criminology, Indigenous studies, gender studies, critical criminology, southern criminology and green criminology, it will be of great interest to scholars and students of criminology, social movement theory and social sciences, as well as those involved in activism and with a stand against criminalization.

Valeria Vegh Weis is an Argentinean/German Criminologist and Criminal Lawyer. She teaches Criminology and Transitional Justice at Buenos Aires University, UBA, and National Quilmes University (Argentina) as well as State Crime in Nazi Germany at Freie Universität Berlin (Germany). She is currently a Research Fellow at the Zukunftkolleg at Universität Konstanz, where she researches on the role of human rights and victims' organizations in resistance to state crime. She is also an Associate Researcher at the Max Planck Institute for Legal History and Legal Theory, where she directs the research group on Transnational Criminal Law in Transatlantic Perspective (1870–1945) together with Prof. Dr. Karl Härter.

Vegh Weis holds a Ph.D. in Law and an LL.M. in Criminal Law from UBA and an LL.M. in International Legal Studies from New York University. She has held different fellowships including the Alexander von Humboldt (Germany), the Fulbright and the Hauser Global (USA).

Her first book *Marxism and Criminology: A History of Criminal Selectivity* (BRILL 2017, Haymarket Books 2018) was awarded the Choice Award by the American Library Association and the Outstanding Book Award by the Academy of Criminal Justice Sciences. She is also the co-author of *Bienvenidos al Lawfare* with Raúl Zaffaroni anc Cristina Caamaño (Capital Intelectual 2020) which was translated into Portuguese and English, as well as many articles and book chapters in the topics of criminology, transitional justice and criminal law. She has 15 years of experience working in criminal courts and international organizations.

Routledge Studies in Crime and Society

Sexual Violence on Trial
Local and Comparative Perspectives
Edited by Rachel Killan, Eithne Dowds and Anne-Marie McAlinden

Harm and Disorder in the Urban Space
Social Control, Sense and Sensibility
Edited by Nina Peršak and Anna Di Ronco

Serial and Mass Murder
Understanding Multicide through Offending Patterns, Explanations, and Outcomes
Elizabeth Gurian

Mass Shootings and Civilian Armament
Alexei Ansin

Criminalization of Activism
Historical, Present, and Future Perspectives
Edited by Valeria Vegh Weis

Elderly Sexual Abuse
Theory, Research, and Practice
Eric Beauregard and Julien Chopin

Desistance from Sexual Offending
The Role of Circles of Support and Accountability
Kelly Richards

Oppressed by Debt
Government and the Justice System as a Creditor of the Poor
Edited by Saul Schwartz

For more information about this series, please visit: www.routledge.com/Routledge-Studies-in-Crime-and-Society/book-series/RSCS

CRIMINALIZATION OF ACTIVISM

Historical, Present, and Future Perspectives

Edited by Valeria Vegh Weis

Routledge
Taylor & Francis Group

LONDON AND NEW YORK

"Who protects us from the police?" Photo taken during feminists protests against the police in Argentina in February 2021, following the femicide of Ursula Bahillo and the brutal police repression against her friends and relatives when they were demanding justice Art Cover by Federico Raposo Aloe (Argentina)

First published 2022
by Routledge
Park Square, Milton Park, Abingdon, Oxon OX14 4RN

and by Routledge
605 Third Avenue, New York, NY 10158

Routledge is an imprint of the Taylor & Francis Group, an informa business

British Library Cataloguing-in-Publication Data
A catalogue record for this book is available from the British Library

Library of Congress Cataloging-in-Publication Data
Names: Vegh Weis, Valeria, editor.
Title: Criminalization of activism : historical, present, and future perspectives / edited by Valeria Vegh Weis.
Description: Abingdon, Oxon ; New York, NY : Routledge, 2022. | Includes bibliographical references and index.
Identifiers: LCCN 2021032349 (print) | LCCN 2021032350 (ebook) | ISBN 9780367700126 (hbk) | ISBN 9780367700119 (pbk) | ISBN 9781003144229 (ebk)
Subjects: LCSH: Criminology. | Human rights workers.
Classification: LCC HV6025 .C736 2022 (print) | LCC HV6025 (ebook) | DDC 364--dc23
LC record available at https://lccn.loc.gov/2021032349
LC ebook record available at https://lccn.loc.gov/2021032350

ISBN: 978-0-367-70012-6 (hbk)
ISBN: 978-0-367-70011-9 (pbk)
ISBN: 978-1-003-14422-9 (ebk)

DOI: 10.4324/9781003144229

Typeset in Bembo
by SPi Technologies India Pvt Ltd (Straive)

CONTENTS

List of illustrations   *xiii*

Preface by Dario Melossi   *xiv*

List of contributors   *xvii*

Acknowledgements   *xxiv*

Introduction   1

PART I
Theoretical approaches on the over-criminalization
of dissent   **17**

1   Politics of exception: criminalizing activism in Western
    European democracies   19
    Katharina Fritsch and Andrea Kretschmann

2   A social control perspective for the study of environmental
    harm and resistance   30
    Alida Szalai

3   The criminalization and "innovation" of resistance: looking
    at the Italian case   42
    Verónica Marchio

Part II
Historical experiences on the over-criminalization of dissent   49

4 Avoiding and amplifying the criminal label in the
   roman republic and medieval England   51
   Matt Clement

5 The criminalization of low-rank castes: a historical
   perspective of mahad movement in India (1927–1937)   61
   Kruthi Jagadish Kumar, Praveenrao Bolli, and
   Myrna Cintron

6 "Loyal spear-carriers": police violence in the Queensland
   anti-apartheid movement, 1971   71
   Paul Bleakley

7 The theorem of national solidarity: Italy and the "7 Aprile"
   case: the criminalisation of left-wing dissent   81
   Vincenzo Scalia

Part III
Current cases of over-criminalization of dissent in
the Global North   91

8 Resistance to survive: the criminalization of the Black
   Lives Matter movement   93
   Teresa Francis Divine and Ginny Norris Blackson

9 Between crime and war: the security model of
   protest policing   103
   Paul A. Passavant

10 Fighting for the right to save others: responses by civil
   society to the criminalization of solidarity in the
   mediterranean sea post–2015   115
   Christal Chapman

11 Media representation of Belgian youth protests: the
   making of "Climate Truants"   130
   Mafalda Pardal, Celine Tack and Frédérique Bawin

12 Criminalization as strategy of power: the case of
    Catalunya 2017–2020   141
    Ignasi Bernat and David Whyte

13 Notes from the Field I: State denial to harass the messengers:
    The case of OSPDH/SIRECOVI   153
    Alejandro Forero-Cuéllar and Daniel Jiménez-Franco

Part IV
Current cases of over-criminalization of dissent in
the Global South   **159**

14 Social protest and punitive treatment in argentina:
    an analysis from Latin American critical criminology   161
    Gabriela L. Gusis and Rodrigo F. Videla

15 Colombia's murderous democracy pre- and
    post-covid-19: the assassination of social leaders and the
    criminalization of protest   170
    Natalia Ruiz Morato

16 Violence and violations of rights against leaderships in
    the Brazilian Amazon   180
    Paula Lacerda and Igor Rolemberg

17 An analysis of the criminalisation of socio-environmental
    activism and resistance in contemporary Latin America   191
    Israel Celi Toledo, Roxana Pessoa Cavalcanti, and Grace Iara Souza

18 Notes from the field II: the judicial persecution in the
    Amazonian Indigenous struggle—"El Baguazo"
    —Amazonas-Perú   201
    Saúl Puerta Peña-Pueblo Awajun

Part V
Challenges for a critical agenda on the
over-criminalization of dissent   **205**

19 Artificial intelligence and the criminalisation of activism   207
    Mark Cowling

20 Covid cops: a recent history of pandemic policing
during the coronavirus crisis 216
Greg Martin

21 Punitive feminism (or When and why did we start
dividing the world between good and evil, rather than
between oppressed and oppressors?): Punitive Feminism 232
Tamar Pitch

22 Genocidal activism and the language of criminality:
reflections on the duality of the Nazi era and the avoidance
of engagement with histories of social and political
activism at the nuremberg trials 246
Wayne Morrison

Index *257*

ILLUSTRATIONS

Figures

I.1 Under- and over-criminalization   3
I.2 Case Example I   5
I.3 Case Example II   7
11.1 Timeline of the 2019 youth climate protests in Belgium   133

Tables

5.1 Indian Constitution   65
5.2 Types of Violence Met by Low-Rank Castes for Accessing
     Water in the State of Maharashtra, India, from 1995 to 2011   67
11.1 Search Results   132
14.1 Formal and Subterranean Criminal System   165

PREFACE

Between private troubles and public issues

One of the great, even if unfortunately, now half-forgotten sociologists of the last century, did famously write that one of the uses of "sociological imagination" is the capacity to read "public issues" within "private troubles" (Mills 1959). It is the essence not only of sociology but also of political life to turn what I might see as my "private troubles" into "public issues", that I therefore share with many others. From biography to history. Or, as one of my mentors in Santa Barbara, Dick Flacks, used to say, indeed inspiring himself to C. Wright Mills, from "making life" to "making history" (Flacks 1988). Such a transformation is at the very roots of political consciousness and organizing. At the end of the 19th century, in the Po Valley of Italy, among the very first organizations of the working class, especially among the most destitute, the daily workers, a motto started circulating, "United we are everything, divided we are canaille!". The proletarian who is overwhelmed within his own private troubles is canaille, riffraff, rabble. In one of the most lucid insights of Foucault's "sociology" (Foucault 1975), he is nothing but a "delinquent", when he tries to round up his miserly income by preying on other poor people in his milieu. He is the product of the prison and of the police, who are happier than ever to transform dangerous "illegalities" into a useful "delinquency". Like the protagonist of Jean Genet's *Journal du Vouleu* (1949)*r*, he loves his policeman; he is his mirror-image. Nobody knew all this better than the early (very young) organizers of the Black Panther Party. When Bunchy Carter and John Huggins in Central LA or Fred Hampton in the South Side of Chicago were working with street gangs to help them see the "public" side of their "private troubles", what else were they doing, if not the perennial work of the political organizer, the work of helping the self-understanding of so many Black youths in the inner city streets to develop toward a kind of "class consciousness" (Lukacs 1923)? This is why they had to be stopped.

And barbarously assassinated. And the crimes of their murders were but the first in a very long series indeed, that would then accompany the aftermath of the downfall and destruction of the Black Panthers in the streets of so many American cities, and the concomitant rise of "the crack cocaine epidemic" that followed that demise. During which, so many young Black men lost their lives or ended up in prison, among a renewal of gang warfare—the Bloods and the Crips!—of which the guardians of order complained loudly but that they had actively helped to bring back!

A tough, hardened criminal, in fact, may harm a few individual members of the ruling class, but he is so unbelievably useful to that class as a whole! Jean Genet's love for his police officer was no doubt dutifully reciprocated! Like in J. Edgar Hoover's waiting room, where one of the most precious souvenirs in the relic collection of the father and master of the FBI was the death mask of John Dillinger, the gangster who had been Hoover's main antagonist in the early 1930s, but indeed so incredibly useful to his ascent in power at the head of the FBI! Of course, Marxists as well as Marx-oriented political organizers, have always been suspicious of the "Lumpen element". And yet, as my father used to tell me, during the war and the Resistance the outlook of political party organizers on those who lived in the Pratello neighborhood of Bologna—at the time the place of the local underworld—started to change, because all the traditional skills of the underworld were suddenly in high demand: how to hide and protect a fugitive, where to find lockpicks, how to forge documents, where to get contraband weapons, all the traditional trades of the *malavita* were now suddenly precious instruments of the armed struggle and also the outlook on those who had these skills, and were sharing them, started to change. Not only this, but the comrade-in-arms was obliged by the circumstances to start thinking in ways that were not too dissimilar, after all, from those of the most hardened criminal. *A la guerre comme à la guerre!* Then, decisions of life and death become technical decisions, not much different if one is a patriot, a terrorist, or a mafioso. Indeed, only political victory and defeat often decide whether the fighter is one or the other. German troops hung signs around the neck of the partisans that they had assassinated which read "Achtung Banditen!" But it did not last long, and their chiefs would be paraded in front of a court in Nuremberg as the worst criminals and put to justice. Probably the most popular President of the Italian Republic, Sandro Pertini (1978–1985), had spent many years in prison under the Fascist regime. And, more recently, Nelson Mandela, when, on 10 May 1994, became president of the Republic of South Africa, declared, "We, who until a short time ago, were considered outlaws, have today the rare privilege of welcoming the world's nations to our land."

A struggle for definition of what is a crime and what is a legitimate act of state goes on indefinitely. That is the place where "processes of criminalization" originate! The answer to the Brechtian question about the difference between a gangster and a State officer is the result of struggle (where, certainly, mass media and social networks are increasingly powerful weapons!). As David Matza stated in the closing pages of *Becoming Deviant*, the separation and distinction between political theory and a science of criminology intended as ancillary to law and politics is a fundamental *dispositif* of power and governance. Leviathan can go ahead about its business "even if it goes to war and massively perpetrates activities it has allegedly banned from the world" such as murder and mayhem. But the observer in the public will say "that is a different matter altogether". "So says Leviathan" —Matza concludes—"and that is the final point of the collective representation." (Matza 1969: 197)

Dario Melossi (University of Bologna)

References

Flacks, Richard 1988 *Making History.* New York: Columbia University Press.
Foucault, Michel 1975 *Discipline and Punish.* New York: Pantheon, 1977.
Genet, Jean 1949 *The Thief's Journal.* New York: Grove, 2018.
Lukacs, Georg 1923 *History and Class Consciousness.* Cambridge, MA: MIT Press, 1971.
Matza, David 1969 *Becoming Deviant.* Englewood Cliffs, NJ: Prentice-Hall.
Mills, C. Wright 1959 *The Sociological Imagination.* New York: Oxford University Press.

CONTRIBUTORS

Exploring organized dissent and its over-criminalization is a complex endeavor that demands a multifaceted analysis. Facing this challenge, this book was made possible by contributions from a variety of impressive scholars and activists from different disciplinary backgrounds who were either invited directly by the editor or selected through an open call for chapters. The resulting volume encompasses thought-provoking research by experts in the field of criminology and social movement theory as well as members from grassroot organizations engaged in organized dissent. Moreover, many of the scholars and academics contributing to the book are also activists and dissenters themselves, which allows for a book rich in unique multi-dimensional perspectives.

Responding to the call for proposals, a significant number of chapters are co-authored by Northern and Southern authors. The authors here are from or work in Latin-America (Argentina, Brazil, Colombia, Ecuador, Perú, and Trinidad and Tobago), Europe (Austria, Belgium, France, Germany, Hungary, Italy, Spain, The Netherlands and the UK), Australia, India and the USA. This geographic diversity made it possible to assemble varied views from contrasting realities. The impulse to incorporate authors from the Global South, despite the language barriers involved, is aimed at overcoming the extended reality of Northern scholars theorizing about Southern realities without giving a voice to the latter. Instead, the book was written with the conviction that involving those with a profound understanding of the social, cultural and economic features of their specific locality might open new perspectives and possibilities.

I am proud of the gender, racial, regional and academic age diversity of the contributors here. While some chapters are written by accomplished senior scholars with vast experience in the field, others are authored by doctoral and postdoctoral researchers early in their career, providing the book with novel and fresh perspectives. More than half of the authors are female, which is unfortunately not yet common: women are still under-represented in scholarly research and publications, despite having equally relevant skills and experience as their male peers. Although it could be further improved, we have also sought to achieve racial diversity among the authors. Notably, because gender and intersectional perspectives in academia not only deal with the greater inclusion of women, LGBTQI+ and racial minorities but also include exploring the role of gender and race, these dimensions are highlighted in many of the chapters. Given that gender and race are crucial aspects of the criminalization of protest, their analysis is indispensable for a comprehensive understanding of the phenomenon.

Frédérique Bawin has been working at the Institute for Social Drug Research at the University of Ghent since 2015, and currently holds the position of Post-Doctoral Researcher. In 2020, Frédérique completed her PhD, which examined self-reported medicinal cannabis use. Her research interests include patterns of substance use, psychoactive medicines and environmental justice.

Ignasi Bernat is a sociologist who has worked in different universities in the UK and Catalonia. He is currently a Post-Doctoral Teaching Fellow in the Department of Applied Social Sciences at the University of Winchester. He has researched crimes of the powerful, state and corporate power and the criminalization of migration. Ignasi Bernat and David Whyte have co-edited the book *Building a New Catalonia: Self-determination and Emancipation* (Barcelona and Edinburgh: Pollen and Bella Caledonia).

Ginny Norris Blackson is the Linfield University's University Librarian and Director of Libraries, Archives and Multimedia Services. An Appalachian refugee and self-identified Radical Hillbilly Feminist, she was raised on her grandparent's tobacco farm in rural Kentucky. She holds a BA and a MLIS from the University of Kentucky. She is a recipient of the American Library Association's 2018 "I Love My Librarian" award, the Smithsonian Libraries' 2016 Neville-Pribram Mid-Career Educators award and the Alaska Center for the Book's 2015 Sue Sherif Literacy award for Contributions to Alaska Literacy.

Paul Bleakley is a Lecturer in Criminology at Middlesex University. He received his PhD in Criminology from the University of New England, Australia in 2019, where he received a federal government research grant to complete his thesis on the impact of historical corruption on the relationship between police and marginalized subpopulations. He has published extensively on various areas of police corruption, policing of protest and child sexual abuse. Paul has published in journals such as *Crime, Law and Social Change*, *Criminal Law Forum*, *Criminal Justice Studies*, *Critical Criminology* and *The Police Journal*. His first book, *Under a Bad Sun: Police, Politics and Corruption in Australia*, is about historical police corruption in Queensland and was published by Michigan State University Press in 2021.

Praveenrao Bolli is a Doctoral student in the Department of Justice Studies in the College of Juvenile Justice and Psychology at Prairie View A&M University.

He earned a MA in Sociology at Prairie View A&M University, India. His research interests include citizen police relationships, disadvantaged neighborhood and juvenile delinquency, social structures and hierarchies.

Israel Celi Toledo is the Director of the Constitutional Law Program at the Universidad Técnica Particular de Loja in Ecuador. He is the author of the book *Neocontitucionalismo en Ecuador: ¿Judicialización de la política o politización de la justicia?* (Universidad Andina Simón Bolívar, 2017). He works in the areas of constitutional law, social movements and human rights in Ecuador and Brazil. Israel is pursuing a PhD in Political Science at Universidade Federal do Rio Grande do Sul in Brazil. His earlier work has focused on participatory democracy, constitutional making and human rights. He is currently focused on the political economy and cultural dimensions of Indigenous activism in Latin America.

Christal Chapman is an attorney-at-law with over 13 years' experience, having been called to the Bar of her native Trinidad and Tobago in 2007. She has worked as an attorney at the Office of Procurement Regulation, the Children's Authority and the Equal Opportunity Commission in that country. She has worked as a Lecturer in international law at the Institute of International Relations, the University of the West Indies in Trinidad and Tobago. She holds an LLM in International Development Law and Human Rights from the University of Warwick and a MA in Development Studies from the International Institute of Social Studies in The Hague. Her MA thesis was awarded the 2020 Han Entzinger (Erasmus Migration & Diversity Institute) Master Thesis Award. Her research interests focus on issues surrounding migration and diversity as well as social protection and inequality.

Myrna Cintron is an Associate Professor in the Department of Justice Studies in the College of Juvenile Justice & Psychology at Prairie View A&M. She earned a PhD in Criminology from Florida State University and has over 20 years of teaching and research experience. Her broader research and teaching interest include people from minority backgrounds in the criminal and justice systems and particularly those with Latino roots. Her recent work addresses unaccompanied children crossing the US border and police-youth interaction.

Matt Clement is a Senior Lecturer in Criminology at the University of Winchester, UK. He has worked as a teacher, community worker and mentor for young people in the criminal justice system. He has since taught at several universities part-time before coming to the University of Winchester in 2013. He has published on knife crime, austerity, state violence and social movements including the monograph *A People's History of Riots, Protest and the Law* (2016).

Mark Cowling is a retired Professor of Criminology and Marxism at Teesside University. He is the author of *Marxism and Criminological Theory: A Critique and a Toolkit* (Houndmills: Palgrave, 2008) and two further single-authored books. He has also singly or jointly produced six edited books. He is the editor of an annual journal *Studies in Marxism*, Volume 16 of which is appearing in 2021.

Alejandro Forero-Cuéllar is a Professor at the Deparment of Criminal and Criminology and a researcher of the Observatorio del Sistema Penal y los Derechos Humanos at University of Barcelona. He has a PhD in Law and Political Science from the same university. He is a consultant in the European Union program EUROsociAL.

Teresa Francis Divine is an Associate Professor at Central Washington University in the Department of Law and Justice. She holds a BA in Political Science from the University of New Mexico, a JD from Mississippi College, a MS and an LLM in Criminal Law from SUNY Buffalo. Born and raised in the Bronx, past family issues allow her to share her first-hand vivid stories about urban life with students and the community. Teresa's life experience has made her dedicated to the success of students of color.

Katharina Fritsch is a Post-Doctoral Researcher at the Department for European Policy and the Study of Democracy at the Danube University Krems. She is also an Associated Post-Doctoral Researcher at the Centre Marc Bloch and has been working as a lecturer at the University of Vienna. Her research and teaching interests lie in the field of critical diaspora and migration studies, postcolonial and decolonial studies, intersectional approaches, protest and democratization processes. Her PhD dissertation—an analysis of political and cultural mobilizations of the Comorian diaspora in Marseille as ethicized biopolitics—is about to be published in the Routledge Studies on African and Black Diaspora series.

Gabriela L. Gusis is an Adjunct Professor of Criminal Law and Criminology at Universidad de Buenos Aires, UNDAV, UNLP and UNR. She holds a post-graduate degree in Constitutionalism from UCLM), another one in Critical Studies on Law and Human Rights from CLACSO and is now pursuing a Master in Sociology of Criminal Law at UNLP and a PhD in Legal Sciences at Universidad San Carlos de Guatemala. She heads the Secretariat at the *Asociación Latinoamericana de Derecho Penal y Criminología* (ALPEC) and at the Department of Criminal Law and Criminology at Universidad de Buenos Aires.

Daniel Jiménez-Franco is a Lecturer in the Department of Psychology and Sociology and a researcher at the Laboratory of Legal Sociology at the University of Zaragoza (Spain). He is also the co-coordinator of the European Group for the Study of Deviance and Social Control. He has a PhD in Legal Sociology and Political Institutions.

Andrea Kretschmann is Professor of Cultural Sociology at Lüneburg University, Germany and a Research Associate at Centre Marc Bloch in Berlin. As a sociologist and a criminologist, she works in the fields of critical security studies, police studies, socio-legal studies, political sociology and cultural sociology. She is a co-editor of the *Kriminologisches* Journal (Journal of Criminology), the *Zeitschrift für Rechtssoziologie* (Journal of Socio-Legal Studies) and the book series *Verbrechen & Gesellschaft* (Crime

& Society). She recently published a book on Pierre Bourdieu's legal thought (*Das Rechtsdenken Pierre Bourdieus*, 2019) and edited a volume on social movements in the legal domain (*Bewegungen im Recht, Zeitschrift für Rechtssoziologie*, 2020).

Kruthi Jagadish Kumar is a Doctoral student in the Department of Justice Studies in the College of Juvenile Justice and Psychology at Prairie View A&M University. She earned a MS in Criminology and Criminal Justice Science from the University of Madras, India, and a BA in Journalism, Psychology and Women's Studies from Bangalore University, India. Her research interests include crime reporting in print media, forms of challenges met by transgender people, child abuse, courts and police youth interaction.

Paula Lacerda is an anthropologist and Associate Professor at the University of the State of Rio de Janeiro in Brazil, teaching undergraduate and graduate students. She is currently researching socio-political dynamics involved in demands for reparation in situations of human rights violations, especially based on the gender dynamics mobilized in the face of state structures in the Brazilian Amazon.

Verónica Marchio is a law graduate at the University of Bologna with a thesis in the sociology of deviance. She attended a Master in Critical Criminology at the University of Padua and meanwhile she had her 18 months practice period to become a lawyer. She is currently finishing her PhD with a thesis on Preventive Justice in Italy. She is also a political activist and collaborates with the political journal *Commonware*.

Greg Martin is an Associate Professor of Criminology and Socio-Legal Studies at the University of Sydney, Australia. He has published widely in criminology, law and sociology, and is the author of *Understanding Social Movements* (Routledge, 2015), *Crime, Media and Culture* (Routledge, 2019), and co-editor of *Secrecy, Law and Society* (Routledge, 2015). He is the founding editor of the book series, *Emerald Studies in Activist Criminology*, an Associate Editor of *Crime Media Culture*, and a member of the Editorial Board of *Social Movement Studies* and *The Sociological Review*.

Wayne Morrison is Professor of Law at Queen Mary, University of London, where he currently teaches courses in criminology and jurisprudence along with his seminar on Law, Modernity and the Holocaust. He was the Director of the University of London's distance learning programs for law (1999–2009), which fitted with his global sense of intersectional identities and immersion in multiple flows of knowledge, perspectives, fears and power. Originally from New Zealand, his research and publications span criminological and legal theory and tend to focus on issues of globalization, culture, identity, making normatively visible the otherwise hidden from view aspects of human interaction, subjectivity and the "other". Increasingly, he writes in a style theory returns to its origins, that is to the experiences of traveling and contemplation and recounting to audiences' interpretations and lessons learnt.

Mafalda Pardal is a Post-doctoral Researcher at the Research Foundation Flanders and an Assistant Professor of Criminology at Ghent University, Belgium. She has been a visiting researcher at the Catholic University of Uruguay. Her research interests focus on illicit markets and drug policies, as well as on social movements and resistance.

Paul A. Passavant is the author of *Policing Protest: The Post-Democratic State and the Figure of Black Insurrection* (Duke University Press, 2021). He is also the author of *No Escape: Freedom of Speech and the Paradox of Rights* and the co-editor of *Empire's New Clothes: Reading Hardt and Negri*. Passavant teaches at Hobart and William Smith Colleges in the USA.

Roxana Pessoa Cavalcanti is a Senior Lecturer in Criminology at the University of Brighton, author of the book *A Southern Criminology of Violence, Youth and Policing* (Routledge, 2020). She works in the areas of critical criminology and critical theory, theorizing social inequalities relating to class, gender and ethnicity. Her earlier work has focused on urban violence, state crime, human rights, the politics of crime control, policing and insecurity in Brazil. She is currently researching the gendered dimensions of activism and the criminalization of resistance movements in Latin America.

Tamar Pitch held the Chair of Philosophy of Law at the University of Perugia, where she also taught sociology of law. She also had teaching positions in the USA, Canada, Mexico, Argentina, Morocco and Chile. She is the editor of the journal *Studi sulla questione criminale*. In 1999 she was awarded the Distinguished International Scholar Award by the American Society of Criminology and in 2007 she received the *Capalbio* award for non-fiction. Her main research topics are criminal justice, fundamental rights and gender and the law. She published *Responsabilità limitate* in 1989 (translated into English and Spanish); *Un diritto per due* in 1998 (translated into Spanish), *La società della prevenzione* in 2006 (translated into Spanish and English) and *Contro il decoro. L'uso politico della pubblica decenza* in 2013 (translated into Spanish)

Saúl Puerta Peña-Pueblo Awajun is the Head of the Indigenous Community Awajun (Perú). He is a social activist, particularly involved in the Bagua social conflict. He is a defender of ancestral justice. He is the former head of a grassroot interethnic organization focused on the defense of the mother earth in Perú (*Asociación Interétnica de Desarrollo de la Selva Peruana*, AIDESEP).

Igor Rolemberg is a Doctoral student at the École des Hautes Études en Sciences Sociales in co-supervision with the Federal University of Rio de Janeiro. He is interested in studies on social mobilization in Eastern Amazon and researches the role of confessional activists in formulating public problems about land reform and deforestation.

Natalia Ruiz Morato is an Alexander von Humboldt Post-doctoral Fellow at the Georg-August-University in Göttingen, Germany. She was a Residential Fellow at the Wilson Center in Washington DC and an Associate Professor at LaSalle

University in Colombia. She was also an independent consultant in law and development for public and private institutions on issues related to international development, ethnic and Indigenous rights and social and environmental justice.

Vincenzo Scalia is a Reader in Criminology at the University of Winchester. He worked with Dario Melossi, Massimo Pavarini and David Nelken on urban security projects. He taught criminology in Bologna, Macerata, Roma, Padova and Palermo. Vincenzo has also thought and researched o in Mexico and Argentina. He has published more than sixty articles in four languages on the topics of prisons, juvenile deviance, organized crime and policing.

Grace Iara Souza is a Research Fellow at the Latin America and the Caribbean Centre at the London School of Economics and Political Science and a Fellow of the King's Brazil Institute at King's College London. Using political ecology as a lens, she is concerned with how development and environmental policies affect Indigenous and non-Indigenous peoples. Her research focuses on human security and political ecologies of development, conservation and peasant societies, with a particular interest in historical invisibility, agency and forms of resistance, power dynamics, social policies, funders and drivers of deforestation, payment for ecosystem services and ethnic identities in Brazil.

Alida Szalai is a PhD candidate at Eötvös Loránd University in Budapest. She holds a MA in criminology from the same university. Her Master's thesis examined the global patterns of land-grabbing from a critical and green criminological perspective. Her doctoral research explores resistance, social mobilization and social control related to environmental harms and crimes. Her teaching interests deal with criminal policy and social movements, globalization and late modernity, community crime prevention, crimes of the powerful and green criminology.

Celine Tack is a graduate student in criminology at Ghent University, where she engaged in a project examining media representation of youth climate protests in Belgium, in the context of a research internship. Currently, Celine is pursuing a MA in investigative journalism at the University of Gothenburg in Sweden.

Rodrigo F. Videla is an activist for a preventive criminology (@criminologia-cautelar) and a lawyer from Universidad de Buenos Aires. He has a post-graduate degree in criminal law from Universidad Torcuato Di Tella in Argentina where he is pursuing an LLM. He teaches and researchers at Universidad de Buenos Aires.

David Whyte is Professor of Socio-Legal Studies at the University of Liverpool. His research and teaching interests are focused on the connections between law and corporate power. His latest book *Ecocide* (Manchester University Press, 2020) explores the role of the corporation in the climate crisis. Other recently published books are *The Violence of Austerity* (Pluto, 2017 ed. with Vickie Cooper) and *Corporate Human Rights Violations: Global Prospects for Legal Action* (Routledge, 2017 with Stefanie Khoury).

ACKNOWLEDGEMENTS

I am thankful to the institutions, colleagues, family and friends that made this book possible. The Alexander von Humboldt Stiftung and my host and friend at Freie Universität Berlin, Kirstin Drenkhahn, provided me with the time and academic freedom to conduct my core research on state crime while also engaging with topics that are at the heart of my motivations as a scholar, for which this book is a foremost example. I am also extremely grateful to CLACSO "*Memorias Colectivas y Prácticas de Resistencia*" (Collective Memories and Practices of Resistance), a critical, horizontal and through-provoking working group of activists and scholars focused on the role of grassroot organizations in the pursue of human rights.

Life has lately brought me a new friend and a big thanks go to him. David O. Friedrichs has been a permanent source of inspiration, knowledge and critical exchange of ideas. My appreciation goes all the way back to Fernando Lizarraga, my PhD supervisor in Argentina, with whom I was then able to dig into the concepts of criminal selectivity, over-criminalization, under-criminalization and historical perspectives in criminology, that are today re-explored within this book. This goes along with my continuous gratitude to all the critical thinkers that inspired me along the way from both sides of the equator. This work would not have been possible either without the permanent inspiration of great scholars such as Raúl Zaffaroni and Boaventura de Sousa Santos, who have continuously pointed out the relevance of learning from the epistemologies and practices of the Global South and particularly from those emerging from social movements. My appreciation also goes to my home universities in Argentina, Buenos Aires University and Quilmes National University.

A huge thanks go directly to the contributors of this book, both old friends and new, who managed to respond to endless backs and forth, comments and revisions, who had the commitment to condense years of fieldwork and reflection in 5,000-word chapters and, not least, who had followed the deadlines even amid a global

pandemic that altered our lives to the core. I am particularly grateful to those contributors that had to overcome language barriers to write their chapters. I also want
to thank to the generous reviewers who collaborated in the process. A special thanks
go to John Lea, with whom I debated the idea for this book and who accompanied
me in the first moments of the project, although life circumstances did not allow
him to go all the way through.

Last, but not least, I want to dedicate this book to the social activists and the
human rights movement from Argentina, Latin America and worldwide whose lessons to keep on struggling despite repression are an inspiration for the present and
future generations. Particularly, I want to dedicate this book to those who have been
killed at the hands of the criminal justice systems while fighting for their rights. We
owe them all a better future. Critically thinking our present might be, hopefully, a
promising starting point.

INTRODUCTION

285 eyes. These many were lost at the hands of police brutality in Chile at the end of 2019. At the time, massive protests took place calling for reform to scrap the constitution passed by the dictator Agustin Pinochet 40 years previously.

These almost 300 blinded eyes are no exception. Modern constitutions hold the right to protest as part of the rule of law and a pillar of democracy. However, in disarticulating the division between past and current times, and between democracy and repressive regimes, a critical historical overview reveals that the actions of the criminal justice system and social protest have always been systematically interrelated. This means that the right to dissent, which is at the core of democracy, has been often approached as a disruption and as a target of law enforcement, in the Global South as well as the Global North.

Despite the striking nature of this state of affairs, research on the topic is lacking. This collaborative book fills the gap by digging into past and present experiences of the criminalization of activism and dissent as well as into related challenges that might appear or deepen in the near future. This work seeks to foster attention on this phenomenon's specificities within the fields of historical and critical criminology. With an intersectional and interdisciplinary approach, the book intends to foster further dialog among different fields within critical criminology, including Indigenous studies, feminist criminology, LGBTQI+ studies, Southern criminology and green criminology.

Building upon these different perspectives, the book uses the term over-criminalization in place of simply criminalization. This choice of words deserves brief clarification: critical criminologists from both sides of the Equator have long identified the systematic unfairness of criminal justice systems and have shown how crime control rarely focuses on society's most harmful behaviors but rather on those affecting hegemonic socio-economic interests. This systematic unfairness can be referred to as "criminal selectivity" and involves instances of "primary criminalization" and "secondary criminalization" (Baratta 1986, 133–4; Becker 1962, 37; Zaffaroni et al. 2000, 7).

DOI: 10.4324/9781003144229-1

Primary criminalization describes the primary filtering process through which only a small portion of negative social behaviors or social harms are legislated. In other words, it describes the filtering system which labels only some harmful conduct as criminal behavior. Of course, this filtering process is framed within existing hegemonic social values. This means that acts that are morally reprehensible but that do not harm the existing social order, such as refusing to help someone asking for food on the street, are not criminalized in the law. Instead, survival strategies of such a person (e.g., leaving waste on the street while searching for food) are often criminalized as an offence against public order.[1] The result of these choices at the level of primary criminalization might be described as "unequal legal treatment of social harms" or, shortly, "inequality under the law".

In turn, the notion of **secondary criminalization** consists of a second filtering mechanism, responsible for selecting which of the countless behaviors corresponding to the criminal law addressed in the primary filtering process will be effectively criminalized. This secondary filter has also been conceptualized as "selective enforcement" and is accomplished by three instances that can be referred to as "law enforcement profiling", "court discretion" and "differential penalization" (Vegh Weis 2017b). These instances are not bias-free either: the targeted individuals are usually those who correspond to "the aesthetic public image of the offender, with classist, racist, age and gender components" (Zaffaroni et al. 2000, 9). At the other extreme of the selective process, the authors of state, white-collar, organized, or war crimes, who do not match the threatening image of the offender, are rarely targeted by enforcement agencies.

Yet one key question remains unanswered. What mechanisms define if a particular behavior falls on either side of these two filters? The concepts of **under-criminalization** and **over-criminalization** help clarify what is left under the sights of crime control at both the primary and the secondary levels (Vegh Weis 2017a). Under-criminalization refers to the restrictive criminal treatment of behaviors perpetrated by privileged sectors of the population—defined not only in relation to their class but also to their race, gender, sexual orientation, religious and ethnic belonging—regardless of the social harm involved in their behavior. Under-criminalization can be found in the limited legislative treatment of those behaviors usually perpetrated by these privileged sectors (**primary under-criminalization**) and in their limited prosecution by law enforcement agencies including the police, courts and prisons (**secondary under-criminalization**). In contrast, over-criminalization refers to the emphatic prioritization of criminal treatment of those behaviors perpetrated by especially vulnerable sectors of the population regardless of the scarce social harm that their behaviors cause. Over-criminalization is reflected in the increasing legislative treatment of those behaviors usually perpetrated by these underprivileged groups (**primary over-criminalization**) and via their excessive persecution by law enforcement agencies (**secondary over-criminalization**). Figure I.1 helps to clarify these notions.

How are these categories connected to the topic of the book? Indeed, state responses to organized dissent might be one of the most striking examples in which under- and over-criminalization are interrelated. Not all dissent, of course: as with any phenomenon, the state approach to dissent differs according to the socio-demographic

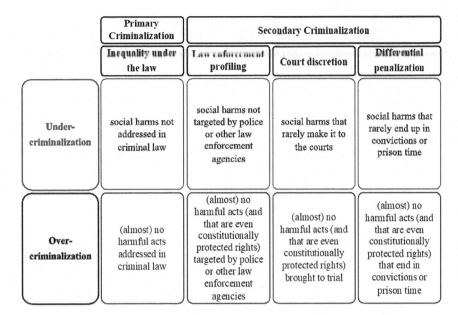

	Primary Criminalization	Secondary Criminalization		
	Inequality under the law	Law enforcement profiling	Court discretion	Differential penalization
Under-criminalization	social harms not addressed in criminal law	social harms not targeted by police or other law enforcement agencies	social harms that rarely make it to the courts	social harms that rarely end up in convictions or prison time
Over-criminalization	(almost) no harmful acts addressed in criminal law	(almost) no harmful acts (and that are even constitutionally protected rights) targeted by police or other law enforcement agencies	(almost) no harmful acts (and that are even constitutionally protected rights) brought to trial	(almost) no harmful acts (and that are even constitutionally protected rights) that end in convictions or prison time

FIGURE I.1   Under- and Over-Criminalization

features of the protestors. Violence and over-criminalization increase when protestors are "the others" (e.g., the poor, Indigenous peoples, people of color, low-rank castes) and their allies. Quite different is the state response, as the concluding chapter of the book shows by exploring Nazi Germany, when activists belong to mainstream subsets of society. A clear example of this selective approach to dissent can be seen in Argentina a decade ago: large farm owners protested policies aimed at cutting their revenues by blocking roads for weeks and leaving the country in chaos, but neither the mainstream media nor the criminal justice system labeled these events as criminal, as is usually the case with popular demonstrations (El País 2008, Zunino 2018). The differential approach to White and Black protestors in the USA also further elucidates the selective treatment of dissent. After the White protest at the Capitol on 6 January 2021 (Leatherby et al. 2021), even recently elected US President Joseph Biden acknowledged on social media that "No one can tell me that if it had been a group of Black Lives Matter protestors yesterday that they wouldn't have been treated very differently than the mob that stormed the Capitol" (quoted in Booker 2021).

So, how do under- and over-criminalization interplay in the dissent of the disadvantaged? Throughout history, "those protesting have been over-criminalized, and those benefiting from the illegal seizures that generated the protestor's discontents have seen their actions under-criminalized—largely due to the consolidated ruling class's increasing levels of control over the state and its laws" (Part II, Chapter 4). Indeed, to fully understand the over-criminalization of dissent, it is necessary to take a step back because protest and activism are usually one of the last resorts of disadvantaged groups when more institutionalized channels—including the justice system—are unresponsive. In this regard, criminal justice systems in the Global South as well as in the Global North have steadily tended to under-criminalize the crimes and harms perpetrated by powerful actors. Countries in Western Europe do not do enough to prosecute smugglers and human trafficking (Part III/Europe Chapter 10), and countries in North America, Latin America and Europe do not seem to be doing much to prosecute corporations harming the environment (Part III Chapter 11, Part IV Chapters 16 and 17), groups undermining peace (Part IV, Chapter 15), land-grabbers (Part IV, Chapters 16 and 17) or those reinforcing structural racism (Part III, Chapters 9 and 10). This means that behaviors that affect nature, peace, or basic human rights are generally not acknowledged by the criminal justice systems. The disparity between the social harm produced by those behaviors and the limited or non-existent criminal justice response is striking.

It is as a result of this under-criminalization of the powerful that the disadvantaged often dissent. Thus, it is not rare that activist gatherings, protests and demonstrations emerge as informal grassroots mechanisms to foster accountability for relevant social harms that are not seriously considered by the state. Unfortunately, as will be shown throughout the book, governments do not tend to respond to grassroots dissent by acknowledging the prior under-criminalization of the powerful or addressing the concerns of the protestors. Instead, over-criminalization of dissent is widespread. Even in circumstances where protesters peacefully exercise their constitutional rights to freedom of expression, it is not unusual that the response of governments follows that of the criminal justice system, emphatically criminalizing behaviors that can hardly be considered crimes.

How is this done? Primary over-criminalization of activism relies on expanding the definition of ordinary offenses ranging from abstract accusations such as social disorder, disobedience, violating the freedom to work, disruption of transportation and vandalism, as well as petty crimes including damage to public property when stepping on grass or painting a slogan on a wall. For example, the current fight for better wages and working conditions led by the White Mask movement in Italy has been framed as "extortion" and criminalized as such (Part I, Chapter 3).

It is also not rare that primary criminalization takes place via emergency-based and exceptional laws targeting dissent after conceiving it as a "danger" or a "threat" to social order. This happened in Australia with the 1970s Traffic Act (Part II, Chapter 7), and even throughout Western Europe during the fight against communism in the 1970s (Part II, Chapter 7) and "with the recent *Ley mordaza* in Spain, the *état d'urgence* in France, new police laws in several German states and many emergency measures related to the Covid-19 pandemic" (see Part I, Chapter 1, *see also* Chapter 2). Moreover, by invoking an emergency, the right to protest itself can be criminalized, as demonstrations regularly become subjected to permissions that can be suddenly revoked, transforming legal protests into criminal gatherings under the banner of "public safety" (Part II, Chapter 6). This phenomenon fosters a vicious circle of criminalization: "prejudging protest to be criminal leads to preventative policing of protest. By aggressively targeting protesters for arrest regardless of any violations of the law, protest policing goes beyond mere law enforcement" (Part III, Chapter 9).

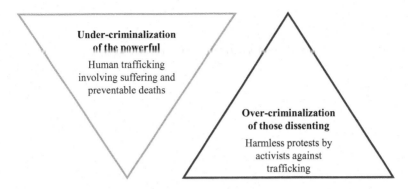

FIGURE I.2 Case Example I

Exacerbating this, global threats including terrorism have been specifically used to legitimize the politics of exception that broadens the scope of criminal law worldwide at the expense of the right to protest. This is the case with the primary over-criminalization of those assisting unlawful immigrants in Europe: "They're using laws intended for international criminal organizations that are earning money from trafficking, smuggling, prostitution and slavery to prosecute humanitarian workers and volunteers who are just trying to save lives" (Open Democracy 2019, quoted in Part III, Chapter 10). In Latin America, in a similar vein, the Colombian government issued a statute as early as 1978 broadly criminalizing "all rioting, insubordinate movement[s], or illegal assembl[ies] related to the crime of terrorism" (Part IV, Chapter 15). Let us take the example of the case study in Part III Chapter 10 to visualize this dynamic (Figure I.2).

In short, either via ordinary offences or special laws, the lens of primary over-criminalization reveals the disproportional attention criminal law pays to protests and dissent given the social harm that they produce (if any). Moreover, the fact that dissent should not be regarded as a crime at all considering its framing as a constitutional right in most modern democracies is sufficient grounds to describe its penal regulation as primary over-criminalization.

What happens, then, at the level of secondary over-criminalization? The use of arguments of emergencies and global threats to expand crime control also has effects, opening the door for police to confront protesters in a way that would be considered an illegal assault under normal conditions (Part II, Chapter 6). In the USA, the Black Lives Matter movement has been under surveillance following counter-terrorism criteria: "by treating BLM protests as a movement akin to an insurgency, the policing of protest in the USA manifests hybrid tendencies that exceed law enforcement but stop short of conventional war on a battlefield" (Part III, Chapter 9). In Colombia, the situation is no less shocking: only considering 2002–2010, the government issued more than 7,000 selective detentions of peasants, Indigenous peoples, members of community boards and even human rights activists as presumed terrorists without judicial orders (Part IV, Chapter 15).

Furthermore, emergencies and global threats have been invoked to foster the use of artificial intelligence and internet surveillance as part of law enforcement's purview (Part V, Chapter 19). This means that "moderate and peaceful social movements attract increased police intelligence surveillance" (Part I, Chapter 1). The Black Lives Matter movement is again a key example, with the FBI conducting intelligence gathering and considering "specific associations, online activity, and violent anti-White rhetoric when deciding whether a person is a Black Identity Extremist" (Part III, Chapter 8). Moreover, online policing can be also used as soft punishment to silence protestors. To exemplify, in Italy, the case against the White Mask protestors "was never brought to court, (but) the authorities pre-emptively asked Facebook to remove the page" (Part I, Chapter 3).

At the level of secondary over-criminalization is where the differences between the Global South and North become more dramatic. While over-criminalization rarely includes the excessive use of force in Western Europe (Part III, Chapters 10–12), the cases of Brazil, Argentina, Colombia, Ecuador, Perú and India show that the excessive (or *deadly*) use of force by law enforcement in the context of protest is all but a rule. Indeed, the situation in the Global South shows that the killing or assault of protestors without further criminalization has happen beyond just in isolated events. In Brazil, in 2017 alone, 71 leaders and members of social movements were killed (Part IV, Chapter 16). The expansion of this phenomenon is so great that a new criminological concept might be needed to describe it, e.g., *repressivization* (Part IV. Chapter 14). This term fills a conceptual gap, covering instances when law enforcement confronts activists with unrestricted violence but not with criminal proceedings, where the term criminalization might not be the most accurate. Indeed, in these cases, there is no detention, criminal prosecution or processes framed within the rule of law, but direct violence, including physical injuries and, not rarely, death.

How does this look in USA? Although the country is part of the Global North in terms of socio-economic development and of institutional structure and functioning. However, when dealing with people of color, the US criminal justice system has much more in common with the permeability to violence that characterizes the South than with the institutionalized and formalized over-criminalization of the North. Shockingly, a criminal justice system can be so racially divided that those softer methods of crime control—approximating the situation in Western Europe—are applied for White citizens but direct use of violence is systematically applied when dealing with African Americans—a modality more resembling that of the Global South. Notably, the over-criminalization (and repressivization) of protest in the USA, as elsewhere, affects both men and women but the latter "often are erased from the demonstrations, discourse, and the demands for social justice" (Part III, Chapter 8).

The final aspect of the under/over-criminalization dynamic in dissent involves the state response to law enforcement's use of deadly force against activists. The Global South and the USA both show that is not uncommon to observe a pattern of *secondary under-criminalization* of the police when using excessive force, even if the result is the killing of those dissenting. The suppression of protest and even the use of deadly force by police "are characterized by the impunity of the perpetrators and

2015	2017	2015-2018	2018

Social harm by the powerful	**Under-criminalization of the powerful**	**Protests by activists**	**Over-criminalization of activism**
Oxec company involving two dam constructions on the Cahabón river that caused heavy social and environmental harm in Guatemala	Not criminal justice response to these harms. The Constitutional Court allowed the company to continue the construction under the condition that within the next 12 months it would hold the formal consultation required by law, which they did without involving all the affected communites	The Indigenous Group *Resistencia Pacífica de Cahabón* develop legal and activist strategies to thwart the investments of the Oxec company	The leader of *Resistencia Pacífica de Cahabón* was sentenced to seven years and four months of imprisonment for allegedly false accusation of illegal detention and aggravated robbery which allegedly had happened back in 2015 + subjected to pretrial detention (even the UN issued a notice of concern about the exaggerated measure)

FIGURE I.3   Case Example II

a high level of hidden figures" (Part I, Chapter 2). Paradoxically, it is also not rare that follow-up demonstrations take place to confront the under-criminalization of the killings and that the police's use of deadly force is repeated in these contexts, stressed by the cover image where demonstrators ask "Who protects us from the police?".

Let us take the example of the case study in Part I, Chapter 1 to examine these categories (Figure I.3).

Many chapters shed light on the fact that the over-criminalization of dissent has not just been aimed at the banning of individual activists. Instead, the goal usually goes deeper, intending to de-legitimatize and defame entire protests or movements in the eyes of the population. This defamation process involves an engagement between the criminal justice system and the mainstream media to expose a distortive, de-contextualized and violent or disruptive image of those labeled as a criminal threat. This was true in the case of the over-criminalization of the communists in Italy in the 1970s (Part II, Chapter 7) as much as of Indigenous leaders in Latin America (Part I, Chapter 2; Part IV, Chapters 16 and 17), Catalonian political representatives today (Part III, Chapter 12), and, at some point, even the Fridays for Future movement (Part III, Chapter 11). Gender is a particularly relevant instrument for de-legitimizing popular leaders, as misogynist characterizations are used to minimize the relevance and seriousness of female-led struggles (Part IV, Chapter 16).

Could it get worse? The future of the over-criminalization of dissent is not promising, and it will hold external and internal challenges for those who oppose the status quo through activism and protest. From an external standpoint, protest policing is becoming more militarized and increasingly uses control technologies to restrain, disassemble, pre-empt, or incapacitate protests, as seen in the policing of the Black Lives Matter movement, for example (Part III, Chapter 9). The paradoxical role of artificial intelligence is that it can lead to polarization and insecurity and thence to further activism, while at the same time "it can also facilitate its repression via intelligent criminalization" (Part V, Chapter 19). From an internal standpoint, challenges also arise. Should a critical perspective aimed at confronting the over-criminalization of dissent and the defense of the freedom to protest without criminal consequences also apply to right-wing groups (Part V, Chapter 22)? How can we engage in activism aimed at defending a transformative agenda towards racial and gender equality and confront those who undermine it without recurring to the same tools that have been violently reproducing inequality and undermining critical activism in the first place, i.e., crime control and punitivity (Part V, Chapter 21)?

With this overview in mind, it is time already to dig into the specificities of the different sections of the book. **Part I** is devoted to **Theoretical approaches on the over-criminalization of dissent** and aims at exploring conceptual tools to better understand the suppression of social protest through the criminal justice system. The first chapter, **Politics of exception: criminalizing activism in Western European democracies**, written by **Katharina Fritsch and Andrea Kretschmann**, argues that the criminalization of protest in Western democracies increasingly takes place through "politics of exception", including legal provisions, political processes, discourses and practices. These politics of exception are characterized mainly by three logics of governing: the inter-twining of different states of exception—including both formal states of emergency and "petty" states of exception, —an expansionary logic of "securitization" and mechanisms of Othering. The authors rely on criminology, political theory and postcolonial perspectives to expose how politics of exception reflect a qualitative rather than a quantitative change in governing practices. Moreover, they propose that this change indicates a broader shift in the state's approach to protest and in its understanding of democracy. Central to such politics, they argue, is the framing of protest as a *destabilizing other* rather than an integral part of the existing democratic political order.

A social control perspective for the study of environmental harm and resistance, written by **Alida Szalai**, inquires if the criminological theory can help to better understand the criminalization of environmental activists and land rights defenders as well as the social, institutional and cultural dynamics behind this process. Szalai argues that, while most episodes of activists' criminalization occur in the Global South, reactions to resistance and environmental movements are adopting a punitive and repressive character worldwide. Addressing this global challenge, the chapter argues that the study of environmental resistance within a green-cultural criminological framework could contribute to a deeper understanding of power relations and competing interests behind criminalization. By extending the notion of social control as it is used in the study of crime control to the study of resistance, the chapter distinguishes between formal and informal control of environmental harm and of the resistance against it.

Finally, **The criminalization and "innovation" of resistance: looking at the Italian case**, written by **Verónica Marchio**, discusses the two mechanisms through which political struggle has been managed by the state: criminalization and socio-political innovation. Both sections include examples of criminalization and innovation in Italy to provide an empirical foundation to the analysis, including the novel protest movement known as "Il Padrone di merda" (The "shitty" boss) which consists of people staging protests outside workplaces in which the employers were accused of exploiting their workers. The movement—also known as the "White Masks" because of the masks the protesters wear—was started after a group of young people in Bologna, Italy only a few years ago.

Part II discusses the **Historical experiences on the over-criminalization of dissent** throughout the 20th century in England, India, Australia and Italy. The overview allows identifying similar criminalization mechanisms even though distant historical periods and geographic locations. In **Avoiding and amplifying the criminal label in the roman republic and medieval England, Matt Clement** goes all the way back to the Roman republic of the 1st century BCE, to expose how, even then, the senators passed what they called "the ultimate decree"— "to see the state comes to no harm"—when threatened by political opposition from below. Ever since, Matt argues, the language employed by the mainstream political machinery of the state, as relayed by the media, describes perceived threats of radicalized ideas and actions as harmful acts, and their perpetrators as criminals. The author analyzes government reactions to protest movements based on the notion of over-criminalization, which includes a process of stigmatization that works to undermine the protestors' "legitimacy" and justify recourse to repressive acts. This discourse constitutes a "politics of fear", where victims of the system are labeled perpetrators—carriers of a dangerous radicalism that must be controlled for the public good. By comparing two protest movements and their repression from the pre-modern era, this chapter assesses how criminalization processes changed across historical epochs.

The criminalization of low-rank castes: a historical perspective of mahad movement in India (1927–1937), written by **Kruthi Jagadish Kumar, Praveenrao Bolli and Myrna Cintron**, explores India's historical patterns in the over-criminalization of riots and experiences of resistance from a Hindu religious and caste struggle perspective. In India, social class is part of the caste system. India follows a strict caste system, which is purely based on class stratification. The chapter discusses the origins of the caste system regarding the Hindu religious scriptures and the language used to over-criminalize the low-rank castes. The chapter particularly details this process of overcriminalization, which included the condemnation in accessing water. The authors narrate how dissent led to the formation of the Mahad Movement led by B.R. Ambedkar, who played a significant role in creating equality in accessing natural resources such as water and establishing it in the Constitution of India.

In **"Loyal spear-carriers": police violence in the Queensland anti-apartheid movement, 1971, Paul Bleakley** focuses on how the 1971 tour of Australia by the South African Springboks rugby union team was a flashpoint for anti-apartheid protest and the criminalization of activism across the country. Paul argues that nowhere was this the case more than in Queensland, where the ultra-conservative Bjelke-Petersen government was in power from 1968 to 1987. In preparation for the Springboks' arrival, Bjelke-Petersen announced the institution of a state of emergency which gave the Queensland Police Force sweeping powers to take repressive action against anti-apartheid activists. The stage was set for violent clashes between protesters and the police, with Bjelke-Petersen vowing to not take disciplinary actions against officers accused of using excessive force. The provocative, state-sanctioned police violence that occurred during the Springboks protests marked the beginning of a campaign to repress protest in Queensland, culminating several years later in the right to conduct street demonstrations being stripped away altogether. In this chapter, the author explores the context that led to the criminalization of the anti-apartheid demonstrations in Queensland, as well as the reasons why the police response to protesters was inordinately violent and aggressive.

Finally, **The theorem of national solidarity: Italy and the "7 Aprile" case: the criminalisation of left-wing dissent**, written by **Vincenzo Scalia**, analyzes the criminalization of the left-wing movement Autonomia Operaia, in 1979, in Italy. By drawing on the category of deviance amplification proposed by Stanley Cohen, the author proposes three stages of the criminalization process: the defamation of the extreme left, followed by their isolation, provides the possibility of enacting the third stage, that of repression. The active role of the Italian Communist Party in connection with the magistrates is well emphasized. The conclusion drawn by the author is that the judicial repression of the left-wing opposition produced political effects that still perdure at the national and local levels. Particularly, the author argues that the criminalization of left resistance has restricted, in the long-range, the expansion of the left and has made room for populism.

Part III is entitled **Current cases of over-criminalization of dissent in the Global North** and includes two chapters on the USA and three on Europe. The first one is **Resistance to survive: the criminalization of the Black Lives Matter movement**, written by **Teresa Francis Divine and Ginny Norris Blackson**, which brings an intersectional perspective to the study of the Black Lives Matter Movement in the USA from the perspective of two authors who are directly involved in the struggle from an activist and a scholarly perspective. The authors reveal that Black bodies still stand up to injustice and death at the hands of police. In a historical overview, they analyze the Civil Rights Movement and the myth of Black forgiveness in an effort to glimpse changes in activism among Black youth. To do so, the authors support the continuing relevance of the British Marxist historian's conception of "social crime" as an alternative form of protest in the changing contexts of industrial capitalism and representative democracy. The chapter also explores changes in social attitudes toward Black activists, from the nonviolent activist of the late-20th century to the Black Lives Matter born in the 21st century. The analysis necessarily includes the current criminalization of victims and witnesses to police brutality, as well, as the criminalization of the Black Lives Matter movement.

In **Between crime and war: the security model of protest policing**, **Paul A. Passavant** also looks at the Black Lives Matter movement but from the perspective of the criminalizing police. In the USA, Paul argues that the security model of protest policing includes militarization and increasing use of technologies of control as an effort to defeat protesters and prevent the assembly of a political subject. The chapter uses a case study of Memphis, Tennessee's Police Department (MPD), which redirected its Office of Homeland Security from counterterrorism to a political intelligence gathering that targeted the Black Lives Matter Movement. The MPD's monitoring of the movement exemplifies the security model of protest policing in its efforts to anticipate protests, track protesters, associate protest-related risk, and contain the effects of protest. By focusing on the possibility of protest, it is argued, the MPD's conduct is oriented to the control of urban space, and to prevent the assembly of a political subject or the appearance of political antagonism.

The following three chapters focused on Europe. The first of them explores the criminalization of dissent concerning the Mediterranean See deaths. In **Fighting for the right to save others: responses by civil society to the criminalization of solidarity in the mediterranean sea post-2015, Christal Chapman** analyzes the offence of "facilitating entry" of irregular migrants into the EU. This criminal offence has been applied not only to human smugglers and traffickers but also to humanitarian workers and volunteers, who have found themselves criminalized since the 2015 EU Refugee Crisis. This chapter analyzes the several ways in which civil society has mobilized against this practice of criminalizing humanitarian actors who bring migrants into Italy and Greece, following search and rescue operations in the Mediterranean Sea. Christal conceptualizes the on-going problem, the criminalization of humanitarian assistance as a form of "lawfare". The chapter addresses the range of governmental action constituting criminalization (both formal and informal) and considers how humanitarian actors justify their actions and challenge their criminalization through both legal and non-legal mobilization. In addition, the chapter aims at highlighting the myriad ways in which political decisions in the field of migration management taken at a national or regional level can have both intended and unintended consequences, for humanitarian actors, for European society and for migrants too.

Media representation of Belgian youth protests: the making of "Climate Truants", Mafalda Pardal, written by **Celine Tack and Frédérique Bawin**, explores the criminalization of environmental activism in Belgium today. The chapter is framed within green cultural criminology, which calls for attention to this intersection between culture, crime and the environment. Within this framework, the authors analyze the media representation of the 20-week climate protest cycle mobilized by young people in Belgium, composing a dataset of 382 Dutch-written news articles. The chapter argues that the media reported on the development of the protests in Belgium and that the protesters were an important voice included in that reporting. However, substantive climate-related issues were rarely featured. The media coverage was primarily centered on a debate about whether protesters should be skipping school to engage in the protest actions. Although there were no cases of formal protest criminalization, the authors' analysis uncovered a media narrative that tended to contribute to a de-legitimization of the protests and their actors. These findings are in line with other analyses of media representation of youth climate protests in Europe which raises the question of whether this type of depiction is also occurring in other regions of the world.

Finally, **Criminalization as strategy of power: the case of Catalunya 2017–2020**, written by **Ignasi Bernat and David Whyte**, explores the case study of the movement for independence in Catalonia to illustrate how the criminalization of resistance is a feature of the state's capacity to fabricate the social order. In this case, the authors argue, the criminalization runs at the level of appearance rather than essence and seeks to *fabricate* the riot, the protest and the strike as "crimes" devoid of political or social content. It does so by hailing the protagonists as "common criminals" and their actions as a threat to a peaceful, law-abiding society. The authors conceptualize this process as "blanket criminalization" and apply it to the different stages of criminalization that Catalonian resisters experienced.

Part IV is titled **Current cases of over-criminalization of dissent in the Global South** and includes four case studies in Argentina, Colombia, Brazil and Ecuador, providing a large overview of the criminalization processes in Latin America today. **Social protest and punitive treatment in argentina: an analysis from Latin American critical criminology**, written by **Gabriela L. Gusis and Rodrigo F. Videla**, builds upon the Latin American critical criminology developed by authors such as Aniyar de Castro and Zaffaroni in the 1970s. Based on categories such as social protest/political dissidence, primary and secondary criminalization by Zaffaroni and subterranean criminalization by Aniyar de Castro, the chapter exposes the existence of different (punitive) tactics for social control including criminalization and "repressivization". The chapter includes a case study that deals with the events known as the "Avellaneda Massacre". On 26 June 2002 in Buenos Aires, Argentina, two social activists, Darío Kosteki and Maximiliano Santillan, were killed by the police. The case is relevant because it shows the specific punitive tactics that run in the global margins, with law enforcement agents using deadly force as part of their contention techniques. The study does not reflect on how disadvantaged social groups have resisted conditions they consider unjust, but on the link between those resistant strategies and the government tactics and techniques for the administration of pain.

The next chapter deals with **Colombia's murderous democracy pre- and post-covid-19: the assassination of social leaders and the criminalization of protest**, written by **Natalia Ruiz Morato**. This chapter is a historical and socio-legal study of the right to protest in Colombia that finishes with the impact of the Covid-19 pandemic. Even though the country is historically considered a democracy untainted by dictatorships, it has suffered from one of the bloodiest armed conflicts of the 20th century, which served as a buffer preventing social reform. Even following the successful negotiation of the 2016 Peace Agreement, there has been an increase in social protests, killings of social leaders and police violence—all of which have been worsened by the Covid-19 pandemic. This chapter explores the criminalization and stigmatization of social protest (2018–2020) as part of this development. It also evaluates the implications and difficulties of the Supreme Court's ruling STC7641 of 22 September 2020, that protects the right to protest in times of pandemic.

Violence and violations of rights against leaderships in the Brazilian Amazon, written by **Paula Lacerda and Igor Rolemberg**, explores the criminalization of environmental activism in Brazil. This contribution aims to discuss and analyze the scenario of violence and violations of rights against leaderships that have acted in the Brazilian Amazon during the democratic period from 1988 to 2020. The authors argue that different forms of violence and violations are the result of mutual reinforcement between practices of under-criminalization and over-criminalization. The authors understand that these overall practices are accompanied by extrajudicial executions and tactics for morally de-legitimizing leadership. The chapter includes the study of empirical material, dossiers and complaints elaborated by human rights and environmental protection entities, the media, and interviews with leaders from the Amazon, which are a result of over ten years of fieldwork and exchanges between the authors and these groups. The chapter concludes that there are continuities and ruptures in the characteristics of violence and violations of rights committed against social movements' leaders in Amazon.

The fourth chapter is also linked to environmental activism in Latin America. Under the title **An analysis of the criminalisation of socio-environmental activism and resistance in contemporary Latin America**, Israel Celi, **Roxana Pessoa Cavalcanti and Grace Iara Souza** examine the criminalization and resistance of Indigenous populations in Brazil and Ecuador as part of contemporary Latin America. The chapter explores how the process of colonization and expropriation is continually re-enacted through dispossession, racist discourses, and practices of over-criminalization, in the context of extractive economies. Starting with an analysis of the historical background of criminalization in Latin America, the chapter then uses qualitative data from two case studies. It draws on research with grassroots Indigenous organizations and a decade of observation of socio-environmental politics in Brazil, in combination with a qualitative analysis of the criminalization of socio-environmental activism in Ecuador. Through a critical analysis of government documents, academic literature and the discourses of both activists and powerful members of the state in the region, it sheds light on the need for further research into the criminalization of dissent and forms of resistance. The central argument is that colonial dynamics are reproduced in processes of persecution and criminalization of socio-environmental activism.

This section finishes with **Notes from the field II: the judicial persecution in the Amazonian Indigenous struggle—"El Baguazo" —Amazonas-Perú**, written by **Saúl Puerta Peña–Pueblo Awajun**, who is an Indigenous activist and protagonist of the struggle to defend the Amazonia against the state and corporations.

Part V is **Challenges for a critical agenda on the over-criminalization of dissent**, which includes the challenges of punitivism from the left, the use of artificial intelligence as a policing tool against dissent, the Covid-19 pandemic and right-wing activism.

The first chapter is **Artificial intelligence and the criminalisation of activism**, written by **Mark Cowling**. This work starts by defining artificial intelligence and noting some of its developments over the next few years. Mark acknowledges that social media fostered by artificial intelligence eases the organization of activism, as the Arab Spring (also known as the Facebook Revolution) exposes. Here also, Black Lives Matter appears as a key example. On the other hand, the chapter argues, artificial intelligence can be also be devoted as a method of repression. Facial recognition technology can be used to identify demonstrators, as done by US and British police forces. The problem is that artificial intelligence can be used to label individuals as dangerous, meaning that they are likely to be stopped aggressively, which in turn may lead them to resist, thus proving that they are violent. Thus, artificial intelligence opens the possibility of intimidating peaceful demonstrators and even of wrongfully targeting.

The next chapter is **Covid cops: a recent history of pandemic policing during the coronavirus crisis**, written by **Greg Martin**. This contribution provides a recent history of policing everyday life and protest during the Covid-19 pandemic. Globally, it is argued, government responses during the crisis sought to balance civil rights and freedoms with government intervention in the face of rising rates of coronavirus infection. Protests occurred over general lockdown measures as well as more specific issues such as the mandatory wearing of masks, as also occurred with anti-mask protests during the Spanish flu pandemic of the early 20th century. As with measures introduced to stem the spread of Spanish flu, fines were a key tool of pandemic policing during the Covid-19 crisis. To enforce restrictions on mass gatherings specifically, police employed a combination of fines, public health legislation and criminal law, effectively criminalizing dissent. However, looking at Australia, the chapter exposes that, far from amounting to a blanket ban on protest rights, courts, not unlike governments, sought to balance public health risks with protest rights. Moreover, considering the stage of the pandemic, courts sometimes upheld protest rights while determining rights to protest were deferred though not extinguished.

In **Punitive feminism (or When and why did we start dividing the world between good and evil, rather than between oppressed and oppressors?): Punitive Feminism, Tamar Pitch** offers an intersectional analysis on the relationship between feminist protest and the criminal justice system. Feminists have been very critical of the way penal law and court proceedings have dealt with harms of which women are the prevalent victims, and have been pushing for significant changes, also by introducing new crimes and new sanctions. This last move, however, Tamar argues, has contributed to a re-legitimation of the criminal justice system, after its discredit due to the antiauthoritarian movements of the 1960s and 1970s. The shift in the feminist lexicon from "oppression" to "victimization" and the insistence on the issue of "violence" may be seen as effects of, but also as contributors to, the centrality of the criminal justice system and its discourses in today's political arena. The chapter describes a contemporary punitive turn taken by a part of the feminist movement, focusing on two present-day struggles: the fight to reach a universal ban on surrogate motherhood and the fight to introduce everywhere the so-called "Nordic model" in dealing with prostitution.

Finally, in **Genocidal activism and the language of criminality: reflec-tions on the duality of the Nazi era and the avoidance of engagement with histories of social and political activism at the nuremberg trials, Wayne Morrison** explores activism within the Nazi movement in Germany. This seems to be a historical case study but, facing the increasing relevance of right-wing extremist groups in Europe (and worldwide) it is important to analyze this chapter from a present-day prism. Wayne calls attention to the fact that thousands who made up the early members of the Nazi regime shared feelings of being lost, of fearing for the future of Germany, of carrying, as an effect of World War I, a suspicion of betrayal, along with immense desire to do good for Germany. The author argues that even though they used aggressive tactics and engaged in identity cultural politics, the term "civil society activ-ists" is still wholly appropriate for these individuals and loose groupings. How those who out of fear of theoretical and existential anarchy, began as activ-ists but ended becoming agents of extermination in practice involved twisted paths, but many trod them. Answering Howard Becker's call to take a stand as criminologists, Wayne argues that we would do well to avoid stereotypes and simply correctional criminology when we seek, as we must, to take sides and commit our energies.

The chapter concludes with a thought-provoking piece by my friend and colleague Wayne Morrison. Hopefully, with it, readers will have reached a more profound understanding of the historical and global framings of organized dissent and gained some direction towards paying more attention to how criminal jus-tice systems have been unreservedly turning rights into crimes. As shown by the wide range of contributors and perspectives, this book also calls for raised awareness among the academic community of the need to foster gender- and racially sensi-tive analysis in our topics of research as well as ensuring equality regarding gender, region, academic age and race among the participants of our scholarly endeav-ors. No less relevant, the co-authorship of many of the pieces by authors from the Global South and North, as well as activists and scholars, sheds light on the enriching outcomes possible when we cross disciplinary and regional boundaries to engage in intersectional and global conversations.

Note

1 The primary filtering process is twofold. On the one hand, only certain harmful behav-iors are subjected to criminal sanctions. These are the offences generally perpetrated with simple or primitive resources, that demand easier evidence gathering, produce low social-political conflict, and are typically committed by the most vulnerable subsets of society. In contrast, those behaviors that are more complex, that demand higher levels of know-how to conduct the investigation, that do not produce social unrest, and that are usually committed by upper social status individuals, are not the core of the legislative process. On the other hand, among the legislated behaviors, they are attached to different punitive consequences, which not only respond to the involved social harm but also class and racial interests.

References

Baratta, A. (1986) *Criminología Crítica y Crítica del Derecho Penal*, Buenos Aires, Siglo XXI, 2001.

Becker, H. (1962) *Outsiders. Hacia una sociología de la desviación*, Madrid, Siglo XXI.

Booker, B. (2021) Protests in White and Black, and the Different Response of Law Enforcement, *NPR*, January 7, 2021, https://www.npr.org/people/348744480/brakkton-booker

El País (2008) El conflicto del campo colapsa Buenos Aires, July 16, https://elpais.com/internacional/2008/07/15/actualidad/1216072821_850215.html

Leatherby, A., Ray, A., Singhvi, A., Triebert, C., Watkins, D. and Willis, H. (2021) How a Presidential Rally Turned Into a Capitol Rampage, *NY Times*, January. 12.

Vegh Weis, V. (2017a) *Marxism and Criminology. A History of Criminal Selectivity*. Boston: Brill, 2017.

Vegh Weis, V. (2017b) Emergencies Blind Reason: When 'Fast on Crime' Undermines 'Smart on Crime', *Washburn Law Journal*, 57, 2, 2018, pp. 337–365.

Zaffaroni, R., Alagia, A. and Slokar, A. (2000) *Derecho Penal. Parte General*, Buenos Aires, Ediar.

Zunino, E. (2018) *La cobertura mediática del conflicto campo gobierno de 2008 en la prensa gráfica argentina*. Bernal, UNQ.

PART I

Theoretical approaches on the over-criminalization of dissent

1

POLITICS OF EXCEPTION

Criminalizing activism in Western European democracies

Katharina Fritsch and Andrea Kretschmann

In liberal democracies, states are only allowed to use exceptional measures to a limited extent. They can temporarily suspend the constitution, but solely when confronted with a systemic threat. Nonetheless we currently see an increase of what we refer to as "politics of exception", that is, the use of exceptional regulations in the legal and political realm of contemporary constitutional democracies. Recent examples include the *ley mordaza* in Spain, the *état d'urgence* in France, the new police laws in several German states as well as many of the emergency measures related to the Covid-19 pandemic. In all these instances, a "politics of exception" also includes a criminalization of public street protest. This chapter argues that this phenomenon—which encompasses legal discourses as well as political processes and practices,—is instrumental for maintaining and reorganizing state power by framing protest as a *destabilizing Other* rather than as an integral part of the existing political order. In doing so, states make use of their heaviest weapon, that is, criminal law.

To explore the issue, we draw on three disconnected research strands. *Political theory* discusses the state of exception as an integral part of the tools and regulations of modern states when dealing with crises. *Criminology* argues that the governing of protest always takes place under exceptional terms, even when there is no formal state of exception. *Post-colonial studies* show how a politics of exception has historically been part of the modern state in its colonial practice. So, we will first discuss the criminalization of protest by drawing on the concept of "large and petty states of exception" as proposed by Kretschmann & Legnaro (2017, 2018) Second, we will argue that the criminalization of protest is creeping from the social margins towards the societal center, leading to an intensified criminalization of protest and de-democratization. Third, we discuss how the logic of the exception becomes indistinguishable from mechanisms of *Othering*. We argue that through the politics of exception much current protest is marked as a *hostile Other*, and hence subjected to the latter's historic social configurations, including those from (post-)colonial

DOI: 10.4324/9781003144229-3

orders. This leads us to conclude that politics of exception do not stand for the opposite of liberal democracy but are an intrinsic part of the latter's own operating principle.

Large and petty states of exception

While "large states of exception" encompass the formal declaration of a state of emergency by state actors, "petty states of exception" refer to daily exceptional practices enacted by the executive branch (Kretschmann & Legnaro 2017). From a political theory perspective, one can argue that states of emergency are increasingly used for the handling of various kinds of crises (Lemke 2017). Criminological perspectives add an important nuance: contemporary politics of exception also run beyond a formal state of emergency at a microlevel (Kretschmann & Legnaro 2017, 2018), for instance, through (indefinite) imprisonment without trial (Jobard 2017). Finally, post-colonial perspectives emphasize that both large and petty states of exception mirror the relation of Western statehood with colonial rule, that is, a rule of law including its own suspension with regard to colonized subjects, considered as the *other* side of its governmentality (Mbembe 2011, Bancel, Blanchard & Vergès 2003)

In political theory it is commonplace to comprehend a formal state of emergency as a legal–political instrument when facing a crisis, that is, as a provision which is accompanied by a shift of powers from the legislative to the executive branch and by the restriction of basic rights and freedoms (Lemke 2017, 2). Scholars understand formal states of emergency as an expression of crisis due to economic, ecological, or social problems internationally and nationally (Belina 2018). Here, the state of emergency serves as *ultima ratio*. However, due to the history of European fascism, Western states have become more reluctant to introduce exceptional policies, given their potential tendency towards authoritarianism (Agamben 2004, 9). Since Schmitt's (1922, 2004, 13) right-wing interpretation of the decision over a state of exception as equaling political sovereignty in the sense of a totalitarian state, the latter is also associated with despotic regimes (Linz 2009). One should add that all politics of exception are grounded in different historical, including colonial, conditions. While in France, for instance, the implementation of a formal state of emergency has been used fairly frequently, in Germany it faces high hurdles (Kretschmann & Legnaro 2017).

How do politics of exception relate to the regulation of protests? Where states govern protest through states of emergency, they frame it as a fundamental threat to public order, signaling a readiness to counter it. This was clearly visible in France, where the freedom to assemble was severely restricted or even suspended during the recent *état d'urgence* (2015–17). Demonstrations such as those against labor law reforms were partially banned, activists were placed under house arrest and police powers were extended, for example, those enabling house searches (Jobard 2017).

Post-colonial perspectives emphasize the parallels of such current politics of exception with colonial governing (Stoler 2011, 201). It is argued that "imperialism … provided the main arena in which the state of exception was practiced most vigorously, systematically and violently" (Shenhaw 2012, 19), marked by unlawful police practices, violent biopolitics, and use of coercion and force by the state in a variety of practices. Clearly, today's politics of exception are embedded in colonial legacies for example, in the context of France, where contemporary politics of exception, among others, reflect the police *dispositif* implemented during the Algerian war of independence (1954–62) (Mbongo 2017).

Conversely, criminology has investigated how practices of exception have become increasingly visible in criminal policy, even outside states of emergency. Kretschmann & Legnaro (2017, 321) argue that exceptional legal provisions and police practices have become common *within* the rule of law, thus gradually shifting its meaning, turning the rule of law into a "state of exception of the second order". Similarly, Fassin discusses instances of racial profiling during routine policing as "petty states of exception" (Fassin 2014) and thus as manifestations of a security order that governs through exception by dismantling civil liberties, particularly through preventive measures. With regard to policing of protests, this exceptionality becomes apparent in a lower degree of tolerance before a police intervention is triggered (Ferret & Mouhanna 2005) or the application of preventive measures that *de facto* turn into repression. This is the case when demonstrations are banned because of a forecast of a risk of violence, when preventive detention deprives individuals of the presumption of innocence or when even moderate and peaceful social movements attract increased police intelligence surveillance (Dopplinger & Kretschmann 2014). As such, these politics no longer conform to classical principles of the rule of law (Jobard 2017), thus becoming effectively "illiberal".

Large and petty states of exception, however, are not merely juxtaposed, but rather interlock by complementing each other discursively and practically (Kretschmann & Legnaro 2017). They share the common premise of extraordinary threats to the state or the nation, which in turn legitimates politics of exception. Petty states of exception prepare large ones by permanently setting perceptions of threats for which large states of exception are the only logical consequence in the case of more extraordinary occurrences that are framed as "dangerous". Inversely, formal states of emergency are frequently an occasion for exceptional legal provisions to be permanently transferred into ordinary law. For instance, in France, legal elements of the *état d'urgence* have been largely transferred into ordinary (criminal) law (Jobard 2017).

Such a 'departure' from the rule of law also raises concerns over the preservation of democracy. Criminology regards the tendency to criminalize protest through politics of exception as a development towards a condition of "post-rule of law" (Kretschmann & Legnaro 2017). This resonates with perspectives in political theory on the relation between formal states of emergency and de-democratization processes, resulting in a "securitization" of Western societies (Agamben 2004, 22). Postcolonial perspectives contribute to such debates, since they contest a narrative about a contemporary shift from "democratic" to "undemocratic" regimes by bringing into focus those subjects who have always been denied democratic rights, both historically in the context of colonization and today in the form of migration regimes and border control (Castro Varela & Dhawan 2015).

Within this framework, protest is governed by a *complex structure of exceptions*. The history of Western modern statehood shows that this 'departure' from the rule of law is not a new phenomenon. However, the literature demonstrates that there is a *qualitative* change that indicates a shift in the state's approach to protest and thus also in its material understanding of democracy. In the context of protest policing, this change in particular affects protest emanating from the center of society, including liberal protest groups.

Exception as expansion

The regulation of protest through politics of exception follows an expansionary logic: more and more parts of the social are connoted as "threats" reflecting (in-) securitization processes (Agamben 2004, 22). This "securitization" (Buzan, Waever & Wilde 1998) of protest is. As detailed above, political activism is increasingly subjugated to intelligence gathering by police, as well as criminalization through the criminal justice system. With Bonß (2011), one might understand such tendencies as part of late modern societies that perceive (in-)security as an uncontainable phenomenon. This contrasts with modern societies, where dangers are perceived to be manageable since they can be known, recognized, and therefore dealt with. This notion corresponds with the short and singular phase of "penal welfarism"', which adopted an inclusionary logic underpinned by welfare state policies: the criminal justice system was understood as having the aim to balance social inequalities and unequal opportunities that may lead to crime and deviancy (Garland 2001). This period overlapped with the implementation of forms of protest policing based on communication and dialogue, while at the same time repressive forms of protest policing were also further developed (Kretschmann 2014).

In late modern societies threats are perceived as difficult to foresee and thus volatile and non-containable. The current governing of protest by means of exception reflects this kind of perception of security, insofar as protest is treated increasingly as an incommensurate and particularly intense threat. The notion of an "uncontainable and borderless security space" mirrors the neoliberal state, whose borders are blurred in the course of globalization. The latter is complemented by a discourse on international organized crime framed as a threatening backdrop, which in turn fuels policies of internal *security*. Crime control, which in the past was primarily conceived as reactive, aimed at punishing criminal offences, becomes preventive, and is transformed into a *security* policy. Problems framed in social security terms during penal welfarism are now rephrased as problems of criminal policy. The societal focus shifts towards (in-)security *in potential*, leading to practices aimed at controlling potentially dangerous spaces, locations, situations and populations, while no longer necessarily differentiating between legal and illegal behavior.

This shift results in societies entering a state of perceived overall insecurity, especially with regard to public space. This includes public protest, so that the increased notion of dangerousness described above no longer only applies to protest at the "extremist" margins, but increasingly also to protests located in the center of society (Belina 2018). Consequently, even protests that are classified as peaceful can be considered a security 'problem'. Furthermore, demonstrators now often appear as *Others* and hence as enemies who are not engaging in political participation but rather intent on destroying the state. Policing protest becomes less an ordinary public order issue and more a way of dealing with potential public disorder, since diffuse dangers are lurking everywhere. In view of an always open, never pacifiable space, this has striking similarities to colonial policing (Blanchard 2014), for instance, if one considers the increased density of control and regulation that marks protests as criminogenic, dangerous and disruptive activities (Kretschmann 2016) and the tendency to displace them spatially (Coaffee 2016). In effect, "far from policing the margins, the police are now controlling large blocks of the population" (Brewer et al. 1996, 43).

This dovetails with findings from Noakes & Gillham (2006) for the USA that can be adapted to the European context: For late modernity, they discover a shift in protest policing which they name "strategic incapacitation". With it, they emphasize a new, almost "pre-emptive" policing approach that prevents or restricts protest, closely monitors protest and collects data on protesters irrespective of concrete dangers. At the judicial level, draconian punishments are handed out in individual cases (Hunold & Wegner 2018), for instance, activists engaging in civil disobedience might end up on terror lists, as was the case in Austria (Kretschmann 2012). Thus, in recent years, liberal protests have been increasingly harshly policed and been met by demands for self-policing. One might introduce a distinction here between the different spatial environments that protests take place in. Protesters in a securitized context, for example, central urban spaces, can appear as "space invaders" (Puwar 2004). Conversely, when protest is in areas already perceived as "dangerous", that is, the periphery in European cities (Fritsch 2021), it is more likely to be seen as a potential threat. Protest then also becomes insecure(d), resulting in a higher likelihood of harsher policing. It has been shown that when police operate in the mode of eventualities, this leads to earlier intervention. Escalatory tendencies in protest policing (Joyce & Wain 2014, 274) and its militarization (Fillieule 2020) can also be situated in this securitized context. Both developments follow developments in crime policy while also being event-driven, for example, in the aftermaths of 9/11 or the Bataclan attacks.

The notion of blurred security and the securitization of public space resonates with power mechanisms in colonial contexts (Mbembe 2011, 28), where politics of exception "tended to erupt at any time, on whatever pretext and anywhere". It certainly is important not to fall into simple analogies between colonialism and contemporary politics of exception. Rather, a post-colonial perspective on the criminalization of protest would link these phenomena to historical and contemporary processes of the criminalization of marginalized groups—both in the Global South and North—and shows how politics of exception have always been and continue to be part of the (intersectional) violence of the modern state. Against this background, protest policing increasingly adopts a logic of counterinsurgency, as can be observed in the contexts of anti-colonial struggles (Rigouste 2011, 57–63).

However, current politics of exception are no "return" or transfer of practices, but rather represent the relation of "illiberalism" and bourgeois democracy and their intensification in form of an expansionary logic.

Since the security logic outlined above has an inherent tendency to perpetuate itself, politics of exception begin to evolve independently to a greater extent than in the preceding phase of penal welfarism. Lemke 2017, 3) emphasizes that exceptional regulations can operate independently from crisis regulation as—we would add here: postcolonial neoliberal—governance, leading to an autonomation of effects. This becomes apparent when observing a tendency where protests are seen less and less as a legitimate expression of political will, but rather as a danger to order *per se*. Criminalization through politics of exception then not only reflects the maintenance of order, but also the *production* of order through exceptional practices. However, this order reflects a departure from liberal democratic principles. The disruption of order caused by protest (as conceptualized from a political theory perspective) (Rancière 2002) is no longer acceptable and welcome as part of democratic participation and negotiation. Rather, protest is seen as interrupting the neoliberal and post-colonial order.

Exception as othering

Finally, we argue that securitization, and its expansion processes are accompanied and shaped by an *Othering logic*, both as condition, and effect of politics of exception. When protests are discursively marked as "non-democratic", activists tend to be seen and treated as state enemies rather than citizens, as was the case with the Gilets Jaunes in France in 2018 and 2019 (Rucht 2019) or parts of the G20 protests in Germany in 2017 (Mullis 2018). The same is true for the European "war on terror" (Pantazis & Pemberton 2009). The focus on *Othering* processes shows that an expansionary logic in protest policing does not affect "all" equally, rather, it has differentiating effects, resulting in differentiated vulnerabilities among activists. However, *Othering* is not a new phenomenon: for decades, criminological literature has pointed out that the marginalized are monitored far more by the police than other sections of the population (Wacquant 2009). Post-colonial theory situates *Othering* within (post-)colonial contexts (Spivak 1999), primarily shaped by racialization and ethnicization, but intersecting with other social categories like gender, class, or dis- and ability. Current post-colonial neoliberalism leads to an intensified governing of protest through *Othering* along these lines.

The aftermath of 9/11 intensified existing tendencies in criminal policy towards tough and/or intensified policing worldwide, including in Europe. As a result, well-known *Othered* figures were reinforced, particularly "male, young, foreign". From a post-colonial perspective, the focus on the "Muslim man" as a synonym for "terrorist" or (sexual) "offender" reflects genealogies of gendered and ethicized *Others* (Spivak 1999). *Othering* thus presents a form of governing through exception that is part of the historically embedded discursive, geopolitical and economic relations between the "West" and the "Rest" (Hall 1992). It continues to shape forms of inclusion and exclusion in contemporary Western societies, thereby linking up with the securitization of the poor in advanced neoliberalism (Wacquant 2010). This entanglement of class and ethnicization increases the focus on ethnicized groups, whereby new legal provisions and jurisprudence, as well as police practices allow for intensified investigation and punishment of politically motivated crime, mainly in the area of "Islamist" terrorism (Holzinger 2017). As discussed earlier, such dynamics also result in increasing criminalization of other political protest groups, including (White) liberal bourgeois protest.

The politics of exception draw on these figures for the *Other*, anticipate, or produce them. Intensified counterterrorism policies and the increased criminalization of some forms of protest can be linked to broader *Othering* logics. Central to this is the construction of "internal" and "external enemies" (Rigouste 2011), being repeatedly reframed and sometimes blurred (Holzinger 2017, 284–285). If terrorists mostly continue to be represented as "external enemies", protest groups, if criminalized, are framed as "internal enemies." Both figures have in common— although with different severity effects—that they are marked as threats to (liberal) democracy, the constitution, or the entire state, which makes them legitimate targets of heightened policing. Intersectional *Othering* practices are thus part of state order mechanisms, as the *demos* constantly defines and re-forms itself internally and externally through the exclusion of *Others*.

Othering also relates to the fact that police behave differently towards different protest groups (Earl et al. 2003). For instance, when dealing with a protest, the degree of tolerance by the police for violations of agreements varies depending on the protest they are dealing with (Mansley 2013, 55). In particular, the police's assessment of the legitimacy of a protest is considered to be crucial for the choice of police strategy (Waddington 2003). Next to demonstrations by marginalized groups and those directed against powerful interest groups, protests associated with a tendency towards violence make the use of forceful tactics more likely (Della & Reiter 1998). Della Porta & Peterson (2005) also note a lower level of willingness to negotiate on the part of police at transnational and anti-globalization protest, and among these, anti-capitalist protests.

In view of this unequal treatment, the politics of exception do not expand "democratically" but create new borders between an "us" and the "*Others*", according to the social and political connotations of a protest. It is well-established that individuals and social groups are at different risk of police violence (Thompson 2018); obviously this also applies to the context of protests. In addition, along with the development of communicative and de-escalating approaches to protest policing, differentiated policing practices come into place, where delinquency and deviancies are no longer attributed to a demonstration as a whole but only to violent segments or individuals. Consequently, this creates new lines of division between protesters while potentially leading to coalitions between police and some activists. Whereas in the past, violence was in some respects considered legitimate by a broad spectrum of people, today it is universally rejected, partly due to the fact that the police tend to heavily problematize violence —often even when present only to the slightest degree (Wood 2014).

The phenomenon of criminalization of protests through the politics of exception is characterized by *Othering* occurring also to liberal protest segments and no longer only affecting the political margins. Often, protest groups are considered as extremist or potentially violent and thus posing a (potential) threat to security (Kretschmann 2021)—mostly without factual basis. Thus, the police's intensified focus on prevention can effectively result in repression. However, despite the increase in politics of exception, dialogical, de-escalate and non-confrontational doctrines—developed since the 1980s—continue to characterize the most part of protest policing (Della Porta & Reiter 1998). Oriented towards agreements and compromises between police and protesters, such policing is designed to protect the protesters' rights and to minimize disruptions of public order. *Radical Othering*, although on the increase, therefore, still only applies to a part of protest policing. However, its creeping into the regulation of protest is one side of a criminal policy coin: Garland's (2001) thesis of a "complementary criminal policy", which is also applicable to the context of Europe (Sack 2010), can offer an insight into the differential application of politics of exception in the context of protest (Kretschmann 2021). Garland describes how a justice system underpinned by welfare state principles that sought to bridge the social divide has been transformed into a neoliberal penal regime characterized by a managerial approach. The latter treats different offenders according to different criminal policy philosophies and standards, resulting in some groups of offenders being perceived not as citizens but as enemies. The same applies to the policing of protest when it is governed by politics of exception. The literature describes these developments in the criminal justice system as a criminal law of the enemy (in favor of this perspective, see Jakobs 2004), showing parallels to colonial criminal policies (Blanchard 2014), as it places groups outside of civil law (Linhardt & Moreau de Bellaing 2017) and thus citizenship. While some types of protest are *de facto* handled according to these principles (Le Roulley & Long 2018), most others face dialogical forms of protest policing as part of a complementary logic.

Conclusions: exception as de-democratization

In Western democracies, citizens should only face state practices of exception if the state or its basic functions are threatened. As we have shown, large and petty states of exceptions are nevertheless on the increase in these societies, a development which in turn leads to the criminalization even of liberal protest outside of periods of crisis. Drawing on political theory, criminology and post-colonial approaches, we have shown that politics of exception are characterized mainly by three logics of governing: the entanglement of large and petty states of exception, an expansionary logic and mechanisms of *Othering*. The result is a (partial) marking of protest as the *Other* to democracy and consequently de-democratization processes.

The politics of exception find their discursive justification by combating protest labeled as a threat to the state in order to (re-)establish security. In this regard, petty states of exception reflect a constant defense of "normality", while large states of emergency react to a sudden rupture of order. Such politics have substantial side effects, as the criminalization of protest through exception diverts attention from underlying social conflicts and results in a regime of securitization with the result of a depoliticization of protest (Agamben 2004). Thus, the effects of a neoliberal transformation become evident in the return of state sovereignty, as order is restored through the public demonstration of power, even if only temporarily.

Effectively, "security"—in its proliferation and as a mechanism of *Othering*—serves as an agent in creating a line between "us" and "them", at the same time, it increases societal cohesion, even if politics of exception mark more and more protest forms— even parts of the political center—as an *Other*. As a result, a growing number of protests and activists are considered potentially dangerous and hence in need of tougher policing. This logic of expansion, however, differentiates between social groups or strata, making protesting ever more difficult for already marginalized groups and actors.

The criminalization of protest reflects a goal of state power: the prevention of political conflict in order to secure power. This goes along with a restriction of the political public sphere and/or its reshaping, as political actors eventually adapt their behavior since making use of freedom of expression can lead to being observed or punished. However, in order to investigate these effects of criminalization through exception, not only on the theoretical but also on an empirical level, further research is needed. In this regard, the question at stake is how protesters react to such changes in protest policing and whether new forms of action and new coalitions might arise between protest groups that are negatively affected by politics of exception, for instance in the form of intersectional alliances.

References

Agamben, G. (2004) *Ausnahmezustand*, Suhrkam: Homo Sacer Frankfurt a. M.

Bancel, N., Blanchard, P. and Vergès, F. (2003) *La République Coloniale*, Paris: Albin Michel.

Belina, B. (2018) Perioden der Kriminalisierung im und durch den (west-) deutschen Staat, in: Jens Puschke and Tobias Singelnstein (eds.), *Der Staat und die Sicherheitsgesellschaft*, Wiesbaden: Springer VS, 171–191.

Blanchard, E. (2014) French Colonial Police, in: Gerben Bruinsma and David Weisburd (eds.), *Encyclopedia of Criminology and Criminal Justice*, 8, New York: Springer, 1836–1846.

Bonß, W. (2011) (Un-)Sicherheit in der Moderne, in: Peter Zoche and Stefan Kaufmann and Rita Haverkamp (eds.), *Zivile Sicherheit*, Bielefeld, 43–70.

Brewer, J., Guelke, A., Hume, I., Moxon-Browne, E and Wilford, R. (1996) *The Police, Public Order and the State. Policing in Great Britain, Northern Ireland, the Irish Republic, the USA, Israel, South Africa and China*, 2. Aufl., London: Palgrave Macmillan.

Buzan, B., Waever, O. and Wilde, J. (1998) *Security. A New Framework for Analysis*, Boulder and London, Lynne Rienner.

Castro Varela, M. and Dhawan, N. (2015) *Postkoloniale Theorie: Eine kritische Einführung*, 2. ed., Bielefeld.

Coaffee, J. (2016) Normalising Exceptional Public Space Security. The Spatial Fix of the Olympic Carceral, in: Mattias De Backer and Lucas Melgaço and Georgiana Varna and Francesca Menichelli (eds.), *Order and Conflict in Public Space*, Abingdon: Routledge, 15–36.

Della, P. and Reiter, H. (1998): *Policing Protest: The Control of Mass Demonstrations in Western Democracies*, Minneapolis.

Della Porta, D. and Peterson, A. (2005) Editorial, *Policing and Society*, 15, 3, 233–234.

Dopplinger, L. and Kretschmann, A. (2014) Die Produktion gefährlicher Räume, *juridikum*, 1, 19–29.

Earl, J., Soule, S. and McCarthy, J. (2003) Protest Under Fire? Explaining the Policing of Protest, *American Sociological Review*, 68, 4, 581–606.

Fassin, D. (2014) Petty States of Exception: The Contemporary Policing of the Urban Poor, in: Maguire, M., Frois, C. and Zurawski, N. (eds.) *The Anthropology of Security*, London: Pluto Press, 104–117.

Ferret, J. and Mouhanna, C. (2005) *Peurs sur les villes*, Paris: Presses universitaires de France.

Fillieule, O. (2020) *Protest in a Time of Pandemic*, Vienna: Paper brief of IWM.

Fritsch, K. (2021) *The Dispositive of Communitarisation and Ethnicised Biopolitics. Cultural and political mobilisations of 'Franco-Comorian diaspora' in Marseille*, London: Routledge, forthcoming.

Garland, D. (2001) *The Culture of Control*, Oxford: Oxford U.

Hall, S. (1992) The West and the Rest: Discourse and Power, in: Ders. and Bram G. (Hrsg.), *Formations of Modernity*, Cambridge: Polity Press, 275–320.

Holzinger, M. (2017) Transnationaler Terrorismus und Ausnahmezustand, in: Lemke, Matthias (ed.), *Ausnahmezustand. Theoriegeschichte – Anwendungen – Perspektiven*, Wiesbaden: Springer VS, 283–300.

Hunold, D. and Wegner, M. (2018). Protest Policing im Wandel? Konservative Strömungen in der Politik der Inneren Sicherheit am Beispiel des G20-Gipfels in Hamburg, *Kripoz*, 5, 291–298.

Jakobs, G. (2004) Bürgerstrafrecht und Feindstrafrecht, in: *HRR-Strafrecht*, 5, 88–95.

Jobard, F. (2017) Der Notstand in Frankreich: Tragödie oder Farce?, [online], https: and www.rosalux.de and publikation and id and 14771 and der-notstand-in-frankreich-tragoedie-oder-farce and [08.07.2019].

Joyce, L. and Wain, N. (2014) *Public Order Policing, Protest, and Political Violence*, Basingstoke and New York: Palgrave Macmillan.

Kretschmann, A. (2012) Das Wuchern der Gefahr. Einige gesellschaftstheoretische Anmerkungen zur Novelle des Sicherheitspolizeigesetzes 2012, *juridikum*, 3, 320–333.

Kretschmann, A. (2014) Katalysator Wirtschaftskrise? Zum Wandel von Protest Policing in Europa, in: *Bürgerrechte and Polizei (CILIP)*, 106, 52–62.

Kretschmann, A. (2016) Die Polizei in Gewaltdynamiken: Eine sozialtheoretische Annäherung, *juridikum*, 4, 504–515.

Kretschmann, A. (2018) Ausnahmezustände, in: *Kriminologisches Journal*, 50, 3, 204–211.

Kretschmann, A. (2021) Les villes artificielles comme espaces de formation de l'ordre: l'entrainement au « worst case scenario » des polices européennes, in: *Carnets des géographes*, im Erscheinen.

Kretschmann, A. and Legnaro, A. (2017). Ausnahmezustände: Zur Soziologie einer Gesellschaftsverfassung, *Prokla*, 47, 3, 471–486.

Kretschmann, A. and Legnaro, A. (2018): Ausnahmezustände, Kriminologisches Journal, 50(3), 204–2011.

Le Roulley, S. and Long, J. (2018) Terrorisme, violences politiques et maintien de l'ordre: L'ultra gauche comme cible de la terreur instituée?, *Journal des Anthropologues*, 154–155, 3, 137–160.

Lemke, M. (2017) Was heißt Ausnahmezustand?, in: Matthias Lemke (ed.), *Ausnahmezustand*, Wiesbaden: Springer VS, 1–9.

Linhardt, D. and Moreau de Bellaing, C. (2017) La doctrine du droit pénal de l'ennemi et l'idée de l'antiterrorisme: Genèse et circulation d'une entreprise de dogmatique juridique, *Droit et société*, 3, 97, 615–640.

Linz, J. (2009) *Totalitäre und autoritäre Regime, 3. Aufl.*, Potsdam: Berliner Debatte.

Mansley (2013) *Collective Violence, Democracy, and Protest Policing*, Abingdon and New York: Routledge.

Mbembe, A. (2011) *On the Postcolony. Studies on the History of Society and Culture*, Berkeley: University of California Press.

Mbongo, P. (2017) Die französischen Regelungen zum Ausnahmezustand, in: Matthias Lemke (ed.), *Ausnahmezustand. Theoriegeschichte – Anwendungen – Perspektiven*, Wiesbaden: SpringerVS, 129–166.

Mullis, D. (2018) G20 in Hamburg. Politik, Unvernehmen, Ausnahmezustand und das Ende der Postdemokratie, *sub\urban*, 6, 1, 29–50.

Noakes, J. and Gillham, P. (2006) Aspects of the 'New Penology' in the Police Response to Major Political Protest in the United States, 1999–2000, in: Donatella della Porta and Abby Peterson and Herbert Reiter (ed.), *The Policing of Transnational Protest*, Aldershot: Ashgate, 97–116.

Pantazis, C. and Pemberton, S. (2009) From the 'Old' to the 'New' Suspect Community: Examining the Impacts of Recent UK Counter-Terrorist Legislation, *British Journal of Criminology*, 49, 5, 646–666.

Puwar, N. (2004) *Space Invaders: Race, Gender, and Bodies out of Place*, New York: Berg Publishers.

Rancière, J. (2002) *Das Unvernehmen*. Suhrkam: *Politik und Philosophie*. Frankfurt a. M.

Reiter, H. (1998) *Policing Protest: The Control of Mass Demonstrations in Western Democracies*, Minneapolis and London: University of Minnesota Press.

Rigouste, M. (2011) *L'ennemie intérieur. La généalogie coloniale et militaire de l'ordre sécuritaire dans la France contemporaine*, Paris: La Découverte.

Rucht, D. (2019) Die Gelbwestenbewegung. Stand und Perspektiven, *ipb Working Papers*, Berlin.

Sack, F. (2010) Der weltweite 'punitive turn': Ist die Bundesrepublik dagegen gefeit?, in: Hans-Georg Soeffner (eds.), *Unsichere Zeiten. Herausforderungen gesellschaftlicher Transformationen*, Wiesbaden: SpringerVS, 229–244.

Schmitt, C. (2004) [1922]: *Politische Theologie. Vier Kapitel zur Lehre von der Souveränität*, 8. ed., Berlin: Duncker and Humblot.

Shenhaw, Y. (2012) Imperialism, Exceptionalism and the Contemporary World, in: Marcelo Svirsky and Simone Bignall (eds.), *Agamben and Colonialism*, Edinburgh: Edinburgh University Press, 17–31.

Spivak, G. (1999) *A critique of Postcolonial Reason. Toward a History of the Vanishing Present*, Calcutta and New Delhi: Seagull.

Stoler, A. (2011) Beyond Sex. Bodily Exposures of the Colonial and Postcolonial Present, in Anne Berger and Eleni Varikas (eds.), *Genre et Postcolonialismes. Dialogues Transcontinentaux*, Paris: Editions des archives contemporaines, 185–214.

Thompson, V. (2018) "There is no justice, there is just us!": Ansätze zu einer postcolonial-feministischen Kritik der Polizei am Beispiel von Racial Profiling, in Loick, Daniel (ed.) *Kritik der Polizei*, Frankfurt and New York: Campus, 197–219.

Wacquant, L. (2009) *Bestrafen der Armen: Zur neoliberalen Regierung der sozialen Unsicherheit*, Opladen and Berlin and Toronto: Budrich Unipress.

Wacquant, L. (2010) Crafting the Neoliberal State: Workfare, Prisonfare, and Social Insecurity, *Sociological Forum*, 25, 2, 197–220.

Waddington, A.J. (2003) Policing Public Order and Political Contention, in: Tim Newburn (ed.), *Handbook of Policing*, Cullompton: Willan, 394–421.

Wood, L. (2014) *Crisis and Control. The Militarization of Protest Policing*, Toronto: Pluto Press.

2

A SOCIAL CONTROL PERSPECTIVE FOR THE STUDY OF ENVIRONMENTAL HARM AND RESISTANCE

Alida Szalai

In 2018, the human rights activist leader of the *Resistencia Pacífica de Cahabón* (Peaceful Resistance of Cahabón), Bernardo Caal Xól, was sentenced to seven years and four months of imprisonment in Guatemala. Caal represented the rights of the Q'eqchi' Indigenous communities in Santa Maria Cahabón municipality, and from 2015 had taken partially successful legal steps to thwart the investments of the Oxec company involving two dam constructions on the Cahabón river that caused heavy social and environmental harm. The accusations against Caal were illegal detention and aggravated robbery based on the testimonies of employees connected to the construction.

Building upon this case, a necessary question arises: how can criminologists engage with the problem of the criminalization of environmental activists and land rights defenders[1] to better understand the underlying structural and cultural dynamics? While the vast majority of criminalization and repression of activists and defenders occurs in the Global South, emerging trends indicate that environmental activists face increasing risk and danger in the Global North as well, exposing this topic as a worldwide phenomenon (Article 19, 2014; 201). This chapter outlines a theoretical perspective to explore the grassroot reactions to environmental harm as well as the state and private reactions to resistance and social mobilization. The understanding is that studying the social control of environmental harm and resistance using a green-cultural criminological framework could contribute to a deeper understanding of power relations, competing interests and the political and cultural dynamics underlying the reproduction of environmental harm.

By broadening the criminological scope to include the concept of socially mediated harm (Hillyard et al. 2004; Pemberton 2007; Michalowski 2009), contemporary power dynamics through which harm is controlled and resisted could be revealed. Studying the interactions between the formal and informal social control of crime is a well-established criminological tradition (Cohen 1985; Garland 2001; Ferrell, Hayward & Young 2008; Borbíró 2011). By extending the notion of social control, usually applied

DOI: 10.4324/9781003144229-4

to the study of crime control, it is possible to distinguish between formal and informal control of both environmental harm and the resistance against it. In this context resistance is seen as a form of "informal control of environmental harm", while the criminalization of activists as a type of "formal, institutionalized control of this resistance".

Environmental harm, resistance and the corresponding social control mechanisms are aligned with the traditions of cultural criminology based on an emerging trend in green-cultural approaches (see, e.g., Brisman & South 2012, 2014; Ferrell 2013; Natali & McClanahan 2017). Part 2 of this chapter asserts a green-cultural approach for analyzing the control of environmental harm and its resistance. Part 3 provides an analysis of the social control perspective and the implications of global law and local orders (Bauman 1998). Finally, the chapter presents the case of Bernardo Caal Xól and the broader post-colonial context in which it is embedded to illustrate the particularities of this phenomenon in the Global South.

A green-cultural framework for the study of social control of environmental harm

When Lynch (1990) introduced the term "green criminology", he emphasized that it bears a twofold task. On the one hand, it reflects the methodological and theoretical basis of the existing and well-established criminological traditions[2] and, on the other, it strengthens a novel, green perspective in criminological thinking, which encompasses the study of environmental crimes and harms. Ever since, green criminology, originating from the traditions of critical criminology, is a constantly developing perspective, offering diverse, inter- and multi-disciplinary approaches and various typologies for studying environmental crimes and harms (South, Brisman & Beirne 2013).

The legal-illegal divide is a main concern amongst criminologists studying environmental issues (White 2009). Halsey & White (1998) describe a legal-procedural and a social-legal approach. The legal-procedural approach is mainly concerned with harms regulated by national and international legal practices. In contrast, a social-legal understanding of harms identifies environmental issues that could be subject to criminological investigation more broadly. This approach opens up criminological study to reach beyond those environmentally harmful practices and acts in relation to which the present legal control mechanisms, including criminal law, have developed so far (see, e.g., Halsey & White, 1998; White 2010; Lynch et al. 2013; Hall 2015). The latter approach, defining the scope of criminological investigation, is essential for the social control perspective, since both activism and resistance could target environmentally harmful activities which are not or only weakly regulated and sometimes even fostered by the state, for instance hydraulic fracturing (Doyon & Bradshaw 2015; Steger & Drehobl 2018). The focus of this study, therefore, is framed in a grey zone, where the everyday practices of corporations, private actors and of the state are behind serious environmental and social harms (Hall 2015).

The recent proposals of the engagement of green criminology with cultural criminology could be an important step in exploring yet uncovered aspects of environmental harm (Brisman & South 2014). Cultural practices shape our perceptions of nature and vice versa (Abram 1997), an interrelationship that plays a crucial role in shaping both the formal and the informal control of environmental harm. For cultural criminology, the extensive control of almost every aspect of social life in late modernity could provoke some form of resistance (Ferrell 2003). Although in this case, resistance is partly a reaction to the "uncontrolled" spheres of social life, such as the global economy and its consequences for social and environmental justice. According to Ferrell, Hayward & Young (2008, 13) "the inequitable dynamics of law and social control remain essential to the maintenance of political power, and so operate to prop up the system that produces them". Power relations underlying environmental harm and conflict shape the forms of control of environmental harm and resistance. The control of the resistance could prove to be a key element for maintaining and reproducing the system that is beneficial for some while having detrimental effects on social and environmental justice.

The social control of environmental harm and resistance at the crossroads of global law and local orders

Those challenging the unwanted proliferation of environmentally harmful industries are increasingly victims of violent and legal retribution (Rasch 2017). While this is increasingly true worldwide, the Global South and marginalized communities are especially hard hit. According to the 2020 Global Witness report, 212 land and environmental defenders were killed in 2019, the highest rate ever. The victims were defending the environment and their own land from invasion by environmentally harmful industries such as mining, logging, agribusiness and hydroelectricity (Global Witness 2020). These violent crimes against defenders are characterized by the impunity of the perpetrators and a high level of hidden figures (see, e.g., Lynch, Stretesky & Long 2018; Ruggiero 2020). The other pressing issue is the criminalization of individuals and groups involved in resistance and social mobilization which, according to a recent analysis of the Environmental Justice Atlas (Scheidel et al. 2020), affects a growing number of activists and defenders throughout the globe.[3]

The state and corporate control of environmental activism and resistance, such as cases of criminalization, ban on protests, and, in some instances, the deployment of excessive police or private security force against activists and protesters, can be seen in the Global North as well. In the UK, three anti-fracking activists were jailed in 2018 for blocking trucks carrying drilling equipment. The appeal court dismissed the 16- and 15-month sentences on the ground that they were manifestly excessive. In 2019, another three anti-fracking activists were given suspended prison sentences because they were breaking a ban on demonstrations (BHRRC 2018b; Global Witness 2019). In Germany, activist moved into the remaining part of the Hambach forest, because an energy company, RWE, wanted to expand its coalmine located nearby. The forest became a symbolic battle ground for climate activist and a precedence for corporate counterinsurgency since the activists were forcefully removed by the police several times from 2012 (Brock & Dunlap 2018). In Hungary, environmental activists who stood against the construction of large public buildings in the City Park, and were assaulted by private security guards, had been charged with breaching the peace and sentenced to more than 200 hours of public duty (EEB 2019). However, the most severe cases of physical violence, i.e., the assassination of defenders, accumulated in the countries of the Global South, where Indigenous environmental and land-rights defenders are the most exposed to both violent crimes and criminalization (Global Witness 2019; Scheidel et al. 2020).

If we consider these repressive reactions to environmental activism as a form of social control, it is important to study the wider context in which they are embedded, namely the study of environmental harm and its control. This means, that we need to investigate, on the one hand, those global as well as local economic interests and cultural practices that lead to a particular environmental harm and, on the other hand, the social control of environmental harm involving a *formal* as well as an *informal* dimension.

The *formal control* of environmental harm embraces national and international environmental laws and policies together with human rights law—such as rights linked to a clean and healthy environment, the right to water or the right to adequate food (Knox & Pejan 2018). The question arises whether we can speak of an *effective* formal control of environmental harm at all. According to Rojas-Páez (2014) international agreements and law reflect the logic of capitalism; therefore, the formal control of environmental harm aligns with this perspective. It does not provide sufficient protection against the destructive, profit-driven forces of the global market, the main driving forces behind environmental harms and crimes (Lynch et al. 2013; Ruggiero 2013; Ruggiero & South 2013; White 2013). While the institutionalized control and enforcement varies across regimes, the logic of neoliberal capitalism tends to predominate in environmental issues. Moreover, the practical enforcement of environmental regulations, criminal or human rights laws is threatened by the sometimes-competing interests of business and other powerful actors (Hall 2015) and could depend largely on the socio-economic situation of the victims (Lynch 2016).

The frequently experienced ineffectiveness, weakness, or the absence of institutionalized control of environmental harms and crimes could lead to alternative *informal forms of control* mechanisms, for instance, to resistance and social movements.[4] From this perspective, the resistance and the struggle of environmental and human rights activists is an engagement to foster social control of the experienced socio-environmental harm. Social control is intertwined with different aspects of power. Not just with "power over", but with "power to" as a transformative capacity (Lukes, 2005; Svarstad, Benjaminsen & Overå 2018). The understanding of social control within labeling theory "moves toward the productive ideas of power, a critical concept for interpreting control and dissent" (Fernandez, 2008, p. 22). The conceptual framework outlined in this chapter builds upon these productive ideas of power by understanding activism and resistance against environmental harm as a form of *informal social control* that aims to achieve environmental and social justice in a particular socio-environmental conflict and has the transformative capacity to do that. In a broader sense it also includes transnational environmental movements concerned with climate change. To understand resistance as a form of informal control, which seeks to complement the formal control mechanisms of environmental harm and challenges the economic and cultural roots these harms spring from, highlights the transformative power dimension of social mobilization.

How does formal-informal social control relate to criminalization of resistance? The formal social control of resistance could be understood as a form of over-criminalization as well (Vegh Weis 2017). In this case, the state's failure to enforce environmental regulations and to protect the rights of the affected communities "is translated in the over-criminalization of those whose rights have been neglected" (Vegh Weis 2017, 227), and those who resist environmentally harmful practices. The criminalization of environmental activists occurs in diverse contexts with distinct historical, cultural and political backgrounds. Nevertheless, it is an instrument to weaken the resistance against socio-environmental harm and natural resource exploitation, in which the state plays a key role (Rojas-Páez 2014; Sieder 2017). It is not isolated that authorities keep the leaders of Indigenous communities in pre-trial detention for two years, before it turns out that the causation lacks sufficient proof (Human Rights Council 2018). Furthermore, the state quite often runs a campaign of defamation and labels the communities, activists and thus the resistance itself as extremists or eco-terrorists. This is how it attempts to legitimize the criminalization and the violation of human rights in the name of economic development and private profit (Raftopoulos 2017).

To shed more light on the control of environmental activism we should consider Bauman's idea of the conflict between "global law" and "local orders" from a criminological perspective (Bauman, 1998). He argues that the growing flexibility of the market at the global level goes hand in hand with the growing control of social and economic activity at the local level. This contributes to the extra-territoriality of certain groups of society, the elite, while the vast majority of society is at times forced to endure the constrains of locality (Bauman 1998). The question arises whether this pattern of growing control at the local level as a result of the increasing global flexibility of the market implies a stronger connection between, on the one hand, the crimes and harms of the powerful, and, on the other, the increased control of those who are trying to resist and change their, or others' locality by bringing social and environmental justice at the forefront of their endeavors. Environmental harm and the surrounding control mechanisms can hence be understood as part of this conflict of the global law and local orders.

The criminalization of environmental activists and defenders is an extreme manifestation of this conflict, which in some regard can be understood as an intersection of victimization. Land and environmental defenders could be victims of both environmental harm and of formal, institutionalized control mechanisms imposed by the state. We could discover the "asymmetric distribution of freedom" (Ruggiero 2015, 69) underlying this intersection, where the extra-territoriality of the elite symbolizes freedom, while on the local level, the victims of environmental harm are compelled to live with the consequences of the global flexibility. According to Ruggiero (2015) the asymmetric distribution of freedom could trigger a dynamic, which allows the powerful to control their own criminality, and empowers them to resist criminalization as well as to impose criminal labels on others. This complex dynamic implies a dimension where upholding the privileges, including impunity, requires the extension of certain control mechanisms, including criminalization, especially when dissent and resistance arise.

Could we identify some kind of relation between the crimes of the powerful and the strengthening control of those who raise their voices and fight against the very systems, norms and practices, without which the economic and political elite could not realize their interests and achieve their goals? If we view this interplay of forces from the perspective of control mechanisms targeting the resistance against environmental harm, we could examine this possibility. Now let us for the moment consider the implications of global law and local orders, which sheds light on the interests of the market and state actors. To attract capital and maintain "business as usual" for economic growth, the state has vested interest to control the local social and economic activity in the way required by neoliberal market principles (Bauman 1998; Harvey 2007; Fisher 2009), which is reflected in environmental regulations as well. The resistance, therefore, against a particular environmental crime, environmentally harmful activity or investment could threaten the interests of those who are the beneficiaries of the harmful activity. To cope with this risk, the state together with private agencies could use different forms of control mechanisms targeting activists and social movement.

A case study: The imprisonment of Bernardo Caal Xól, defender of the Cahabón river[5]

In Latin America, and in the Global South overall, these tendencies of criminalizing land and environmental rights defenders have been underpinned by investment projects and the over-exploitation of natural resources, which is illegal in a vast majority of cases (Zaitch, Boekhout van Solinge & Müller 2014). The exploitation of natural resources carried on uninterrupted during colonialization; nonetheless, we are witnessing an intensification of it in the last few decades (Carrington et al. 2019). The expansion of extractive industries and their proliferation to new areas, such as hydro-electricity has negative impacts on human rights endeavors of the region and becomes a constant source of socio-environmental conflicts (Raftopoulos 2017). Sometimes whole Indigenous communities live in fear because of the threats and attacks performed against them if they are resisting environmentally harmful development projects and Investments (Birss 2017; Rasch 2017), thus challenging the "systems and forms of control responsible for environmental harm" (Brisman & South, 2014, p. 90). Communities involved in resistance have to face criminalization and even the use of armed state or private security forces against them. If there is no grassroots or international civil organization to provide help for the affected community, it is difficult to even find out about these instances (Birss, 2017; Scheidel et al. 2020).

In Guatemala, seven hydroelectric power plants operate presently on the river Cahabón and its seven tributaries. The case Caal stood for was directed against the legitimacy of the Oxec I and Oxec II. plants run by the Oxec S.A. company because of the environmental damage they had been inducing (PBI Guatemala n.d.). As a form of informal social control of the environmentally harmful investment, Caal submitted his complaint regarding the construction permit of the Oxec I and Oxec II. hydroelectric plants in the name of the Q'eqchi communities to the Supreme Court in December 2015. According to this suit, the construction of the dams violates the right of the members of the community to life, health, environment and drinking water. Moreover, the legal steps regulated by international law indispensable to implementing such an investment have not taken place at all. One of the core requirements of these precluding legal steps is to consult Indigenous communities whose livelihood could be affected by the investment. The petitioners proposed the suspension of the construction until the formal consultation required by the ILO Convention 169. takes place. The Supreme Court decided in favor of the community in January 2017 and suspended the construction of the dam until the consultation in question took place. The same sentence had been reinforced by the Constitutional Court a month later and the construction was halted. In May, nevertheless, the Constitutional Court retracted the suspension and allowed the company to continue the construction under the condition that within the next 12 months it would hold the formal consultation required by law. Civil society and grassroots organizations stood up for the case and claimed that the consultation process held by the company was inadequate since it did not involve all the affected communities, and because the authorities disregarded the consultation held by the communities where the vast majority voted against the construction of the dams. Despite the resistance of the local communities the Oxec hydroelectric plant is in operation to this day (BHRRC 2018a) and the construction of Oxec II was completed in less three years (Ghassemi 2020).

The resistance of the Q'eqchi' communities tried to enforce the formal control mechanisms of environmental harm, therefore threatened the investment and the interests of the company and the state. As a reaction, it triggered formal, institutionalized control targeting the resistance. Four people working on the site of the project filed formal complaints at the Public Prosecutor's Office against Caal for illegal detention and aggravated robbery, which allegedly happened back in 2015.[6] As a result, the Cobán Tribunal ordered his pre-trial detention in February 2018 and sentenced him to seven years and four months of imprisonment in November that year. Prior to his arrest, "he had been subjected to acts of intimidation and a campaign of defamation on social media" (Human Rights Council 2018, 11). Caal and human rights organizations persevered that these charges were false and only served to silence him, for he was a key person of the social mobilization against the construction Furthermore, he has filed two lawsuits against Oxec.

In this case different forms of resistance control, criminalization and labeling through the media were employed. These control mechanisms, notably Caal's imprisonment, set off a wave of indignation all over the country, and many Indigenous communities together with human rights organizations have demanded for him to be released. The organizations and the communities believe that Caal was imprisoned because he had led a successful resistance against the construction of the Oxec plants. After the visit of the United Nations Special Rapporteur for Indigenous Rights in Guatemala, the UN issued a notice of concern about the exaggerated measure of the more than seven years of imprisonment sentence, especially in view of the fact, that the charges had been principally based on the testimony of the employees working for the company in charge of the constructions (OHCHR 2018). The sentence against the leader is seemingly an attempt to discredit and silence Indigenous people from their legitimate practice of law, which is by no means an isolated case (OHCHR 2018), and sheds light on the interplay between the informal control of environmental harm and the formal control of the resistance. As Bernardo Caal Xól said in an interview:

> The question I ask is "where should we go to complain?" If I am punished for protecting q'eqchi' peoples' rights and I am imprisoned for filing complaints against those who dispossess and hijack our rivers and mountains, where else can we go to complain? What else can we do to tackle discrimination and the racism that prevails in the system? There is no place we can go to complain because they are infringing on our rights.
>
> (PBI 2018, 8)

Many Indigenous people in Guatemala are criminalized because they are protecting their land and natural resources traditionally belonging to them against development projects that cause serious environmental damage and social harm (Sieder 2017; Human Rights Council 2018). Until governments aim to meet the increasingly growing demand for energy, and corporations gain profit from extractive industries and agribusiness, Indigenous and rural communities have to live with the consequences of environmental harm and they find themselves at the frontline of socio-environmental conflicts (Böhm 2016; Carrington et al. 2019).

Conclusion

The roots of the different forms of practices aiming to control the resistance and endeavors of activists could be intertwined. Threats, economic retribution, violence, criminalization of dissent, prosecution without clear charges and bribery are all means by which the elite protects its interests and upholds the status quo (Ruggiero, 2020; Fernandez, 2008). It is not extraordinary for authorities to use anti-terrorism procedures and rhetoric to justify their punitive measures when targeting environmental activists (Article 19, 2014; Mireanu, 2014; Lynch, Stretesky & Long, 2018; Global Witness, 2019). These measures all point to the structural violence that land defenders and environmental activists face throughout the world (Moore et al. 2015; Scheidel et al. 2020).

The control of environmental harm and resistance could be examined as a complex web of social control (Ferrell 2003) formed by the specific context of the case as well as by the wider political, economic, cultural and social factors. To situate local experiences within global patterns and structures (Young 2011), the criminological perspective outlined in this chapter is concerned with the nature of underlying control mechanisms and their implications on the reproduction of environmental harm. By studying the underlying control mechanisms from a green-cultural criminological perspective, we could explore the reactions to environmental harm and resistance in a way that connects the study of environmental harm with cultural criminology' inquiries into "the presence of power relations, and the emergence of social control, at the intersections of culture and crime" (Ferrell 1999, 408). The aim of this social control perspective is to reveal the interactions between these various forms of control and to understand their consequences. What has been demonstrated in the chapter is a rather modest beginning in applying this approach, although developing it further could highlight novel ways in which the resistance as a transformative capacity threatens the interests of the powerful and could contribute to a more subtle understanding of the dynamic interplay between power and resistance in environmental conflicts.

Notes

1 "" Environmental defenders are individuals and collectives who protect the environment and protest unjust and unsustainable resource uses because of social and environmental reasons. They may include Indigenous people, peasants or fisherfolks whose lives and livelihoods may be threatened by environmental change or dispossessions, as well as environmental activists, social movements, journalist, or any other who actively defend the environment because degradation has reached for them unacceptable levels"" (Scheidel et al. 2020, 1)
2 The contribution of studies on white-collar, corporate and state crime to the study of environmental crimes and harms are essential (Lynch, 1990)
3 The analysis of 2,743 environmental conflicts from the Environmental Justice Atlas found that land and environmental rights defenders face a high rate of criminalization (20% of cases), physical violence (18%), assassinations (13%) (Scheidel et al. 2020).
4 In this regard I am talking about overt resistance, including activism, which, according to the sociologists Hollander and Einwohner (2004) is a visible resistance recognized by both targets and observers and one which is intended to be recognized as such. Although, in a broad sense we can also talk about the "everyday resistance" against environmental harm and against the cultural norms of consumer society not only as a reaction to the weakness of the formal control, but as a response to our culturally reinforced wasteful use of natural resources. This form of resistance can also trigger reactions of control from the part of state agencies (Brisman 2010). For instance, Jeff Ferrell wrote about his experiences as a daily trash picker. Sometimes he encountered aggressive police and private security reactions and in one zone he gained the reputation of a "known troublemaker" in the eyes of the police as a dumpster diver (Ferrell 2013). This also illustrates the diversity of reactions to the destruction of the environment, and that every reaction which potentially causes a disruption in the norms maintaining late capitalism will eventually be subjected to an attempt of control at some level.
5 Bernardo Caal Xol, defender of the Cahabón River. Peace Brigades International (PBI) https://peacebrigades.org.uk/sites/peacebrigades.org.uk/files/Bernardo%20Caal_0.pdf
6 According to the charges, the employees of a cable television company affiliated with Oxec were unable to pass through the crowd during a meeting held by the communities affected by the project. Thousands attended this meeting and people were standing on the road; thus, the workers were stuck in their truck for a few hours. Meanwhile a drill, a tool box and some optic cable went missing (OHCHR, 2018).

References

Abram, D. (1997) *The Spell of the Sensuous. Perception and Language In A More-Than-Human World*. New York: Vintage Books.

Article 19 Free Word Centre (2014) *A Dangerous Shade of Green: Threats to Environmental Human Rights Defenders and Journalists in Europe*.

Bauman, Z. (1998) *Globalization the Human Consequences*. Cambridge: Polity Press.

BHRRC (2018a) *Oxec S.A. lawsuit (re consultation for hydroelectric plants, Guatemala)*, accessed 30 September 2020, https:// www.business-humanrights.org/en/latest-news/oxec-sa-lawsuit-re-consultation-for-hydroelectric-plants-guatemala/

BHRRC (2018b) *UK: Three anti-facking activists become first environmental campaigners to be jailed for protest since 1932*, accessed 30 September 2020, https://www.business-humanrights.org/en/latest-newsanduk-three-anti-fracking-activists-become-first-environmental-campaigners-to-be-jailed-for-protest-since-1932/

Birss, M. (2017) 'Criminalizing Environmental Activism', *NACLA Report on the Americas*, 49(3), 315–322.

Böhm, M.L. (2016) 'Transnational Corporations, Human Rights Violations and Structural Violence in Latin America', *Kriminologisches Journal*, 48(4), 272–293.

Borbíró, A. (2011) 'Kriminálpolitika és bűnmegelőzés a késő-modernitásban' phD. thesis.

Brisman, A. (2010) 'The Indiscriminate Criminalisation of Environmentally Beneficial Activities', in White, R. (ed.) *Global environmental harm: Criminological perspective*. Portland: Willan Publishing, 161–192.

Brisman, A. and South, N. (2012) 'A Green-Cultural Criminology: An Exploratory Outline', *Crime, Media, Culture*, 9(2), 115–135.

Brisman, A. and South, N. (2014) *Green Cultural Criminology. Constructions of Environmental Harm, Consumerism, and Resistance to Ecocide*. Abingdon: Routledge.

Brock, A. and Dunlap, A. (2018) 'Normalising corporate counterinsurgency: Engineering consent, managing resistance and greening destruction around the Hambach coal mine and beyond', *Political Geography*, 62, 33–47.

Carrington, K. et al. (2019) *Southern Criminology. New Direct*. Oxon és New York: Routledge.

Cohen, S. (1985) *Visions of Social Control. Crime, Punishment and Classification*. Cambridge, UK: Polity Press.

Doyon, J.A. and Bradshaw, E.A. (2015) 'Unfettered Fracking: A Critical Examination of Hydraulic Fracturing in the United States', in Barak, G. (ed.) *The Routledge International Handbook of the Crimes of the Powerful*. Abindgon: Routledge, 235–246.

European Environmental Bureau (2019) *The Harrassment of Environmental Defenders in the European Union. A Case Study Report*.

Fernandez, L.A. (2008) *Policing dissent: Social control and the anti-globalization movement, Policing Dissent: Social Control and the Anti-Globalization Movement*. London: Rutgers University Press.

Ferrell, J. (1999) 'Cultural Criminology', *Annual Review of Sociology*, 25, 395–418.

Ferrell, J. (2003) 'Cultural Criminology', in Schwartz, M.D. and Hatty, S.E. (eds) *Controversies in Critical Criminology*. Cincinnati: Anderson Publishing Company, 71–84.

Ferrell, J. (2013) 'Tangled up in green: Cultural criminology and green criminology', in South, N. and Brisman, A. (eds) *Routledge International Handbook of Green Criminology*. Oxfordshire: Routledge, 349–364.

Ferrell, J., Hayward, K. and Young, J. (2008) *Cultural Criminology: an invitation, Cultural Criminology. An Invitation*. London: Sage.

Fisher, M. (2009) *Capitalist Realism: Is There no Alternative?*. Winchester: John Hunt Publishing.

Garland, D. (2001) *The Culture of Control*. Chicago: The University of Chicago Press.

Ghassemi, H. (2020, April) Oxec II. Hydroelectric Project Helping to Energise Guatemala, *NS Energy*, accessed 25 September 2020, https://www.nsenergybusiness.com/news/oxec-ii-hydroelectric-project-guatemala/

Global Witness (2019) *Enemies of the State?*, https://www.globalwitness.org/en/campaigns/environmental-activists/enemies-state/

Global Witness (2020) *Defending Tomorrow*, https://www.globalwitness.org/en/campaigns/environmental-activists/defending-tomorrow/.

Hall, M. (2015) *Exploring Green Crime. Introducing the Legal, Social and Criminological Contexts of Environmental Harm*. London: Palgrave Macmillan.

Halsey, M. and White, R. (1998) 'Crime, Ecophilosophy and Environmental Harm', *Theoretical Criminology*, 2(3), 345–371.

Harvey, D. (2007) *A Brief History of Neoliberalism*. Oxford University Press.

Hillyard, P. et al. (2004) *Beyond Criminology: Taking Harm Seriously*. London: Pluto Press, Fernwood Publishing.

Hollander, J.A. and Einwohner, R.L. (2004) 'Conceptualizing Resistance', *Sociological Forum*, 19(4), 533–554.

Human Rights Council (2018) Report of the Special Rapporteur on the Rights of Indigenous Peoples, *Human Rights Council*, https://www.ohchr.org/en/issues/ipeoples/srindigenouspeoples/pages/sripeoplesindex.aspx.

Knox, J.H. and Pejan, R. (2018) *The Human Right to a Healthy Environment*. Cambridge: Cambridge University Press.

Lukes, S. (2005) *Power: A Radical View. Second*. London: Palgrave Macmillan.

Lynch, M.J. (1990) 'The Greening of Criminology: A Perspective on the 1990s 2.', *Critical Criminology*, 3–4, 11–12.

Lynch, M.J. (2016) 'The Ecological Distribution of Community Advantage and Disadvantage: Power Structures, Political Economy, Communities, and Green-State Crime and Justice,' *Critical Criminology*, 24(2), 247–262.

Lynch, M.J., Stretesky, B. and Long, M.A. (2018) 'Green criminology and native peoples: The treadmill of production and the killing of indigenous environmental activists', *Theoretical Criminology*, 22(3), 318–341.

Lynch, M.J. et al. (2013) 'Is It a Crime to Produce Ecological Disorganization? Why Green Criminology and Political Economy Matter in the Analysis of Global Ecological Harms', *British Journal of Criminology*, 53., 997–1016.

Michalowski, R.. (2009) 'Power, Crime and Criminology in the New Imperial Age', *Crime, Law and Social Change*, 51(3–4), 303–325.

Mireanu, M. (2014) 'The criminalisation of environmental activism in Europe', *Studia Universitatis Babes-Bolyai Sociologia*, 2, 87–103.

Moore, J. et al. (2015) In the National Interest? Criminalization of Land and Environment Defenders in the Americas, *MiningWatch Canada*, https://miningwatch.ca/sites/default/files/inthenationalinterest_fullpaper_eng_1.pdf.

Natali, L. and McClanahan, B. (2017) 'Perceiving and Communicating Environmental Contamination and Change: Towards a Green Cultural Criminology with Images', *Critical Criminology*, 25(2), 199–214.

OHCHR (2018) *Guatemala: UN Experts Concerned Indigenous Leader Convicted in Retaliation for Opposition to Oxec Hydro Project*, accessed 30 September 2020, https://www.ohchr.org/EN/NewsEvents/Pages/DisplayNews.aspx?NewsID=24031/LangID=E

PBI Guatemala (2018, May) *Bernardo Caal Xol, defender of the Cahabón River*, accessed 30 September 2020, https://peacebrigades.org.uk/sites/peacebrigades.org.uk/files/Bernardo%20Caal_0.pdf

PBI Guatemala (n.d.) *Peaceful Resistance Cahabón*, accessed 30 September 2020, https://p guatemala.org/en/who-we-accompany/peaceful-resistance-cahab%C3%B3n

Pemberton, S. (2007) 'Social Harm Future(s) Exploring the Potential of the Social Harm Approach', *Crime, Law and Social Change*, 48(1), 27–41.

Raftopoulos, M. (2017) 'Contemporary Debates on Social-Environmental Conflicts, Extractivism and Human Rights in Latin America', *International Journal of Human Rights*, 21(4), 387–404.

Rasch, E.D. (2017) 'Citizens, Criminalization and Violence in Natural Resource Conflicts in Latin America', *European Review of Latin American and Caribbean Studies*, 103, 131–142.

Rojas-Páez, G. (2014) 'Whose Nature? Whose Rights? Criminalization of Social Protest in a Globalizing World', *Oñati Socio-Legal Series*, 1, 1–12.

Ruggiero, V. (2013) 'The environment and the crimes of the economy', in South, N. and Brisman, A. (eds) *Routledge International Handbook of Green Criminology*. Oxfordshire: Routledge, 261–271.

Ruggiero, V. (2015) *Power and Crime*. London: Routledge.

Ruggiero, V. (2020) 'Killing Environmental Campaigners: Manifest and Latent Justifications', *Criminological Encounters*, 21(3).

Ruggiero, V. and South, N. (2013) 'Green Criminology and Crimes of the Economy: Theory, Research and Praxis', *Critical Criminology*, 21(3), 359–373.

Scheidel, A. et al. (2020) 'Environmental Conflicts and Defenders: A Global Overview', *Global Environmental Change*, 63(April).

Sieder, R. (2017) Indigenous Sovereignties in Guatemala: Between Criminalization and Revitalization, *NACLA Report on the Americas*.

South, N., Brisman, A. and Beirne, P. (2013) 'A guide to a green criminology', in South, N. and Brisman, A. (eds) *Routledge International Handbook of Green Criminology*. Oxfordshire: Routledge, 37–42.

Steger, T. and Drehobl, A. (2018) 'The Anti-Fracking Movement in Ireland: Perspectives from the Media and Activists', *Environmental Communication*, 12(3), 344–356.

Svarstad, H., Benjaminsen, T.A. and Overå, R. (2018) 'Power theories in political ecology', *Journal of Political Ecology*, 25(1), 350–363.

Vegh Weis, V. (2017) *Marxism and Criminology. A History of Criminal Selectivity*. Leiden: Brill.

White, R. (2009) 'Researching Transnational Environmental Harm: Toward an Eco-Global Criminology', *International Journal of Comparative and Applied Criminal Justice*, 33(2), 229–248.

White, R. (2010) 'Transnational Environmental Crime and Eco-Global Criminology', in Shoham, S.G., Knepper, P., and Kett, M. (eds) *International Handbook of Criminology*. New York: Taylor & Francis Group.

White, R. (2013) 'Eco-global criminology and the political economy of environmental harm', in South, N. and Brisman, A. (eds) *Routledge International Handbook of Green Criminology*. Oxfordshire: Routledge, 243–260.

Young, J. (2011) *The criminological imagination*. Cambridge: Polity.

Zaitch, D., Boekhout van Solinge, T. and Müller, G. (2014) 'Harms, crimes and natural resource exploitation: A green criminological perspective on land-use change', in Maarten, B., Lorenzo, P., and Mostert, E. (eds) *Conflicts over Natural Resources in the Global South*. London: CRC Press, Taylor & Francis Group, 91–108.

3

THE CRIMINALIZATION AND "INNOVATION" OF RESISTANCE

Looking at the Italian case

Verónica Marchio

This chapter analyzes the theoretical relation between "crime" and "politics", with the aim to discuss the logic of the criminalization of activism and introduce the concept of socio-political innovation. To do this, the chapter uses theories and concepts related to critical criminology, the sociology of deviance (Melossi 2008) and *Operaismo* or "Italian political workerism" (Wright 2002; Alquati 1994).

Whereas "crime" is an instrument of social government (Melossi, Sozzo & Sparks 2017; Simon 2007), which indicates a "break" in peace and social order, including deviance, "politics" has instead often been emptied of its potential for rupture by legal and social sciences, and considered to be an element of pacification rather than as a space of conflict. Instead, when the "political" is freed from institutional boundaries, it can generate conflicts and produce enemies higher up the social hierarchy. "Crime" and "politics" are, therefore, dialectically connected and traversed by power relations. Quoting Mills (1959), Melossi & Selmini states that: "the ability of the ruling class to define the main social conflicts as "criminal" rather than "political"—as "private troubles" rather than as "public issues"—is a sure sign of its hegemony, a hegemony, however, that is not only constructed ideologically through persuasion but is deeply rooted in the reality of social relationships" (2009, 156).

This chapter focuses on how a "political" phenomenon of activism has historically been managed through two mechanisms: criminalization and socio-political innovation. The first section analyzes the classical mechanism of criminalization. The second section examines the way in which protests are formed and transformed, introducing the concept of socio-political innovation. Both sections include examples in Italy to provide an empirical foundation to the analysis.

DOI: 10.4324/9781003144229-5

Criminalization of resistance in Italy

In many different historical and political periods, the political struggle (for instance, of solidarity, micro resistances, or urban disorders) has been considered a crime and effectively criminalized. The two most relevant categories through which the criminalization of resistances has been practiced in Italy are, on the one hand, "public order" and "public security", understood as something to preserve, and, on the other hand, "violence" and "disorder" as elements of social danger to be fought against.

The criminalization of the "social question" has a long history in Italy—from the unification of Italy onward (Palidda 2000)—with both criminal and preventive justice (Ashworth & Zedner 2014) historically used for the management of political crime or urban disorder. Recently some of those measures from the past have been revived (Petrini 1996) as well as new policing tools experimented with (Selmini 2020). Italy has more than 50 years of experience in the management of "public order" (Della & Reiter 1998; Gargiulo 2015). This experience inspires and informs both the capacity to sentence people in the courts and the possibility of intervening before the dangerous behavior would manifest itself in a public space or on the streets, be it an occupation of buildings or the emergence of new types of protest.

Let us consider a recent Italian example of the criminalization of resistance that demonstrates both the power to bring political struggle to a criminal court and the attempt to identify and criminalize new unpredictable political behaviors. The case refers to a recent political movement known as "*Il Padrone di merda*" (The "shitty" boss); people staging protests outside workplaces in which the employers were accused of exploiting their workers. The movement—also known as the "White Masks" because of the masks the protesters wear—started after a group of young people in Bologna, Italy, shared stories of their experiences at work and began noticing the similarities between them. The movement is made up mostly of precarious workers: students, young workers, freelancers, young people doing internships or in work trial periods. This specific social segment no longer has trust in political institutions such as trade unions, parties and formal worker organizations because those institutions have not taken their problems seriously and have made promises which are impossible to keep. This new resistance practice is now being used in several Italian cities, drawing attention to employers who don't pay wages and national insurance contributions, as well as to those who have harassed or abused their workers. The group started as a Facebook page in which workers who were not yet in the group spontaneously shared testimonies about their bosses' behavior, which were then published on Facebook. These workers then met each other to decide how to publicly shame the businesses involved. The tactic that they chose collectively was to put on white masks and stand in front of the business letting people know what the employers had done. Once on the spot, a few of them would plaster the windows and doors with stickers stating "*Questo posto ha un padrone di merda*" (This place has a "shitty" boss), while another worker would read out the employee's testimony through a megaphone. Usually, curious passersby would stop and watch while, sometimes, the owner would confront the protesters, trying to grab the megaphone and tear off the protesters' masks. Besides receiving complaints through the Facebook page, activists also see allegations made against bad employers in local newspaper reports or on social media. The group uses its stickers to alert the public that a place is accused of exploiting workers both in order to discourage customers and because they believe that the warning might convince employers to act more fairly in the future[1].

This movement was soon felt as a threat by criminal and political institutions. A few months after it started, a snack bar owner, accused by the "White Masks" of not paying his employees, asked the city authorities to block the group's Facebook page, arguing that he had been slandered by false accusations. Although the case was never brought to court, the authorities pre-emptively asked Facebook to remove the page. But the public Facebook page remained live and still exists. In 2016, the US State Department sent a message to Italian prosecutors dissuading them from asking Facebook to reveal the identities behind anonymous profiles in defamation cases, because the statements written on the social network, however defamatory, are covered by the principle of freedom of opinion. The first criminalization attempt—through a defamation charge—failed.

The second attempt was more serious and had coercive and punitive consequences for the workers. This time the business was a beauty salon. The worker who had testified against the salon brought to the public action her employment tribunal injunction which certified that she was owed €8,000 by the salon. Consecutively the "White Masks" carried out at least three actions in front of the salon. Many of the videos show the owners pushing workers around, demonstrating their nervousness about the worker's testimony. During the third action police intervened arresting one of the workers on site but releasing him soon after. The criminalization happened a few months later when, the day after the end of the first Italian Covid-19 lock down, five workers were banished from the city as a preventive measure related to a serious criminal accusation. The court decided to accept the prosecution charge of attempted extortion, an accusation usually related to "organized crime" that in Italy leads to sanctions of between seven and 20 years of prison. The court also decided to pre-emptively prohibit the beauty salon worker from approaching the business. Following this action by the court and further steps taken by the prosecution, the group received a lot of solidarity from the community and continued to take action against other bosses. On Facebook the group points out how many workers have managed to get their salaries back thanks to this form of protest. Nevertheless the five workers are still banned from the city and so the political campaign and resistance against the extortion charges continues. It is important to note that the criminalization of the "White Mask" movement signifies the identification of the demand for rights and the payment of wages with the crime of extortion. This is both a traditional political criminalization and a way of equating new protests (not accompanied by the political mediation of traditional institutions) with common criminality. The aim of such an identification clearly is the depoliticization of new forms of struggle.

Socio-political innovation

Political struggle has not only been criminalized but, insofar as it is a sociological and political object of study, has also been emptied of its conflictual character. To describe this process, the present section proposes the concept of socio-political innovation. This concept could be defined as the state ability to re-channel certain behaviors considered politically or economically dangerous to an end that is not their own, appropriating the social and material conditions that determined them, and breaking down and individualizing ends and subjectivities. "Innovation", thus, consists in the ability to re-absorb transgressions and antagonism, but also to control counter individual or social roles and goals. It is useful to make use of the Mertonian conception of "innovation" in a double sense. On the one hand (with his critical functionalist theory of crime), Merton (1969) developed the concept of "*anomie*" to describe this imbalance between cultural goals and institutionalized means. He argued that such an imbalanced society produces "*anomie*" because there is a strain or tension between the goals and means that produce unsatisfied aspirations. Innovation is thus one of the ways people must adapt when faced with strain; innovation results in crime because the individual uses socially unapproved or unconventional means to obtain culturally approved goals. On the other hand, with the concept of "Sociological Ambivalence", Merton (1976) argued that people face frustration and "*anomie*" also performing their conventional and approved social roles. The accumulation of ambivalence and frustration results in the production of counter social roles, goals and standards by the individuals.

The concept of socio-political innovation proposed in this chapter consists, therefore, in the state ability to control, re-absorb and make functional those counter roles, standards, goals and expectations. Innovation by the state, which is based on the absorption of social behaviors and resistances, involves also a process of normalization with the function of neutralizing politically dangerous behaviors and valorizing others.

As shown by the example of the "White Mask", through criminalization political practice clashes with authority, whereas, through innovation, the field of action unfolds mainly within the relationships between the various parts of the social composition, on both material and symbolic levels. "Innovation" is therefore directly connected to the production and reproduction of certain social relations, echoing what Melossi & Selmini write about the dialectic of the criminal and the political. Whether one or the other is dominant, depends on the extent of the state's capacity at that time to discipline social relations.

To better explain the concept and practice of socio-political innovation, it is useful to highlight that its principal consequence is the production of "social disciplining". Theoretically speaking, "social disciplining" works to build specific subjectivities and specific social relationships, it assigns and produces roles and destroys others in order to deprive those same subjectivities of the possibility of engaging in a politicization that is "against"[2]. Social discipline acts in different places and ways, being articulated as a security motive and thus depoliticizing the issue of security as related to quality of life. It can be used as an instrument to create divisions and fragmentation of social aggregates, for example, those formed in solidarity (or to resist) against the precariousness and flexibility of the labor market.

A good Italian example of "socio-political innovation" is the current management of the struggle related to the use of public or private abandoned buildings. The "*Lotta per la Casa*" (housing struggle) is a form of protest used over the last four decades in Italy, especially in the country's biggest cities. From the 1980s onwards, the struggles of occupied "Social Centers" gave birth to numerous social and political engagements and countercultures. As a result of multiple recent police led evictions of such places, there are now very few explicitly social or residential squats left in Italy. Nevertheless, political groups have continued to put pressure on public institutions, especially with regard to the possibility of having places and structures within which to continue their socio-political activities. The demand for "alternative" spaces has been re-absorbed by institutional politics over the years, and those that were previously occupied either no longer exist or are now covered by formal or informal contracts that bind groups and movements to only take part in activities and struggles that are emptied of any conflictual character. There is, thus, a kind of blackmail: if you break the deal, you lose the space. The innovation process has tended to normalize these spaces and the activities of the groups that use them. This re-absorption is thus also expressed by a process in which student groups or "student collectives" have been forced to become formal associations, making them more predictable and easier to control.

Conclusions

The chapter argued that the category of "crime" is an excellent means for managing political activism. By drawing the boundaries of the legitimacy of social and individual behaviors, criminalization acts to divide society, delimiting a sphere of acceptable and unpunished crimes at the top of the class composition, while fragmenting the class at the bottom. Where necessary, the state defines political behaviors as criminal, and where useful, it accepts and normalizes deviant behaviors or practices as political. Criminalization is not the only instrument to control political struggle. The chapter discussed the concepts of socio-political innovation to argue that it is also important to consider the way in which the state simply reabsorbs conflicts without the need to use visible force or exert power.

Notes

1 See the following articles: https://www.theguardian.com/cities/2019/sep/16/horrible-bosses-masked-activists-publicly-shame-businesses-in-bologna, https://narratively.com/the-masked-vigilantes-coming-for-your-horrible-boss/
2 The term "against" often recurs in the political works of the Italian militant and sociologist R. Alquati, in some way also circumscribing the political as a struggle between opposite parties.

References

Alquati R. (1994), *Camminando per realizzare un sogno comune*, Torino: Velleità Alternative.

Ashworth A. and Zedner L. (2014), *Preventive Justice*, Oxford: Oxford University Press.

Della P.D. and Reiter H. (1998), *Policing Protest. The Control of Mass Demonstrations in Western Democracies*, Minneapolis: University of Minnesota Press.

Gargiulo E. (2015), Amministrare nell'ombra. Discrezionalità e opacità nella gestione della sicurezza, in *Matrix: proposte per un approccio interdisciplinare allo studio delle istituzioni*, edited by Giuseppe Ambrosino & Loris De Nardi, Verona: Qui Edit.

Melossi D. (2008), *Controlling Crime, Controlling Society: Thinking About Crime in Europe and America*, Cambridge: Polity Press.

Melossi D. and Selmini R. (2009), Modernisation of institutions of social and penal control in Italy-Europe: The new crime prevention, in *Crime Prevention Policies in Comparative Perspective*, edited by Adam Crawford, London: Routledge.

Melossi D., Sozzo, M. and Sparks R. (2017), *Travels of the Criminal Question Cultural Embeddedness and Diffusion*, London: Hart Publishing.

Merton R.K. (1969), *Social Theory and Social Structure*, New York: The Free Press.

Merton R.K. (1976), *Sociological Ambivalence and Other Essays*, New York: The free Press.

Mills C.W. (1959), *The Sociological Imagination*, Oxford: Oxford University Press.

Palidda S. (2000), *Polizia postmoderna. Etnografia del nuovo controllo sociale*, Milano: Feltrinelli.

Petrini D. (1996), *La prevenzione inutile. Illegittimità delle misure praeter delictum*, Napoli: Jovene.

Selmini R. (2020), *Dalla sicurezza urbana al controllo del dissenso politico. Una storia del diritto amministrativo punitivo*, Roma: Carrocci Editore.

Simon J. (2007), *Governing through Crime. How the War on Crime transformed American Democracy and Created a Culture of Fear*, Oxford: Oxford University press.

Wright S. (2002), *Storming Heaven: Class Composition and Struggle in Italian Autonomist Marxism*, London: Pluto Press.

PART II

Historical experiences on the over-criminalization of dissent

4

AVOIDING AND AMPLIFYING THE CRIMINAL LABEL IN THE ROMAN REPUBLIC AND MEDIEVAL ENGLAND

Matt Clement

The language employed by the mainstream political machinery of the state, as relayed through their advocates in the media, labels perceived threats of radicalized ideas and actions as "harmful acts" and their perpetrators as "criminal". "Over-criminalization" is especially evident in government reactions to protest movements, as will be explored below using examples from ancient Rome and medieval England. As Vegh Weis emphasizes, this distortion and amplification of these so-called "crimes" is matched by a parallel "original under-criminalization" of acts of violence conducted in public for the purposes of repression and intimidation by state agents, in partnership with those who rule societies (Vegh Weis 2018). Her account focuses on capitalism, the system of accumulation beginning in 16th century Western Europe (Dimmock 2015), and she is quite specific about how her terms apply:

> [T]he social sectors favored by original under-criminalization were the monarchy, the feudal lords, and the rising mercantile bourgeoisie. Together, or in conflict with each other, they exercised crime control in Europe and the colonies.
>
> (Vegh Weis 2018, 61)

Capitalism can only come about through the dispossession of those working what had been known in various societies as "common land", and just as the rulers and rising classes benefit from their under-criminalization in the process of stealing this land, at the same time, "over-criminalization targeted those peasants when they tried to defend their communal and customary ownership" (Vegh Weis 2018, 64). Whilst the development and working through of these two concepts is central to this account, and undoubtedly enhances the spectrum of theoretical criminology through this historical materialist sociology of deviance, this chapter will attempt to extend the use of these concepts into other forms of state society, namely the

DOI: 10.4324/9781003144229-7

"ancient world" of the Roman republic in the 2nd century BCE, and "feudalism" in 14th century England. It concludes that these concepts can be applied here, but that their scale and effectiveness is necessarily of a different order.

Ancient Rome became a republic when the citizens deposed its king–Tarquin–for tyranny or personal rule. The government was now to be composed of *Senatus Populus Que Romanus (SPQR)*—meaning "the senate and the people of Rome" (Beard 2015). As the republic grew from a small city state in the 6th century BCE to a continental power with a growing empire 400 years later, the social conflicts built into this arrangement were becoming clearer. (Brunt 1971). Only the rich could become senators and they were an elite who believed they alone should rule. The senators were content for the rest of the citizens—the *plebeians*—to play a part in the theater of government by attending the popular assemblies in the city's forum. The plebeians were even allowed to cast their votes for or against bills proposed by senators speaking from the rostrum set before the crowd, although the rules still parceled up their votes into sections known as "tribes" that were weighted in favor of the richest. The benefit of these limited elements of democracy was that the rulers gained a "mandate", that is, some civic endorsement for their actions, backed up by other public measures, such as the most powerful Romans sponsoring vast free banquets and entertainments to win favor by showing their "magnificence". Thus, they ruled by a mixture of fear and consent and this state of affairs won much acclaim from the likes of Polybius, the Greek thinker who praised Rome's "mixed republic" for effectively combining authority and democracy in what he thought was the right proportions. (Polybius 1979)

In truth, this was not a case of a cleverly designed model balancing these competing pressures. The "mix" emerged out of the struggle between the patricians and the plebeians. A strike organized by plebeians had seen the bulk of the city's small population withdraw from the Capitoline Hill, seat of the city's main temple and senate house and many of the houses of the rich, and camp out on the neighboring Aventine Hill until the "fathers of Rome" conceded their right to representation in the political body. This won them the creation of "Tribunes of the People" —a group they could elect themselves and who had the right to veto any law the senate proposed. The senators calculated they could allow this innovation as votes in the forum were still taken by a show of hands, and they believed they could use their servants and other "retainers" to let the people know which way they should vote by the traditional forms of encouragement, a combination of bribery and intimidation.

In the year 137 BCE, the struggle went slightly further and the vote for ballots to be cast in secret was won. The stage was set for another confrontation between the interests of the wealthy—the 1% of their day—and those of the mass of Romans who had found a new cause in the struggle for the right to common land. Plutarch sets the scene, explaining:

> Of the land which the Romans gained by conquest from their neighbors, part they sold publicly, and turned the reminder into common, this common land they assigned to such citizens as were poor and indigent…But when the

wealthy men began to offer larger rents, and drive the poorer people out, it was enacted by law that no person whatever should enjoy more than five hundred acres of land.

(Plutarch 1912)

At this point, the wealthy defied the law and used their riches to grab more and more land regardless. Obviously, their convenient belief that they alone were the lawgivers facilitated this "under-criminalization" (Vegh Weis 2018). This process of accumulating property through expropriating the peasants was a fundamental change to the way in which the Roman republic had operated. As Marx describes, from the 6th century right down to the late 2nd century BCE "small-scale peasant agriculture and independent handicrafts were…the economic bases of the classical commonwealth in its palmy days…before slavery had gained effective control of production" (Marx 1933, 351). As a result, the poor were illegally deprived of their rights with calamitous consequences every time land has been enclosed right across the globe in future centuries. Following Rome's conquest of Carthage (Tunisia) in 145 BCE the process of accumulation and robbery in Italy expanded, "there were comparatively few freemen remaining in all Italy, which swarmed with workhouses full of foreign-born slaves. These the rich men employed in cultivating the ground of which they dispossessed the citizens" (Plutarch 1912, 998). The people were devastated and looked for redress. In 133 BCE they elected Tiberius Gracchus as tribune of the people in the hope he would champion their cause, "setting up writings upon the porches, walls and monuments, calling upon him to reinstate the poor citizens in their former possessions" (Plutarch 1912, 998). His speech was made in the forum—the vast public arena at the heart of the city with the mass of the people surrounding him:

> The savage beasts in Italy have their dens, their places of repose and refuge, but the men who bear arms, and expose their lives for the safety of their country, enjoy nothing more than the air and the light, and, having no settlements of their own, are constrained to wander from place to place with their wives and children…They fought, and indeed were slain, but it was to maintain the luxury and the wealth of other men. They were styled masters of the world, but in the meantime had not one foot of ground which they could call their own.

This was an explosive political situation. Tiberius the Tribune—in the name of the people—was demanding the law be respected, thousands endorsed his call (Richardson 1976). Plutarch acknowledges as much, explaining how: "an harangue of this nature, spoken to an enthusiastic and sympathizing audience, by a person of commanding spirit and genuine feelings, no adversaries at that time were competent to oppose." (Plutarch 1912, 999). The state in ancient Rome was not in the exclusive control of its ruling class. All of the control over who commanded armies, elected leaders, the public treasury and the operation of the laws was supposed take place in the forum under the active supervision of the people of Rome, as Millar explains, "fundamental issues about the shape and military activity of the empire were being brought for decision before the crowd...all secured by mass voting in the Forum". (Millar 1998 170, 172). Of course, the rich did not accept restrictions upon their power so this conflict could only be resolved by force.

The grouping of the rich tried to label Tiberius, they "endeavored to seduce the people, declaring that Tiberius was designing a general redivision of lands, to overthrow the government, and put all things into confusion". They then worked on his fellow tribune, Marcus Octavius, with the aim of getting him to use his power of veto to prevent the law being acted upon. This only made things worse though, as "Tiberius, irritated at these proceedings, presently laid aside this milder bill, but at the same time preferred another, which, as it was more grateful to the common people, so it was more severe against the wrongdoers, commanding them to make an immediate surrender of all lands which, contrary to the former laws, had come into their possession." (Plutarch 1912, 999). So, when the people backed Tiberius Gracchus and voted to depose Marcus Octavius, he "was dragged out in an ignominious manner. The people at once assaulted him, whilst the rich men ran in to his assistance...the law concerning the lands was ratified...The great men of the city were therefore utterly offended" (Plutarch 1912, 1001). Tiberius still had the people's mandate and proposed further reforms, that money coming into the treasury "should be distributed amongst such poor citizens as were to be sharers of the public lands" (Plutarch 1912, 1002), and two further measures, "making the years of serving in the war fewer than formally and granting liberty of appeal from the judges to the people" (Plutarch 1912, 1004) as well as including broader layers of the citizens on juries.

Consent and coercion in the public arena were now working on the side of the people and threatening that the land seizures of the wealthy would be outlawed by laws acting in their interests. For the rich, this situation had to be reversed. Not only must this drive to criminalize them be prevented, but also those that advocated it must themselves be criminalized: They must "learn the lesson" that the "people" cannot arbitrate justice. A sympathizer told Tiberius that "the rich men, in a sitting of the senate...had come to a final determination amongst themselves that he should be assassinated, and to that purpose had a vast number of their friends and servants ready armed to accomplish it" (Plutarch 1912, 1005). Gracchus's allies prepared to defend him. But were outnumbered by this noble lynch mob and their retainers. Leading senator Nasica rose from his seat in the chamber:

> "Since the consul', said he, 'regards not the safety of the commonwealth, let everyone who will defend the laws, follow me.' He then, casting the skirt of his gown over his head, hastened to the capitol, those who bore him company, wrapped their gowns about their arms, and forced their way after him... furnished themselves with clubs and staves from their houses...Thus armed, they made their way towards Tiberius, knocking down those they found in front of him...Tiberieus tried to save himself by flight...a tribune, one of his colleagues,

was observed to give him the first fatal stroke by hitting him on the head with the foot of a stool. Of the rest there fell above three hundred killed".

(Plutarch 1912, 1000)

The belief of Nasica and his fellow murderers that they were "defending the laws" epitomizes their mindset. What you could call the *habitus*—or social character—of the senatorial rulers of Rome. Nasica effectively invoked the *senatus consultum ultimum, that is,* the "ultimate decree" which authorized them to override the consul and the written law and take whatever measures necessary to "see that the state comes to no harm". Such measures were likely to breach citizens' rights and liberties: In this case, by murdering the only tribune of the people who was advocating their cause. "States of emergency" such as this have featured regularly in subsequent history as justifications for crimes of the powerful. Indeed, because authorized by the state, they claim they are therefore legitimate and, therefore, under-criminalized, however violent or criminal the actions that follow in their wake. Vegh Weis has shown how violence associated with primitive accumulation into the hands of the most powerful was integral to state formation processes during the transition to capitalism from the 16th century onward, arguing "the concept of original under-criminalization shows how limited the legislation and prosecution of harmful behaviors committed in rural Europe and the colonies really were, regardless of their criminogenic character" (Vegh Weis 2018, 39). The crimes of Rome's rulers would be replicated by nobles and merchants, with the aid of church and state over the next 2,000 years, providing the fuel for the primitive accumulation of capital through the destruction of the sustainable economies of the poor across the globe.

A second example of how rulers maintain social control in the face of campaigns for social justice can be found in the events taking place in southern England in 1381 that have become known as the "peasants revolt". This account draws on the principal contemporary source available, the chronicles of Sir John Froissart. He begins by stating his intention is to describe: "How the Commons of England rebelled against the Noblemen" and is in no doubt this is a very serious matter:

> In the youth of King Richard there fell in England great mischief and rebellion, and movement of the common people, by which England was at a point to have been lost without recovery, there was never realm nor country in so significant risk as it was in that time, and all because of the ease and riches that the common people were of
>
> (Newbolt 1902, 93)

It appears this is to be another "condition of England" social document, such as became extremely popular on the 19th century as writers and readers sought to come to terms with their changing times (Carlyle 1829, Engels 1844). A study of history and sociology is combined to explain circumstances and point out their causes. As a noble person himself, Froissart perceives a "problem" of insufficient punishment and repression—hence their "mischief and rebellion". The condition of the commons is one of "ease and riches", indicating that he believes there is a surfeit of confidence and combativity—what would later be called "class consciousness" in their outlook.

In reality, the immediate cause of the revolt was the imposition of a poll tax, ordered by the government to pay for warfare in France (Barker 2009). The brutality employed by the royal tax collectors stirred up the revolt, whilst many other injustices imposed upon the peasantry were brought into sharper focus in the light of this latest outrage as various histories recount (Oman 1989, Cohn 2013, Barker 2014, Clement 2016, Empson 2018). Froissart alludes to this also, stating: "There was a usage in England, and yet in divers' countries, that the noblemen have great right over the commons" (Newbolt 1902 93). It is impossible to appreciate the true sense of actions like the 1381 Peasant's Revolt without recognizing how the oppression and injustice meted out by the powerful cliques around the monarch made life so hard for everyone else. Whereas in Rome's late republic, and also in the Athenian democracy in the 5th century BCE, all citizens had a say in the making of the laws (Millar 1998, Patriquin 2015), in feudal Europe, the monarch and their allies in the nobility and the church had wrested exclusive control of the state and its machinery of justice (Linklater 2016). A key measure to over-criminalize the laborer occurred in 1351, when the state legislated to prevent people from raising their wages. The statute set a maximum wage commensurate with wages paid before the Black Death—the European pandemic known as "the plague"—specifically the wage paid in 1346. It also mandated that all able-bodied men and women work and imposed harsh penalties for those who remained idle. By the Statute of Labourers, the Justices of the Peace gained the power "compelling the service and regulating the wages of all sorts of workmen" (Harding 1984, 182). It stated:

> Each and every man and woman in our realm of England, of whatever condition, free or servile, who are strong in body and under sixty years of age, if they are not living by trade or exercising a special craft, do not have property to live from or land to cultivate and are not already in the service of others, shall be bound to serve anyone who requires their services to work suitable to their status.
>
> (Harding 1984,185)

Being forced to take the wages paid five years ago was felt to be a form of wage slavery. Those without property were to be made to serve, and if they refused their master, they were liable to imprisonment. It was a crime not to work as directed by the propertied, who were the masters. Thus, class oppression was the seedbed for the revolt. It should be recalled, however, that the reason the law was introduced was due to the vast shortage of labor that followed this 14th century pandemic. People were quitting their "obliged" occupation for one that was paid better as desperate landowners and master craftsmen sought replacements for the millions who died from the plague across the continent.

Doubtless, as a noble, Froissart approves of this pattern of domination, but also sees the problem, reminding his (noble) readers "there be more of these people in England than in any other realm" (Newbolt 1902 94). Froissart was originally from

Flanders, scene of a large 13th century peasant revolt. Metal workers in Paris revolted in the 1350s and textile workers in Florence rioted and fought for political rights 1378 (Cohn 2006). But Paris and Florence were both city states, where the local authorities had sufficient support from their leading institutions to police the rebellious crowd. Would this be the same in the nation state of England? Large numbers of commoners could get out of the control of their rulers: England was full of "villeins" or bondmen tied to the nobles who would be "made free" (Hilton 1973). Froissart gives an idea of their labors "to thresh and to fan…to make their hay, and to hew their wood" demonstrating how the powerful rely upon this growing mass of the population, stating "thus the noblemen and prelates [high priests] are served by them, and especially in the country of Kent, Essex, Sussex and Bedford." Clearly, he believes "serving" can be seen both as an obligation to their betters but also a sign of how interdependent are noble and commoner, which allows the latter to air their grievances, "these countries began to stir because they said they were kept in great bondage…they maintained that none ought to be bond" (Newbolt 1902 94). Once you add in numbers of sympathetic commoners in the capital, Froissart states "there were in London of their unhappy opinions more than thirty thousand" (Newbolt 1902 102). They "assembled them together and sent word to the foresaid countries [counties—as above] how they should find London open to receive them…they rose…to the number of sixty thousand" (Newbolt 1902, 96–97). Froissart also reveals the ideology that informed the peasant's revolt, claiming that many listened to the sermons of "hedge priest" John Ball who preached a kind of "liberation theology"— a version of Christianity that interpreted the faith in the name of the people:

> We be all come from one father and mother, Adam and Eve, whereby can they say or shew [show] that they be greater lords than we be?…they dwell in fair houses, and we have the pain and travail [work]…and by that cometh of our labours they keep and maintain their estates.
>
> (Newbolt 1902, 96)

The establishment already recognized the subversive nature of this creed. It was pioneered by former Oxford scholar, John Wycliffe, whose believers were labeled "Lollards". In 1380, Wycliffe was prosecuted for his denunciations of papal power and calls for a reformation that would amend the corruption of the Church—testament to the fear his ideas generated: He wrote "God cannot give civil dominion to man for himself, and his heirs, in perpetuity … Charters of human invention concerning perpetual civil inheritance are impossible". One scholar concludes "it was nothing if not easy to read into Wycliffe's philosophy ideas for a program of devastating revolution" (Aston 1960, 2). As Froissart recalls the great march of the peasants through Kent, the reader gains a sense of the significance of this medieval social movement, and the enthusiasm that accompanied the revolt:

> When the men of Kent marched into Canterbury all the common people made great feast, for all the town was of their assent…And when they came

to Rochester, they had there good cheer, for the people of that town…were
of the same sect.

(Newbolt 1902, 100–101)

They ransacked the Savoy—the riverside palace of the Duke of Lancaster and stood in
their 10,000s on the bank of the River Thames at Mile End facing the king, when one
of his retainers killed their leader, Wat Tyler, when "negotiations" broke down. Many
men, trained archers from the King's armies now in the peasant's "army" raised their
bows to retaliate. If they had unleashed them, who knows what would have resulted?

But in this feudal period, the oppressed were not convinced that they needed
to turn "the world upside down" as later 17th century radicals believed (Hill 1973).
Reforming existing institutions like the monarchy still appeared a choice to them, and
Ball had concluded his earlier sermon advising the peasants, "Let us go to the king,
for he is young, and shew him what bondage we be in, and shew him we will have
it otherwise, or else we will provide us of some remedy." (Newbolt 1902, 95). In that
light, many chose to believe young Richard's promise that they should have charters
of rights to take back to their villages, their departure split up the vast host of peasants
and allowed the authorities to gradually regain control of the capital. The hopes of the
peasants were not yet extinguished: In Cambridgeshire, messengers rode up and down
the county proclaiming that the king had freed all serfs and that no one for the future
owed suit or service to his lord. In a score of villages there were bonfires of charters.
Essex sent a deputation back to the king "with a demand for the ratification of the
promises made at Mile End". Richard told them the pledges made counted for nothing, having been extorted by force, announcing: "Villeins ye are still, villeins ye shall
remain" (Oman 1989, 84). Nobles and bishops led troops of soldiers who pursued and
punished the rioters wherever they found them, some slain, some dispersed.

Conclusions

Although both revolts described here were defeated and the rebels punished, some
historians have noted the contrast between these earlier eras and "modernity", that
is, capitalism in terms of the sheer scale of punishment meted out. The rulers of
republican Rome or medieval Europe punished the rebels, but their measures appear
moderate compared to their later equivalents. In Rome, hundreds were killed in the
Forum, but not enough to prevent many further uprisings and riots over the next
century. As the plebeians without property became integral to the Roman army,
leaders emerged who backed their claims for "peoples" rights, from Marius to Julius
Caesar (Wiseman 2016). In England, hundreds were certainly punished following
the 1381 peasants' revolt, but most deaths were "exemplary". These pre-capitalist
rebels were certainly subject to over-criminalization, just as the accumulation by
the rich that sparked their rebellions was under-criminalized. But it is important to
note the contrast in the *scale* of punishment compared to the violence of the modern world that was emerging in Europe in the 16th century and beyond. Surveying
revolts across Europe, Cohn points out:

Instead of capital punishment issued to a select number of popular ringleaders, such as the decapitation of eight of the leaders of the 1382 Parisian hammer men... monarchs by the mid-fifteenth century began to engage in massacres of the innocents—sacks of cities, with the rape, pillage, and murder of thousands of women and children.

(Cohn 2015, 432)

Perhaps, one of the worst cases of brutal "over-criminalization" was in the early 16th century. Cohn cites "one battle during the German Peasant's War—that of *Francherhaus*—when 50,000 peasants were slaughtered and with nearly twice that number of peasants facing death during the two-year rebellion" (Cohn 2015, 433). The violence was carried out through a combination of slaughter on the battlefield, and legally sanctioned punishment as villages were sacked and populations executed. Once again, this is a question of class. Before the advent of capitalism, many of these revolts saw the population below the ruling figuration of monarch, noble and church uniting in protest. Rulers had to be careful who they suppressed as they needed to win allies amongst the merchants and emerging middle classes. But, as the business class expanded and allied with the modernizing state it switched sides. Now, merchants, bourgeois, nobles and monarchs united to subject all revolts from peasant and artisan to a more violent process of demonization, suppression and criminalization of the oppressed. In terms of crime and punishment, just as in all other aspects of the impact of capitalism, Marx is surely correct when he states of:

[T]he domination of capital over labor. Whilst, therefore, from one point of view it may be regarded as a historical advance and as a necessary developmental factor in the economic evolution of society, from another point of view it must be looked upon as an instrument of civilized and refined exploitation.

(Marx 1933, 386)

The purpose of this study has been to illustrate how throughout history processes of revolt have been both stimulated and repressed by the actions of the economically powerful elements controlling states and territories. Those protesting have been over-criminalized, and those benefiting from the illegal seizures that generated the protestor's discontents have seen their actions under-criminalized—largely due to the consolidated ruling class's increasing levels of control over the state and its laws. The advent of capitalism accelerated and consolidated this criminal selectivity, molding it to the contours of contemporary class domination. It continues apace into the 21st century, threatening the very sustainability of the planet in the process.

References

Aston, M. (1960) Lollardy and sedition, 1381–1431. *Past and Present*, 17, 1–45.
Barker, J. (2009) *Conquest: The English Kingdom of France*, London: Little Brown.
Barker, J. (2014) *England Arise: The People, the King and the Great Revolt of 1381*, London: Little Brown.

Beard, M. (2015) *S.Q.P.R: A History of Ancient Rome*, London: Profile

Brunt, A. (1971) *Social Conflicts in the Roman Republic*, New York: Norton

Carlyle, T. (1829) *Signs of the Times* http://www.victorianweb.org/authors/carlyle/signs1.html

Clement, M. (2016) *A People's History of Riots, Protest and the Law: The Sound of the Crowd*, London: Palgrave Macmillan

Cohn, S. (2006) *Lust for Liberty: The Politics of Social Revolt in Medieval Europe 1200–1425*, Cambridge, MA: Harvard

Cohn, S. (2013) *Popular Protest in Late Medieval English Towns*, Cambridge: Cambridge University Press

Cohn, S. (2015) 'Authority and popular resistance' In H. Scott (Ed.), *The Oxford Handbook of Early Modern European History 1350–1750 II: Cultures and Power*, Oxford: Oxford University Press

Dimmock, S. (2015) *The Origin of Capitalism in England 1400–1600*, Chicago: Haymarket

Empson, M. (2018) *Kill all the Gentlemen: Class struggle in the English Countryside*, London: Bookmarks

Engels, F. (1844) *The condition of the working class in England.* Available at https://www.marxists.org/archive/marx/works/download/pdf/condition-working-class-england.pdf

Harding, A. (1984) 'The revolt against the justices' In R. Hilton and T. Aston (Eds.) *The English Rising of 1381* Cambridge: Cambridge University Press

Hill, C. (1973) *The World Turned Upside Down*, London: Temple Smith

Hilton, R. (1973) *Bond Men Made Free*, London: Temple Smith

Linklater, A. (2016) *Violence and Civilization in Western States-Systems* Cambridge: Cambridge University Press

Marx, K. (1933) *Capital*, London: J.M. Dent and Co.

Millar, F. (1998) *The Crowd in Rome in the Late Republic*, Ann Arbor: University of Michigan

Newbolt, H. (1902) *Froissart in Britain*, London: James Nisbet

Oman, C. (1989) *The Great Revolt of 1381*, London: Green Hill

Patriquin, L. (2015) *Economic Equality and Direct Democracy in Ancient Athens* New York: Palgrave Macmillan

Plutarch (1912) *Lives of the Greeks and the Romans* London: Modern Library.

Polybius (1979) *The Rise of the Roman Empire*, Harmondsworth: Penguin

Richardson, K. (1976) *Daggers in the Forum: The revolutionary lives and violent deaths of the Gracchus brothers*, London: BCA

Vegh Weis, V. (2018) *Marxism and Criminology. A History of Criminal Selectivity*. Brill 2017 (republished by Haymarket Books 2018)

Wiseman, T. (2016) *Julius Caesar*, Stroud: History Press

5

THE CRIMINALIZATION OF LOW-RANK CASTES

A historical perspective of mahad movement in India (1927–1937)

Kruthi Jagadish Kumar, Praveenrao Bolli, and Myrna Cintron

The chapter focuses on the over-criminalization of Mahar, a specific caste in India, by the Mahad Movement in the city of Mahad, where the first social movement for caste equality in Indian history took place (Samel 1999). The goal of the Mahad Movement (1927–1937) was to give access to drinking water to the low-rank castes (Shirke 2012) in the context of social (Hindu caste system) and religious (Hinduism) ideologies that over-criminalized the low-rank castes in their struggle to access water. Following Vegh Weis (2017, 2019), over-criminalization refers to regular everyday practices subjected to over-inclusive regulations, despite the minimal social detriment they generate.

This chapter is divided into different sections. The first discusses India's caste system and the historical over-criminalization of low-rank castes (2nd century to 21st century). The second section introduces the low-rank castes struggle to access water and the role of the Mahad Movement as a pioneer action in the long road to social justice against the domination of high-rank castes and Hindu legal repressive measures (Kumar 2016, Shirke 2012, Samel 1999). The third section focuses on Dr. B.R. Ambedkar, who was the leader of the Mahad Movement and rejected the Hindu law, laying the foundation of equality against the Hindu caste hierarchical system (Kumar 2016, Krishna 2019).

India's caste system and over-criminalization

The caste system is an unavoidable concept in understanding any movement in India (Pomohaci 2013). Caste is derived from the Hindu hierarchical system, which is broadly divided into two levels. The datum of caste comes from Hinduism's two-level hierarchal system. The first level is the Varna system which refers to a skin color, that is, the color established a division between the high-rank and the low-rank castes (Vallabhaneni 2015). The second level consists of the sub-classification

DOI: 10.4324/9781003144229-8

of castes under the Varna system. Although there is no constructive definition for caste, it illustrates the social stratification of race, breed, customs, physical features and other differences found by the division (Vallabhaneni 2015). Caste being a sub-classification under Varna, also includes lifestyle and tradition in the caste-related occupations, it keeps endogamy and membership in a caste is based on birth and associated with higher or lower ritual status. (Ketkar & Ketkar 1909, 46, as cited by Subedi 2013). Brahmins were the priest class, and they uphold the Hindu belief system and the caste hierarchy system (Gould 1960). The caste system was solidly structured after the Hindu religious script Manusmrithi (also called as Manava Dharma Shastra), named after its writer, Manu (Macdonnel 1914). The Manusmrithi was drafted between 200 B.C. and 200 A.D. (Ketkar & Ketkar 1909, Macdonnel 1914, Vallabhaneni 2015) and became a social and religious law book for Hindus (Desai 2014) as well as a guiding principle for a whole social system that is unequal and discriminatory (Ketkar & Ketkar 1909). The institutionaliza-tion of caste hierarchy fostered inequality, prejudices and over-criminalization as breaks of the regulations constitute criminal offenses, that can even receive the death penalty (Bapuji & Chrispal 2020, Lerche 2008, Macdonnel 1914). Indeed, criminalizing language can be seen in how the Chandala caste was given its name in the hierarchal caste system: untouchables. These are not allowed to read and listen to the religious scriptures (Manu IV-99, as cited by Vallabhaneni 2015) and, if they do so, punishments include cutting the tongue and poring hot oil into the ears to forcefully impair hearing (O'Hanlon 1982). For any attempt of low-rank castes to remember the scriptures, the punishment consists of splitting the body into two halves because only high-rank castes can read the religious scriptures (Ambedkar 1946, Franco & Sarvar 1989). The Hindu scripture uses specific ter-minology to over-criminalize low-rank castes for actions that do not cause social harm and that are part of the everyday life of the upper-castes. In this regard, crimi-nal selectivity can serve to describe how to the system's characteristic select, punish and over-criminalize a particular group and under-criminalize others (Vegh Weis 2017, 2019). Ambedkar (1946) compared the caste system with Roman law since it also had divisions between privileged and underprivileged populations. However, Roman law respected the "equality before the law", so the same punishment was applied in response to similar crimes, regardless of who committed them—at least not in the letter of the law. In Hindu religious law, regulations discriminate and exploit the low-rank caste while they protect the high-rank caste's position. For example, in the early 19th century, as Russel (n.d. quoted in O'Hanlon 1982) states, Hindu religious scriptures condemned contact of the low-rank castes with high-rank castes. In the city of Poona, low-rank castes were banned from coming on the streets between 9am and 3pm to avoid physical contact. In case a low-rank caste person accidentally faced a Brahmin from the priest caste, they had to bow down to minimize their shadow and avoid visual contact (O'Hanlon 1982). Fukazawa (1968, 1971) states that the failure of a low-rank caste individual to hide his or her shadow was punishment by forced labor. These punishments were issued by caste councils or by high-rank caste members.

Low-rank castes struggle for water

Since the beginning of the 18th century, low-rank castes experienced the worst forms of discrimination in accessing fundamental resources such as food, housing and education (Channa 2005, O'Hanlon 1982). The cultural norms were constructed so that low-rank castes should not wear clothes, eat in clean utensils of copper or brass pots and wear gold or silver jewelry. The low-rank castes were not just prohibited from the latter, but also from accessing clean drinking water (Daily 2009). As Vegh Weis (2017) writes, these actions conformed "criminalized survival strategies", that is, everyday surviving strategies became crimes. Any attempt of low-rank caste individuals to access education was punished by being tied to an elephant's feet (Rao 2014). Low-rank castes also experienced geographical isolation as their neighborhoods were in the outskirts of villages to avoid that the high-rank caste Hindus became "polluted" with the air of low-rank caste neighborhoods. Low-rank castes were not allowed to leave their assigned work either. If any low-rank caste family moved to a different neighborhood or changed their assigned work, the case was referred to the Panchayat so that they received the proper punishment (Wankhade 2014, O'Hanlon 1982). Panchayat used several methods in assigning punishments for low-rank caste disobedience, including excommunication, which involved ending their social acquaintance even within their own caste, the confiscation of properties and business and the prohibition to work (Fukazawa 1968). If the excommunicated person had any married daughters, they would be disapproved at their in-law's place and sent back to their father.

By 1901, the first Indian census verified that India had a total of 2,378 main castes and tribes, from which the majority were low-rank castes (Olcott 1944). During the early 1900s, European missionaries supplied food, water, education, health and economic assistance to their members. Indeed, a considerable number of low-rank castes converted to Christianity to escape discrimination (Ganguly 2009). Between 195,000 to 667,000 outcastes converted into Christianity between 1917 and 1926. To confront this tendency, liberal Hindus opted to provide similar services to low-rank castes (Olcott 1944). However, the low-rank caste's socio-cultural position did not change much, they remained in the lower rank of the socio-cultural hierarchy and segregated from the upper caste (Ganguly 2009). Despite their conversion, the low-rank castes remained untouchables and the missionary's struggle to access water for the low-rank castes was curtailed by the Hindu high-rank castes (Adagale 2017). Moreover, the high-rank castes persistently polluted the low-rank castes' drinking water by disposing their trash and excreta, making it unfit for human consumption (Kumar 2016, Javaid et al. 2014).

Dr. Bhimrao Ramji Ambedkar and the Mahad movement

Dr. B.R. Ambedkar, born on April 14, 1891, had a western educational background and supported British policies when they allowed to foster equality among Indians (Rajasekhariah & Jayaraj 1991, Chakrabarty 2016). Particularly relevant was the 1923 decision of the British government to organize that all public state properties and resources could be accessed by all the citizens irrespective of their caste (Adagale 2017, Deepa 2017, Samel 1999). Three years later, the Mahad city's municipal committee passed an order to keep the Chavdar water tank open for the public. Although the order was passed, it became a nominal effort because no low-rank caste members dared to exercise the given right (Deepa 2017).

As the law failed in its implementation, Dr. Ambedkar and other activists met the low-rank caste families and explained the aims of the Mahad Movement, concentrating on the importance of water as a valuable source of life (Kumar 2016). Dr. Ambedkar also organized a conference to schedule future action plans against caste discrimination and in favor of status mobility for low-rank castes (Deepa 2017, Jilova 2019, Kumar 2016, Shirke 2012). A total of 10,000 people from low-rank castes took part in the first conference (Deepa 2017, Majid & Zahid 2014, Samel 1999). On the last day of the Mahad conference, participants walked towards the water tank (Samel 1999), and around 3,000 people drank water from the city's public water (Kumar 2016). They were attacked and brutally beaten with bamboo sticks (Samel 1999, Shirke 2012) and the clash led to riots (Jilova 2019). The conference and the later actions have been described as the starting point of the Mahad Movement.

The Mahad Movement successfully broke the 1,000 years' rule of Hinduism (Sarkar 2006: 341, as cited by Majid & Zahid 2014). Since Hinduism's high-rank castes considered that the low-rank castes had polluted the tank with their touch, the conservative high-rank caste Hindus performed a religious water cleansing ritual (Pooja) to purify the tank (Majid & Zahid 2014, Samel 1999). They also filed a petition in the high court, saying that the Chavdar water tank was private property, and the low-rank castes had trespassed. After the violence occurred, the city government repealed the decision and declared the Mahad tank as private property and not open to low-rank castes. (Hardtmann 2009, as quoted by Majid & Zahid 2014).

As a result of these actions, a census report of 1931 mentioned that people from low-rank castes were still prohibited from accessing water, using government roads, use of wells and reservoirs, Hindu temples, cremation grounds, private businesses such as tea shops, hotels and entertainment areas (Olcott 1944). In the year 1932, a low-rank caste man was beaten by high-rank caste women when he drank water from the well (Kumar 2016). To confront this unfairness, the Mahad Movement presented legal proceedings and won the case in 1937. After a decade-long struggle to access natural water resources, the Bombay high court verdict said that the Mahad water tank was public, marking the Mahad Movement's success (Deepa 2017).

After the Mahad Movement's legal success, the movement extended its goals to other untouchable issues such as temple entry (Kumar 2016). In the two cities of Maharashtra state, around 15,000 low-rank castes tried to gain access to Shree Rama temple (Hindu god) and Parvathi temple (Hindu goddess). High-rank castes closed the temple entrance, which led to violent riots. High-rank castes attacked the low-rank castes with sticks, throwing stones and slippers. The two individuals from low-rank castes who came close to the temple doors were assaulted by high-rank castes (Tejani 2013). Later high-rank castes closed the temple permanently, assuming that the god was polluted by the presence of low-rank castes (Majid & Zahid 2014, Tejani 2013).

A breaking point took place after India gained its independence. Then, Dr. Ambedkar was appointed to draft the Constitution, and he used this opportunity to place special emphasis on the empowerment of the low-rank castes (Abraham 2002, Lerche 2008). Dr. Ambedkar's contributions to the Constitution can be found with the principles of equality, fraternity, social democracy, social justice and economic plans. The Constitution of India promises equal rights and equal justice for every citizen in the nation irrespective of religion, region, caste, creed, gender, and/or birth (Abraham 2002, Jilova 2019). Dr. Ambedkar's attempts to achieve social change and wipe out caste differences are seen in Part III and Part IV of the Constitution that cover the fundamental rights and directive principles safeguarding all Indian citizens, as mentioned in Table 5.1 (Kumar 2016, Jilova 2019).

TABLE 5.1 Indian Constitution

Part	Articles	Description
Part III Fundamental Rights	14	Right to equality – The State shall not deny to any person equality before the law or the equal protection of the laws within the territory of India.
	15	The State shall not discriminate against any citizen on grounds only of religion, race, caste, sex, place of birth or any of them.
	15 (2b)	The use of wells, tanks, bathing ghats, roads and places of public resort maintained wholly or partly out of State funds or dedicated to the use of the general public.
	16	Equality of opportunity for all citizens in matters of public employment
	17	"Untouchability" is abolished and its practice in any form is forbidden. The enforcement of any disability arising out of "Untouchability" shall be an offense punishable in accordance with law.
	19	Right to Freedom – All citizens shall have the right – to freedom of speech and expression, to assemble peacefully and without arms, to form associations or unions, to move freely throughout the territory of India, to reside and settle in any part of the territory of India and to practice any profession, or to carry on any occupation, trade or business.

(Continued)

TABLE 5.1 (Continued)

Part	Articles	Description
	25	Right to Freedom of Religion – Subject to public order, morality and health and to other provisions of this Part, all persons are equally entitled to freedom of conscience and the right to freely profess, practice and propagate religion.
	26	Subject to public order, morality and health, every religious denomination or any section thereof shall have the right to manage religious affairs.
	30	All minorities, whether based on religion or language, hall have the right to establish and administer educational institutions of their choice.
Part IV Directive Principles of State Policy	45	The State shall endeavor to provide, within a period of ten years from the commencement of this Constitution, for free and compulsory education for all children until they complete the age of fourteen years.

Source: Government of India 1950

Yet, even after the Constitution was passed, incidents of violence, humiliation, verbal and physical abuse across the country for accessing water perdured (Jilova 2019, Kumar 2016, Majid & Zahid 2014). Adagale (2020) finds violence committed against the low-rank castes for accessing water even today.

Table 5.2 shows the types of violent acts perpetrated against low-rank caste residents who accessed water in the state of Maharashtra between 1995 and 2011. Overall, 13 cases are mentioned in Table 5.2, in which, the kind of violence committed includes poisoning the water source, verbal and physical abuse, vandalism and murder. From the case status column, it is seen that out of 13 cases, in only one case charges were filed and three cases were not reported to the law enforcement agency, the accused were acquitted in three cases, two were convicted, two cases were pending in the court, and only one case received stay orders from the high court. Notably, there is no significant difference in terms of the violence committed between the villages with a below-average population size of low-rank castes (also known as scheduled castes or Dalit's) and the above average population size of low-rank castes (Adagale 2020). Table 5.2 illustrates how the social hierarchy and high-rank caste domination still exist, and the social weakness of low-rank castes regardless of the supporting Constitution even in the 21st century.

TABLE 5.2 Types of violence met by low-rank castes for accessing water in the State of Maharashtra, India, from 1995 to 2011

Numerical Strength	Village	Total population	Percentage of scheduled castes population (low-rank castes)	Nature of the crime	Current status of the case
Below Average Population of Dalits	Dagadi Shahajanpur	1,103	7.43	Poring of poison into the water source	Charge-sheet filed
	Gawandara	2,253	8.88	Abusing the victim for irrigating land	Accused acquitted
	Kuslamb	2,760	8.99	Verbal abuses	Accused convicted
	Ashti	243,607	10.20	Murder	Pending in the court
	Ganjpur	1,255	8.76	Victims prohibited from accessing water	Non-registered case
	Vanjarwadi	989	2.22	Physical violence	Accused acquitted
Above Average Population of Dalits	Ghodka Rajuri	2,257	12.54	Abuses hurled and physical assaults	Compromised (no charges filed)
	Wantakli	2,004	21.26	Physical violence, burning the victim's house	Stayed by the High Court
	Ranmala	1,044	18.97	Beating the victim for not releasing water	Accused convicted
	Mali Pargaon	2,529	20.13	Murder	Accused acquitted

(Continued)

TABLE 5.2 (Continued)

Numerical Strength	Village	Total population	Percentage of scheduled castes population (low-rank castes)	Nature of the crime	Current status of the case
	Kiti Adgaon	4,767	16.15	Mob attack on Dalits (low-rank castes)	Non-registered case
	Rui Dharur	2,866	21.11	Beating	File closed
	Jategaon	4,564	17.81	Physical violence	Pending in the court

Source: Amended from Adagale 2020, p.405

Conclusions

This chapter discussed the Varna system and its subdivision of castes. Based on these hierarchies, the chapter discussed the over-criminalization of the low-rank castes in Hinduism and how it curtailed the accessibility to natural resources to the low-rank castes for centuries. As mentioned, in 1927, Dr. Ambedkar questioned caste untouchability and started the Mahad Movement demanding access to public water resources to all castes. Dr. Ambedkar also injected equality ideas into the Indian Constitution, modeling further water policies in Independent India (Kumar 2016). However, the study conducted by Adagale (2020) shows that, although Dr. Ambedkar laid the groundwork for an equal and democratic society, the country failed in implementing the constitutional rights to safeguard the low-rank castes from discrimination. The need to enforce constitutional rights irrespective of caste and individual interests is still pending.

References

Abraham, L. (2002) Notes on Ambedkar's water resources policies. *Economic and Political Weekly*, 37(48), 4772–4774.

Adagale, R. (2020) Water and violence against dalits in Maharashtra: A multi-case approach, *Social Change*, 50(3), 399–415.

Adagale, R.D., (2017) *Caste and access to water: Case studies of caste discrimination and atrocities against Dalits in Beed district of Rural Maharashtra.* Ph.D. Tata Institute of Social Sciences.

Ambedkar, B. R. (1946) *Who were the Shudras?.* Bombay: Thackers.

Bapuji, H. and Chrispal, S. (2020) Understanding economic inequality through the lens of caste. *Journal of Business Ethics.* 162, 533–551.

Chakrabarty, B. (2016) B.R. Ambedkar and the history of constitutionalizing India. *Contemporary South Asia*, 24(2), 133–148.

Channa, S.M. (2005). Metaphors of race and caste-based discriminations against Dalits and Dalit Women in India in Harrison, F. V. (ed). *Resisting Racism and Xenophobia: Global Perspectives on Race Gender and Human Rights* AltaMira Press pp 49–66

Daily, L.A. (2009) *Constructing a New Nationalism from Below: The Dalit Movement, Politics and Transnational Networking. M.L.A.* University of South Florida.

Deepa, B. (2017) Mahad satyagraha: Dr. Ambedkar's speech to enlighten Dalit women on social and cultural rights. *International Journal of Research in Education and Psychology*, 3(1), 20–26.

Desai, L. (2014) The language of rights is alien to Hindu religion. *Studia Bioethica*, 7(1), 33–38.

Franco, F. and Sarvar V.S.C. (1989) Ideology as social practice: The functioning of varna. *Economic and Political Weekly*. 24(47), 2601–2612.

Fukazawa, H. (1968) State and caste system (jāti) in the eighteenth century Maratha kingdom. *Hitotsubashi Journal of Economics*. 9(1), 32–44.

Fukazawa, H. (1971) A note on the corvée system (veṭhbegār) in the eighteenth century Maratha kingdom. *Hitotsubashi Journal of Economics*. 11(2), 1–10.

Ganguly, D. (2009) Pain, personhood and the collective: Dalit life narratives. *Asian Studies Review*. 33, 429–442.

Gould, H.A. (1960) Castes, outcastes, and the sociology of stratification. *International Journal of Comparative Sociology*. 1(2), 220.

Government of India (1950) *The Constitution of India*.

Hardtmann, E. M. (2009) *The Dalit Movement in India: Local Practices, Global Connections*. Oxford: Oxford University Press.

Javaid, U., Majid, A. and Zahid, S.F. (2014) Low caste in India (Untouchables) *South Asian Studies*. 29(1), 7–21.

Jilova, N.K. (2019). Thoughts and constitutional provisions of Dr. B.R. Ambedkar to social justice. *Journal of the Gujarat Research Society*, 21(2), 257–261.

Ketkar, S.V. and Ketkar, S.V. (1909) The history of caste in India. *In Evidence of the Laws of Manu on the Social Conditions in India During the Third Century A.D.* Taylor and Carpenter. 1, 1–212.

Krishna, S. (2019) Engaging Ambedkar on inclusive discourse: countering exclusion towards social reconstruction. *IASSI Quarterly*. 38(1), 139–153.

Kumar, V. (2016) History of Indian environmental Movement: A study of Dr. B.R. Ambedkar from the perspective of access to water. *Contemporary Voice of Dalit*. 8(2), 239–245.

Lerche, J. (2008) Transnational advocacy networks and affirmative action for Dalits in India. *Development and Change* 39(2), 239–261.

Macdonnel, A. (1914) The early history of caste. *The American Historical Review*. 19(2), 230–244.

Majid, A. and Zahid, S. (2014) Low caste in India (Untouchables). *South Asian Studies*. 29(1), 7–21.

O'Hanlon, R. (1982) A tyranny against nature-the untouchables in western India. *History Today*.

Olcott, M. (1944) The Caste system of India. *American Sociological Review*. 9(6), 648–657.

Pomohaci, M. (2013) The influence of the political, social and religious measures upon caste during British India. *International Journal on Humanistic Ideology*. 6(1), 105–128.

Rajasekhariah, A. and Jayaraj, H. (1991) Political philosophy of Dr. B. R. Ambedkar. *The Indian Journal of Political Science*. 52(3), 357–375.

Rao, V. (2014) A century of consolidation and resistance: Caste and education in Maharashtra 1818–1918. *Nehru Memorial Museum and Library Occasional Paper*. 54.

Samel, S. (1999) Mahad Chawadar tank satyagraha of 1927: Beginning of Dalit liberation under B. R. Ambedkar. *Proceedings of the Indian History Congress*. 60, 722–728.

Sarkar, D. R. (2006) *Dalit in India, Past and Present.* India: Serials Publications.

Shirke, S. (2012) The attitude of British government towards Mahad Chavdar tank satyagraha. *Proceedings of the Indian History Congress.* 73, 1435–1436.

Subedi, M. (2013) Some theoretical considerations on caste. *Dhaulagiri: Journal of Sociology and Anthropology.* 7, 51–86.

Tejani, S. (2013) Untouchable demands for justice or the problem of religious 'non-interference': The case of temple entry movements in late-colonial India. *Journal of Colonialism and Colonial History*, 14(3).

Vallabhaneni, M. (2015) Indian caste system: Historical and psychoanalytic views. *The American Journal of Psychoanalysis.* 75(4), 361–381.

Vegh Weis, V. (2017) Marxism and Criminology: A History of Criminal Selectivity. *Brill.* 104, 368.

Vegh Weis, V. (2019) Towards a critical green southern criminology: An analysis of criminal selectivity, indigenous peoples, and green harms in Argentina. *International Journal for Crime, Justice and Social Democracy.* 8(3), 38–55.

Wankhade, D. M. (2014). Geographies of untouchability and caste discrimination in India. *Zero Mile.* 1(1), 1–8.

6

"LOYAL SPEAR-CARRIERS"

Police violence in the Queensland anti-apartheid movement, 1971

Paul Bleakley

Often mischaracterized as a stalwart bastion of Australian conservatism in the 20th century, in reality the state of Queensland boasted one of the country's most robust activist movements in the early 1970s. National leaders of the radical New Left such as Brian Laver and Mitch Thompson called the state capital Brisbane home, directing the efforts of protest organizations like the Society for Democratic Action (SDA) and Civil Liberties Co-ordinating Committee (CLCC) in opposition to the repressive policies of conservative Country Party premier Johannes "Joh" Bjelke-Petersen. Assuming power in August 1968, the arch-traditionalist Bjelke-Petersen was a leader in constant conflict with the radical movement that was appearing in the era, both in Queensland and around the world more broadly (Laver 1968, Wear 2002). For the premier, the protest movement posed an existential threat to the social fabric of Queensland: not only were local New Left style groups like the SDA and the CLCC linked to the much-despised Communist Party of Australia, the long-haired and marijuana smoking youths who were most outspoken against the Bjelke-Petersen government reflected a general relaxing of collective morals that was an anathema to the premier, the pastoralist son of a Lutheran minister (de Lange, 1967a, Wear, 2002). Using the apparatus of the state to repress left-wing protesters was a core element of the premier's platform from his earliest years in government, supported on a practical level by a Queensland Police Force (QPF) who stood ready to serve—or, rather, enforce—the government's political agenda.

First, the government set out to use the legal system to tighten restrictions on protest via the *Traffic Act*, a move that attracted great opposition from local activists (The Courier-Mail 1967, Brennan 1983). When it came to the 1971 Springboks' tour, the Bjelke-Petersen government went even further: more than just restricting the legal rights of anti-Apartheid demonstrators, the premier's emergency declaration suspended civil liberties and gave police enhanced powers to deal with protesters

DOI: 10.4324/9781003144229-9

in an initiative-taking manner, resulting in widespread (often unrestrained) police violence. The state of emergency was not responsible for prompting the police riots of July 1971: the premier made clear through his rhetoric on the protests that police were expected to take decisive action against protesters and, in his conversations with the Police Union, Bjelke-Petersen was open in his stance that police accused of excessive force would not be disciplined for incidents that occurred during the state of emergency (Evans, 2004, Condon 2013). The government held up their end of the bargain, with no police facing legal or departmental action despite the litany of assault allegations against them during the Springboks' tour. In return, the police held up their end of the bargain as well: under the protection of the state, the QPF took full advantage of the disciplinary freedoms afforded under the state of emergency to force protesters off the streets, using a concerted strategy where force was intended as both a general deterrent and, as suggested in the historical record, a reprisal for non-conformity.

Though the stage was set for conflict in the years before, the arrival of the South African Springboks rugby union team for their Australian tour in July 1971 proved a flashpoint for clashes between protesters and police, running under explicit orders from the state government. Unwilling to allow the New Left to hijack the event with demonstrations against the segregationist policies of the South African government, Bjelke-Petersen issued a pre-emptive state of emergency that effectively gave police *carte blanche* to repress dissent using whatever means at their disposal, an order later described as "a mind-bendingly draconian move, virtually suspending civil liberties" (Evans 2004, 278). Nevertheless, the anti-Apartheid protesters refused to buckle in the face of the state's attempts to silence them, creating an atmosphere of escalating tension that inevitably led to an outburst of frenzied police violence across several nights of protest (Cowen 1971, Evans 2004).

The Springboks' tour was not the first case of police-protester clashes in Queensland, nor would it be the last—Bjelke-Petersen served another 16 years as state premier after the Springboks tour and, for much of that time, called on the police to silence alternative voices in the state to reinforce his "vision" for Queensland. What makes the Springboks case important, however, is in the precedent it set for suppression of protest moving forward. It showed a premier willing to change the standard rules of engagement for policing protest to legitimize the extreme violence perpetrated by police officers. Another key factor was that, rather than simply ignoring excessive force complaints, as was the case in the past, in this occasion Bjelke-Petersen called a state of emergency as a purposeful move to suspend the principles of due process and, moreover, incited the police to take aggressive measures in dispersing planned demonstrations. As this chapter shows, the response to the Springboks protests was not only a case of the state government criminalizing activism, but instead a matter of actively decriminalizing police misconduct committed in service of the state's political agenda. Bjelke-Petersen's actions during the Springboks tour offer relevant lessons for the contemporary policing of activism, highlighting the significant risks inherent in giving police free reign to combat protest, even in situations considered a "state of emergency".

On a collision course: the radical movement rises in Brisbane, 1960s–1971

Even before Bjelke-Petersen became premier in 1968, there was an established tradition of socio-political conservatism in Queensland that was partly reinforced by the absence of a truly progressive leftist movement. The political left, mostly represented by organizations like the Australian Labor Party (ALP) and trade unions, were themselves conservative compared to other leftist groups around the world. The central conflict within the Queensland left was not between traditionalist Marxists and radical intellectuals, as it was elsewhere. Instead, it was a struggle for control between two equally conservative subsects: on one side the workers' rights campaigners of the "Old Left" and, on the other, socially conservative Catholics who dominated the state's ALP (Wanna & Arkley, 2010).

Because of this status quo, there were few avenues for radical activists to practice their campaigning until the mid-1960s, at which point the global rise of the New Left began to filter into a burgeoning student protest movement based on Brisbane's university campuses, driven by activist groups such as the SDA and the CLCC. Just as C. Wright Mills predicted in his 1960 "Letter to the New Left" shifting ideas on how best to achieve social change was driven in Brisbane (as elsewhere) by "the young intelligentsia ... thinking and acting in radical ways" (Mills, 1960: 18). Rather than perpetuating a myopic focus on conventional Marxist labor concerns, the Brisbane New Left turned attention to broader issues of socio-political equity, from demanding increased rights for disenfranchised populations to anti-imperialist campaigns against nuclearization or the Vietnam War (Mills 1960, Miller 1994).

Unique to Brisbane was the fact that, at the end, a coalition was formed between Old and New Left over the struggle for the right to political protest which, though not banned, had been severely curtailed under the state's *Traffic Act 1949 to 1965*. When conservative premier Frank Nicklin did not negotiate over reforms to these restrictions in 1967, his actions prompted the disparate subgroups within the Queensland left to combine in a series of protests demanding change (Brennan, 1983, The Canberra Times, 1967). The *Traffic Act* protests were, in many ways, the zenith of the Queensland protest movement and, when Bjelke-Petersen inherited the role of premier the following year, the Queensland progressive movement was enjoying its greatest success in 20 years.

The energizing effect that New Left groups had on Brisbane's protest movement inevitably attracted the attention of the QPF, who saw the student radicals as a potential threat to security and social cohesion in Queensland. There was, from an international perspective, some cause for concern: the SDA was inspired by an analogous organization in the USA, the Students for a Democratic Society (SDS). Like the SDA, the SDS handled a pivot in the US protest movement in the early 1960s, turning away from traditional Marxist causes in favor of New Left concerns—indeed, the focus on "Vietnam, conscription, education, civil liberties, aborigines [sic], conservation, local government etc." was an explicit part of the SDA's foundational mission statement (Radical Times, n.d.: 2). Not only was the SDA modeled on the SDS, but there were also clear ties between the two groups, with US students and academics like Ralph Summy at the University of Queensland playing a guiding role in the group's formation (Radical Times, n.d., Piccini, 2011). In 1969, the US SDS would evolve into the Weather Underground, a militant splinter cell that would be responsible for perpetuating violent acts of protest around the USA for much of the 1970s and be labeled a domestic terrorist group (Varon 2004). While this was definitively not the trajectory that the SDA would take in Queensland, there was a fear among many in government that there was enormous potential for escalation in the student movement which required diligent surveillance and monitoring by the QPF.

Responsibility for checking the SDA fell to the force's Special Branch, an intelligence-gathering section of the QPF formed in response to the Communist threat several decades earlier (Jones, 1948). Surveillance was focused on a property known as SDA House in inner-city Highgate Hill, where Special Branch operatives watched both comings-and-goings of student radicals from outside and, in some cases, inserted operatives to observe and record SDA meetings. The results of the infiltration only seemed to confirm the police view that the New Left radicals were on the same extremist path as their US compatriots: A Special Branch report produced in March 1967 noted visits to SDA House by Communist Party national president Laurie Aarons and, later in July 1967, another report recorded SDA leader Brian Laver as stating "they [the SDA] cannot exclude drug addicts and beatniks from their membership" (de Lange, 1967a: 2, 1967b). The information gathered in this monitoring process opened the door for the QPF to partake in unconventional practices designed to harass the SDA. After Laver's statements on "drug addicts and beatniks" were reported to the QPF hierarchy, the practice of using the *Health Act 1937* as a cover for raiding SDA House began: officers from Special Branch were, for a short-term of a few hours, seconded to the Drug Squad. The Drug Squad was able to use the provisions of the *Health Act* to enter any property where drug use was suspected and having entered SDA House on this basis, the Special Branch had free reign to search for material that could be used to compromises the group's political activities (*The Courier-Mail* 1967, 13). For the Queensland police, running in the shadow of the Cold War, the resultant perception of the New Left protest movement was one of anti-Australian Communists who did not reflect the traditional values accepted by most Queenslanders. Groups like the SDA were, thus, exposed to a labelling process—an "othering"—through which the QPF constructed student protesters as an enemy, rather than part of the community they were sworn to protect.

As noted above, the SDA and other New Left groups in Queensland were concerned with a vast variety of socio-political issues, from Vietnam to environmental conservation. Central to the New Left's ideological standpoint was a commitment to civil rights, and just treatment for all. For this reason, the segregationist Apartheid imposed by the South African government became a *cause célèbre* for New Left activists around the world, including in Queensland. Since 1948, a racial caste structure was in place in South Africa that reinforced *baasskap* (or "white supremacy") through a restriction of public services and limitation of socio-economic opportunity for non-White South Africans (Louw 2004). Global condemnation of Apartheid escalated in the early 1960s, partly the result of the Sharpeville massacre but also in conjunction with the expanding internationalist perspective adopted by the New Left. The international anti-Apartheid movement succeeded in forcing South Africa out of the British Commonwealth in 1961 and, later, South Africa was suspended from the 1964 Summer Olympic Games based on claims of racism in the country's sporting world (Nixon 1992, Klotz 1999). The ban on South African participation was reinforced in 1970, when the country's failure to address the allegations raised in 1964 caused them to be expelled from the Olympic Games altogether. In spite of these acts, there remained much for the New Left to protest while outwardly expressing a disapproval of Apartheid, nations like Australia stopped short of agreeing to sanctions or trade bans against South Africa—a common demand of the New Left anti-Apartheid movement (Thorn, 2006). It was in this context that, in 1971, the all-White South African Springboks rugby union team set out on a six-week tour of Australia. Despite being banned from international events like the Olympic Games, the Australian government rejected calls to prevent the Springboks tour going forward. With the South African team's arrival fast approaching, the 1971 tour swiftly became a rallying point for the New Left across Australia. However, it was the pre-emptive actions of an already antagonistic premier Joh Bjelke-Petersen in Queensland that set the stage for some of the most violent clashes between police and protesters in modern Australian history.

A "state of emergency": the state prepares for battle with anti-Apartheid protesters

Though anti-imperialism and civil rights were, in general terms, formative parts of the New Left agenda in Queensland, the anti-Apartheid movement in the state officially began on 14 May 1971 when a meeting at the University of Queensland decided that the upcoming Springboks tour would serve as a focal point for anti-racist protest (Radical Times, n.d.). The decision to oppose the tour came at a time of heightened activism, only six weeks prior to the third Moratorium rally in opposition to the Vietnam War was held, where five thousand protesters took to the streets of Brisbane under the direction of the protest movement. The strength of the Moratorium was no doubt a consideration when the premier pre-emptively announced a state of emergency on 13 July 1971 in response to the planned anti-Apartheid protests. Bjelke-Petersen said he decided on the state of emergency order after consultations with QPF Commissioner Whitrod, who told him the Springboks match planned for Brisbane on 24 July would have to be played at an alternative venue because police were unable to secure the usual site for rugby union matches. Referring ambiguously to the anti-Apartheid protests, the premier described the state of emergency as necessary "in the face of the threat of real violence and defiance of law and order with subsequent dangers to life and property" (The Canberra Times 1971a, 1).

The premier's power to impose a state of emergency was bestowed under the *Transport Act*, giving the government the ability to take control of private assets for public use and—importantly—providing police with broad powers to arrest any person they believed posed a risk to "public order". The augmentation of police powers was a major factor in Bjelke-Petersen's declaration: in his announcement, he cited Whitrod's public safety concerns as a trigger for his decision and, in turn, asked the QPF to reassign more than 450 police from regional Queensland to Brisbane for the duration of the Springboks visit to supplement police in the capital (*The Canberra Times* 1971b, 1). In addition to his public directive to police to keep the public order, Bjelke-Petersen also made his orders clear via informal communications with the Queensland Police Union. The premier promised union executives that police would "not be penalized for any action they take to suppress" the anti-Apartheid demonstrations (Condon 2013, 245). With regional police flocking to the nearby Enoggera army barracks to be billeted, the message quickly filtered through the rank-and-file that Bjelke-Petersen had given the QPF *carte blanche* to use whatever force they considered necessary to disperse protesters. The premier, in effect, offered police immunity for violence when it took place in pursuit of his political agenda—this "green-light" for the use of excessive force reinforced the increasingly prevalent view that the QPF were "loyal spear-carriers" for the state government, rather than independent arbiters of sociolegal order (Whitton 1989, 10). Though this was a belief that had long been held in the radical protest movement, the state of emergency (and, later, events of the Springboks tour) further expanded the public understanding of the close ideological links between government and police.

Police violence in the name of "law and order", 21–24 July 1971

The first flashpoint between police and protesters occurred on 21 July, a day before the Springboks team even arrived in Brisbane. Before beginning the anti-Apartheid demonstrations planned to greet the South African team, protesters turned their attention to marching in opposition to Bjelke-Petersen's state of emergency, seen as an unprecedented attack on free speech in Queensland. An official permit was issued allowing the demonstrators to march along a designated route from the University of Queensland campus to the Roma Street Forum, a public space where the protest would end with speeches from some of Brisbane's best-known activists like Brian Laver and Mitch Thompson (Queensland Police Force [QPF] 1971a). At some point during this march, however, the route changed when some protesters deviated from Roma Street Forum to approach Parliament House instead. There is no evidence that this was a planned strategy on the part of protest organizers: indeed, police radio logs from 21 July show that protest leaders Laver and Thompson were at the Forum awaiting the marchers' arrival when the route-change occurred, showing that the original plan for the rally remained set to that point (QPF 1971a, 1). Whether planned or not, the changing course of the march triggered the intervention of the Public Order Squad, a non-permanent unit of officers trained to respond to major cases of civil unrest (Hodges, 1971). The Cowen report notes that, even at this early stage of the protests, police were forceful in their dispersal efforts. One protester told Cowen he was "kicked in the buttocks by a policeman" and another told of how "he was accosted by police who kicked, kneed and punched him, pulled his hair, and pushed him to the ground" (Cowen 1971, 2). Notably, none of the protesters who alleged excessive force was used against them reported that police first directed them to disperse before engaging them physically. Under the usual Police Rules, there is an impetus on police to issue this dispersal order and allow protesters a reasonable amount of time to comply before forcibly removing them. However, these professional rules were suspended under the state of emergency, opening the door for police to confront protesters in such a way that (under normal conditions) would be considered an illegal assault. Ordinarily, the *Police Rules* said officers must give fair warning before using force and, especially, before drawing batons. In the state of emergency, these rules were suspended, and police were able to act with virtual impunity in their campaign to clear the streets.

The events of the 21 July protest set the tone for an even more violent clash the following night at the Tower Mill Motel, where the Springboks team stayed for the duration of their tour. Protesters gathered outside the motel to await the Springboks arrival, at which point the assembled group were infiltrated by undercover Special Branch officers who acted as *agent provocateurs* "ready to start something extreme to provoke conflict" (Evans 2004, 280). Use of covert agents to target the protest community was not unusual, as highlighted by the infiltration of SDA House that began several years earlier (de Lange 1967b). In this case, however, police were not just checking the activities of protesters: the allegation is that they were intentionally causing trouble in an otherwise peaceful crowd with the aim to give police at the motel reason to order their dispersal. If so, the plan worked: at around 6pm, Inspector Stanley Hambrecht gave the dispersal order after conferring with Special Branch officers embedded in the crowd (Hambrecht 1971, 58). Unlike the day prior, there was an order to disperse in this case—however, in this case the police did not give protesters time to leave the area peacefully and, instead, rushed the assembled group and "indiscriminately assaulted many persons" as they fled into the adjacent Wickham Park (Cowen 1971, 4).

During the clash in the park, victims of police violence reported to Cowen that numerous comments were made by officers that suggested deeper political motivations for the extreme response: several reported being called "nigger loving bastards" while being beaten by police, and another reported police saying the protesters would now "think twice about making fun [of the police]" (Cowen 1971, 6–7). The protesters who alleged they were beaten by police were, in some ways, fortunate: others sustained serious injuries after being chased or, in some recounts, thrown over a fifteen-foot cliff that marked the boundary of Wickham Park (Cowen, 1971, 5–6). Even when the area around Tower Mill Motel was cleared, the police violence did not end when some fleeing protesters sought refuge in the nearby Trades Hall, police laid siege to the building. The official police record suggests that the clash was triggered because police officer Lindsay Daniels was being "held by demonstrators in the Trades Hall" as a hostage (QPF 1971b, 56). The Cowen report tells a different story: witnesses said that a police officer (with a badge number that matches Daniels) chased protesters seeking refuge into Trades Hall and launched a violent attack on one, student activist and future Queensland premier Peter Beattie (Cowen 1971, 8). Even though Beattie suffered serious injuries, he was nevertheless charged with disorderly conduct while still recovering in hospital. Daniels, on the other hand, received the benefit of the premier's largesse and, true to the promise made by Bjelke-Petersen before the protests began, was not disciplined for hospitalizing Beattie (QPF 1971c, 64).

As protesters reeled from the ferocity of the police charge at Tower Mill Motel, planned demonstrations on the next night were comparably restrained and brief. On the day after, when the Springboks match was scheduled to be played, protests resumed in earnest. On the afternoon of 24 July, more than four thousand protesters gathered in a city park—initially, the plan had been to march on the match venue but (while some demonstrators did attend the playing field) embedded Special Branch officers reported that the protesters had changed their mind and, instead, would set out for the site of their clash with police at Tower Mill Motel two nights prior (QPF 1971d). With consideration for the tensions the 22 July clash had provoked, Police Commissioner Whitrod personally took control of the scene at the motel. Again, conflict between police and protesters seemed unavoidable: police guarding the hotel were reported to chant "paint them red and flog them dead" at protesters, an allusion to their perceived Communist sympathies (Cowen 1971, 10). Other witnesses claimed that, as in earlier clashes, police "grinned with anticipation" as they awaited a dispersal order from Whitrod (Cowen 1971, 11–12). The circumstances of this dispersal order are unclear: while Whitrod claims he only gave the order to disperse after a noise complaint from staff at the nearby Holy Spirit Hospital, police radio records indicate otherwise—these records show that Sister Eunan from the hospital contacted Whitrod at 5:55pm, however Whitrod had already given orders to commence dispersal almost an hour earlier at 4:41pm (Whitrod 1971, 3). Once again, the result of dispersal was extreme violence conducted with the explicit intent to send a message to the Queensland protest community that dissent was no welcome in the state. By issuing the state of emergency, Bjelke-Petersen gave police political cover to take this action. By (erroneously) justifying the 24 July dispersal by citing noise complaints that did not actually come until almost an hour later, Whitrod provided his own form of cover for the actions of officers under his command on the night of the Springbok match.

Conclusions

The response to the Springboks protests in Queensland was that of a conservative government in ideological lockstep with a police force that served at its pleasure. In the period leading up to the protests, the state government opposed public marches that conflicted with their traditionalist political agenda. What the events around the 1971 Springboks protests highlight is the risk posed when police are used as the "spear-carriers" of a government that is explicitly opposed to any public protest that challenges their socio-political dominance (Whitton 1989, Evans, 2004). In such a case, there is not only a risk of activism being criminalized, but the excessive actions of police to repress dissent being *decriminalized*. Even before Bjelke-Petersen became premier, the SDA and CLCC fought government plans to limit their ability to conduct public marches. The rationale then was then, as it continues to be in contemporary times, that large-scale protest had the potential to turn to riot and needed to be controlled. The *Traffic Act* did just that, mandating permit fees for every sign carried and giving police on the ground the power to revoke an approved permit at any time, even after the demonstration began. In practice, a cycle of criminalization appeared: activists had permits approved and, after commencing a legal protest, that approval was revoked, and the march suddenly became a criminal gathering. In calling the state of emergency, the premier stripped away what few rights to protest remained in Queensland, under the banner of public safety.

Based on earlier experience with the protest movement, Bjelke-Petersen was fully aware that such restrictions would not stop the most committed of protesters from proving and, thus, it was just as important to provide police with as much coverage as possible to enforce the rules set out in the emergency declaration. The premier gave a green light to use violence as a policing strategy. He emboldened the QPF to pursue the state government's interests in repressing protest, a context that would continue in the state for the rest of the 1970s as the Bjelke-Petersen government restricted the right to protest even further to the point where, between 1977 and 1979, all political street marches were outlawed (Brennan 1983). The Springboks tour was more than a mere skirmish in the ongoing war between the government and protesters—it was a battle in which the protest community showed their willingness to persevere despite government crackdowns and, in turn, the state government's willingness to go to extreme lengths to win the fight against left-wing dissent. It emphasizes the fact that risk lies not only in the criminalization of activism, but the open decriminalization of police misconduct when it is used to pursue a governmental agenda to repress protest. The events of 1971 echo through not just Queensland's socio-political history, but in cases of police violence around the world where governments have similarly endorsed the extreme use of force to assert the public order.

References

Brennan, F. (1983) *Too Much Order With Too Little Law*. Brisbane: University of Queensland Press.

Condon, M. (2013) *Three Crooked Kings*. Brisbane: University of Queensland Press.

Cowen, Z. (1971) *Report to the Premier on the Springbok Tour Protests*, 31 August. Queensland State Archives Item ID318773, Correspondence – police.

De Lange, L. (1967a) *Leo de Lange to Frank Bischof*, 4 July. Queensland State Archives Item ID540961, Protest demonstrations – general.

De Lange, L. (1967b) *Leo de Lange to Frank Bischof*, 6 July. Queensland State Archives Item ID540961, Protest demonstrations – general.

Evans, R. (2004) Springbok tour confrontation. In: R. Evans and C. Ferrier (Eds.), *Radical Brisbane: An Unruly History*. Brisbane: Vulgar Press, pp. 277–284.

Hambrecht, S.H. (1971) *Official Log*, 22 July. Queensland State Archives Item ID381772, Correspondence – police.

Hodges, A.M. (1971) Public order squad, police department. *Parliamentary Debates (QLD)*, 31 March: 3393–3394.

Jones, A. (1948) Communists in public service. *Parliamentary Debates (QLD)*, 1 September: 197–198.

Klotz, A. (1999) *Norms in International Relations: The Struggle Against Apartheid.* Ithaca: Cornell University Press.

Laver, B. (1968) Behind Student Action. *Australian Left Review* 1(13) 22–25.

Louw, E. (2004) *The Rise, Fall and Legacy of Apartheid.* Westport: Greenwood.

Miller, J. (1994) *Democracy Is In The Streets: From Port Huron to the Siege of Chicago.* Cambridge: Harvard University Press.

Mills, C.W. (1960) Letter to the new left. *New Left Review* (5) 18.

Nixon, R. (1992) Apartheid on the run: The South African sports boycott. *Transition* (58) 68–88.

Piccini, J. (2011) "'A group of misguided way out individuals': The old left and the student movement in Brisbane: 1966–70," *Queensland Journal of Labour History* (12) 19–33.

Queensland Police Force. (1971a) *Police Radio Transcript*, 21 July. Queensland State Archives Item ID381772, Correspondence – police.

Queensland Police Force. (1971b) *Official Log*, 22 July. Queensland State Archives Item ID381772, Correspondence – police.

Queensland Police Force. (1971c) *Official Log*, 23 July. Queensland State Archives Item ID381772, Correspondence – police.

Queensland Police Force. (1971d) *Official Log*, 24 July. Queensland State Archives Item ID381772, Correspondence – police.

Radical Times. (n.d.). Introduction to a detailed history of the movement for social change in brisbane. *Radical Times.* Available at: http://radicaltimes.info/PDF/history64-74.pdf (accessed 12 August 2020)

The Canberra Times. (1967). Campus Politics *The Canberra Times*, 20 July: 2.

The Canberra Times. (1971a). Confusion over emergency. *The Canberra Times*, 15 July: 1.

The Canberra Times. (1971b). Queensland in State of Emergency. *The Canberra Times*, 14 July: 1.

The Courier-Mail. (1967). Govt. civil liberty view criticised. *The Courier-Mail*, 5 October: 13.

Thorn, H. (2006) *Anti-Apartheid and the Emergence of a Global Civil Society.* Basingstoke: Palgrave Macmillan.

Varon, J. (2004) *Bringing the War Home: The Weather Underground, Red Army Faction and Revolutionary Violence in the Sixties and Seventies.* Berkeley: University of California Press.

Wanna, J. and Arkley, T. (2010) *The Ayes Have It: The History of the Queensland Parliament, 1957–1989.* Canberra: ANU E-Press.

Wear, R. (2002) *Johannes Bjelke-Petersen: The Lord's Premier.* Brisbane: University of Queensland Press.

Whitrod, R.W. (1971) *Police Radio Transcript*, 24 July. Queensland State Archives Item ID318773, Correspondence – police.

Whitton, E. (1989) *The Hillbilly Dictator*, Crows Nest: ABC Books.

7

THE THEOREM OF NATIONAL SOLIDARITY

Italy and the "7 Aprile" case: the criminalisation of left-wing dissent

Vincenzo Scalia

The *7 Aprile* marked a watershed in contemporary Italian history. The arrest of 22 members of the political grouping *Autonomia Operaia* across the country on 7 April 1979 (thus giving the name to the case), triggered a massive wave of repression of left-wing activists, as more than 60,000 individuals were investigated in the early 1980s with 10,000 interrogated via preventive arrests and subsequent detention for political reasons reaching a peak of 5,000 people (Prette 1994).

The Padua prosecutor, Pietro Calogero, issued a warrant against both intellectuals and the political leaders of the *Autonomia*, such as Toni Negri, Oreste Scalzone, Franco Piperno (Fiorentino & Chiaramonte 2019) and 19 others. Calogero claimed that the 92 left-wing armed groups that were active in Italy between 1969 and 1979 (Moroni 1995) were bogus front organizations directed by a Central Committee based in Padua, formed by academics, journalists and political leaders, whose Supreme Commander was Toni Negri (Palombarini 1982). The evidence for this, according to Calogero's investigation, was to be found in the clear winding down of the organization *Potere Operaio* in 1973.

Negri and all the other members of this group were members of *Autonomia*, which was not a political party, but a cluster of committees (*collettivi*), radio stations and journals who defined themselves as autonomous from any organized party and group (Clement & Scalia 2016). Workers, feminists, LGTBQI+ activists and intellectuals were part of this network aimed at creating a *new subjectivity* to promote a radical transformation of society in the wake of the new class structure created by the economic crisis of 1973 (Negri 1993).

The Prosecutor of Padua rejected this view. His attitude was soon to be shared by his colleagues in Milan, Armando Spataro, and in Rome, Achille Gallucci, who engineered a massive clampdown on left-wing activists. The three prosecutors believed that *Potere Operaio* had never ceased to exist, and that its alleged dismantling really entailed its transformation into a clandestine structure, active in promoting,

DOI: 10.4324/9781003144229-10

planning and executing terrorism across Italy. The kidnapping of President Aldo Moro in 1978 was, of course, the key example of terrorist action, and Toni Negri was accused of being the person who telephoned the Moro family to communicate the Red Brigades' plans and requests. The *Teorema Calogero* (Calogero Theorem), as the accusation was named, would later be refuted during a criminal trial, as it was proved that Negri had a Veneto accent, whereas the man on the phone (the Red Brigades leader, Mario Moretti, as it was eventually found out) had a Central Italian accent. In fact, all the *7 Aprile* evidence against the defendants was legally dubious, as the prosecution relied upon the interpretation of some articles written by the defendants in *Autonomía* journals such as *Metropolis*.

The *7 Aprile* case clearly had a political agenda which reached beyond the mere judicial aspect. First, because its outcome was the repression of the radical opposition to the left of the Italian Communist Party (PCI), in the process wiping away for good any alternative to the traditional left forces. Mass arrests and investigations marred the reputation of left-wing groups, as well as increasing fear and mistrust among its members. Following the pattern of over-criminalization (Vegh Weis 2018), left-wing political activists were prosecuted using judicial tools instead of other democratic means. Second, this case showed that the PCI was at the heart of this repression—a strong advocate of prosecution against the members of *Autonomia* (Ginsborg 1992, Violante 1982). Communists supplied the ideological justification for the state of emergency laws, the pre-trial detentions and mass arrests as tools to be used against those who threatened the democratic state. The use of exceptional tools exposes the limits of liberal democracy. On the one hand, due process of law is claimed to be the only legitimate tool of contemporary states. On the other hand, when the capitalist foundations of liberal democracies are pushed to the boundaries, criminalization using exceptional tools takes over. Finally, the *7 Aprile* case inaugurated a disturbing tendency of Italian magistrates to actively intervene inside the political contradictions of the country, which reached its peak during the *Tangentopoli* corruption scandal of the 1990s (Nelken 2001). Because of this, the division of powers a democratic state should rely upon is violated. The crisis of the political system, as well as Italy's economic decline, have given the magistrates a significant role in Italian politics, making room for the rise of penal populist 5-Star movements.

This chapter analyzes the development of the *7 Aprile* case in three stages. By drawing on the concept of *deviancy amplification* forged by Stanley Cohen (1971), three stages of development will be shown. First, *isolation*, that is, the widening of the gap between the increasingly institution-oriented PCI and the radical left. Second, *repression*: as the economic crisis of late 1970s got worse, the protests grew more radical, with the PCI siding with the law-and-order demands orchestrated by mainstream public opinion. Third, *defamation*: left wing opponents, in particular the members of *Autonomia Operaia*, became increasingly marginalized and labeled within Italian society. The conclusion shows that the criminalization of left-wing dissent and the overweening power of magistrates has made room for the rise of populism in Italy.

Isolation. The historical compromise and the *Untorelli*

Stanley Cohen (1971, 20) emphasizes how the gap between society's insiders and outsiders widens as the former refuse to recognize the values, the interests and the aims of the latter, thus increasing repression and marginalization. Because of this, the outsiders will cling to their deviant identity and increase their resentment against the insiders. Cohen's scheme provides a useful tool to analyze the Italian case. The social and political movements of 1968 opposed not only to the clerical-fascist pattern which still hegemonized the country at the time (Crainz 2004), but was also critical of the traditional left, and of the working-class movement (Scalzone 1990). Between the 1950s and 1970s, Italy had undergone to a deep transformation, out of which new demands had appeared. As the country modernized, and the ideological grip of the Catholic church weakened over the mass of the population, women, students and workers generally became more assertive. This promoted a deep democratization of social relations in Italy: demands for higher wages and better working conditions matched the protests asylums and prisons, as well as the feminist battles for legalizing abortion and divorce, and the abolition of the sexist criminalization of female adultery. The traditional left, the PCI, was ready to meet most of these demands, as its electoral growth throughout the first half of 1970s demonstrates.

However, the gulf between the Communists and the social movements of 1970s originated in their different aims: while the PCI by now aspired to "Eurocommunism", epitomized by their own participation in government, and the full enactment of the Constitution of 1948 (Ingrao 1993), the New Left longed for a radical, revolutionary transformation of the country, inspired by the guerrilla movements of Vietnam and Latin America, while they also opposed the Soviet bloc. The economic crisis of 1973, coupled with the coup against the socialist Chilean government, embittered the gulf between the two sides of the Left. The PCI (Partito Comunista Italiano), under the input of leader, Enrico Berlinguer, proposed an alliance with the "democratic forces" of the country (Berlinguer 1973), that is the DC(Democrazia Cristiana), to prevent the risk of authoritarian upheavals. The New Left rejected this strategy—claiming that it was not possible to defend democracy with a party, that is DC, rife with ex-fascists, siding with organized crime in the south, and manipulating terrorist actions to their own advantage (Various Authors 1973). Moreover, the economic crisis gave the left the chance to fight for a revolutionary change many in Italy had been longing for since the end of World War II.

Since the expulsion of the *Manifesto* dissenters in 1969 (Garzia, 1985), the PCI reacted quite violently against left-wing opponents, either inside or outside the party. This was also the case after 1973, with the isolation taking place in two stages. First, the New Left members had to face negative propaganda against them, which spanned from a general lack of political understanding to the more relevant infamous accusations of being paid for by the CIA and working as *agents provocateurs* on behalf of the Fascists. When the *Manifesto* group decided to create a newspaper, which is still active, *l'Unità*, the PCI paper, published a front-page article whose title was: *Chi li paga?* (Who pays them?). The active hostility by the PCI militants ensued, consisting of banning New Left militants either from demonstrations or from party events through the action of protection squads. As a former New Left militant remembers: "Party squads started cordoning the demonstrations off. It was impossible to approach the demonstration without being wrenched away from it [W1]".

Their isolation and stigmatization from 2 million PCI militants, coupled with some institutional measures, such as the *Legge Reale* (Reale Act), which was unanimously endorsed by the Italian parliament in 1975, and allowed the police to shoot direct during the demonstrations (Della Porta & Reiter 2003). During the DC-PCI National Solidarity government, in 1977, the so-called *Cossiga decree*, issued by the then Ministry of Interior and Future President of the Republic, Francesco Cossiga (Miliucci 1997), introduced serious restrictions to public demonstrations and preemptive actions against political activists. The killings of young left-wing militants Claudio Varalli, Francesco Lorusso and Giorgiana Masi between 1975 and 1977 by the police, as well as the closure of left-wing radio stations such as Bologna's Radio Alice, and the call of PCI secretary Enrico Berlinguer for democratic forces to gather against the *untorelli* (ciphers) of the movement, marked a definite watershed, as the distance between the two sides turned into fierce mutual hostility.

The new left movement started considering the PCI as a governmental force to oppose, not only because of their agenda of "national solidarity", but also due to the secretary of the communist-backed trade union CGIL, Luciano Lama, in 1977 claiming the right of employers to sack workers to defend profit rates. In the Bologna conference of 1977 *Mai più senza fucile* (No more without a gun) became the slogan of a movement which openly discussed the need to engage in armed struggle to fight the system. Attacks against local branches of both the PCI and CGIL became frequent. On 17 February 1977, students and militants ejected Lama from the University of Rome, while he was trying to give a speech, taking by surprise the PCI and CGIL protection squads.

Three months later, in Milan, an urban guerrilla action shocked Italian public opinion, with the *Autonomia* militants Marco Ferrandi and Giuseppe Memeo producing their guns and killing the police anti-riot agent, Antonio Custra, while another militant fired at the headquarters of *Assolombarda*—the Lombard Entrepreneurs Association. Political marginalization, judicial prosecution, growing unemployment and social distress combined to create an atmosphere of desperation and despair, and use of heroin spread across the younger generations (Colaprico 2008). A feeling of generalized frustration spread among the New Left militants, now hegemonized by *Autonomia Operaia*. Many activists started considering the armed struggle as their last chance to prevent reaction (Segio 2005). This choice neglected a realistic analysis of force relations, that is, the state use of violence to overpower the resistance while it also neglected the attempt to gain the consent of Italian society, or at least of some parts of it. The Red Brigades (BR) were the only group who did this, as they claimed to be the vanguard of the working class, a self-appointment that not only proved to be flawed, but also provoked the state repression towards that vast majority of the New Left who deemed the BR an old-fashioned Stalinist group.

Repression. Magistrates and questionnaire

On 7 April 1979, the front page of the main Italian newspapers discussed the arrest of the leaders of *Autonomia Operaia*. The charges against the defendants were serious, as they drew on the Penal Law enforced in 1930 by the Fascist regime, the so-called *Codice Rocco* (Rocco Act—named after the Minister of Justice who drafted it). The allegations of being members of armed groups (*banda armata*), plotting against the state (*cospirazione*) and promoting terrorist attacks against the government (*insurrezione armata contro i poteri dello Stato*) stunned public opinion (Bocca 1982), as all the defendants were long-term members of the intellectual community, with some of them enjoying an international academic reputation. This was certainly the case for Toni Negri, who was arrested just after returning from a series of lectures he had given in Paris, at the invitation of Louis Althusser. Calogero used these charges with the specific aim of accusing the leadership of *Autonomia* of being the leadership of the Italian terrorist movement and organizing the abduction and killing of Moro. There was no evidence proffered to back up these accusations, as no weapons had been found and no other records could be traced.

If it were true that the defendants, both in their academic and in their journalistic works, advocated the need of an uprising against capital and the government, nevertheless, their project radically differed from that of the BR. Whereas the latter advocated the construction of a new Communist Party that promoted the revolution under their centralized supervision, *Autonomia Operaia* drew on the widespread rebellion against the existing social and political order within society. The idea of both Negri and the others was that a decentralized, plural rebellion of workers, women, LGBTQI, students, unemployed and the marginalized, no matter whether they were armed, would cause the capitalist state to collapse (Negri, 1993, 1996, Berardi 2001). The *mass illegality* the leaders of *Autonomia* cherished spanned from measures such as the occupation of flats to the sabotage of factory production, from mass looting in shops to the refusal to pay bills, from the so-called *right to luxury* (Ruggiero 2003) to mass riots. It was supposed to be a decentralized, territorial riot, not focused on industrial workers, tailored on the needs of what they called the new proletariat.

However, the magistrates were not willing, or able, to spot the difference, as all the defendants faced extended periods of pre-trial detention (Amnesty International 1987), up to five years, raising the indignation of international public opinion at such measures in a western democracy. Those charged were also held in special prisons, facing tough living conditions and prison staff brutalities (De Vito 2009). Such lengthy periods of detention were possible under the "emergency laws" enforced after the Moro Affair, which allowed the state to hold prisoner *incommunicado* (that is, without informing either their families or their lawyers) for up to 96 hours (Della Porta 1996). Oreste Scalzone, leader of the Rome *Autonomia*, suffered from ischemia and hepatitis because of imprisonment, and weight loss which reduced him to 39 kilos. Moreover, the special prisons were rife as members of the Red Brigades, who tried to take up the leadership of political prisoners, often used violence (Fenzi

2000, Franceschini 1989). Conflicts between the prisoners of *Autonomia Operaia* and the BR detainees became frequent. Not even the protests the harsh conditions of detention could bridge this political gap, as in 1980, when a revolt led by the BR broke out in the prison of Trani, near Bari, and the *Autonomia* members detained there refused to participate, although they also faced the harsh retaliation which followed the repression of the revolt.

The repression stage was also enacted within the fabric of broader society. In early 1979, the Turin PCI, distributed a questionnaire among its members. Communist militants were asked if they knew someone who could be a member of a terrorist organization, and to report the suspected person immediately to the local party or trade union branch, who would report the case to the police (Revelli 1993). This questionnaire was part of the policy to "isolate the violent and the provocative" which encouraged the members of PCI to actively cooperate with the police to report alleged or real members of terrorist organizations. In other words, through the circulation of the Questionnaire, the PCI required its members to side with the repressive stance that both police forces and magistrates were conducting under the political direction of the National Solidarity-inspired governments. The rift between the working class and the New Left movement, as well as inside the workers' movement itself, enlarged because of this collaborative policy. There were also tragic episodes like that of 24 January 1979. Guido Rossa, a PCI and CGIL member, steelworker of Italsider in Genoa, was killed by the BR for reporting a work colleague to the police, and eventually testifying against him. Despite the differences and rivalries between BR and *Autonomia*, the resentment of the PCI against all the extra-parliamentary left-wing forces triggered suspicion and spite against the latter, partly because of their engagement in attacks against PCI militants and premises.

The 7 *Aprile* trial ended with the acquittal of all the defendants, although some of them, such as Negri, faced sentences for *concorso morale* (moral cooperation) in minor crimes as robberies, brawls and clashes during demonstrations. In any case, the 7 *Aprile* case achieved its aim of de-legitimizing *Autonomia Operaia* before society, as well as clearing away the Left opposition.

Defamation (or the destruction of the militant fabric)

Mass arrests, long pre-trial detentions and criminalization had the consequence of destroying the public reputation of many defendants. In 1988, Toni Negri, who had managed to flee to France four years earlier, was banned from teaching in Italian universities. Soon after his arrest, the prominent left-wing publishing house Feltrinelli, whose founder was an activist who died whilst committing a terrorist attack (Galli 2003), decided to burn all Negri's published books. It took 15 years before other publishing houses retrieved the destroyed manuscripts and re-published them (Negri 1996). Such an inquisition-like attitude of criminalizing intellectual activities alongside their authors traces its roots to the catholic subculture of the country, which, based on a fascist criminal code, makes it possible to be "repentant" and to issue sentences for "moral cooperation", so that one can get sentenced because of mere group membership. Moreover, the concept of *moral responsibility* legitimates the stigmatization of intellectuals and reducing the freedom of speech, so as to label them with the responsibility for choices made by others. This is the case of the *cattivi maestri* (bad teachers) rhetoric, which tries to make up for the lack of judicial evidence about effective involvement with the creation of another accusation. The definition of *cattivi maestri*, forged in 1977 by the right-wing journalist Indro Montanelli (www.ilgiornale.it), refers to those intellectuals who, even if not involved in active terrorist acts, had written articles and books that were deemed influential on the political choices of 1970s youths, thus leading them into terrorism. This aspect, according to Montanelli, lately followed also by more liberal intellectuals and politicians, holds the *7 Aprile* defendants *morally responsible* for armed struggle and terrorism in Italy.

Additionally, the label of being "bad teachers" caused the exile of many New Left protagonists of the 1970s, either to France or Latin America. Many others withdrew from public life, also to escape judicial consequences. Some protagonists of that period recall those memories:

> It was unbelievable. The night before, you had a drink overnight with that person. The day after you came across the same person, and he, or she, turned their face away, pretending they had not seen you. Why? Because you were friend with someone who had been arrested. And people did not want to be in troubles [W2].

> Anything that could compromise you…a present, a rubric containing names, could get you troubles. You know, we knew each other, going to the same osterias, attending the same parties, living in the same flats…it took nothing to be suspected [W1].

> It was the end…really the end…we had a place in the center of Bologna, we used it as our headquarters. Not only for political initiatives. Parties, conferences, aperitifs…comrades without a place to sleep stayed there. Never empty. After 7 April, just the chosen few [W3].

Once again, there was a double level of articulation of the criminalization process. The institutional and the societal dynamics were interrelated in a treacherous way as the mere "association" was enough to present charges and even to justify convictions. A relational pattern relying on mutual suspicion developed and its consequences were the destruction of friendship, solidarity and trust, which make up the construction of a political community. In this respect, the declarations of supergrasses, or *pentiti* (repentant) played a key role. These ex-members of left-wing organizations who collaborated with the magistrates sometimes pushed their collaboration into invention, as their declarations were not always totally accurate:

I spent 4 years and a half in pre-trial detention. Just because C told the magistrate I had done that robbery, and I had not. It took 4 years for the magistrates to interrogate those who could testify I was with them on the day of the robbery. They had a "pentito" they could not de-legitimize…and I lost 4 years and a half of my life. And I am lucky. Others were convicted…[W4].

This late declaration sheds light into the limits of the so-called "favorable treatment laws", awarding a reduction of the conviction for those members of political groups who chose to collaborate with the magistrates. It also exposed the unequal treatment as "repentant" testimonies that could be used as the basis of a conviction. This was particularly true for the Italian penal system of the 1980s, which was based on the inquisitorial system, before being replaced in 1988 by the accusatory format (Damarska 1993). Once prosecutors considered an accusation valid, the defendants could only try to refute them. In any case, the *pentiti* catalyzed the removal of historical memory, mainly for reasons of survival, and provided a relevant contribution to the criminalization of the 1970s generation, thus paving the way for the neoliberal turn, which took over from the 1980s onwards. Exile, heroin and the retreat into private life, completed the informal punishment of a generation that still suffers from the negative bias of mainstream public opinion and over-criminalization to undermine radical politics. The stigmatization of left-wing dissents is even sharper when is conducted through the use of allegedly legal means, such as police and magistrates operating under laws voted by the Parliament and enforced by the government. In this case, mainstream public opinion legitimizes the policies of repression. If nowadays the younger generations of Italians think that the neo-fascist bombs were indeed put by the BR, is also because of the 7 *Aprile* case.

Conclusions

The age of *riflusso*, that is of rolling-back into private life, made its way into the Italian society. The criminalization of left-wing opposition and the entrance of PCI into the government weakened the opponents of the industrial reconstruction of the following years, which started in 1980 with FIAT dismissing 23,000 workers (Polo 1993). This was the beginning of a large-scale firing process. Many big factories closed or were down-sized while manufacturing moved to small-sized, family-based factories located in the so-called Northeast of the country, the Veneto area (Bonomi 1998). Meanwhile, a post-industrial Milan paved the way to individualism and hedonism, thus making way for the rise of Berlusconi, Veneto and rural Lombardy, while former peasants turned into factory bosses and provided the ideological backbone for the rise of the Northern League.

The use of special emergency laws and conspiracy-based accusations to repress the radical left cleared the left opposition and gave magistrates a significant role in the Italian political arena. Resentment against economic crisis, moral panics, political corruption and organized crime led to a rise in the demand for enhanced security (Baratta 2002) which was directed to the courts and the legal process. The idea that the crisis of ideologies had to be replaced by morality crusades without any political connotation (Dal Lago 1996) became increasingly popular among Italian public opinion. Therefore, the economic collapse of 2008, coupled with the conviction of Berlusconi for different crimes were faced by a weakened Left unprepared to propose a political alternative. The PCI had changed its name three times in 20 years and its members became increasingly marginal and unpopular. The populist 5-Star Movement filled this political vacuum by mixing some traditional aspects of the Left agenda with environmentalism and a strong anti-corruption rhetoric, relying on penal populism and conveyed through the massive use of IT, specifically, the so-called Rousseau platform (Stockman & Scalia 2019).

The *7 Aprile* case shows how criminalization of political dissent is, in the long range, a counter-productive strategy, as it undermines the foundations of civil society, and makes a community weak in periods of crisis. Moral panic and penal populism might follow. The *7 Aprile* case mirrors what happened in other countries. Turkey, for example, has been experiencing the populist policies of Erdogan after years of left-wing opposition repression and similar trends can be traced in Latin America and the Middle East.

References

Amnesty International (1987) *Il Caso 7 Aprile*. Rome: Amnesty International Italia.
Baratta, A. (2002) *La Bilancia e la Misura*. Rome: Editori Riuniti.
Berardi, F. (2001) *La nefasta Utopia di Potere Operaio*. Rome: Deriveapprodi.
Berlinguer, E. (1973) Riflessioni sul Colpo di Stato in Cile. *Rinascita*, (4), 4–35.
Bocca, G. (1982) *Il Caso 7 Aprile*. Milan: Feltrinelli.
Bonomi, A. (1998) *Il Capitalismo Molecolare*. Turin: Einaudi.
Clement, M. and Scalia, V. (2016) "1968 and the Birth of a New Criminology", in Clement, M. *A People's History of Riots, Protests and the Law. The Sound of the Crowd*. Basingstoke: Palgrave.
Cohen, S. (1971) *Folk Devils and Moral Panic*. London: Routledge and Kegan Paul.
Colaprico, G. (2008) *Milano Calibro 38*. Milan: Garzanti.
Crainz, G. (2004) *Il Paese Mancato*. Rome: Donzelli.
Dal Lago, A. (1996) *Nonpersone*. Milan: Feltrinelli.
Damarska, M. (1993) *Le Due Facce della Giustizia*. Bologna: Il Mulino.
De Vito, C. (2009) *Camosci e Girachiavi*. Bari: Laterza.
Della Porta, D. (1996) "Le Brigate Rosse." *Annali della Storia d'Italia*, (16), 676–751.
Della Porta, D. and Reiter, H. (2003) *Polizia e Protesta*. Bologna: Il Mulino.
Fenzi, E. (2000) *Armi e Bagagli. Diario delle BR*. Genoa: Costa and Nolan.
Fiorentino, D. and Chiaramonte, X. (2019) *Il Caso 7 Aprile*. Verona: Mimesis.
Franceschini, A. (1989) *Mara, Renato ed Io*. Milano: Rizzoli.
Galli, G. (2003) *Il Partito Armato*. Milan: Rizzoli.
Garzia, A. (1985) *Da Natta a Natta*. Bari: Dedalo.
Ginsborg, L. (1992) *Storia d'Italia 1943–1991*. Turin: Einaudi.
Ingrao, L. (1993) *Le Cose Impossibili*. Rome: Editori Riuniti.
Miliucci, V. (1997) *Una Sparatoria Tranquilla*. Rome: Odradek.
Moroni, L. (1995) *Le Parole e la Lotta Armata*. Milan: Shake.
Negri, A. (1993) *Marx oltre Marx*. Rome: Manifestolibri.

?gri, A. (1996) *I Libri del Rogo*. Rome:Deriveapprodi.

elken, D. (2001) "Tangentopoli" in Barbagli, M. and Garri, U. (ed.) *La Criminalità in Italia*, pp. 55–67.

Palombarini, G. (1982) *7 Aprile. Il Processo e la Storia*.Venice: L'Arsenale.

Polo, G. (1993) *Restaurazione Italiana*. Rome: Manifestolibri.

Prette, R. (1994) *La Mappa Perduta, I*. Rome: Sensibili alle Foglie.

Revelli, M. (1993), *Lavorare in Fiat*. Milan: Garzanti.

Ruggiero, V. (2003) *Movimenti nelle Città*. Turin: Bollati Boringhieri.

Scalzone, O. (1990) *Il Secondo Biennio Rosso*. Milano: Sugarco

Segio, S. (2005) *Micciacorta. Una vita in Prima Linea*. Rome: Deriveapprodi.

Stockman, C. and Scalia, V. (2019) "Democracy and the 5 Star Movement." *European Politics and Society*, https://www.tandfonline.com/doi/abs/10.1080/23745118.2019.1705564.

Various Authors (1973) *La Sinistra Extraparlamentare in Italia*. Rome: Samonà e Savelli.

Vegh Weis, V. (2018) *Marxism and Criminology. A History of Criminal Selectivity*. Boston: Brill.

Violante, L. (1982) *Magistrati*. Turin: Einaudi.

PART III

Current cases of over-criminalization of dissent in the Global North

8

RESISTANCE TO SURVIVE

The criminalization of the Black Lives Matter movement

Teresa Francis Divine and Ginny Norris Blackson

In the 21st century there is no longer legal segregation or sundown towns in the USA. Unlike in the past, Black people may do as they please, there are no Black sections where people must sit in on the train, plane, or bus. Upward mobility is possible and Black people can be prosperous. Black people are the racial group still facing the largest numbers of poverty. But the poverty rate of 18.8% in 2019 is the lowest since 1959 (Creamer 2020). The Black middle class is real. Black people do not feel the fear of physical violence from all White people they come across anymore. The original Voters Rights Act was passed 55 years ago and has strengthened our democracy. Following the election of President Obama, many Black children believe they too can be president of the USA. Yet, regardless of education or economic status Black people still face the threat of death whenever they interact with the police.

This threat is ever present and requires the "talk" that teaches Black children how they should behave to protect themselves from White society's violence. The "talk" is the conversation Black folks must have with their children to also needed to inform Black children on how to behave in an encounter with the police. Black people are told to follow directions, do not make any sudden movements and stay calm. Since the murder of Trayvon Martin in 2013, the Black Lives Matter movement has supplied a venue for people to speak out against institutional racism and police brutality. But how safe is it for Black people to take part in the movement? Is a criminal record the cost of free speech and peaceful assembly for Black people in the USA?

Resisting the criminalization of blackness

Standing up for change requires even more civil disobedience. John Lea, in the article *Social Crime Revisited*, discussed a classic theory in the UK that has essential elements. The first theoretical element from the article shines a light on the idea

DOI: 10.4324/9781003144229-12

that a crime is not just an incident to be punished; it can have a mission behind it. A mission that aids others or creates positive change in society. Lea writes "social crime can serve as a starting point for the exploration of the complex ways in which protest or survival strategies interface with violence and oppression" (Lea 1999, 322).

After slavery in the USA, Black Codes were enacted to support the social hierarchy and keep Black people in their place. According to Race, Law and American Society by Gloria J. Browne-Marshall, slavery was abolished except for the punishment of crime. The abolition of slavery and the enactment of the 13th amendment was a bit of a compromise. No slavery or involuntary servitude was allowed, but other forms of punishment of freed slaves continued. The enactment of the 13th amendment invoked freedom and simultaneously revoked it (Browne-Marshall 2007, 56–57). Once free, many Black people were subjected to vagrancy laws enacted to criminalize homelessness. They also restricted Blacks' right to travel were restricted, those who did travel were often forced to produce identification and other documents. When one did not have a home or a job one could be charged with trespassing and jailed. Once convicted of the most minor offenses, one could be sentenced to hard labor. After reconstruction, these Jim Crow laws, named after white minstrel shows, were challenged by the people through marches and sit-ins that challenged unjust systems through nonviolent resistance.

In 1947, the Congress of Racial Equality, known as CORE (Chama 2019), decided to draw attention to racial segregation in public transportation systems in the southern cities of the USA. They first created the Journey of Reconciliation. However, this first campaign was not considered to be successful. It would later inspire the 1961 Freedom Rides (Browne-Marshall 2007, 239). There were 13 men and women both Black and White who were the original "Freedom Riders". The Freedom Riders rode buses across the South. These riders were brutally attacked in the Alabama towns of Anniston and Birmingham and beaten by mobs of White people. One of their buses was firebombed. The federal government was forced to step in to protect the Freedom Riders. In turn, James Farmer and CORE stood up and challenged Boynton v. Virginia, which declared that the restaurant-serving interstate buses could not discriminate (Browne-Marshall 2007). Because the buses and the restaurants catered to interstate passengers, these services must be subject to the same discrimination prohibitions as the transportation itself (Boynton v. Virginia, 1960). The courage of the Freedom Riders and other civil rights activist helped change the discriminatory laws in the USA.

According to Peniel Joseph in the article *Why Black Lives Matter Still Matters* (Joseph 2017), the beginnings of the Black Power Movement has been viewed differently by different scholars. Of course, in the eyes of Malcolm X, Black people would be justified to defend themselves from the violence against them by any means necessary. The Black Power Movement gave us not only the gun carrying Black Panthers, but it created militant college students that became empowered to make change through civil disobedience at universities. Muhammed Ali protested the Vietnam war and refused to fight for a country that mistreated Black People.

The important discussions about the achievements of the Black Power Movement must include using racial consciousness as a weapon used to promote institutional change. Transforming "negros" (sic) into proud Black people was essential. Black is beautiful, an intentional self- love awakening was a strategic move that brought a broad spectrum of positive racial identity (Joseph 2017, 18). Joseph explains the Black Power Movement inspired changes in the literature, art and poetry in the USA. The movement created a wave of Black scholarship in higher education. It helped to elect Black public officials in all levels of government. Without the Black Power Movement, the USA would not have a national Black History month or a Martin Luther King holiday. Furthermore, would there be breakfast for children across the country if not for the Free breakfast program developed by the Black Panthers? Joseph goes on to argue there would be no songs like Public Enemy's *911 is a joke*, or *Lemonade* by Beyoncé, or even Barack Obama without the Black Power movement (Joseph 2017, 18). Even after the civil rights movement, considered by some as the most one of the most prolific movements in our history, the Black community still suffers from a great deal of injustice and inequality ingrained in society (Wells-Barnett 2012). The resistance against the police existed during the Black Power Movement and still permeates. The fact that no matter the reason, law enforcement is used as a weapon to silence the Black community.

During this historic process, the violence against Black people played out on national television and there was sympathy for Southern Blacks, who lived under this apartheid. They were only asking to move freely. However, the narrative about Black protest changed in the 1980s and 1990s as part of the War on Drugs and the guise of gang violence. Black people in cities were the cause of the crime and certainly the cause of the state violence against them. The new narrative includes all Black people, men and women, young and old, and it is deadly. Black people are among the countless low-income and homeless people abused by the police targeted for their poverty. Black women are stereotyped and harassed at the same rate as Black men. They have also been victims of the war on drugs. Their bodies are viewed as vessels for drugs ingested, swallowed and/or hidden on their person. Black women's homes are stereotyped drug factories or dens of danger and violence (Crenshaw et al. 2015, 295).

Changes also permeate resistance. Black Lives Matter (BLM) is different from the Civil Rights movement of our past. Yes, it is grassroots like the movements from the past, and focuses on racial justice and equality. However, as said in the New Republic it does have a hierarchy and has been criticized as not having a single easily identifiable goal. Furthermore, the Black Lives Matter movement is seen as not devoting itself to bringing about a substantive legal and legislative change (Joseph 2017). The BLM movement created by three queer, Black women in 2013 is much more inclusive than the Civil Rights Movement. It is also much more democratic than the Black Panther movement. The activists of the BLM are queer and feminists. BLM makes direct links to eradicating the marginalization of women. A movement born from the hashtag #BlackLivesMatter, the use of social media has allowed the movement to decentralized and become inclusive. The decentralized structure allows for real participation and power-sharing with the LGBTQI+ community, and all of society through social media. Also, they were able to create local chapters and articulated a broader agenda (Joseph 2017).

However, repression did not change. According to the ACLU, the FBI is still creating problematic scenarios for the Black Community. This intelligence assessment was sent out to at least 18,000 law enforcement agencies. The ACLU requested the assessment from the FBI. However, they were only able to obtain a heavily redacted document in response to their Freedom of Information Act request. The FBI created fake groups of Black people who are a danger to the law enforcement community. The group they created is called the Black Identity Extremist. The FBI believes this group is motivated to target law enforcement officers. The document aids in racial profiling of Black people who raise their voices, and it appears FBI is manufacturing a threat (ACLU 2019). Moreover, the government has used surveillance as a weapon to investigate and prosecute Black people for constitutional protected activity. On 3 August 2017, a document leaked to *Foreign Policy* magazine and later by Young Turks was quite revealing. It appears the FBI is wrongly grouping together Black folks who are perceived to be standing up against racism and injustice in the USA. The FBI considers specific associations, online activity and violent anti-White rhetoric when deciding whether a person is a Black Identity Extremist (Levin 2017).

There are no practical options other than protest. No matter the improvements we have made since the freedom rides. Mass incarceration and police brutality still loom over the Black community. Tabloid papers are one of the reasons BLM does not get the community support as discussed by John Lea in *Social Crime Revisited*. According to reporter Brian Chama's, crime news feature Black people committing crimes against Whites, often discrediting the movements (Chama 2019, 206). BLM is also viewed as a criminal organization and even responsible for behavior that leads police assassinations. Many people in the Black community know these things without an academic study.

Resisting when Black lives don't matter

All Black people are not safe driving. Black women are racially profiled on the streets and roads by the police. Black people in the USA face the challenge of staying alive while trying to change a system designed for and by Whites. From the criminalization of Black people to continue free and forced slave labor under the 13th amendment to the prison industrial complex that profits from the incarceration of hundreds of thousands of Blacks. The legacy of Jim Crow and the historical role that police played in its enforcement, have led to modern police forces that still view Black people as a menace to society. This history has led to the execution of Black people by police for even the smallest infractions.

Sandra Bland, a civil rights activist, was pulled over on 10 July 2015, in Waller County, Texas for not signaling a lane change. The police video shows her slammed to the ground surrounded by police. She is heard asking why they slammed her head to the ground. She used her voice as a form of resistance, and she is arrested for assault. Three days later, it was reported that she committed suicide. Her friends and family think otherwise (Crenshaw et al. 2015, 253–254). Sandra Bland had an activist project she called "Sandy Speaks": a series of videos where she spoke mind about injustice. Sandra was known by her family as a woman who had a voice and honed her voice while growing up with five sisters, all of which spoke their mind (McFadden 2018). Many believe she paid dearly for speaking up.

The narrative that Black people are criminal just because of where they live, resonates in the death of Brenna Taylor. She was a 26-year-old aspiring nurse, when on 13 March 2020 the police in Louisville, Kentucky, raided her home in the middle of the night. Her boyfriend thought they were criminals: the police functioned as criminals entering a home without knocking or announcing themselves (Sullum 2020). While Brenna's death has not resulted in criminal charges for the officers, a clear example of under-criminalization based on racial bias (Vegh Weis 2017), the same cannot be said for those who took part in 100 days of continuous protest for justice in Louisville, who were severely over-criminalized (Vegh Weis 2017). These protests lead to daily arrest in Louisville, including 130 people in one day following the grand jury's announcement that charges would not be filed against the offices involved in her death (Kim 2021). Moreover, Brenna's partner, Kenneth Walker, who was the only non-police witness to her death, was arrested and charged with attempted murder for legally firing his gun in defense of his home. He was held by police and interrogated for hours to retroactively criminalize him. He was only released and the charges dropped after public outcry; however, he faces the possibility of being recharged at any time.

In terms of gender, the situation is even more striking. Events in 2014, sparked a movement with the murders of Michael Brown, Eric Garner and Tamir Rice and their names and their stories faces made national news. 2014 also marked the unjust police killings of several Black women including Gabriella Nevarez, Aura Rosser, Michele Cusseaux and Tanisha Anderson (Crenshaw et al. 2015). Black women are killed and harmed by the police as equally as Black men, but often are erased from the demonstrations, discourse and the demands for social justice. Black women are the first to hit the streets and resist the violence by the police. Black women have every reason to stand up and scream their faces off regardless of the consequences. The report *Operation Ghetto Storm* found that 313 Black people were killed by police, security guards and vigilantes in 2012. The report concluded that Black people of all genders were being killed every 28 hours. However, the report is often cited as a Black man is killed every 28 hours erasing Black women from the dialogue. This fear of violence and death still looms over Black women too (Crenshaw et al. 2015).

Including Black women in the conversation, counting their bodies and stating their names mean Black lives really do matter. Our collective outrage must include Black women and girls for the violence by the state against Black communities. Because not knowing who they are or that it is happening is fatal to the movement. Black women have consistently played leadership roles in social movements, for example, Rosa Parks in the Civil Rights movement and Angela Davis as a leader of Black Power movement, and now supporting the Black Lives Matter movement. Yet, the victimization and consequences that Black women face is left out of the conversation. Instead, when Black women are asked to take the podium, they, too, speak about their fears of losing their sons, brothers, partners and comrades (Crenshaw et al. 2015). This form of discrimination is amplified when Black women are poor, transgender, gender-nonconforming, or thought to be involved in criminal activity (Crenshaw et al. 2015).

One of the saddest victims in this fraudulent narrative of the Black threat is the death of Elijah McClain (ACLU 2019, Andone 2020). On 30 August 2019, in Aurora, Colorado, Elijah was walking home from a convenience store waving his arms (Tompkins 2020). A "911" caller thought he looked suspicious wearing a ski mask. He was then attacked by the police. He was grabbed and put into a choke-hold. In the struggle he threw up twice and apologized both times. While he did not die in the street, his apologies did not spare his life. When the ambulance arrived, he was given the powerful sedative ketamine. On his way to the hospital, he went into cardiac arrest. He was 23 years old. Meanwhile, newspapers reported that "he violently resisted" the police. This language has been used repeatedly to remove liability and place blame on Elijah for his own demise, even as the bodycam showed Elijah attempting to comply with police. A year later, after the protests erupted, 2,000,000 people signed an online petition to demand further investigation. Only because of the widespread grassroot initiatives and Elijah's family fight, the Governor asked the Attorney General to conduct an independent investigation and the City of Aurora commissioned an outside study of the police department (Andone 2020. Tompkins 2020).

Just a few months afterward, a new case of under-criminalization appeared (Vegh Weis 2017) when a group of four officers posed for photos near Elijah's memorial mimicking the choke-hold he was put in that eventually caused his death. One was an officer who took part in the incident in which Elijah lost his life. Three of the officers in the photos were fired and one resigned. No criminal charges were ever filed against the officers involved in Elijah's death but the same cannot be said for those who protested for answers and justice. In June 2020, protests began outside the Aurora Police Department headquarters and moved to block interstate traffic. A man who drove his Jeep into the crowd of protesters faced no charges. Later that month, riot police were deployed at a peaceful violin concert as a memorial for Elijah. A federal class action lawsuit against the police detailed the indiscriminate use of chemical agents, projectiles and batons against protesters (Tabachnik 2020).

Years later, the death of George Floyd would send the USA into a tailspin. In the middle of the Covid-19 pandemic, when most things are shut down, a Black man is still in danger of violence by the police. On the evening 25 May 2020, George Floyd bought a pack of cigarettes from Cup Foods, a grocery store in Minneapolis. He was suspected of passing a counterfeit $20 bill which a store employee reported (BBC News 2020). Floyd was pinned face down on the ground in handcuffs by white officer Derek Chauvin, his final moments captured on several cell phones. Chauvin places his left knee between his head and neck for eight minutes and

46 seconds causing his death. When the video of his pleas and his death hit social media, people took to the streets all over the country. From Minneapolis, Portland, Seattle to New York City, unrest swelled over a death that was intentional and blatant. Even within the pandemic, there were demonstrations everywhere. Young and old, Blacks and Whites, faced the tear gas and the rubber bullets and other aftereffects as well, while Donald Trump called BLM protesters terrorists and promised violence against them (Dewan 2020).

Even when the tear gas might affect people regardless of race, the criminalization of protest disproportionately effects young people of color. While 93% of the BLM protest was peaceful (Mansoor 2020), media and government spokespeople still regularly refer to protesters as violent agitators that threaten our very society. According to a Pew Research Center survey, 41% of BLM protesters were younger than 30 years. The ethnic background of protesters was 17% Black, 22% Latinx and 46% White. A smaller survey looking at protesters in Washington DC, New York City and Los Angeles found the median age of protesters was 29 years. About 25% of protesters were 24 or younger. During protests in Chicago from 29 May through 31 May, 2,172 people were arrested by the Chicago Police Department. The *Chicago Reader* reported that, of those arrest in Chicago, 70% were Black and 10% were White. That same weekend in Atlanta, 48 of the 82 protesters processed into Fulton County jail were Black (Chan 2020). D'Angelo Sandida is just one example of the criminalization of protest. After he watched George Floyd call out on his mother, he felt sick to his stomach. He felt a need to get involved. The 24-year-old, six-foot-four Black man headed to join protest in downtown Indianapolis. By that evening D'Angelo Sandida was arrested for violating curfew and resisting arrest. He had a clean driving record much less of a criminal record. Now, he faced a $5,000 fine and up to a year in jail (Chan 2020, 58).

According to Crowd Counting Consortium, which collects data from news reports, the demonstrations against police brutality led to more than 7,800 arrests in the USA in May and June of 2020. Further, the Associated Press tallies more than 10,000 protesters were arrested in just the first 10 days after George Floyd's death (Crowd Counting Consortium 2020). In Detroit, a woman was chased, detained and handcuffed by city council member Eddie Kabacinski for placing Black Lives Matter stickers on a Trump campaign sign (Hall 2020). Prosecutors in Utah charged protesters with felony criminal mischief that also used state criminal enhancement laws for gang violence. The charges could lead to life sentences for those charged for splashing red paint and breaking windows. One of individuals charged saw the use of the felony offense as, "far beyond just the enforcement of the law, it feels retaliatory," (Whitehurst 2020). Many of those arrested are starting to come to terms with the repercussions of their decisions to take part in a major moment in history. The young protesters of color will face consequences on top of prosecution. Including costly fines, loss of employment and legal stigma that could cost them their ability to obtain housing, jobs and occupational licenses (Chan 2020, 58).

Even those who bear witness to police violence face criminalization for their attempts to tell the truth. On Sunday 14 July 2014, Eric Garner broke up a fight outside a convenience store in Staten Island, NY. When plainclothes police arrived, they were much more interested on Eric rather than the fight he had helped to stop. It has been argued that the police focused on Eric because of his size and his clear frustration with the police. Police were convinced Eric was selling loose cigarettes. When more police arrive, Eric was taken down by his neck. One officer held him while a second officer leaned on his body and then his neck. Eric plead for his life trying to tell the two officers that he could not breathe. Eric's death in the middle of the sidewalk was captured on camera. Following the release of the video, protests erupt all over the city.

After the police and media paint Eric as a career criminal who was selling illegal cigarettes, police next set their sights on Ramsey Orta. Ramsey, a friend of Eric, recorded Eric's death on his mobile. Orta said once the recording of Garner's death went public, he was target for harassment by the police. In 2016, Otra told *Al Jazeera* he was arrested eight times in a two- year span (Johnson 2020). Eventually, Ramsey Otra was arrested for having a handgun and selling heroin to an undercover officer. Behind bars, he was transferred multiple times and it made it difficult for his friends and family to contact him. He has accused correction officers of abuse and intimidation. He is in and out of solitary confinement. The week before Eric died, Ramsey captured another brutal beating with a baton by police. The organization We Cop Watch has kept a close watch on his incarceration and has fought hard for his release. He was finally released in July 2020 after serving four years. He will remain under court supervision until January 2022 in another striking example of over-criminalization, that is, the application of criminal law for a behavior that not only did not produce social harm, but it is even framed within the Bill of Rights (Vegh Weis 2017).

Resisting the criminalization of the future

The Red Record: Tabulated Statistics and Alleged Causes of Lynching in the United States from 1865 to 1872 recorded merciless murder of hundreds of Black men and women during the period. In this landmark work, Ida B. Wells builds on the three reasons Fredrick Doulas gave for the lynching of Black people during reconstruction in the USA. First, Black people could be lynched for even the possibility of inciting a riot. Because of Black newfound freedom, Whites thought any gathering of Black people could turn into race riots and must be stamped out. The wires sent to the north often said that a riot caused the harm, Black people were the only ones killed and Whites went unharmed (Wells-Barnett 2012). Second, Black people were lynched by Whites who opposed giving rights and power to the former. Whites feared Black domination and believed that they would lose White dominance to the Black vote. The KKK, Regulators and lawless mobs intimidated and murdered Black people one by one and by the dozen. Finally, the rape of White women was used to justify lynching. The charge came when Christian White women began to teach Black people to read and write and, of course, Christian values. The Southern White men believe that it is impossible for a voluntary alliance to exist. Therefore, an alliance is proof of force. Furthermore, these killings were not only in southern areas but all over the country in cities and towns of New York State, Kentucky and Kansas

(Wells-Barnett 2012, 6). This period was followed by the Black Codes of Jim Crow. Black people could be arrested for being where "they didn't belong" or not showing the proper respect for White people. Charges against protesters have included trespassing, unlawful assembly, violating curfew, destruction of property, camping on government property, not following the orders of a police officer and felony charges.

Has this changed? Just as Jim Crow was used to subjugate Black people to White rule, the criminalization of Black Lives Matter protesters creates a criminal class for those who might try to challenge White systems. Over 1,000 people died because of their interactions with police in 2019 (Sterling 2020). While few, if any, police officers faced arrest for their role in these deaths, tens of thousands of people in the USA and across the world have been arrested for protesting the same deaths. Young activities of color are being charged with all types of misdemeanors and felonies around the country. Activists are criminalized by the media as rioters, terrorists and even called police killers. While the main perpetrators of the crimes of assault murder continue to harass grief-stricken youth in the streets. Instead of seeing police as protectors, young people of color continue to suffer under the Jim Crow legacy that the police continue to enforce. The arrest of BLM protesters has clearly shown the legacy of Jim Crow in the US legal system.

Thus, we have the right to vote and the legal right to come and go as we please. The law appears to be on our side, but our bodies are still not safe. It may not be exactly a race riot that is feared, we are still under suspicion by the police of illegal activity on the streets and the roadways as we are continuously and consistently racially profiled in this country. Although we are disenfranchised 1.2 million people who are incarcerated by felony convictions, we are still voting and trying to fight back racism and fascism with actions at the ballot box. It is legal to marry whoever you want in this country. However, White women know that they can call the police on Black men at any time and his life will be in jeopardy. While Black women risk their own lives when calling the police for help. The police continue their violence against youth who are crying for change. Everyday arresting and criminalizing young people who just want it all to stop.

References

ACLU (2019) *Leaked FBI documents raise concerns about targeting black people under 'black identity extremist' and newer labels.* [Online]. Available at: https://www.aclu.org/press-releases/leaked-fbi-documents-raise-concerns-about-targeting-black-people-under-black-identi-1 [Accessed December 2020].

Andone, D. (2020) *Elijah McClain died after a police encounter almost one year ago. Here's what happened since.* [Online] Available at: https://www.cnn.com/2020/08/24/us/elijah-mcclain-one-year/index.html [Accessed December 2020].

BBC News (2020) *George Floyd: What happened in the final moments of his life.* [Online] Available at: https://www.bbc.com/news/world-us-canada-52861726 [Accessed December 2020].

Boynton v. Virginia (1960) USSC 364 U.S. 454

Browne-Marshall, G. (2007) *Race, Law, and American Society: 1607 to Present.* New York: Taylor & Francis Group.

Chama, B. (2019) The Black Lives Matter movement, crime and police brutality: Comparative study of New York Post and New York Daily News. *European Journal of American Culture*, 38(3), pp. 201–216.

Chan, M. (2020) The price of protest. *TIME Magazine*, 21 September, 196(11 and 12), pp. 56–61.

Creamer, J. (2020) *Inequalities Presist Despite Decline in Poverty For All Major Race and Hispanic Origin Groups*. [Online] Available at: https://www.census.gov/library/stories/2020/09/poverty-rates-for-blacks-and-hispanics-reached-historic-lows-in-2019.html [Accessed December 2020].

Crenshaw, K., Ritchie, A., Anspach, R., Gilmer, R. and Harris, L., (2015) *Say Her Name: Resisting Police Brutality Against Black Women*. New York: African American Policy Forum.

Crowd Counting Consortium (2020) *Collective Action and Dissent under COVID*. [Online] Available at: https://sites.google.com/view/crowdcountingconsortium/dissent-under-covid [Accessed 30 January 2020].

Dewan, A. (2020) *Trump is calling protesters who disagree with him terrorists. That puts him in the company of the world's autocrats*. [Online] Available at: https://www.cnn.com/2020/07/25/politics/us-protests-trump-terrorists-intl/index.html [Accessed January 2020].

Hall, C. (2020) *Warren councilman faces criminal charges for 'arresting' woman over Trump signs*. [Online] Available at: https://www.freecom/story/news/local/michigan/macomb/2020/10/28/warren-councilman-faces-misdemeanor-charges/3755256001/ [Accessed January 2021].

Johnson, S. (2020) Ramsey Orta In and Out of Solitary confinement, abused by officers. *New York Amsterdam News*, 2 January.

Joseph, L. (2017) Why black lives mattter still matters. *New Republic*, 248(5), pp. 16–19.

Kim, S. (2021) *More Than Twice As Many Arrested Protesting Breonna Taylor Verdict Than in Capitol Riots*. [Online] Available at: https://www.newsweek.com/us-capitol-riots-washington-dc-protesters-arrested-breonna-taylor-protest-arrests-1559773 [Accessed January 2021].

Lea, J. (1999) Social crime revisited. *Theoretical Criminology*, 3(3), pp. 307–325.

Levin, S. (2017) *FBI terrorism unit says 'black identity extremists' pose a violent threat*. [Online] Available at: https://www.theguardian.com/us-news/2017/oct/06/fbi-black-identity-extremists-racial-profiling [Accessed January 2020].

Mansoor, S. (2020) *93% of Black Lives Matter Protests Have Been Peaceful, New Report Finds*. [Online] Available at: https://time.com/5886348/report-peaceful-protests/ [Accessed December 2020].

McFadden, S. (2018) *In Life and After Her Death, Sandra Bland Taught Others About Activism*. [Online] Available at: https://www.vice.com/en/article/nepqyk/sandra-bland-docu-mentary-hbo [Accessed 19 January 2021].

Sterling, A. (2020) *Forbes*. [Online] Available at: https://www.forbes.com/sites/amysterling/2020/07/01/police-killed-over-1000-american-civilians-in-2019/?sh=1950b30e667e [Accessed December 2020].

Sullum, J. (2020) End the war on drugs. *Reason*, 52(5), pp. 32–34.

Tabachnik, S. (2020) *Aurora police hit with federal lawsuit over response to Elijah McClain rally last month*. [Online] Available at: https://www.denverpost.com/2020/07/23/aurora-police-federal-lawsuit-elijah-mcclain-protest/ [Accessed January 2021].

Tompkins, L. (2020) Here's what you need to know about Elijah McClain's death. *New York Times*, 16 August.

Vegh Weis, V. (2017) *Marxism and Criminology. A History of Criminal Selectivity*, Boston: Brill

Wells-Barnett, I. (2012) *The Red Record Tabulated Statistics and Alleged Causes of Lynching in the United States.*. Denham springs, LA: Cavalier Classics.

Whitehurst, L. (2020) *Utah protesters face charges with potential life sentence*. [Online] Available at: https://www.pbs.org/newshour/nation/utah-protesters-face-charges-with-potential-life-sentence [Accessed January 2020].

9
BETWEEN CRIME AND WAR

The security model of protest policing

Paul A. Passavant

In the USA, studies of protest policing often frame the policing of protest as criminalizing protest (Dunn et al. 2003). Recent scholarship also refers to the militarization of protest policing (Wood 2014). These two vectors—the criminalization of protest and the militarization of protest policing—point to a process of institutional transformation. Policing protest is becoming a disturbing hybrid. On the one hand, prejudging protest to be criminal leads to preventative policing of protest. By aggressively targeting protesters for arrest regardless of any violations of the law, protest policing goes beyond mere law enforcement. On the other hand, although protest policing is increasingly militarized in the USA, the policing of protest stops short of total war conducted by a disciplined military force on a battlefield. More than crime but less than conventional war, the policing of protest in the USA since the late 1990s might be described as the security model of protest policing.

The forward edge of the security model of protest policing expresses two tendencies, both of which exceed ordinary law enforcement. The policing of protest is increasingly militarized, with police seeking to defeat protesters. Police also increasingly use what philosopher Gilles Deleuze (1992) describes as technologies of "control" to prevent the assembly of a political subject in the streets to confront a state formation we might characterize in terms of neoliberal authoritarianism (Passavant 2021). These two tendencies are intertwined in practice: the execution of military drone strikes require surveillance and tracking of the strike's subject. Both the tendency of increasingly militarized protest policing and the tendency to utilize control technologies, represent the forward edge of the security model of protest policing, and they are deployed by police against Black Lives Matter (BLM) protests.

In this chapter, I contend the policing of protest in the USA may be described in terms of the security model of protest policing. I focus on the Memphis, Tennessee Police Department (MPD), which redirected its Office of Homeland Security (OHS) from counterterrorism to political intelligence gathering that focused

DOI: 10.4324/9781003144229-13

heavily on those it associated with BLM. This case study is exemplary of the security model of protest policing in terms of its reliance on intelligence gathering for the purpose of expecting protests, tracking protesters and associating fragments of protest-related risk. Such intelligence gathering focusing on the possibility of protest is geared to pacifying and controlling urban space, it is geared to preventing the assembly of a political subject and the appearance of political antagonism.

The security model's forward edge

When a video recording circulated of Minneapolis police officers needlessly killing George Floyd, a Black man, on 25 May 2020, an uprising estimated to be the largest social movement in US history spread almost at once to cities across the country (Buchanan, Bui, & Patel 2020). Over 93% of the protests were peaceful (Kishi & Jones 2020). While the protests were entirely peaceful, the same could not be said for the police response to those demonstrations ("NYPD Says it Used Restraint" 2020). While some of the police abuse of force was simple brutality, like pushes, punches, body slams and use of batons, there was also a significantly militarized response to the protests.

For example, in Washington, DC on 1 June 2020, police from several agencies, supported militarily by the National Guard, brutalized peaceful protesters in Lafayette Square to remove them from the area so President Trump could be photographed in front of a nearby church while holding a bible "demonstrating toughness" (Baker et al. 2020). Without an audible warning to disperse, police in riot gear rushed demonstrators using shields, batons and chemical irritants, as well as flash and smoke grenades (Baker et al. 2020). Military helicopters flown by the National Guard conducted shows of force against protesters by flying low and shining searchlights directly onto demonstrators in a maneuver more typically deployed against insurgents in a combat zone (Gibbons-Neff et al. 2020). In Portland, Oregon, Portland police and federal agents used batons and fired projectiles—many having chemical irritants—against passive protesters. Unidentified federal agents abducted protesters, taking them away in unmarked vans (Olmos, Baker & Kanno-Youngs 2020). Federal agents patrolled Portland streets wearing camouflage and tactical gear, blocks away from any federal building they may have been legally justified in guarding, to arrest protesters on federal charges (Baker, Fuller & Olmos 2020). Among the federal forces deployed to Portland was a group known as BORTAC, a Border Control unit that some compare to a police force such as the SWAT unit, and others compare to a special force unit within one of the armed services (Olmos, Baker & Kanno-Youngs 2020, Pilkington 2020). By treating BLM protests as a movement akin to an insurgency, the policing of protest in the USA manifests hybrid tendencies that exceed law enforcement but stop short of conventional war on a battlefield. These are the hybrid institutional tendencies the security model of protest policing stands for.

Deploying military power against protesters implies a more aggressive use of force and different rules of engagement. It also communicates hostility and enmity. Control technologies may be less spectacular in their communications. A mobile telephone invisibly sets surveillance in motion when it is used—for it to function, its location must be known to the system. A mobile phone's communications with a cellular system, then, can be used to track a cell phone's location. It also makes mobile phones vulnerable to police use of cell site simulators—such as Stingrays, manufactured by the Harris corporation—to check, capture or disrupt cellular communications (Scahill & Williams 2015).

As theorized by Deleuze, control technologies fragment, divert, control or condition points of system access, manage or minimize risk to a system, create graduated stages of system access, disable access, or use aggregations of data produced by our participation in communicative capitalism to calculate risk levels to systems (Deleuze 1992, Dean 2004). They create lines of association and reflexively construct probabilities and possibilities of threats. Control technologies are post-disciplinary in the sense that they do not train, normalize, or correct subjects with an aim of integrating subjects as productive members of society, as forms of disciplinary power would (Foucault 1995). With their fragmenting tendencies, control technologies function according to a logic of subjective and social disintegration: they prevent the formation of a political subject, its appearance or assembling power (Passavant 2021).

By deploying technologies of control, police can monitor and manage protesters, and displace or disassemble the appearance of a political subject. For example, on 11 August 2011, after a Bay Area Rapid Transit (BART) police officer shot and killed a homeless man in a subway station, BART thwarted an expected protest by shutting down wireless communication services in its downtown San Francisco stations (Cabanatuan 2011). The BART action engendered protests and unfavorable comparisons with authoritarian regimes that shut down internet or cellular services to maintain state power without legitimation from citizens (Elinson 2011). With protesters often displaced to marginalized locations and forced to use social media to communicate grievances, BART's disabling of internet and cellular communication shows how the assembly of a political subject and the public appearance of political antagonism can be disabled by denying access to key communicative systems.

The Memphis Police Department and Black Lives Matter

Memphis residents sued the city on 22 February 2017. They complained of surveillance by the Memphis Police Department (MPD) because the MPD videotaped their demonstrations. The MPD had also created a "blacklist" of 81 persons who could not enter City Hall without a police escort to their destination. Activists involved with BLM were heavily represented on the list. The suit also complained of the city's use of Geofeedia software (Blanchard, et al. v. City of Memphis February 22, 2017).

Memphis was one of the cities that was discovered keeping political intelligence and blocked lists of radicals and subversives in the 1960s. As protest policing became more tolerant during the negotiated management era of the 1970s, 1980s and early 1990s, such surveillance and police conduct was recognized as incompatible with a constitutional democracy, and these cities came under judicial consent decrees barring them from engaging in political intelligence gathering and political disruption. Memphis's consent decree was known as the *Kendrick* Consent Decree. Unlike other major cities, however, Memphis's consent decree had remained unchanged since 1978 when activists filed their 2017 action and sought to have the consent decree enforced.

As their case went ahead, activists and the American Civil Liberties Union of Tennessee learned that MPD monitoring of BLM was more far-reaching than they had initially believed. Although the MPD's Office of Homeland Security (OHS) focused on counterterrorism when it was created, evidence produced during the litigation proved that OHS had become "refocused on political intelligence" (Blanchard and ACLU-TN v. City of Memphis October 26, 2018c, 22). Between 2016 and 2017, time devoted to terrorism threats had diminished, only occupying about 35% of OHS time, while "protests involved much of [OHS] time," according to officer testimony (Blanchard and ACLU-TN v. City of Memphis October 26, 2018c, 22). Consequently, federal judge Jon McCalla found Memphis to be in violation of the *Kendrick* Consent Decree because it conducted forbidden political intelligence practices and "Operated the Office of Homeland Security for the purpose of political intelligence" (Blanchard and ACLU-TN v. City of Memphis October 26, 2018c, 2–3). Judge McCalla also found Memphis to be in violation of *Kendrick* because it intercepted electronic communications and infiltrated groups using a fake Facebook account, failed to familiarize MPD officers with the decree, did not create an approval process for criminal investigations that could implicate First Amendment rights, disseminated information the MPD collected to individuals outside law enforcement, and recorded and maintained a database of protest attendees (Blanchard and ACLU-TN v. City of Memphis October 26, 2018c, 3).

Why did OHS institutional resources become redirected away from counterterrorism to protests? OHS became retooled to focus on political intelligence in response to the 2014 BLM protests in Ferguson (Blanchard and ACLU-TN v. City of Memphis July 24, 2018a, 3429)[1]. The redirection of OHS resources was also in response to protests targeting the MPD due to an MPD officer having killed a teenaged, African American male, Darrius Stewart, who was a passenger in a car pulled over for a broken headlight in July 2015 (Blanchard and ACLU-TN v. City of Memphis July 24, 2018a, 3427). The OHS became the MPD's organizational hub for targeting the BLM movement in Memphis.

The OHS produced and disseminated between one and three Joint Intelligence Briefings (JIBs) daily. The JIBs circulated information on police shootings and deaths, riots and protests, BLM and officer safety. The JIB circulation broadened "exponentially" over time and was forward beyond its circulation list. The list's recipients included not only different components of the MPD, but Shelby County officials, the US military, US Department of Justice, Tennessee Department of Homeland Security, Arkansas Fusion Centers, Memphis Gas and Electric, Shelby County Schools, FedEx, Autozone and St. Jude. Events included public protests, events on private property, a rumored event that turned out to be a hoax, and a BLM activist's complaint about police harassment. The JIBs included "Sensitive and Classified" information such as driver license profiles, juvenile arrest records, mental health histories and photographs (Blanchard and ACLU-TN v. City of Memphis, July 24, 2018a, 3073–3074, 3430). Michael Rallings, MPD Director, instructed OHS to create and maintain a database of protests and demonstrations. The database included protest events with as few as four people. Only two recorded events resulted in any arrests, and none produced any damage (Blanchard and ACLU-TN v. City of Memphis, July 24, 2018a, 3075).

The OHS captured private communications of Memphis residents active in BLM and OHS created a dummy Facebook account under the name of "Bob Smith" to "catfish" activists and convince them to friend the account. Tim Reynolds, who was one of the key officers in the OHS monitoring of BLM, also obtained an undercover phone from the Organized Crime Unit to allow him to communicate surreptitiously with BLM activists by call or text message about planning, preparation and events so the MPD could become more "proactive" with respect to BLM demonstrations (Blanchard and ACLU-TN v. City of Memphis, July 24, 2018a, 3077–3078, 3508ff., 3358).

To support its political intelligence gathering, OHS enlisted the Real Time Crime Center's (RTCC's) resources. The RTCC has a "bank of approximately 30–33 computers on the floor," staffed by officers who work in three shifts. The officers in the RTCC monitored live video feeds from cameras posted throughout Memphis, mobile cameras and a drone. They would manually search social media, and they would use social media collators Geofeedia and NC4 to search and check social media chatter in public posts regarding protests in the Memphis area, and reported findings back to OHS. The OHS would then disseminate this intelligence to precinct commanders and would make sure that protests were covered by officers in uniform or in plainclothes (Blanchard and ACLU-TN v. City of Memphis, July 24, 2018a, 3076, 3410).

Officers in the RTCC would use analysis software, such as Accurint LE Plus and i2 Analyst's Notebook. Accurint creates a visual image of "complex relationships" for police and uses finding information to locate other identifying information (such as telephone numbers or photos), property assets of suspects and information about potential financial distress that can be useful for police investigations. The i2 Analyst's Notebook is a "visual analysis tool" that performs "social network analysis." It creates "network visualizations" by constructing "connections" and organizing them either spatially or temporally. Officers in the RTCC would use the i2 package to create a document mapping events and Memphis residents to each other, scoring the created relationships for their "closeness." The document is titled "Black Lives Matter.pdf" (Blanchard and ACLU-TN v. City of Memphis July 24, 2018a, 3364–3365, "Accurint LE Plus" n.d., "IBM Security i2 Analyst's Notebook" n.d.).

The construction of the blocked list at issue in the complaint against Memphis exhibited this logic of association integral to the use of control technologies embedded within preventative policing. The list began with the names of those who conducted a die-in protest at Memphis mayor Jim Strickland's residence, 19 December 2016. There were no arrests at the protest, but MPD director Rallings instructed the MPD to respond, and the response resulted in the City Hall Escort List and an Authorization of Agency (AOA) (Blanchard and ACLU-TN v. City of Memphis July 24 2018a, 3071–3072, 3522–3528). The AOA was a delegation of trespass authority to the MPD so that if the MPD encountered members of the list on Strickland's property, for example, the MPD could arrest and charge these persons with criminal trespass without Strickland needing to be present. The list was not limited just to those who took part in the die-in protest. It extended to "associates in fact"—those considered to be associated with the protesters through social media contacts, whether they were seen with the individual the MPD had identified as a key activist, or if they had been at other protests, either with the group that organized the die-in or the key individual. The logic of control technologies is an illiberal logic of guilt by association.

In fact, the slightest mention of BLM drew MPD attention and was sufficient for dissemination for further monitoring, flagging, or more proactive intervention by MPD organizational resources—a process that created an ever-extending web of association. For example, an email from Officer Bradley Wilburn to Officer Timothy Reynolds in OHS with the subject heading "Protest Monitoring" observes, "Tami Sawyer is active with Steve Cohen, post below." Steve Cohen is a member of Congress standing for Memphis, and the post in question stated that Cohen called for "cultural training" for police and said that "Black Lives Matter is doing important work." When asked about the email during his deposition and why that social media post might have been sent to OHS, Wilburn responded, "Probably because of the mention of Black Lives Matter." When MPD got wind of a church hosting a community-police dialog, it contacted the bishop to make sure that the event would be "pro-police." A memorial service for Darrius Stewart was also checked by MPD, observing "known individuals" in the crowd and other details until it concluded, and the attendees left (Blanchard and ACLU-TN v. City of Memphis July 24, 2018a, 3248, 3547–3548, 3330, 3339–3357).

BLM also became elided with "lack," as the event "Black Owned Food Truck Sunday" did not escape MPD notice. The MPD prevented Black BLM protesters from entering Graceland during Elvis Week in 2016, keeping them enclosed behind metal barricades and separated from tourists. Meanwhile, a group of mostly White BLM protesters were free to enter the major annual tourism event in Memphis. Local lawmakers articulated concern that the MPD's policing of the event was not "content neutral" because it allowed free movement and expression for those celebrating Elvis, but not to those who were perceived to be BLM speakers. Elvis Presley Enterprises later released a statement communicating support for inclusion and hospitality. The MPD's policing during Elvis Week, which sought to separate BLM from Elvis Week celebrations, were segregating actions where the exercise of First Amendment rights overlapped significantly with race (Blanchard and ACLU-TN v. City of Memphis July 24, 2018a, 3074, Callahan & Beifuss 2016).

The MPD's use of control technologies not only to check but to construct lines of association linked to potential criminalization as part of a practice to pre-empt protest demonstrates a logic of post-democratic policing. Nevertheless, as these lines of association become almost absurd in their breadth—and narrowness—they can tell us something about the state formation of neoliberal authoritarianism through this state's practices of protest policing. The MPD's reaction to BLM is so excessive that it not only chills the exercise of First Amendment rights, but it also expresses core elements of this state formation.

A Power Point presentation created by OHS stands for the MPD's frame of reference for BLM. Titled "Blue Suede Shoes," it addresses BLM protests and MPD intelligence gathering about leading protesters. The presentation opens by referring to the "social climate in the 1960s and the 1970s," and the title of its second slide is "2016: A Year of Social Unrest Reminiscent of the late 1960s and early 1970s" (Blanchard and ACLU-TN v. City of Memphis July 24, 2018a, 3207–3208). The 1960s were a time of civil rights protests, nonviolent civil disobedience and urban riots—triggered by police abuse of force—that expressed outrage at the gap between democratic norms and the reality of deep material inequalities in US cities (National Advisory Commission on Civil Disorders 1968). The MPD is haunted by the specter of Black insurrection (Derrida 1994).

Like the weekly news magazine *U.S. News and World Report*'s editorials on the Civil Rights movement in the 1960s conflating nonviolent sit-ins with crime and violence, or Richard Nixon's speeches during the 1968 presidential campaign conflating crime, protests and riots, "Blue Suede Shoes" and depositions of MPD officers conflate protest, violence and riots or civil disorder (Lawrence 1963, Nixon 1968). The Power Point reports that a BLM protest during Elvis Week could be used to "incite" and "escalate the violence." "Smaller radical groups" in "metropolitan areas across the USA," the Power Point informs its audience, are using "peaceful demonstrations to use violence and destruction to promote or advance their own agendas." A slide finds a woman arrested for standing at Elvis' gravesite one night at 10:30pm yelling "Black Lives Matter!" When she refused to leave, she was arrested and charged with "Disorderly Conduct, Inciting a Riot, and Criminal Trespass" (Blanchard and ACLU-TN v. City of Memphis July 24, 2018a, 3207–3231). When asked about the database of demonstrations in Memphis, the director of the MPD responded by characterizing demonstrations as "civil disturbances," a term typically used to describe a riot or insurrection, until conceding it was "very rare" that "law enforcement had to do anything other than just kind of be there to keep everybody safe" (Blanchard and ACLU-TN v. City of Memphis July 24, 2018a, 3480–3482, "Civil Disturbance Law and Legal Definition" n.d.). Institutionally, the MPD comprehends BLM as an insurrection.

If the MPD understands BLM to stand for a political insurrection, then the use of control technologies for surveillance, intelligence gathering, databases, mapping and weighing possible associations among residents and events, as well as MPD briefings and deployment of institutional assets, begin to make more sense. So also does the "Blue Suede Shoes" Power Point and MPD detective Tim Reynolds's deposition, which express concern that activists are using (or "hijacking") "legitimate community organizations to advance a radical agenda," such as "embarrass[ing] law enforcement to undermine the bond between law enforcement and the community" (Blanchard and

ACLU-TN v. City of Memphis July 24, 2018a, 3222, 3227, 3231). As the US Army field manual *Counterinsurgency* instructs, the struggle between insurgents and counterinsurgents is a struggle for popular support (US Department of the Army 2006, 1–8)[2]. To undermine popular support for insurgencies, the field manual recommends, "Insurgents Must be Isolated from Their Cause and Support" so that "the people [will] marginalize and stigmatize insurgents to the point that the insurgency's claim to legitimacy is destroyed" (US Department of the Army 2006, 1–23). The field manual also advises, "When insurgents are seen as criminals, they lose public support" (US Department of the Army 2006, 1–24). Much like COIN (counter-insurgency) operations conducted by US armed services, the MPD looks to criminalize BLM, separate BLM from community organizations and events perceived as popular, and control police-community dialogs in order to protect the popularity of their own brand's image while pre-empting potentially damaging association. Whether compiling an AOA, separating BLM demonstrators from Elvis fans, arresting a woman for inciting a riot who is chanting a slogan that is anti-violence ("Black Lives Matter!") or contacting a faith leader to receive assurances that the community dialogue to be hosted would be "pro-police," policing in the USA increasingly incorporates the COIN principles of the armed services.

Best practices

The MPD's use of control technologies, and its preoccupation with social media for protest policing, is not unique among police departments in the USA. During the litigation, the MPD released a statement from Director Rallings arguing, "Monitoring these public social media posts is simply good police work" (Statement from Memphis Police Director Michael W. Rallings 2018). After Judge McCalla ruled the MPD had violated the *Kendrick* Consent Decree in terms of political intelligence gathering and ordered a trial on other questions, Memphis gave a legal motion asking that the MPD be relieved of its obligation to the consent decree. In its motion, Memphis contended the "40-year-old document" was "impractical" and "not suited to today's world of social media activity" where "activities must be monitored" for "public safety." "The Consent Decree's … prohibition against modern methods of surveillance," Memphis continued, "is dangerous and untenable in today's world" (Blanchard and ACLU-TN v. City of Memphis August 15, 2018b, 3–4). Memphis's motion was stayed, and Memphis was required to abide by a modified consent decree updated to accommodate the need to protect First Amendment activities from intelligence gathering given the emergence of social media (ACLU of Tennessee v. City of Memphis September 21, 2020). Nevertheless, Memphis is correct to see that the use of control technologies and far-reaching political intelligence gathering done in the name of proactive policing are considered by many today to be best practices.

The Department of Justice's *After Action Assessment of the Police Response to the August 2014 Demonstrations in Ferguson, Missouri* (AAA) criticized certain aspects of the militarized response to the Ferguson uprising for escalating tensions. The AAA, however, is enthusiastic about the use of intelligence, improving intelligence gathering and the use of social media. It finds "intelligence personnel had learned a great deal about threats associated with the Ferguson mass gatherings, particularly from some special-interest groups with an intention to create havoc." It urges policing agencies to "proactively leverage the resources and expertise of fusion centers in response to a critical incident such as that in Ferguson." With respect to social media, the AAA recommends hiring "technologically savvy personnel" capable of using social media both to "share information and to collect intelligence" (IIR and COPS 2015, 83, 85, 131). This enthusiasm for social media monitoring echoes other professional iterations of policing's best practices that urge police executives to "tap into the social media system" (Police Executive Research Forum 2011, 37).

In addition to social media monitoring, control technologies are being embedded within urban infrastructures. When cities host mega-events classified as National Special Security Events, they become eligible for federal money to enhance security. Cities often use this money to buy weapons, vehicles—including armored vehicles—and security cameras. Like the weapons and vehicles, the cameras are still in the city after the event is over. Additionally, many cities are working to integrate private security cameras into police networks. Much stored video recordings, however, are "never watched," and watching live video feeds can be mesmerizing. Because of significant improvements in computer vision due, in part, to a dramatic decline in time needed to train a computer to recognize images, we can foresee the substitution of machines for humans as checks of video feeds, substantially amplifying the density of control technologies. A partnership between the NYPD and Microsoft gives Microsoft access to New York's vast network of security cameras to further develop its video analytics system, which it then plans to market to other cities (Stanley 2019, 3–10).

Military operations and spending stimulate the development of control technologies. Aerial surveillance developed to enable the US military to check large areas, and then rewind and fast-forward footage to track insurgents, was deployed in Baltimore during the uprisings over Freddie Gray's death at the hands of Baltimore police. Offered by Persistent Systems and funded by a private donor, the system can capture an area of 30 square miles and send real-time images to analysts on the ground for up to ten hours a day. The system is described as like "Google Earth with TIVO capability" (Reel 2016).

In summary, Memphis and the MPD are correct to see that maximal monitoring using control technologies I describe as part of the security model of protest policing is a key element of contemporary policing. They are also correct when they find the conflict between contemporary policing's best practices and the constitutional values represented by the *Kendrick* Consent Decree. Memphis and the MPD's discomfort with, if not political opposition to, the values of *Kendrick*, and their approval of contemporary policing's best practices, stands for the broader tendency toward post legitimation, post-democratic policing integral to neoliberal authoritarianism.

Conclusions

Protest policing is becoming more militarized and increasingly uses control technologies to check, disassemble, pre-empt, or incapacitate protests. The policing of the

BLM movement shows both tendencies. The increased use of militarized responses and control technologies reflects how protest policing in the USA may be characterized as a practice of security—an institutional practice treating protesters as something more than criminals while functioning short of total war. In this regard, the policing of BLM protests—whether during the late spring and summer of 2020 or earlier with the MPD's policing of BLM—proceeds like a low-intensity war or a practice of counterinsurgency. In its excesses, this policing of BLM protests shows a haunting, protest policing in the USA is haunted by the spectral figure of Black insurrection.

Notes

1 Blanchard and ACLU-TN v. City of Memphis, "Plaintiff's Undisputed Statement of Material Facts," July 24, 2018, includes hundreds of pages of exhibits and excerpts of depositions. References to evidence will use "Page ID" numbering from the electronic court filing system unless otherwise noted.
2 References are to page numbers, not subsections, unless otherwise noted.

References

"Accurint LE Plus." (n.d.) *LexisNexis Risk Solutions.* Available at: https://risk.lexisnexis.com/products/accurint-le-plus (Accessed 29 December 2020)

Baker, M., Fuller, T., Olmos, S. (2020) "Federal Agents Push Into Portland Streets, Stretching Limits of Their Authority," *New York Times*, July 25. Available at: https://www.nytimes.com (Accessed 26 July 2020)

Buchanan, L., Bui, Q., and Patel, J. (2020) "Black Lives Matter May Be the Largest Movement in U.S. History," *New York Times*, July 3. Available at: https://www.nytimes.com (Accessed 4 July 2020)

Cabanatuan, M. (2011) "BART Admits Halting Cell Service to Stop Protests," *San Francisco Gate*, August 12. Available at: https://www.sfgate.com (Accessed 7 August 2018)

Callahan, J. and Beifuss, J. (2016) "Legislators Ask Why Protesters Blocked from Graceland During Elvis Vigil," *USA Today*, August 16. Available at: https://www.usatoday.com (Accessed 10 July 2019)

"Civil Disturbance Law and Legal Definition." (n.d.) *USLegal.* Available at: https://definitions.uslegal.com/civil-disturbance (Accessed 29 December 2020)

Dean, J. (2004) "The Networked Empire: Communicative Capitalism and the Hope for Politics," in Passavant, A. and Dean, J. (eds.) *Empire's New Clothes: Reading Hardt and Negri.* New York: Routledge, 265–288.

Deleuze, G. (1992) "Postscript on the Societies of Control," *October* 59 (Winter 1992), 3–7.

Derrida, J. (1994) *Specters of Marx: The State of the Debt, the Work of Mourning, and the New International*, trans. Kamuf. New York: Routledge.

Dunn, C., Eisenberg, A., Lieberman, D., Silver, A., and Vitale, A. (2003) *Arresting Protest.* New York: New York Civil Liberties Union, April 2003.

Elinson, Z. (2011) "After Cellphone Action, BART Faces Escalating Protests," *New York Times*, August 20. Available at: https://www.nytimes.com (Accessed 19 July 2019)

Foucault, M. (1995 and 1977) *Discipline and Punish: The Birth of the Prison*, trans. A. Sheridan, New York: Random House.

Gibbons-Neff, T., Cooper, H., Schmitt, E., Steinhauer, J. (2020) "Former Commanders Fault Trump's Use of Troops Against Protesters," *New York Times*, June 2. Available at: https://www.nytimes.com (Accessed 2 June 2020)

"IBM Security i2 Analyst's Notebook" (n.d.) *IBM*. Available at: https://www.ibm.com/products/i2-analysts-notebook (Accessed 29 December 2020)

Institute for Intergovernmental Research (IIR) and Community Oriented Policing Services Office (COPS) (2015) *After-Action Assessment of the Police Response to the August 2014 Demonstrations in Ferguson, Missouri*. Washington, DC: Office of Community Oriented Policing Services.

Kishi, R., and Jones, S. (2020) *Demonstrations and Political Violence in America: New Data for Summer 2020*. Princeton: Armed Conflict Location and Event Data Project and Bridging Divides Initiative, September 2020.

Lawrence, D. (1963) "What's Become of 'Law and Order'?" *U.S. News and World Report*, June 29, 104.

National Advisory Commission on Civil Disorders (1968) *Report of the National Advisory Commission on Civil Disorders*. New York: Bantam.

N.Y.D. Says it Used Restraint During Protests. Here's What the Videos Show. (2020) *New York Times* July 14. Available at: https://www.nytimes.com (Accessed 15 July 2020)

Nixon, R. (1968) "Address Accepting the Presidential Nomination at the Republican Convention in Miami Beach, Florida," August 8. *The American Presidency Project*. Available at: https://www.presidency.ucsb.edu/documents/address-accepting-the-presidential-nomination-the-republican-national-convention-miami (Accessed 12 January 2014)

Olmos, S., Baker, M., and Kanno-Youngs, Z. (2020) "Federal Officers Deployed in Portland Didn't Have Proper Training, D.H.S. Memo Said," *New York Times*, July 18. Available at: https://www.nytimes.com (Accessed 19 July 2020)

Passavant, A. (2021) *Policing Protest: The Post-Democratic State and the Figure of Black Insurrection*. Durham: Duke University Press.

Pilkington, E. (2020) "'These are His People': Inside the Elite Border Control Unit Trump Sent to Portland," *The Guardian*, July 27. Available at: https://www.theguardian.com (Accessed 13 December 2020)

Police Executive Research Forum. (2011) *Managing Major Events: Best Practices from the Field*. Washington, D.C.: Police Executive Research Forum.

Reel, M. (2016) "Secret Cameras Record Baltimore's Every Move from Above," *Bloomberg Business Week*, August 23. Available at: https://www.bloomberg.com (Accessed 26 June 2019)

Scahill, J. and Williams, M. (2015) "Stingrays: A Secret Catalogue of Government Gear for Spying on Your Cellphone," *The Intercept*, December 17. Available at: https://www.theintercept.com (Accessed 22 December 2020)

Stanley, J. (2019) *The Dawn of Robot Surveillance: AI, Video Analytics, and Privacy*. Washington, DC: American Civil Liberties Union.

Statement from Memphis Police Director Michael W. Rallings. (2018) "*City Unseals Documents in Ongoing Lawsuit*," 24 July 2018. Available at: https://memphis.hosted.civiclive.com/news/what_s_new/city_unseals_documents_in_ongoing_lawsuit (Accessed 2 December 2020)

United States Department of the Army. (2006) *Counterinsurgency: Field Manual 3–24*. Washington, DC: Headquarters, Department of the Army.

Wood, L. (2014) *Crisis and Control: The Militarization of Protest Policing*. New York: Pluto Press.

Legal Documents

ACLU of Tennessee v. City of Memphis, U.S.D.C. W.D.T.N. 76 Civ. 00449, "Amended Judgment and Decree 'Modified *Kendrick* Decree,'" (September 21, 2020)

Blanchard and ACLU of Tennessee v. City of Memphis, U.S.D.C. W.D.T.N. 17 Civ. 02120, "Plaintiff's Undisputed Statement of Material Facts," (July 24, 2018a)

Blanchard and ACLU of Tennessee v. City of Memphis, U.S.D.C. W.D.T.N. 17 Civ. 02120, "Motion for Relief from Judgment or Order," (August 15, 2018b)

Blanchard and ACLU of Tennessee v. City of Memphis, U.S.D.C. W.D.T.N. 17 Civ. 2120, "Opinion and Order," (October 26, 2018c)

Blanchard, et al. v. City of Memphis, U.S.D.C. W.D.T.N. 17 Civ. 02120, "Complaint for Enforcement of Order, Judgment, and Decree," (February 22, 2017)

10

FIGHTING FOR THE RIGHT TO SAVE OTHERS

Responses by civil society to the criminalization of solidarity in the mediterranean sea post-2015

Christal Chapman

"Facilitating entry" of irregular migrants into the European Union (EU) is classified as a crime, a crime not limited in its application to human smugglers, but one which has led to the criminalization of humanitarian workers since the 2015 EU Refugee Crisis. Consequent to the EU's decreased search and rescue (SAR) operations in the Mediterranean Sea from 2015 onwards (del Valle 2016), NGOs (Non-Governmental Organizations) have stepped in so that SAR is now exclusively undertaken by civil society. In addition to the reduction of nationally led SAR efforts by EU member states, one must also note the EU's general policy of externalization of border control, whereby agreements have been struck with Libya and Turkey to encourage the retention of migrants within their borders. Given this existing policy of externalization of border control, and particularly the reliance on Libyan and Turkish authorities preventing migrants from reaching EU borders, post-2015 has seen an increase in the cases of criminal charges imposed against humanitarian workers who rescued migrants in the Mediterranean Sea,[1] and thereafter brought them into the EU.

In June 2019, the case of Carola Rackete, captain of the rescue ship Sea Watch 3, came to prominence. After rescuing 53 migrants off the coast of Libya and with the NGO (Sea Watch) having already stated its position that it would not forcibly return rescued migrants to Libya—which was not considered a place of safety,—a decision was taken by the NGO to transport the migrants to the next nearest port, namely the Italian island of Lampedusa. However, due to a ban instituted by the Italian government barring rescue ships carrying migrant people from docking in Lampedusa's port, the vessel was forced to remain in international waters for two weeks. On 29 June 2019, Rackete made the decision to dock in Lampedusa's port, without government permission, noting concerns for the health and safety of those on board. She was after charged with abetting irregular migration and resisting the orders of a warship. However, in February 2020, she was acquitted.

DOI: 10.4324/9781003144229-14

In Greece, there have also been examples of humanitarian actors being charged for their role in easing the entry of rescued migrants onto Greek shores. One such example concerns that of five volunteers—three Spanish firefighters (PROEM-AID) and two Danish aid workers (Team Humanity)—who were conducting SAR operations in Greek waters and were subsequently arrested in January 2016 and indicted on charges of illegal transportation of irregular migrants into Greek territory without authorization (Conte & Binder 2019). The volunteers had been accused by the Hellenic Coast Guard of having smuggled migrants by towing a sinking boat from Turkish waters into the Greek zone. However, on the day when this alleged activity took place, they had not saved anyone. The Judge in their case accused them of using "rescue as a pretext" to pursue smuggling. Despite a long and arduous trial process they were eventually acquitted in May 2018.

This chapter analyzes the ways in which civil society (including NGOs) has mobilized against this practice of criminalizing humanitarian actors who bring migrants into Italy and Greece, following SAR operations in the Mediterranean Sea. For the purposes of this chapter, the term "migrant" is used to refer to both potential economic migrants and asylum seekers. The research drew on 13 semi-structured interviews with researchers, activists and lawyers in different EU member states who supplied insights into current forms of criminalization. Secondary sources including court cases, investigative reports, policy reports and scholarly research, were also consulted. Section 1 begins with an analysis of the ways in which criminalization has been affected—both formally and informally—and conceptualizing such criminalization as a form of lawfare being engaged in by states. Section 2 addresses humanitarians' justification for engaging in SAR, and Section 3 highlights the myriad ways in which they have been legally challenging this criminalization. Section 4 concludes that despite the potential role mobilization, particularly legal mobilization, by civil society can play in reducing these incidences of criminalization, legal mobilization against criminalization of SAR in and of itself may not be sufficient to drop the practice of criminalization entirely. What may be needed is a change in societal thinking as it relates to the perception of migrants.

Section 1: Criminalizing (solidarity) assistance to migrants as a form of lawfare

This section begins with an analysis of the practice of criminalizing solidarity, so as to better understand the ways in which this practice manifests and whether the actions carried out in Italy and Greece against SAR NGOs fit established categories of criminalization of solidarity. The criminalization of solidarity can be defined as demonizing, stigmatizing, posing obstacles to and criminalizing humanitarian aid to migrants (Caritas Europa 2019). Second, the concept of lawfare has been chosen because of its ability to aptly describe and explain the criminalizing actions taken by governments against those engaging in SAR activities. Therefore this concept is used to show how the actions and discourse promoted by the Italian and Greek governments, media and other public figures, have been used to legitimize the scapegoating of civil society generally and SAR NGOs in particular, and the far-reaching consequences this has not only for migrants' rights, but also for the rights of European citizens who choose to engage in SAR activity.

Since the "refugee crisis" of 2015, there has been a significant increase in the number of judicial prosecutions and investigations against individuals related to the criminalization of solidarity (Vosyliūtė & Conte 2019, 31). According to a monitoring exercise conducted by the Research Social Platform on Migration and Asylum (ReSOMA), in 2015 roughly eight cases of criminalization were recorded (Vosyliūtė & Conte 2019, 23). However, as of December 2019, at least 171 individuals had been criminalized for their solidarity towards migrants trying to reach Europe (ReSOMA 2020), and as of June 2019, 83 individuals were investigated or prosecuted exclusively on grounds of easing the entry or transit of migrants (Vosyliūtė & Conte 2019, 25).

Several authors have written on the history of the criminalization of solidarity, with some noting that this is not a 21st century phenomenon but was a regular practice in all regimes that were proto- or entirely totalitarian (Jalušič 2019). "It began several decades ago, with heavy-handed police tactics and, on occasion, prosecution of those individuals (including priests) involved in a sanctuary movement, providing a place of safety for those facing deportation" (Fekete et al. 2017, 3). Additionally, "[it] has historic parallels in the evolution of liberal democracy with the criminalization of slaves escaping from their captors and in the depiction by state authorities of those mobilizing to help fugitive slaves as 'traitors'" (Allsopp 2017, 2).

The notion of "policing the mobility society" describes the effects of criminalization of civil society, particularly of those organizations going beyond humanitarian aid and engaging in critical monitoring of states and or seeking to politically mobilize on behalf of migrants. "Policing" goes beyond traditional surveillance, prevention or traditional criminal law or other pre-emptive criminal law-like approaches, cases of criminal prosecution and sentencing before competent courts. Instead,

> it refers to the wider set of practices and policies employed by the EU and member states which impact (directly or indirectly) civil society's activities and are aimed at (or have the effect of) limiting dissent, monitoring, litigation, or political mobilization against anti-human smuggling policies.
>
> (Carrera et al. 2018a, 239)

There is, indeed, a "continuum of the criminalization of the organized and independent provision of assistance to ("irregular") migrants" (Jalušič 2019, 118). This continuum occurs in five stages. The first stage is "discursive criminalization", which involves public incrimination of civil society (including NGOs) through political and media discourses wherein NGOs are linked to criminals and smugglers and are accused of being pull factors and traitors. Second, there is a "bureaucratic tightening" which means that the space for civic action shrinks. Organizations and volunteers must register, cooperate, inform authorities, and have a duty to report certain occurrences. Third, there is a "banning of access and prohibition of monitoring" which means that many NGOs are no longer granted access to hotpots or zones of entry. Fourth, the "labeling of NGOs and volunteers" takes place, whereby they are labeled as "dangerous" and suitable for persecution. The fifth stage is the direct "criminalization of assistance" as provided for in criminal laws or what might even be called "over-criminalization" (Vegh Weis 2017).

Criminalization of SAR in the Mediterranean takes various forms—both formal and informal—in keeping with Jalušič's continuum. Thus, there were several instances of stage one of the continua, that is, "discursive criminalization", particularly in pre-election periods, whereby "fake news" and conspiracies about humanitarian actors have been spread as well as accompanying outbursts of hate-speech and xenophobic rhetoric towards migrants and those who assist them" (Carrera et al. 2018, 22). An overwhelming lack of public trust for civil society, and for SAR NGOs, arose in Europe (Trilling 2020), which can be linked to the increase in right-wing political parties' popularity and promotion of discourses inciting hate, xenophobia and discrimination.

Stage two of the continuum, that of the "bureaucratic tightening of space for civic action", was illustrated by the Hellenic Coast Guard, which introduced a vetting procedure for SAR NGOs to set up that they meet certain minimum standards (Carrera et al. 2019). Additionally, between April and May 2017, the Italian Senate Defence Committee issued non-binding recommendations to the government, which advocated implementing compulsory registration and background checks for organizations engaging in SAR (Maccanico et al. 2018, 19–20). Thus, one notes the use of administrative measures in effecting criminalization.

The most flagrant illustration of the tightening of action space, along with stage three, that is, "banning of access", was seen with the advent of the "Code of Conduct for NGOs involved in migrant rescue at sea" instituted in July 2017 by the Italian government. All NGOs had to sign the Code if they wished to continue engaging in SAR activity in the Mediterranean. The Code of Conduct sought to circumscribe NGO conduct and mandated allowing law enforcement personnel aboard ships, and the transmission of surveillance data about SAR missions, in addition to other requirements, many of which ran counter to humanitarian principles. Certain NGOs refused to sign the Code and therefore had to stop all SAR activity (e.g., *Médecins Sans Frontières*, Save the Children and Sea Eye), whilst some signed but afterwards greatly decreased their SAR activity, or redeployed their vessels to other areas, for example, Migrant Offshore Aid Station signed but later indicated that their vessel would instead move to conduct SAR in Asia.

Stage four of the continuum, "the labeling of NGOs and volunteers as dangerous", is illustrated with the publication, in 2016, of a leaked Frontex report by the UK Financial Times. The Frontex report had highlighted "concerns" about alleged interactions between SAR NGOs and smugglers operating in Libya while the Financial Times referred to "collusion" between NGOs and smugglers, with this term being after co-opted by an Italian Prosecutor who publicly accused NGOs of criminal activity (Carrera et al. 2019).

The final (fifth) stage along Jalušič's continuum, that of "direct criminalization of assistance" and utilization of criminal law, has also occurred quite often. Examples include the actions of the Italian government in charging captains of SAR vessels, such as Carola Rackete and those charges originating in Greece, for example, the three PROEM-AID volunteers and two Team Humanity workers who were accused of easing migrant smuggling, as highlighted in my introduction.

In terms of conceptualizing this criminalization, I contend that these actions can be viewed as forms of lawfare. The literature reveals that there is no standard definition of lawfare. Some have chosen to define it in military terms[2] focusing on its use to accomplish military objectives and thereby focusing on its use as an actual "weapon", thus, Tiefenbrun (2010, 29) defined it as, "a weapon designed to destroy the enemy by using, misusing and abusing the legal system and the media in order to raise a public outcry against that enemy". Handmaker (2019, 9–10) defines it as "the illegitimate and hegemonic use of law by state and/or corporate bodies to suppress claims and to persecute individual advocates and NGOs", whilst Goldstein (2013) defined it as "the abuse of Western laws and judicial systems to achieve strategic military or political ends". In Latin-America the term lawfare is widely used to describe the biased functioning of the criminal justice systems to legally and politically de-legitimized politicians from the opposite party with the support or encouragement of mainstream media (Zaffaroni et al. 2020).

In addressing the confusion which these varying definitions may tend to bring, Werner (2010, 62) notes that "the meanings of terms such as 'lawfare' are not set in stone, but rather evolve through their use in different social practices". One should also note the importance of not just seeking a single meaning but comparing the varied meanings of the concept so as to explore the different contexts in which it is used and the distinct ways in which it has been framed in these contexts. Within this debate is acknowledgment of the fact that "meaning is not pre-given but produced and reproduced in specific social contexts" (Werner 2010, 71). As such, the meaning which I believe is most apt for this current research is that used by Goldstein (2013, no pagination) where he notes that as a practice, lawfare entails "the negative manipulation of international and national human rights laws to accomplish purposes other than, or contrary to, those for which they were originally enacted". In this case, the concept of lawfare is clearly illustrated using national legislation meant to criminalize and penalize smugglers instead being wielded against those undertaking SAR efforts, even if that had not been the direct intention of lawmakers when the law was initially passed. As noted by Paula Schmid Porras, attorney for the PROEM-AID volunteers, "They're using laws intended for international criminal organizations that are earning money from trafficking, smuggling, prostitution and slavery to prosecute humanitarian workers and volunteers who are just trying to save lives" (Open Democracy 2019).

Finally, Gordon (2014), in dealing with the way the promotion of human rights protection is increasingly being viewed as a security threat (the securitization of human rights), has addressed the ways in which lawfare has moved beyond simply describing phenomena, and how it can also run as a "speech act". The author notes that in describing lawfare as a speech act, the thinking underpinning such an assertion is that "saying something can produce certain consequential effects upon the feelings, thoughts or actions of the audience…and it may be done with the design, intention or purpose of producing them" (Gordon 2014, 317). Thus, I contend that where specific words are used by government actors when describing the actions of those conducting SAR activities, such as "pull factor" or "taxi service", to produce certain feelings in the wider public, this "speech act" would constitute a form of lawfare. Whilst the effects of these speech acts are felt primarily within the public domain, they can be nonetheless used by both prosecutors and judicial officers during court proceedings—as highlighted in my Introduction, where the judge in criminal proceedings against SAR volunteers in Greece accused them of using "rescue as a pretext" to engage in smuggling.

In both Italy and Greece, there has been ongoing negative publicity generated in the media against SAR NGOs, which had the effect of lowering public support and empathy for their cause and the practical consequence of leading to a decrease in private sector funding for these NGOs. Thus, my research has revealed that there have been deliberate attempts to engage in lawfare as "speech acts" which has affected public opinion. Consequently, a distinct challenge that must be overcome is the changing of entrenched attitudes engendered by these discourses. Thus, lawfare has become the framework through which human rights promotion in liberal democracies is being securitized (Gordon 2014, 312), as different securitizing actors, including policy makers and legislators, mobilize the media, shape public opinion, lobby legislators, engage in certain speech acts and introduce laws that engender the limitation of human rights work (Gordon 2014, 311).

Conceptualizing these actions as lawfare, and governments' intentional aim in so doing can also be supported by analyzing the EU's general policy of externalization of migration control. As researcher Sara Prestianni noted in highlighting the shift in policy undertaken by the EU and how this impacted later campaign of criminalization:

> When they decided to externalize SAR [activities] to Libya, in some way NGOs had to be pushed back in the sea and the only way to do that was to create a kind of criminalization around them…One moment in 2016, NGOs were considered something helping …, and they became in a few months the enemy and the people working with the traffickers, but they were always the same people. So, what really changed was the policy and the strategy, which decided to bring out NGOs from the sea and externalize SAR to the Libyan militia and coastguard.
>
> (Prestianni, quoted in Maccanico et al. 2018, 8–9)

Section 2: Justification for humanitarian action

Why is it possible to speak about "over-criminalization"? Because the involved actions by SAR NGOs are not only not necessarily a crime but, moreover, can be classified as an existing duty under international law. The duty to rescue persons in distress at sea is not simply a foundational principle of international law but has been codified in treaties and through historic application (Papanicolopulu 2016). This duty to rescue persons in distress at sea can be found in Article 98 of the UN Convention of the Law of the Seas (1982), which creates a duty to render assistance, so that the master of any ship—be it a humanitarian ship, fishing boat, commercial ship or even state operated vessel—is obliged to render assistance to anyone found in danger at sea, insofar as doing so would not place his ship, passengers or crew in any serious danger (Human Rights at Sea 2019). Article 98 also obliges coastal states to set up and maintain adequate SAR services, including through regional cooperation if necessary. Additionally, the duty to rescue persons in distress at sea can also be found in other international conventions including the International Convention for the Safety of Life at Sea (1974), the International Convention on Salvage (1989) and the International Convention on Maritime Search and Rescue (1979). Significantly, this duty to rescue must be adhered to without discrimination as to persons' race, nationality, age, gender, immigration status or any other characteristic.

Justification for humanitarian protection for migrants found in distress in the Mediterranean Sea is based on the operation of principles of international law, both as it relates to the duty to rescue and to universal human rights law. Recognition of the universal nature of human rights would mean that value is placed on all lives (without distinction as to race or origin) so that one's right to seek asylum, right to non-refoulement, right to a decent standard of living and right to life would be held sacrosanct. The existence of these principles cannot be denied, and as humanitarians mobilize the existing international laws in their favor they find justification for their actions, which I would also argue is borne out by the fact that the trials held for those criminalized, have always ended in acquittals.

Moreover, such justification for SAR, rooted as it is in international law, makes humanitarians' criminalization even more inexplicable, as one questions how those can who are seeking to uphold international law be criminalized—even over-criminalized (Vegh Weis 2017), whilst those who are willing to flaunt international law (including state authorities willing to allow persons to die at sea) are under-criminalized (Vegh Weis 2017). Humanitarians have, however, been fighting this "anomaly" of criminalization of an altogether legal and decent activity, and, in the later section, I seek to address the various ways in which they have not only sought to legally mobilize against their criminalization but are also seeking to hold state authorities to account for their lack of action, or purported willingness to allow migrants to die at sea.

Section 3: Resisting criminalization of solidarity

Whilst the humanitarian actions of SAR personnel have been criminalized by EU member states, particularly Italy and Greece, an equally disturbing trend has appeared, whereby the international human rights violations perpetrated by European authorities (in not providing national SAR operations and actively seeking to discourage SAR by NGOs) have been simultaneously under-criminalized.

Nonetheless, humanitarian workers have not sat idly by and accepted this criminalization but have been actively resisting by utilizing both legal and non-legal strategies. For the purposes of this chapter, however, I focus on their legal mobilization.

Indeed, the increased number of cases of criminalization of humanitarian aid has invariably led to an increase in litigation surrounding this matter before European courts (Lesinska 2019). Thus, one notes not only have civil society actors been involved in cases defending humanitarians against criminalization, but they have also looked to initiate cases against states in an attempt to overturn the under-criminalization of the harms committed against migrants and SAR personnel.

To better understand civil society's legal mobilization, one must have a clear idea of the backdrop against which this mobilization has taken place. Civil society has responded to the increased monitoring and attacks on their operations in many ways. Some NGOs have chosen to leave the humanitarian field, while others have chosen to try to continue operating within the restricted space but operate in a very controlled manner so as to not jeopardize their funding (Allsopp 2017). Whilst increased scrutiny has led to the "silencing" of some actors, others have become very vocal, "framing their work as an immanent critique of national or European values or in extreme cases, as civil disobedience against unjust laws" (Allsopp 2017, 15–16). Moreover, "some civil society groups have suggested that in increasing their scrutiny of NGOs, certain government and EU actors are trying to distract attention away from policy failures and find a common 'scapegoat'" (Allsopp 2017, 17). Lastly, it is also argued that the nature and work of civil society groups in the EU changed during the refugee crisis in that the space for supplying support to migrants expanded to include more informal and loose networks which are increasingly connected across borders (Allsopp 2017).

Legal mobilization has been resorted to at various levels, perhaps due to the fact that civil society has recognized that, "without mobilization of the law, a legal control system lies out of touch with the human problems it is designed to oversee. Mobilization is the link between the law and the people served or controlled by the law" (Black 1973, 126), it also refers to strategic actions undertaken by individuals and or groups in order to engender or resist change in a particular policy area (Cichowski 2011, 80). Legal mobilization in particular has been defined as, "involving the strategic use of law by civic actors to advance human rights, social justice and especially equality as a legitimate political claim" (Handmaker 2019, 11). Legal mobilization therefore encompasses the legitimate use of law as a means of buttressing one's political claims (Handmaker 2019, 9), since without continued mobilization, the law would lose its deterrent power. Consequently, legal mobilization becomes the moral obligation of every citizen whose rights are infringed (Black 1973, 127).

Legal mobilization allows an individual and group to operationalize the law as a shield (Abel 1995) and as a form of counter power, and can even have the added benefit of transforming marginalized groups into political powers (Handmaker 2019). Law can and should be mobilized by both individuals and groups, and as concerns the role of NGOs in legal mobilization, one notes they can act in various capacities, for example, standing for an individual in a claim brought before a court or by providing support for litigation through the production of specialized reports (Cichowski, 2011). Oftentimes civil society plays a crucial role in not just educating vulnerable populations about their rights but also in providing marginalized individuals with the necessary resources to undertake legal mobilization, thus it is important to analyze the role that civil society plays in starting legal mobilization (Gleeson, 2009).

One form of legal mobilization used by civil society in resisting their criminalization is strategic litigation. Strategic litigation is litigation undertaken with the goal of achieving broader societal changes. It actively seeks to effect significant changes in law, practice and public awareness (Scott 2015), and I might argue may even be engaged in when the party initiating the claim is aware that there is a very poor chance of success but, nevertheless, decides to engage in litigation as a means of raising awareness. It is different from normal litigation in that it seeks to combine legal and non-legal tactics to bring about changes in public and political opinions (Lesinska 2019). Thus, it may result in combining litigation strategies with advocacy and communication strategies, including improved public relations and targeted media campaigns (PICUM 2017). One of the clearly found strengths of strategic litigation, is its "ability to incrementally develop the law against real-life scenarios" and the fact that it often entails the identification of legal arguments that go beyond the perceived limitations of existing legal stock (Scott 2015, 48).

Civil society has been faced with unique hurdles and opportunities as they try to engage in legal mobilization against this criminalization of SAR. Not only has civil society been involved in cases defending humanitarian actors, but they have also looked to initiate cases against states at the national level, as a form of strategic litigation. Thus, Carola Rackete filed defamation proceedings in the Italian courts against Former Italian Interior Minister, Matteo Salvini (Balmer 2019), and the Italian NGO Mediterranean also filed a suit in the Italian courts against the Italian government based on a directive signed by former Minister Salvini (InfoMigrants 2019).

Furthermore, there has been a move to file cases at the regional level, namely at the European Court of Human Rights (ECtHR), as part of a campaign of strategic litigation. Consequently, a case was filed against Greece in April 2019, by Salam Kamal-Aldeen, one of the five volunteers (PROEM-AID and Team Humanity), who had been charged and prosecuted by Greece. His case against Greece filed before the ECtHR alleged illegality on the part of the Greek government by its crackdown and arbitrary prosecution of human rights defenders working to make aid to persons in distress at sea (GLAN 2019). In the words of Global Legal Action Network (GLAN), legal advisor Violeta Moreno-Lax (GLAN 2019):

> The Strasbourg Court has now the opportunity to condemn the growing trend in Greece and Europe of criminalizing solidarity. Rescue is not a crime; it is a binding duty under international law. Humanitarian help of persons in distress at sea should never be prosecuted. Attacking civil society constitutes an assault on the main values of democracy.

Additionally, 17 survivors of a fatal incident in which a boat carrying migrants found itself in distress off the coast of Libya, filed an application against Italy in May 2018, with the ECtHR. The application was filed on their behalf by the GLAN and the Italian Association for Juridical Studies on Immigration (ASGI), with support from the Italian non-profit Associazione Ricreativa Culturale Italiana (ARCI) and Yale Law School's Lowenstein International Human Rights Clinic. According to GLAN legal advisor Violeta Moreno-Lax:

> The Italian authorities are outsourcing to Libya what they are prohibited from doing themselves, flouting their human rights obligations. They are putting lives at risk and exposing migrants to extreme forms of ill-treatment by proxy, supporting and directing the action of the so-called Libyan Coast Guard.
>
> (GLAN 2018)

Moreover, there has been concerted activity by lawyers engaging in critical strategic litigation at the international level on the issue of criminalization of humanitarian aid and EU migration policies. Of note is the case filed against the EU at the International Criminal Court (ICC). In June 2019, a case was filed against the EU at the ICC, by Juan Branco, who formerly worked at the ICC and Omer Shatz, an Israeli lawyer. The submission alleges that the EU has committed crimes against humanity, in contravention of Articles 5 and 7 of the Rome Statute of 1998. It is alleged that such crimes were committed (and omitted in the case of withholding SAR activities) from 2014 onwards, as part of a premeditated policy to curb migration flows from Africa to the EU. The attorneys argue that, "without the implementation of the EU's policy of deterrence the crimes against the targeted population would not have ever occurred" and that furthermore, the accused was fully aware "of the lethal consequences of their conduct" (Branco & Shatz 2019, 10–15).

Thus, there has been a noted diversification of the actors involved in the litigation process, as civil society looks to refine its resistance strategies. As such, there has been engagement with scientific agencies specialized in forensic analysis and investigations, which have contributed their skills to the compilation of evidence to be used by litigation teams[3]. Specifically, in the case filed by GLAN against the Italian government, recourse was made to such ability in building evidence to support GLAN's case. Such actions give credence to the notion that, "strategic introduction of expert evidence [from] multidisciplinary perspectives can help to tell a fuller story…it [is] critical to identify a range of relevant partners, allies and experts from disciplines beyond the law" (Duffy 2018, 244,246). It also proves a crucial element of strategic litigation as noted by Lesinska (2019), that being, the ongoing cooperation among different actors, both legal and non-legal.

It is my contention that such cooperation, and the ability to form these loose networks across borders, is a significant situational opportunity which figures out whether the decision is taken to even engage in legal mobilization, particularly given the fact that oftentimes, public opinion is actively being swayed against civil society or anyone seeking to support migrants in these host communities. A significant hurdle, however, is the slow pace with which these cases make their way through courts, thus, one cannot say for certain when these attempts at legal mobilization will yield their expected fruit.

Finally, a further tactic currently employed by civil society is its use of non-legal strategies in conjunction with their legal efforts. Some have noted that, "advocacy and mobilization, rather than litigation, might drive an overall long-term strategy in which litigation only plays a small, though critical part" (Dugard & Langford 2011, 48). Such non-legal strategies have indeed been affected by civil society in this fight against the criminalization of SAR. Independent monitoring efforts have been launched by various civil society organizations and there have been joint statements, letters and press releases—undertaken by academics, INGOs, and other researchers on this issue of criminalization (Vosyliūtė & Conte 2019). Additionally, one notes the establishment of certain observatories, for example, Search and Rescue Observatory for the Mediterranean (SAROBMED) which "collects, analyzes and disseminates data regarding human rights violations in the Mediterranean and such evidence is then used to support evidence-based advocacy, strategic litigation and research-led lobbying and campaigning" (SAROBMED, n.d.). Also noteworthy is the "We are Welcoming Europe" Campaign, a European Citizens Initiative which mobilized more than 200 civil society organizations in Europe calling for an end to the criminalization of humanitarian assistance.

Section 4: Conclusions

Post-2015 has seen an overwhelming increase in the criminalization of solidarity, with the criminalization of SAR being a glaring example of the extent of governmental action. The criminalization of solidarity includes demonizing, stigmatizing, posing obstacles to and criminalizing humanitarian aid to migrants (Caritas Europa 2019). Whilst there has been an undeniable increase in criminalization of those conducting SAR in the Mediterranean Sea, these humanitarian actors have nonetheless legally justified their continued SAR activity. Legal justification can be found in international laws that mandate the provision of aid to those in distress at sea, as well as recognition of the universal nature of human rights that places equal value on all lives without distinction as to race or origin. Despite such justification for their activity, however, a range of criminalizing actions have been taken against those engaging in SAR. These include discursive or "speech acts", encouraging negative publicity and increased suspicion in media coverage to decrease public trust, tightening of the space for civic action, banning access to migrants, labeling NGOs as dangerous, and direct criminalization through the laying of charges. These actions can be conceptualized as lawfare since they involve the negative manipulation of laws to carry out purposes other than or contrary to their original intent (Goldstein 2013). Moreover, I conclude that because of these acts of lawfare being perpetrated against them, humanitarian actors now have no choice but to mobilize if they wish for this phenomenon to cease.

Civil society has looked to mobilize both legally and non-legally, against the increased criminalization of humanitarians facilitating migrants' entry into Italy and Greece subsequent to SAR. Legal mobilization has been undertaken at the national, regional and international levels, and has been preceded or accompanied by varied forms of non-legal mobilization, including ongoing advocacy, demonstrations, public awareness campaigns, joint statements by NGOs and international actors and newly formed observatories and research platforms. The identified ongoing attempts at legal mobilization have yielded success at the national level, but at the regional and international levels have not yet yielded fruit since these matters are presently pending before courts. Many of the non-legal mobilization strategies, such as advocacy and demonstrations, have been underway for some time, having been started soon after the various forms of criminalization first started to manifest. Whilst not discounting the role these non-legal strategies have played thus far or the impact they have had on improving public awareness and garnering more long-term support, the reality is they have not propelled the needed policy and legislative changes.

Furthermore, whilst civil society can justify their SAR activity from a legal and moral perspective and have looked to legally mobilize in response, they continue to be criminalized. Thus, the impact of law and thereby legal mobilization depends on the changing dynamics of the context within which the law is being applied (McCann 2006, 19). Duffy (2018, 5) makes the point that, "litigation is not an ideology: it is a tool. The extent of its impact or influence will invariably depend on how, where, when and perhaps by whom the tool is used". Consequently, attention must be paid to the "unique situational, legal, cultural, institutional and other contexts in which cases arise" (Duffy 2018, 7). In the instance where the political, social and cultural contexts have not changed, and where xenophobic discourses remain prevalent along with populist propaganda, and ongoing EU externalization of migration control and securitization of border policies, a distinct challenge which must be overcome, is the changing of entrenched societal attitudes towards migrants. Consequently, any policy changes which legal mobilization can potentially render may nonetheless be ineffectual. Therefore, whilst legal mobilization has its role to play, it nevertheless has its shortcomings and further research needs to be conducted on the issue of effectively changing entrenched societal attitudes and forms of mobilization that can be used to advance such attitudinal changes.

Notes

1 Migrants departing Libya, other parts of North Africa and Turkey.
2 Gordon (2014) citing Major General Charles Dunlap, noted that Dunlap defined lawfare as a "strategy of using or misusing law as a substitute for traditional military means to achieve an operational objective…law in this context is much the same as a weapon".
3 *Forensic Oceanography*-project that critically investigates the militarized border regime in the Mediterranean Sea. They analyze different data, including audio-visual recordings made by NGOs while at sea to reconstruct events.

References

Abel, R. (1995) *Politics by Other Means: Law in the Struggle Against Apartheid, 1980–1994.* New York: Routledge.

Allsopp, J. (2017) 'Solidarity, smuggling and the european refugee crisis: Civil society and its discontents'. *Diritto, Immigrazione e Cittadinanza (Rights, Immigration, Citizenship)*, fasc. n. 3 and 2017, 1–28.

Balmer, C. (2019) 'German rescue captain to sue Italy's Salvini over migrant comments'. *Reuters World News* 5 July 2019 [online] german-rescue-captain-to-sue-italys-salvini-over-migrant-comments-idUSKCN1U01K4 (Accessed 28th October 2019)

Black, D.J. (1973) 'The mobilization of law'. *The Journal of Legal Studies*, 2, No. 1, 125–149.

Branco, J. and Shatz, O. (2019) '*Communication to the Office of the Prosecutor of the International Criminal Court Pursuant to the Article 15 of the Rome Statute EU Migration Policies in the Central Mediterranean and Libya*'. 1st ed. [PDF] Paris: Dr. Juan Branco and Omer Shatz. Available at: eu-icc-case-EU-Migration-Policies.pdf (Accessed 12th November 2019)

Caritas Europa. (2019) 'The "criminalisation" of solidarity towards migrants'. *Position Paper*. 20th June 2019. eu-caritas-position-paper-criminalisation-solidarity-17-6-19.pdf (Accessed 14th December 2020)

Carrera, S., Allsopp, J. and Vosyliūtė, L. (2018a) 'Policing the mobility society: The effects of EU anti-migrant smuggling policies on humanitarianism." *International Journal of Migration and Border Studies*, 4, 3, 236–276.

Carrera, S., V. Mitsilegas, J. Allsopp and L. Vosyliūtė. (2019) *Policing Humanitarianism: EU Policies Against Human Smuggling and their Impact on Civil Society.* Oxford: Hart Publishing.

Carrera, S., L. Vosyliūtė, S. Smialowski, J. Allsopp, and G. Sanchez. (2018) '*Fit for purpose? The Facilitation Directive and the Criminalisation of Humanitarian Assistance to Irregular Migrants (2018 Update)*'. Brussels: European Parliament Policy Department for Citizens' Rights and Constitutional Affairs.

Cichowski, R.A. (2011) 'Civil Society and the European Court of Human Rights', in J. Christoffersen and M.R. Madsen (eds.) *The European Court of Human Rights between Law and Politics*. Oxford: Oxford University Press, 77–97.

Conte, C. and Binder, S. (2019) 'Strategic Litigation: The role of EU and international law in criminalising humanitarianism'. Discussion Brief published by ReSOMA (Research Social Platform on Migration and Asylum)

del Valle, H. (2016) 'Search and Rescue in the Mediterranean Sea: Negotiating Political Differences'. *Refugee Survey Quarterly*, 35, 22–40.

Duffy, H. (2018) *Strategic Human Rights Litigation: Understanding and Maximising Impact.* Oxford: Hart Publishing.

Dugard, J. and M. Langford (2011) 'Art or Science? Synthesising Lessons from Public Interest Litigation and the Dangers of Legal Determinism'. *South African Journal on Human Rights*, 27, 39–64.

Fekete, L. F. Webber and A. Edmond-Pettitt (2017) *Humanitarianism: The Unacceptable Face of Solidarity*. London: Institute of Race Relations.

GLAN. (2018) '*Legal action against Italy over its coordination of Libyan Coast Guard pull-backs resulting in migrant deaths and abuse*'. Published 8 May 2018. [online] Legal-action-against-Italy-over-its-coordination-of-Libyan-Coast-Guard-pull-backs-resulting-in-migrant-deaths-and-abuse (Accessed 10th August 2019)

GLAN. (2019) '*Case filed against Greece in Strasbourg Court over crackdown on humanitarian organisations*', 18 April 2019 [online] www.glanlaw.org and single-post and 2019 and 04 and 18 and Case-filed-against-Greece-in-Strasbourg-Court-over-Crackdown-on-Humanitarian-Organisations (Accessed 10th August 2019)

Gleeson, S. (2009) 'From rights to claims: The role of civil society in making rights real for vulnerable workers'. *Law and Society Review*, 43(3), 669–700.

Goldstein, B. (2013) '*The Lawfare Project. Lawfare: The Use of Law as a Weapon of War*', [online] www.thelawfareproject.org and what-is-lawfare.html (Accessed 13th September 2019)

Gordon, N. (2014) "Human Rights as a Security Threat: Lawfare and the Campaign against Human Rights NGOs". *Law and Society Review*, 48, 2, 311–344.

Handmaker, J.D. (2019) 'Researching legal mobilisation and lawfare'. ISS Working Paper Series and General Series (641, 1–19) International Institute of Social Studies of Erasmus University (ISS).

Human Rights at Sea (2019) 'Human Rights at Sea: Briefing Note. Human Rights and International Solidarity: Report of the Independent Expert on Human Rights and International Solidarity with Implications for Human Rights at Sea'. [online] HRAS_ Human_Rights_and_International_Solidarity_Special_Rapporteur_Briefing_Note_ August_2019_SP_LOCKED.pdf. (Accessed 24th September 2019)

InfoMigrants (2019) '*Mare Ionio starts latest rescue mission, sues Italian government*'. [online] mare-ionio-starts-latest-rescue-mission-sues-italian-government (Accessed 28th October 2019)

Jalušič, V. (2019) 'Criminalizing "pro-immigrant" initiatives: Reducing the space of human action'. *Two Homelands* 49, 105–123.

Lesinska, M. (2019) 'Strategic litigation of criminalisation cases', Ask the Expert Policy Brief published by ReSOMA (Research Social Platform on Migration and Asylum)

Maccanico, Y., Haye, S. B. and Kenny, S. (2018) '*The Shrinking Space for Solidarity with Migrants and Refugees: How the European Union and Member States Target and Criminalise Defenders of the Rights of People on the Move*'. Amsterdam: Transnational Institute.

McCann, M. (2006) 'Law and social movements: Contemporary perspectives.' *Annual Review of Law and Social Science*, 2, 17–38.

Open Democracy (2019) '*Hundreds of Europeans 'criminalised' for helping migrants – as far right aims to win big in European elections*' [online] published 18 May 2019 hundreds-of-europeans-criminalised-for-helping-migrants-new-data-shows-as-far-right-aims-to-win-big-in-european-elections and (Accessed 21st May 2019)

Papanicolopulu, I. (2016) 'The duty to rescue at sea, in peacetime and in war: A general overview'. *International Review of the Red Cross*, 98 (2), 491–514.

PICUM (2017) '*Defending Migrants' Rights in the Context of Detention and Deportation*'. Brussels: Synthesis Report.

ReSOMA (2020) '*The criminalisation of solidarity in Europe*' [online] https://www.migpolgrou-com (Accessed 26th September 2020)

SAROBMED (n.d.) '*About Us*' [website] sarobmed.org (Accessed 10th October 2019)

Scott, M. (2015) 'A role for strategic litigation'. *Forced Migration Review*, 49, 47–48.

Tiefenbrun, S. (2010) 'Semiotic definition of lawfare', *Case Western Reserve Journal of International Law*, 43, 1, 29–60.

Trilling, D. (2020) 'How rescuing drowning migrants became a crime'. *The Guardian*, 22 September [online] https://how-rescuing-drowning-migrants-became-a-crime-iuventa-salvini-italy (Accessed 22nd September 2020)

Vegh Weis, V. (2017) 'Criminal selectivity in the United States: A history plagued by class and Race Bias', *DePaul Journal for Social Justice*, 10, 2, 1–31.

Vosyliūtė, L. and Conte, C. (2019) 'Crackdown on NGOs and volunteers helping refugees and other migrants'. Discussion Brief published by ReSOMA (Research Social Platform on Migration and Asylum)

Werner, W. (2010) "The curious career of lawfare". *Case Western Reserve Journal of International Law*, 43, 1, 61–72.

Zaffaroni, R., Caamaño, C., and Vegh Weis, V. (2020) *Bienvenidos al Lawfare*, Buenos Aires: Capital Intelectual.

International Conventions

International Maritime Organisation (IMO), International Convention for the Safety of Life at Sea, 1 November 1974, 1184

International Maritime Organisation (IMO), International Convention on Maritime Search and Rescue, 27 April 1979, 1403 UNTS

International Maritime Organisation (IMO), International Convention on Salvage, 28 April 1989, 1953 UNTS 165

UN General Assembly, Convention on the law of the sea, 10 December 1982

11

MEDIA REPRESENTATION OF BELGIAN YOUTH PROTESTS

The making of "Climate Truants"

Mafalda Pardal, Celine Tack, and Frédérique Bawin

On 2 December 2018, a large climate demonstration mobilized in Brussels at the start of the United Nations Climate Change Conference (COP24 Katowice 2018). About 65,000 participants joined what was, at the time, the largest climate mobilization the country had seen (Wouters & Vydt 2019). Nevertheless, a few days later, Belgium became one of the two countries[1] that voted against the revised EU Directive on energy efficiency.[2] It is against this backdrop that two Flemish high-school students launched "Youth for Climate" on Facebook and invited their fellow students to join them in skipping school and protest in Brussels every Thursday until the Belgian federal elections scheduled for May 2019 (Youth for Climate 2019)[3]. They succeeded in mobilizing a cycle of 20 weeks of protest in the country, which "for Belgian norms [was] an unseen wave of grassroots climate protest" (Wouters & Vydt 2019, para. 9). Similar protests were progressively held by students in a range of other countries, across Europe and beyond (e.g., Australia, Canada, Germany, Switzerland, UK, USA, the Netherlands and Norway). The global climate movement has now spread over 106 nations (Cretney & Nissen 2019, McKnight 2020).

Since the (new) youth climate movement is a recent phenomenon, the available research on the protests is limited. Research in this area has explored, for instance, the tactics of climate activists in terms of their successfulness in contributing to social and political change (e.g., motivating other people in taking climate action, increased educational attention to climate change) (Cretney & Nissen 2019, Thomas, Cretney & Hayward 2019, Wouters, de Vydt & Knops 2019). The young protesters' discourse has also been the focus of research, with a particular focus on discourses of resistance (Holmberg & Alvinius 2020, McKnight 2020). Other research examined the profiles and the motives of the young climate protesters in different countries and cities around the world (Wouters et al. 2019, Wahlström et al. 2019, de Moor, Uba, Wahlström, Wennerhag & de Vydt 2020). The recent studies by Jacobsson (2020) and Bergmann & Ossewaarde (2020) are particularly relevant

DOI: 10.4324/9781003144229-15

to our analysis as the authors carried critical discourse analyses of how the youth climate movement in, respectively, Sweden and Germany have been depicted by mainstream media, and we will return to them when discussing our findings.

Green cultural criminology: a call for a critical analysis of the mediated production of environmental phenomena

Green criminology is a critical perspective that pays attention to activities and behaviors that produce environmental harms (Brisman 2010, Brisman & South 2013, Goyes & South 2017, Lynch 2006, South 1998). While some scholars adhere to a strict definition of what constitutes green crimes (according to the scope of applicable laws), some green criminologists have also focused on harms to the environment, regardless of whether the conducts directly or indirectly contributing to such harms are legal or not (Jarrell, Lynch & Stretesky 2014, Lynch & Stretsky 2003, Potter 2010, White 2014). Green criminology is also interested in the study of activities such as protest or "direct action" initiatives, which have the potential to make a positive impact to the environment but are threatened by criminalization or other forms of repression (Potter 2010). In that regard, South (1998) suggested that green criminologists should examine new social movements and their resistance strategies. As Ellefsen (2012, 182) put it: "much work of the green movements is beneficial, and when such lawful activism is repressed by state institutions or others it deserves scholarly attention".

The media can be one of the institutions enhancing or playing down public concern about environmental issues (White 2008). Indeed, this crime-media nexus has been central in cultural criminology studies which, drawing on labeling theory, have examined how certain forms of behavior and or certain individuals or groups are defined as deviants, and the role of the media in constructing such views (Muzzatti 2006, Zaffaroni 2013). Borrowing from this tradition, Brisman & South (2013) underline the opportunities for cross-fertilization between green criminology and cultural criminology perspectives, focusing for instance on the "mediated" presentations of environmental phenomena, including resistance and demand for changes. However, until now, green criminologists have devoted "relatively little attention to the media and political dynamics surrounding the presentation of various environmental phenomena" (Brisman & South 2013, 11). Our analysis seeks to help fill this research gap, by analyzing whether and how the youth climate protests were portrayed in the Flemish written press.

Methods

Data collection

The youth climate protests in Belgium started on 10 January 2019 and were held on a regular basis until the federal elections on 26 May of that year. To capture the entire period of protests, we started collecting data from the first week of January[4] until 2 June 2019. The searches were conducted on *GoPress*, an online database of

TABLE 11.1 Search results

Initial number of articles	*542*
Excluded articles (e.g., duplicates or irrelevant)	160
Final number of hits included in the analysis	**382**

Belgian newspapers (*Vlaamse Regulator voor de Media* 2018). Considering that: (1) the calls for protest came primarily from Flemish[5] students, and that (2) a pilot search in French-written Walloon newspapers produced a relatively small number of results,[6] we decided to conduct our searches in Dutch only, in a selection of Flemish newspapers. From the eight daily Flemish newspapers, we included six in our analysis. The six chosen newspapers have a combined 85% share of the market in Flanders (*Vlaamse Regulator voor de Media* 2018)[7].

We used a combination of search terms: climate march AND policy, climate protest, climate march AND skipping class,[8] following a phase of testing. In Table 11.1, we offer an overview of the number of search results. After the exclusion of irrelevant and duplicate articles, we arrived at a total of 382 news items for analysis. The coded articles provided information concerning 19 student-led protests and three non-student-led protests (which also counted with student participation).

Data analysis

We conducted a content analysis of this media dataset. This is an approach often applied in media studies as it allows for a systematic analysis of media messages (Hesse-Biber & Leavy, 2011, Krippendorff 2013), with a focus on the characteristics of those materials (such as who says what, to whom) and the identification of themes (Mayring, 2000). To develop the codebook used in the analysis, the first two authors carried a test coding of ten (randomly chosen) newspaper articles. After this pilot coding, we discussed the coding process, the codes used and their content and fine-tuned the codebook until reaching agreement. The revised version of the codebook was brought into *NVivo12* for the analysis of the newspaper articles in the dataset. In the next phase, the first two authors coded the content of the news articles independently, and then compared it, discussing divergences in the coding. Subsequently, that process was repeated with the third author also coding in separate and the research team discussing that process thoroughly until reaching a consensus.

An overview of the dataset

As shown in Figure 11.1, the volume of news production covering the climate protests was not stable throughout the period considered. There were mostly peaks after the first protests and news outlets' interest in covering the story seems to have declined after week ten, when the protests significantly gathered less participants.

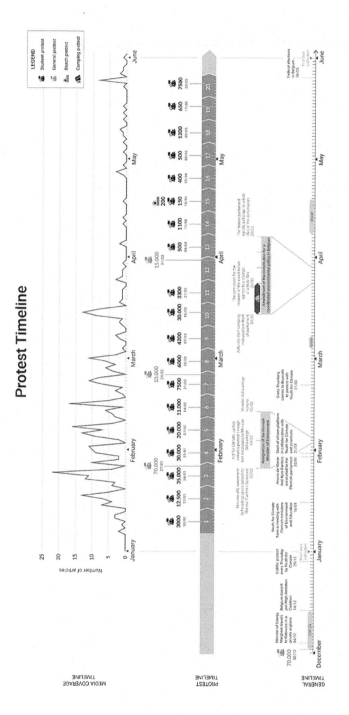

FIGURE 11.1 Timeline of the 2019 youth climate protests in Belgium.

Note: The number of protesters included here is based on the news reporting on the size of the protests

We observed a final peak in the news volume at the very end of the protest cycle, which can be seen in connection with the Belgian federal elections held at the time.

Results

The protests as main event

Offering a description of the protests was the central focus of the majority of the news items in our sample. The Flemish media acknowledged the size and growth of the protests, covered the regional replicas of the national marches in Brussels as well as the international expansion of this youth movement, and the growing support from older students (e.g., from University or College University), or endorsements from other individuals or groups (e.g., Jane Goodall, Leonardo DiCaprio, other adult citizens, school boards). Beyond the weekly marches, we also found some coverage of other protest tactics, including the campaign "sign for my future",[9] or an event where students sought to camp in front of the Parliament in Brussels.[10] Local activities organized by students who were not able to join the main protest events were also featured (e.g., local cleaning up actions, auction of art works or food made by the students to financially support specific climate projects).

The protesters were an important source for the news reporting about the protests, as they were quoted in 177 news articles. Among them, the two young activists who created Youth for Climate in Belgium and set the protests in motion were predominantly featured. Greta Thunberg was mentioned on 59 occasions. Some articles (n=21) seemed to (over-) focus on the leaders of the movement, in some instances idealizing them (using descriptors such as *"climate messiah", "climate icon", "one of the Beatles"* to refer, for instance, to Greta Thunberg's participation in the Belgian events). While this kind of coverage can be seen as positive, it also diverts the attention away from the actual event and claims driving the movement, rather highlighting characteristics of a few of the intervening figures. Politicians' views or responses to the youth climate protests were, to a lesser extent, also included in the media. Among them, the politicians most often mentioned in the newspaper dataset had political responsibilities in relation to the issues at stake (in the field of environment and education). Only a small amount of the articles in our dataset (n=17) were centered on understanding or interpreting the contribution of the youth climate protests for future policies, or what they meant *per se* in terms of social mobilization.

The truancy frames

A recurring theme within our dataset concerned a discussion of whether the protesters, mostly individuals under 18 years old, were entitled to skip school to engage in protest action (this was the main theme of 65 articles)[11]. Article titles illustrate the centrality of this theme, citing students' slogans and banners, including: *"Skipping school? No, fighting for our future"* or *"We skip school because we did our homework, and they didn't"*. Also, institutional actors, such as the Minister of Education, often commented on students' absence from school to participate in the protests. In one of her first reactions, she noted that it was *"positive that young people stand up for climate, but skipping school is not the right method"* (Flemish newspaper *De Standaard*, 15-01-2019, own translation).

The term "truancy" was included 570 times (within 255 news articles), much more often than the word "striking"—which only appeared 63 times in the media items we analyzed. The view opposing the protests claimed that such actions could be organized outside of school hours, while students argued that in that case their actions would have received less attention or would have had less impact. An example of this type of debate is captured in the following dialogue between a reporter and a youth protester: *"Is skipping school the right way to convey that message? 'Would you have been here otherwise?'"* (Flemish newspaper *De Morgen*, 11-01-2019, own translation). As this interaction illustrates as well, the media may have also fed this debate by asking this type of questions.

The implementation of disciplinary action by the schools (or "study punishments")[12] for the students skipping classes was also discussed: we found 62 references to the term across our dataset (within 30 articles)[13]. This debate about whether protesters should skip school to demonstrate in Brussels or in other cities gained another layer when some of the schools took the initiative of organizing or supporting students in attending the marches, in some cases making these compulsory activities. Some of the news reporting characterized this development as: *"the world turned upside down: not being present at the climate march is also skipping school"* or *"skipping school for climate becomes school trip"*. Several article titles played also with the age of participants, infantilizing them—for instance *"Mommy won't let me go to Brussels"* or *"Mommy, can I join the protest?"*. During a week of school holidays, about half of the articles published during that time seemed to question students' actual engagement in the protests, putting forward the idea that during the school holidays the protests also took vacations. Examples of such statements include: *"climate takes (a little) vacation"* or *"it's vacation and climate protests cool down"*.

Beyond the debate about and characterization of the youth protests as "climate truancy", we found other examples of allusion to rule breaking. For instance, a significant portion of the coverage related to the Minister for the Environment, Nature and Agriculture dealt in fact with a controversial statement she made, and which led to her resignation from that post. In a speech to the General Farmers Syndicate (February 2019), the Minister suggested that the student protests were a complot stating that: *"I know who is behind this movement, both of the Sunday demonstrations and the truants on Thursdays. I have been told that by the State Security Service"* (Flemish newspaper *Het Laatste Nieuws*, 05-02-2019, own translation). According to the Minister, the protests were a retaliation by nature organizations. In doing so, the Minister put forward the idea that the protests were a matter for the intelligence services of the country, suggested that the school strikes had a hidden agenda, and again resorted to the language of truancy to characterize the protesters. Additionally, in a few articles, we found reports of protesters leaving garbage behind in the streets. Another example, reported in two articles, relates to a police intervention where a number of students attempting to join the protests were brought back to school from the train station by the police. However, in general, references to police presence at the protests were neutral in tone and often only mentioned with regards to an estimate of the number of protesters and the practical organization of the marches.

What about the climate?

A discussion of climate change issues, its expected consequences or alternative environmental policies was barely addressed in the news covering the climate protests in Belgium. Only a few articles (n=7) were dedicated primarily to discuss climate policy in the country and abroad. The demands for "climate action" voiced by the protesters were the main theme of some of the articles analyzed (n=13). In addition, a group of articles (n=24) focused on concrete initiatives to tackle climate change: including citizens' and protesters' own life choices (e.g., increasingly using public transport, purchasing less clothes, seeking a "zero waste" lifestyle, etc.), policy measures introduced by or discussed within some municipalities (e.g., organizing "plastic free" local markets, buying electric cars and allowing for car sharing, introducing free public transport), or wider proposals (e.g., the amplification of low emission zones in the country, etc.). It is striking that the voices of scientists or other knowledgeable actors about the complexities of climate change and environmental policy were hardly present in the media coverage of the youth climate protests. In our dataset, academics or other scholars were only quoted in 12 articles, but almost none of those were climate scientists.

Discussion

The analysis of the news reporting during this cycle of protests in Belgium offers insights into how the media have dealt with the issue. This is of particular relevance when considering the protests from a green cultural criminology perspective, i.e., critically examining the mediated construction of environmental phenomena—in this case, understanding how protests and protesters calling for increased protection of the environment have been represented in the domestic written press. The protests gathered the gaze of the media for a relatively long period of time. This is remarkable in itself. The youth climate protesters contributed to the news-making of the protests and their voices were often included in the media reports through interviews or citations of their slogans. Although in general the type of protest action developed by the students can be considered as an act of civil disobedience (de Moor, Uba, Wahlström, Wennerhag & de Vydt 2020, Thackeray et al. 2020, Wahlström et al. 2019), no serious public disorder offences were reported by the media. The presence of the police at the protests was also described in neutral terms, and there were no instances of confrontation nor violence.

Nevertheless, the media representation of the youth climate protests was perhaps *not that green*. Content-wise, the news articles paid relatively little attention to substantive issues relevant to the protests and the claims being made by the protesters. Despite the seemingly positive media coverage, most of the reporting focused on describing the protest events *per se*, without offering a more in-depth look into the underlying problems being raised by the protesters. Only a few articles discussed climate change issues. Similarly, and although the students noted the importance of climate policy measures based on scientific research, (climate) experts were barely quoted in the newspapers. This idea of a "light" coverage of the actual issues was also a central finding in a media analysis of youth climate protests in Sweden, as the author noted that: "the event [i.e., protest] is what is made salient, along with the shape, form, location and organization of the strikes", with "the actual social critique" being absent from the news stories (Jacobsson 2020, 8).

Furthermore, a significant part of the media focus lay on students' skipping school to take part in the protests. Not only was this the primary focus of a part of the articles in our dataset, but the theme was also diffusely present in most news articles. There are at least two important implications deriving from this type of representation. The first can be described as an infantilization of the protesters. Their age was often a central element in the reporting, and there were clear attempts to belittle protesters by making humorous references to their need to be granted authorization to travel within the country and join the protests. The seriousness of their engagement with environmental issues was also questioned by the media, especially around the time school holidays took place. Bergmann & Ossewaarde (2020, 283) arrived at a comparable finding in relation to the German media representation of the youth climate protesters. The authors considered that the media used "derogatory ageist language" which ultimately sheds doubt on youth activism.

A second important implication of the focus on the "skipping school" debate, or what Jacobsson refers to as "the pseudo-conflict of whether it is morally defensible to skip school" (2020, 13), relates to the (mediated) construction of the youth climate protests as "climate truancy" and the labeling of protesters as "climate truants". Although the action of students skipping classes to protest was not necessarily portrayed as a negative act, the Dutch term "*spijbelen*" or "truancy" was used manifold—a language that entails a more negative connotation than the perhaps more neutral characterization of "school strike". The media adopted (and to some extent fed the debate using) this language, but also important stakeholders in a position of power seem to have taken a similar approach (i.e., former Minister for the Environment). This narrative diverts the attention from the core concerns that are driving the youth protests and delegitimizes the resistance and the actors of protest. The truancy frame places youth protesters as an outgroup. Bergmann & Ossewaarde consider this a form of "mild criminalization" in the sense that activism is portrayed as absenteeism, as rule breaking: "to question whether it is legitimate to violate the education law (skipping school) for the purpose of protest, mildly criminalizes the youth climate activists" (2020, 273). At the same time, it can also be argued that the particularities of the protest cycle (e.g., age of participants, protest tactics used) and the type of media depiction may have been a double-edged sword. As Holmberg & Alvinius suggest "everyday resistance makes no headlines. However, when a child defies or violates socially constructed rules and conventions such as school attendance and procuring followers all over the world, the action receives major media attention" (2020, 80).

Conclusions

The analysis of the media reporting on the youth climate protests in Belgium did not reveal instances of formal repression or criminalization of the protests nor of the protesters. At first sight, the media coverage of the protests was benign. However, and despite the visibility given to the demonstrations, this mediated construction of the protest action leaves the environmental issues in a secondary place. Moreover, it introduced a more subtle narrative of delegitimization (or "mild criminalization") of the protesters—by creating "climate truants." Our findings seem to resonate with recent analyses of media depictions of youth climate activism in other European countries (e.g., Germany and Sweden). As the protest has increasingly become globalized it will be important to examine how the movement and the youth climate activists are being represented in other regions of the world, and if further or more explicit criminalization is present in other contexts. This may be particularly relevant with regards to the Global South, as some of the most severe impacts of harmful environmental practices are felt in the region (Goyes 2019), and "criminal selectivity" when it comes to environmental issues may be at play (i.e., an over-criminalization of protesters and Indigenous peoples) (Vegh Weis 2019).

Notes

1 The Czech Republic was the other country to vote against the directive, Croatia and Slovakia withheld their vote. All other member states voted in favor of the bill.
2 Directive (EU) 2018 and 2002 of the European Parliament and of the Council of 11 December 2018 amending Directive 2012 and 27 and EU on energy efficiency.
3 Greta Thunberg began skipping school on Fridays to protest outside of the Swedish Parliament beginning in August 2018, being joined by other students (in Sweden and abroad) in what have become known as the 'Fridays for Future' protests.
4 For example, after the announcement by Youth for Climate (29 December 2018) regarding the launch of the protest.
5 Belgium is a federal state, divided into three regions: Flanders, Wallonia and Brussels-Capital. In Flanders the official language is Dutch, in Wallonia the official language is French.
6 The initial search using the same keywords yielded a total of 736 hits in Dutch-written newspapers, against only 128 in francophone newspapers (these are the total figures before checking for duplicates or relevance for the period between 01-01-2019 and 27-02-2019).
7 The two excluded newspapers (*De Tijd* and *Metro*) have arguably less relevance for this study: *De Tijd* is classified as a specialist business newspaper, with limited interest on social issues, *Metro* essentially includes short articles produced by other news agencies (Beckers et al. 2017).
8 In Dutch: klimaatmars AND beleid, klimaatprotest, klimaatmars AND spijbelen.
9 'Sign for my future' was an initiative of *vzw Klimaatmandaat* to bring together citizens, youth, business leaders, non-governmental organizations, the media and academia. They collected signatures demanding action from the next federal and regional governments.
10 On 24 March, together with other environmental organizations, Youth for Climate protested in front of the Parliament in Brussels to pressure the political parties to amend article 7bis of the Constitution. This amendment would be necessary to implement a

coordinated environmental policy in Belgium, but the 2/3 majority required to pass the amendment was not reached.

11 As indicated in the Methods section, although we explicitly run 'skipping class' as keywords, we relied also on a combination of terms that related to policy and climate protest more generally.

12 In the original in Dutch: *"strafstudie"*.

13 In most cases, the students received some form of alternative sanction related to the theme of climate change: they were asked to give a presentation, organize a debate about climate change, brainstorm or propose local climate initiatives, spend extra hours in school to receive lectures about climate, etc.

References

Beckers, K., Masini, A., Sevenans, J., Burg, M.V. D., Smedt, J. D., Bulck, H.V. D., et al. (2017) Are newspapers' news stories becoming more alike? Media content diversity in Belgium, 1983–2013. *Journalism*, 20(12), 1665–1683.

Bergmann, Z., and Ossewaarde, R. (2020) Youth climate activists meet environmental governance: ageist depictions of the FFF movement and Greta Thunberg in German newspaper coverage. *Journal of Multicultural Discourses*, 15(3), 267–290.

Brisman, A. (2010) 'Creative crime' and the phytological analogy. *Crime, Media, Culture, 6*(2), 205–225.

Brisman, A., and South, N. (2013) A green-cultural criminology: An exploratory outline. *Crime, Media, Culture, 9*(2), 115–135.

Cretney, R., and Nissen, S. (2019) Climate politics ten years from Copenhagen: activism, emergencies, and possibilities *Women Talking Politics* (15–19) New Zealand: New Zealand Political Studies Association Te Kāhui Tātai Tōrangapū o Aotearoa.

de Moor, J., Uba, K., Wahlström, M., Wennerhag, M., and de Vydt, M. (2020) Protest for a future II: composition, mobilization and motives of the participants in Fridays for Future climate protests on 20–27 September 2019, in 19 cities around the world. Retrieved 2 April 2020, from https://guub.gu.se/publication/290509

Ellefsen, R. (2012) Green movements as threats to order and economy: Animal activists repressed in Austria and beyond. In R. Ellefsen, R. Sollund and G. Larsen (Eds.), *Eco-Global Crimes: Contemporary Problems and Future Challenges* (181–208) London: Routledge.

Goyes, D.R., (2019) *Southern Green Criminology: A Science to End Ecological Discrimination.* Bingley: Emerald Publishing.

Goyes, D.R., and South, N. (2017) Green criminology before 'Green Criminology': Amnesia and absences. *Critical Criminology, 25*(2), 165–181.

Hesse-Biber, S.N., and Leavy, P. (2011) *The Practice of Qualitative Research.* Thousand Oaks: SAGE Publications.

Holmberg, A., and Alvinius, A. (2020) Children's protest in relation to the climate emergency: A qualitative study on a new form of resistance promoting political and social change. *Childhood, 27*(1), 78–92.

Jacobsson, D. (2020) Young vs old? Truancy or new radical politics? Journalistic discourses about social protests in relation to the climate crisis. *Critical Discourse Studies.*

Jarrell, M.L., Lynch, M.J., and Stretesky, B. (2014) Green criminology and green victimization. In B. A. Arrigo and H.Y. Bersot (Eds.), *The Routledge Handbook of International Crime and Justice Studies* (423–444) Oxon: Routledge.

Krippendorff, K. (2013) *Content Analysis: An Introduction to Its Methodology.* Thousand Oaks: SAGE Publications.

Lynch, J.M. (2006) The greening of criminology: A perspective on the 1990s. In N. South (Ed.), *Green Criminology* (165–169) London: Routledge.

Lynch, M.J., and Stretsky, B. (2003) The meaning of green: Contrasting criminological perspectives. *Theoretical Criminology, 7*(2), 217–238.

Mayring, P. (2000) Qualitative content analysis. *Forum: Qualitative Social Research, 1*(2), art. 20.

McKnight, H. (2020) 'The oceans are rising and so are we': exploring utopian discourses in the school strike for climate movement. *Brief Encounters, 4*(1), 48–63.

Muzzatti, S.L. (2006) Cultural criminology: A decade and counting of criminological chaos. In W.S. DeKeseredy and B. Perry (Eds.), *Advancing Critical Criminology: Theory and Application*, 63–82. Lanham: Lexington Books.

Potter, G. (2010) What is green criminology? *Sociology Review, 20*(2), 8–12.

South, N. (1998) A green field for criminology? A proposal for a perspective. *Theoretical Criminology, 2*(2), 211–233.

Thackeray, S.J., Robinson, S.A., Smith, P., Bruno, R., Kirschbaum, M., Bernacchi, C., et al. (2020) Civil disobedience movements such as School Strike for the CLimate are raising public awareness of the climate change emergency. *Global Change Biology, 26*(3), 1042–1044.

Thomas, A., Cretney, R., and Hayward, B. (2019) Student strike 4 climate: Justice, emergency and citizenshi. *New Zealand Geographer, 75*(2), 96–100.

Vegh Weis, V.V. (2019) Green activism and indigenous claims under the language of criminality: The persecution of argentine indigenous peoples confronting state-corporate environmental harms. *International Journal for Crime Justice, and Social Democracy, 8*(3), 38–55.

Vlaamse Regulator voor de Media. (2018) *Mediaconcentratie in Vlaanderen: Rapport 2018.* Brussel: Vlaamse Regulator voor de Media.

Wahlström, M., Sommer, M., Kocyba, P., de Vydt, M., de Moor, J., Davies, S., … & Buzogany, A. (2019) Protest for a future: composition, mobilization and motives of the participants in Fridays for Future climate protests on 15 March 2019, in 13 European cities. Retrieved 2 April 2020, from https://guub.gu.se/publication/290509

White, R. (2008) *Crimes Against Nature: Environmental Criminology and Ecological Justice.* Devon: Willan Publisher.

White, R. (2014) What is to be done about environmental crime? In B.A. Arrigo and H.Y. Bersot (Eds.), *The Routledge Handbook of International Crime and Justice Studies*, 445–468, Oxon: Routledge.

Wouters, R., de Vydt, M., and Knops, L. (2019) *Klimaatspijbelaars Ontcijferd: Een Beschrijvend Onderzoek Naar De Kenmerken, Drijfveren, Mobilisatie-En Participatiepatronen Van Youth For Climate-Facebooksympathisanten.* Antwerp: University of Antwerp.

Wouters, R., and Vydt, M.D.. (2019) Youth for Climate Belgium: The narrative of an exceptional protest wave. *Mobilizing Ideas* Retrieved 6 November 2019, from https://mobilizingideas.wordpress.com/2019/04/12/youth-for-climate-belgium-the-narrative-of-an-exceptional-protest-wave/

Youth for Climate. (2019) Over ons. Retrieved 6 November 2019, from https://youthforclimate.be/nl/over-ons/

Zaffaroni, E.R. (2013) Estado y seguridad pública: algunas consideraciones básicas. *Metapolitica, 17*(0080), 29–35.

12

CRIMINALIZATION AS STRATEGY OF POWER

The case of Catalunya 2017–2020

Ignasi Bernat and David Whyte

The process of criminalizing people *en masse* has been a continuous feature of the state's capacity to actively produce or fabricate the social order (Neocleous 2000). The logic and practice of criminalization is etched deep into the history of the modern state. Mass criminalization in late medieval Europe appeared as a strategy to uphold property rights, to segregate the poor, to support a class society and to uphold oppressive gender relations (Rusche & Kirchheimer 2003, Sharpe 1982, Smart 1989). This practice spans the long historical continuity between the colonial policing techniques that were evaluated on subjects in the periphery and then brought back to the center (Bell 2013, Brown 2014). As we shall discover later in this chapter, techniques of criminalization enable capitalist states to oscillate between the imposition of naked repression and popular consent-building for the repressive function of the state (Sim et al. 1987).

Precisely the same logics and strategies of criminalization that sought to control landless vagabonds, workers, colonial subjects and migrant people, were developed to simultaneously to control protest and political opposition to the state (Linebaugh 2003). The process of criminalization has always facilitated the production of a range of different "suitable enemies" (Christie 1986) whether they are enemies of the socio-economic order, or enemies of the liberal political order. What unites the criminalization of more overtly political movements and the criminalization used against "street" crime is that both seek a process of de-politicization. Criminalization as a strategy, no matter its targets, always looks to remove political and social content from the acts or types of behavior are criminalized. That is, de-politicizing through criminalization is a tactical state move, a move to displace the conflict from the political to the legal arena. In doing so, it always reduces any immediate crisis of the *social* order (the riot, the protest, the strike) to the level of a threat to *law and* order. This chapter does not argue that criminalization can depolitize struggles. It this is the aim; it is never entirely successful. Rather, it runs at the level of appearance rather

DOI: 10.4324/9781003144229-16

than essence and seeks to *fabricate* the riot, the protest and the strike as "crimes" devoid of political or social content. It does so by hailing the protagonists as "common criminals" and their actions as a threat to a peaceful, law-abiding society. The chapter calls this process "blanket criminalization."

This chapter sets out four key stages in the blanket criminalization of the movement for independence in Catalonia between 2017 and 2020. First, we outline how this social and political struggle emerged. Second, we trace how criminal law categories were applied and enforced to denigrate the leaders of the independence movement, and to discredit their struggle. In the third stage, the state moves to target the most active sections of the population that have the capacity to challenge the status quo. Fourth, we show how criminalization is being normalized as a state strategy. Before we embark on our analysis of those four stages of criminalization in the latter sections of this chapter, we first present an overview of our understanding of the political nature of criminalization as a strategy of power and reflect on how a strategy of blanket criminalization can be readily administered by the contemporary Spanish state.

Criminalization as a strategy of power

If there is one thing that the radical historians of policing and the police have taught us, it is that policing is never solely concerned with law and order, the function of the police in capitalist societies has been a much broader one that regulates social relations. One of the articles of faith in critical criminology is that those who stand outside the law are criminalized, not merely because they threaten the legal order, but because they threaten the *social* order. The reproduction of social class, of oppressive gender roles, and of racism is always predicated on a dichotomy of over- and under-policing (Vitale 2017), or in Vegh Weis (2017) terms, over- and under-criminalization. Whilst the construction of the criminal "other" is part and parcel of modern policing, equally important is the unwillingness to criminalize higher status groups (Alvesalo & Whyte 2007). By upholding particular legal standards over others, and by targeting "dangerous" groups over others, the process of criminalization ensures that the *status quo* is sustained. In capitalist social orders, this means that an equilibrium of social inequality can be upheld through law and lawful means. This is the core function of policing, and individual police officers are well socialized into recognizing the enemies of a peaceful, law-abiding society (Scraton 1987, Corriera & Wall 2018).

The origins of a unified police force in European states are partly found in the need to control a growing urban working class that might threaten both property rights and the *commercial* order. Indeed, the origins of the various forms of law enforcement organization that we now refer to as "police" are found in the market, the factory, the docks and in the railways (Harcourt, 2011). The newly uniformed police forces that enforced the criminal codes and new common law doctrines that emerged in Europe in the late 18th century were necessary to secure the rocky social transition from feudalism to capitalism (Melossi 2008). Property laws, vagrancy laws, rent laws and the laws of the workplace required new forms of magistracy and police to uphold them and ensure that this social transition was viable (Emsley 2001). Modern police forces thus have their roots in a process of rapid anomic transition to a new economic and social order. The role of police in contemporary liberal democratic states is, in the current phase of late capitalism, nominally more defensive: its priority is to keep the social order as secure as possible. This is why we see no difference between the basic process of criminalization that has been applied to "street" criminals, or to resistance movements and movements of political opposition. In its application of strategies of criminalization, the state is not interested in the objective threat of "crime" or "harm" that it targets: rather, it is interested in the potential that its targets have to threaten the *status quo*.

Of course, the process of criminalization adopts a myriad of different forms, but it is always a strategy of power. And because it is always a strategy of power, campaigns of criminalization must be understood within the particular moment of political and social power they emerge from. Policing generally seeks order: not just order in the immediate moment, but a lasting order, an order that must observe a lasting obedience to power. In doing so, it is part of the core function of policing to re-define any riot, protest, mass demonstration or strike as a threat to law and order. Through criminalization, political protest becomes amenable to definition as any number of offences that have no apparent "political" character: public affray, looting or assault (Dadusc 2020). Yet the overall aim of criminalization in *political* situations is not to punish individual citizens for individual legal transgressions. Rather, the purpose is to enforce a blanket criminalization, i.e., a means of imposing control on a large group of people at the same time.

Our concept of blanket criminalization set out in this chapter resembles, but is distinct from, the process of "net-widening" described by Cohen (1985). The latter concept refers to an intended or unintended tendency in Western criminal justice systems to expand its punitive capacity even when initiatives or strategies are "decarceral" or "diversionary". For the targets of those initiatives, the very fact of being known to or processed by the authorities, even in ways that seek diversions from custody or "criminalization", have the effect of expanding the targets that are brought into the "net" of the totality of criminal justice institutions. By being drawn into the "net" of criminal justice, even where this is via explicitly decriminalizing initiatives, still ensures that more people come to the attention of and are processed by the criminal justice system. The final result is, no matter the intentions of state servants, or the architects of such initiatives, more, rather than less, criminalization. Our description of blanket criminalization is quite different. In this description, the criminal justice system looks for very deliberately and consciously to widen its net—not indiscriminately—but in very politically targeted ways. This is not indiscriminate "net widening", but very discriminate "net-casting."

Strategies of blanket criminalization involve a disproportionate use of power and police violence. This use of force by the police tend to escalate public protests. States also tend to use blanket criminalization to cultivate more generalized support for their strategy, bolstering its hegemonic ability to mobilize public opinion against the target group. This may be in the form of cultivating the *primary re-definition* of protestors as deviants in public discourse (Hall et al. 1978), or cultivating support from professional groups such as judges, to mobilize their capacity for intellectual leadership (Ciocchini & Khoury 2018). Paradoxically, then, blanket criminalization provokes popular resistance at the same time as it builds consent for the use of violence against suitable enemies. The Spanish state's response to the Catalan referendum of 2017 supplies a clear illustration of how this paradox comes into play.

Political criminalization and the Spanish state

The starting point for any analysis of the current moment of political and social conflict in Catalonia today, is, as we have pointed out elsewhere, the transition to democracy in 1978 that followed the end of the Franco regime (Bernat & Whyte 2019a). The deep constitutional legacy of Franco profoundly shaped the Catalan conflict. This legacy includes the prominence given to the Monarchy, as the official head of the army and the military in elevating the constitutional principle of Spanish unity. The Spanish Monarchy, after all, was restored by Franco to preserve his legacy (Bernat & Whyte 2019b). A core part of this legacy is that the military occupies a position of cultural and political pre-eminence in Spain. The most recent example of this came with the Covid-19 crisis: the key messages on public safety and public rules were communicated in nightly broadcasts at the initial stages of the pandemic by army generals and military leaders alongside elected politicians. The elevation of those institutions above the rights of ordinary citizens is a direct continuity with the fascist "Principles of the National Movement" (Taibo 2014).

The legal apparatuses of the state have played a significant role in the institutional continuity of Franco's structures of power within the Spanish state. Of particular significance to the constitutional continuity of Franco has been the replication of the way that political control is exerted over the national courts. The Spanish Constitutional Court, for example, is not a jurisdictional body, it is not part of the judicial system, nor is it regulated by the same law that regulates judges and magistrates. Its members do not have to be accredited judges and are chosen directly by the organs of government (the Spanish parliament, central executive and the administrative body for the courts). As we shall see in the following section of this chapter, the Constitutional Court has played a deeply political role in provoking and amplifying the current conflict.

The Audiencia Nacional is the court responsible for starting the prosecution of the nine Catalan political leaders before their cases are passed to the Supreme Court for trial. This court was created in the image of Franco's notorious Public Order Tribunal. The judges are political appointees, the court explicitly deals with issues of conflict considered to be of national significance. The court's authority was established before the 1978 Constitution, having been established by Royal Decree in 1977. It assumes jurisdiction over cases affecting the Spanish nation due to their relevance or scale of threat. The Audiencia Nacional therefore tends to assume jurisdiction over organized crime, significant corruption or financial crimes and crimes of political violence such as terrorism or crimes against the crown. The Audiencia Nacional is therefore a court with a political purpose that predates the Constitutional legal architecture. It is for those reasons that this court can be said to have a distinctly *political* role. This role has been played out in the targeting of Basque political leaders and a string of highly controversial political convictions over the past three decades (Bernat & Whyte 2019b). In a case involving Basque political prisoners in 2018, the European Court of Human Rights found the Audiencia Nacional in violation of Article 6 of the European Convention, which enshrines the right to a fair trial. It was the Audiencia Nacional that ultimately initiated the charges of "rebellion" against the political leaders and supervised the trial of Catalan government officials and the head of the Catalan police force, the Mossos d'Esquadra, for their role in the referendum.[1] The crime of rebellion, used to detain the 12 political leaders, was established in 1900, is the offense specifically revived by Franco to persecute thousands of opponents using his military courts.

The political and institutional structure of Franco's legacy—a phenomenon we call post-Fascism (Bernat & Whyte 2019a)—relies heavily on the state's repressive ability in law to secure the social order. The legal and political apparatuses that are so infused with Franco's legacy continue to shape social relations in Spain. If there is one dominant internal legal logic that binds ruling elites to a specific liberal capitalist project—uniting the armed forces, the monarchy, the financial and corporate class and the criminal justice system—it is the idea that the centrifugal purpose of the state is to defend "Spanish unity" (Bernat & Whyte 2020). Those who threaten or challenge Spanish unity are therefore understood as threatening the entire liberal capitalist project. It is this logic, supported by a highly politicized legal system, that enabled a strategy of blanket criminalization to be mobilized in Catalonia in 2017. In the following sections, we analyze four distinct stages of this strategy.

Stage 1: The emergence of a social and political struggle

The Catalan demand for independence came at the high point of a more general crisis of social and economic conditions. In summary, those conditions were: austerity and fiscal crisis, rising inequality, unemployment, housing evictions, repressive state practices the denial of political autonomy, the denial of political expression (Bernat & Whyte 2019a). This social and political crisis created the conditions that made a challenge to the legitimacy of state power inevitable. This challenge found its expression in a range of social movements (anti-austerity, anti-fascist, anti-evictions, feminist and other solidarity movements) all of which were formative in the rise of a "secessionist" movement for political independence.

A plethora of social protests gave momentum to the *Indignados* movement, which appeared as part of the worldwide Occupy movement in 2011. The housing movement physically blocked evictions: the unemployed workers' movement marched to occupy land and collectivize essential products covering basic needs, demonstrations were organized at the homes of the politicians responsible for those harmful social measures, and, in June 2011, the Catalan Parliament was blocked by anti-austerity protestors forcing the Catalan president to enter via helicopter. Following this demonstration, eight protestors were sentenced to three years of imprisonment (SCS 459/2019 14 October).

Criminalization therefore was a central aspect of the Spanish state's strategy to neutralize opposition to austerity. Since 2011, a number of key reforms in criminal law and the criminal justice system have been introduced to provide legal support to this strategy. Amendments to the Criminal Code and a Law of Citizen Security (known widely as the "Gag Law") introduced new restrictions on the right to protest and political expression in the wake of the financial crisis and the social unrest that ensued (Oliver et al. 2015). Like other European nations, Spain has used anti-terrorism laws widely to criminalize domestic political protests (Bergalli 1997, Brandariz 2007, Jiménez 2019).

This pushback against specific social measures taken by the Catalan Parliament was coupled to a more general undermining of autonomy. In 2010, the Constitutional Court had revoked key elements of the Catalan autonomous statute even after they had been ratified by both the Catalan and Spanish parliaments and validated by the Catalan population in a referendum. The resultant demonstration against the sentence brought more than a million protestors onto the streets under the slogan "We are a nation. We decide". The combination of those decisions by the Constitutional Court certainly helped to give momentum to the independence movement and provoked a series of demonstrations that brought similar numbers onto the streets every year, providing the strength that culminated in the referendum of 1 October 2017.

It is important to note that both of those related movements—the Indignados and the supporters of Independence—experienced criminalization in different forms. The Indignados movement faced police brutality on countless occasions and forced eviction from *Puerta del Sol* in Madrid and *Plaça Catalunya* in Barcelona. They also faced numerous examples of police violence as they occupied buildings and health centers to avoid their closure or indeed blocked evictions. The Independence movement, on the other hand, faced police brutality for the first time on the day of the 2017 referendum. Since then, the movement has faced an ongoing, systematic process of criminalization. It is how this process has played out that is the concern of the rest of this chapter.

Stage 2: Criminalization attacks the head

In the run-up to the 2017 Catalan referendum, websites were closed down, ballot papers were seized by the millions, and post was intercepted and confiscated. The extremity of Spain's response to the referendum was remarkable. Human Rights Watch's (2017) assessment of the police violence of 1 October 2017 concluded that Spanish police engaged in excessive force when "using batons to hit non-threatening protesters and causing multiple injuries." Subsequently, Amnesty International has condemned the trial of the 12 political leaders, arguing that it "contravenes the principle of legality and permits the imposition of disproportionate restrictions on conduct" (Amnesty International 2019, 1). The UN Working Group on Arbitrary

Detention had previously demanded the release of political prisoners. (Reuters, 19 May 2019). In other words, two of the largest human rights NGOs, along with a key UN body have explicitly accused Spain of committing state crimes in its repression of the Catalan self-determination movement. This condemnation has been replicated in a ruling of the EU Court of Justice that the Spanish Supreme Court had no right to judge neither condemn Oriol Junqueras, the vice-president of the Catalan Government during the referendum, due to his subsequent election to the European Parliament. The Court of Justice therefore declared the verdict of 14 October against him null and void and ordered the Spanish Court to release him. At the time of writing, 11 months after the Court of Justice ruling, the Spanish Supreme court has refused to do so.

The Spanish Attorney General started the legal process against two civil society leaders of the largest civil organizations leading the independence movement in the days before the referendum. Those leaders, Jordi Sànchez and Jordi Cuixart were accused of sedition after a crowd protested against a police raid at the Catalan Department of Economy on 20 September. The raid, under the name Operation Anubis was investigating if public money had been used in the preparation of the referendum, a purpose has already been defined as illegal by the Spanish courts. The legal procedure against Sànchez and Cuixart was initiated by the Audiencia Nacional. On 16 October, two weeks after the referendum of 1 October, and the biggest general strike in recent Catalan history on 3 October, Jordi Sànchez and Jordi Cuixart were sent to prison. On 2 November, ten members of the Catalan government that had not already gone into exile were accused of "rebellion" and sent to prison by the Audiencia Nacional. Their crime was signing the declaration of independence for Catalonia.

To describe the acts and motivations of those leaders as "criminal" is a strategy that seeks to denigrate the social and political legitimacy of their struggle and bolster the legitimacy of the Spanish state (a core function of the state, after all, is to control criminals) to use force. However, criminalizing the leaders of the opposition can only ever be a *partial* strategy. This is first because the targeting of individual, high profile leaders, especially if they are charismatic, risks creating symbolic heroes that strengthen grassroots movements. Second, to defeat renegade or counter-hegemonic movements, it is never enough to target the leaders, because they are not the source of the movement's power. And it is for this reason that the Spanish state has generalized the strategy of criminalization.

Stage 3: Criminalization attacks the roots

The sentences imposed against the nine of the 12 political leaders on 14 October 2019 fueled the conflict further. The police violence that followed over the ensuing weeks created a conveyor belt of more political prisoners, many of whom may go to jail for their participation in public demonstrations. A total of 712 town mayors were charged with "assisting the referendum," and many were detained for questioning by the police. The Committees to Defend the Referendum (CDRs)—the grassroots networks organized on the grounds to ensure that the polling stations and ballot boxes were not seized by the police—faced the full force of anti-terrorist laws. On 23 September 2019, the Audiencia Nacional launched Operation Judas, which mobilized no fewer than 500 officers from the national police force, the Guardia Civil, to arrest 11 people accused of terrorism, possession of explosive material and planning bomb attacks. Nine of the 11 arrestees were sent to prison and seven of them spent several months in isolation.

CDR activists and other independence movement activists have also faced very large fines using administrative laws, a huge number of criminal charges have been brought against protestors for civil disobedience actions, and two local town mayors were arrested at their houses, without judicial orders, after being accused of taking part in demonstrations. In April 2018, two other members of the CDRs were accused of terrorism by the Audiencia Nacional. One of them escaped and flew into exile. The other was sent to prison, later released, and then placed on house arrest. It was in the latter case that the amendment to the Criminal Code noted above was used for the first time. The case invoked Amendment 559, which stipulates a prison sentence of up to one year for sharing images or information, by any media, that leads others to commit a public order offense. Tamara Carrasco was the first person ever taken in front of the courts for this offense. She was subsequently found innocent.

After the sentences of the nine political leaders were announced, a wave of direct-action protests emerged, organized by a new civil disobedience organization, Tsunami Democratic. Perhaps most famously, Tsunami Democratic organized the mass protest that blocked Barcelona airport on 14 October 2019 for several hours. They were also involved in other peaceful civil disobedience actions, for example, working with the CDRs to support the General Strike in Catalunya on 18 October by blocking roads across the French and Spanish border into Catalunya. During those weeks of popular unrest, 29 people were sent to prison. The overtly political nature of those detentions was revealed when it was disclosed that the Attorney General passed an instruction to state prosecutors to seek imprisonment for all those who were arrested during those protests. At the time of writing, one is still in prison, and another has been deported to Morocco. Overall, since 2012 at least 2,800 have been imprisoned, arrested, charged, or sued by the courts of justice for their relationship in one way or another to the independence movement. Between September 2017 and December 2019 there were 308 people from the independence movement arrested. If the aim of this process of criminal and civil harassment was to intimidate the independence movement and prevent mass protests prior to the sentencing of the political prisoners, it can hardly be said to have been successful. But if the aim was to create an ideological climate linking the independence struggle to terrorism, thereby justifying the imposition of harsh sentences on the leaders of the movement, then it was clearly more successful.

In Spain, the intensification of criminalization techniques against social movements did not arrive with the Catalan conflict, or indeed, with the anti-austerity movement. Here we distinguish the criminalization of social movements from other Spanish government initiatives to combat political rebellion, such as the long conflict in the Basque Country. However, we would argue that the war against ETA also revealed similar characteristics: it connected an explicit strategy to isolate and target movement leaders, and members of the armed militia, to a more general strategy of criminalizing civil society organizations and movements. As we note above in a very different context, this was done because targeting leaders and the militia alone risked the creation of creating symbolic heroes or martyrs. But in the Basque Country, as in Catalonia, more recently, the strategy of criminalization has also sought to neutralize the elements of the independence movement that connect the social and political dimensions of the struggle. This is why there has been a concerted attempt to target and criminalize a much wider group of elements stretching across the Basque Abertzale Left, including elements that were never connected to armed struggle.

Stage 4: Normalization of criminalization

The tactical movement of criminalization has allowed the state to change the parameters of the debate, which is no longer about the mandate or the demand for independence, but the "threat" of the enemy. Today is no longer possible to represent the independence struggle in the Spanish media as a viable project. This is not to assume that the state it is a monolithically and unidimensional actor but to show that its core elements, the Monarchy, the judiciary and the repressive apparatuses personified in the Guardia Civil, the Spanish National Police and the military, emerged in a moment of deep constitutional crisis to fully exercise and reassert the state's sovereign power through criminalization.

In the Catalan case, we have witnessed a transformation in the repressive practices of the state. The scale and intensity of the police operation in Catalunya in 2017 is unrivalled in recent European history. No similar movement in the past 40 years has seen anything like this level of confrontation on the streets or this level of criminalization. The high judiciary, the state prosecution authorities and the police broadened the interpretations of existing legal precepts. This is highlighted by the suspension of normal legal procedures that prevent the political prisoners from being released on two counts. First, the Attorney General applied to suspend the rights of those prisoners to attend work for limited periods outside the prison, and in doing so ignored all legal precedent. Second, the so-called "third regime of imprisonment" covering parole has been suspended. The Supreme Court, the sentencing court, claimed exceptional powers over parole and early release, by assuming jurisdiction over the prison board. This disrupts a regime of due process that has existed for 40 years of Spain's constitutional democracy. Other examples of this transformation include police raids against activists, journalists and mayors without judicial warrant, as occurred in Girona in January 2018, and the grotesque fabrication of terrorist cases against social movement activists linked to the CDRs and Tsunami Democratic, even though they have never resorted to violence.

The decision of the Supreme Court to uphold the disqualification from office of the elected Catalan President Quim Torra in September 2020 (the court upheld an 18-month period of disqualification for refusing to withdraw pro-independence symbols in the government headquarters *Palau de la Generalitat*) is highly significant. Torra's disqualification signals that the "head" of the movement may face an ongoing process of criminalization. However, there are even stronger signals that the criminalization of the wider, grassroots, movement will continue, and even intensify. In late 2020, several members of the anti-capitalist and pro-independence political party CUP were placed under investigation by the courts, just for participating in the Yes campaign during the 1 October referendum. The public attorney has indicated that they could be prosecuted for misuse of public funds, an offence punishable up to a maximum of four years in prison.

Conclusions

We have argued that the repression of political dissent has been revealed as a core function of the criminal justice system in Spain. As we set out in the first section of this chapter, the function of the police in capitalist societies is not narrowly concerned with "law and order" but captures a much deeper role in securing the social order. Blanket criminalization has always been a core state function, meeting the practical need to enforce property rights and public order, and to uphold a divided and contradictory economic and social order. In Catalonia, this function has been fully revealed in the repression of the independence movement, a movement which threatens the unity of Spain, and therefore the threatens the deeply divided social order that Spanish statehood protects and serves (Bernat & Whyte 2020).

We propose that *all* strategies of mass criminalization, even when they are not directed at political opposition, have a tendency to follow the same four stages set out in this chapter. First, the emergence of an issue of social and political contest or crisis makes repressive state apparatuses appear more necessary and their core function for securing power more visible. This stage might encompass a range of perceived or real threats to the social order: rioting, terrorism, "gang violence", mugging, people trafficking, benefit or tax fraud, "illegal migration", and so on. Those issues are likely to be portrayed as more pressing or immediate, or more of a threat to the social order, when the popular legitimacy of the state is low or is fragile. Normally, such issues are more easily portrayed as "threats" amid anomic or sudden changes in social and political conditions.

Second, the state uses criminal law categories to focus on a narrow group that are deemed responsible for the problem. They may be folk devils, as in the sense of a classical moral panic, or they may be the demonized leaders of gangs, or political movements and so on (Cohen, 2002). Every strategy of criminalization needs its visible symbolic "head". Symbolic targets are likely to be portrayed as relatively powerful even if they are not ("human traffickers", organized begging cartels, leaders of riots and so on). To describe the acts and motivations of those figures as "criminal" removes the social and political context of the conflict and anomic change underlying the conditions that shape "criminal" acts and processes. This, in turn, bolsters the legitimacy of the state's authority.

In the third stage, the state moves to target a wider body of individuals that are claimed to be in involved in the criminal activity. In the context of migration, this means widening the categories of migrants that should be targeted and targeting those officials who are perceived to be tolerating illegal migration or not helping the state (as in the measures introduced in the UK to create a "hostile environment" for migrants). In the context of gangs, this means loosening evidence rules to ensure that those associated with gang leaders or activities can be criminalized (as in the UK joint enterprise laws). In the context of terrorism, that means broadening the range of groups defined as "terrorism" (in the UK, the struggle over the definition of the Kurdish political movement, the PKK, is an example of this).

Fourth, the exceptional rules and practices introduced to deal with temporary crises become permanent, those exceptional powers (or *primary criminalization*, Becker 1991, Vegh Weis 2017) are retained by the state to deal with future problems that arise. This not only bolsters the state's repressive powers, but this reserve capacity of primary criminalization enables future strategies of blanket criminalization to be more easily mobilized and therefore more easily removed of their social and political content. In this sense, what we have described as a process relating to a very particular set of circumstances, is in fact a process that is mobilized in all other forms of criminalization.

In Catalonia, criminal laws, the courts and enforcement agents have embarked upon a remarkably intensive campaign to de-legitimize the struggle for independence. It is so intensive that it threatens the political integrity of the Spanish state itself. Behind the strategy of criminalization, therefore, there is an attempt to secure a particular political order to guarantee a particular social order.

Note

1 Josep Lluís Trapero, head of the Mossos d'Esquadra was removed from his post in October 2017 and accused of colluding with the Catalan government during the independence referendum. He was subsequently acquitted of wrongdoing by the Audiencia Nacional in November 2020.

References

Alvesalo, A. and Whyte, D. (2007) Eyes Wide Shut: The police investigation of safety crimes, *Law and Social Change*, 48.1–2: 57–72.

Amnesty International (2019) Spain: Analysis of the Supreme Court's Ruling in the Case of Catalan Leaders, 19 November, Index number: EUR 41/1393/2019

Becker, H. (1991) *Outsiders: Studies in Sociology of Deviance*, New York: Free Press.

Bell, E. (2013) Normalising the exceptional: British colonial policing cultures come home, *Mémoire(s), identité(s), marginalité(s) dans le monde occidental contemporain*, 10.

Bergalli, R. (1997) The new order in Spain and an Hispanic perspective on the history and meaning of social control. In: Sumner, C. and Bergalli, R. (eds.) *Social Control and Political Order*. London: Sage, 34–51.

Bernat, I. and Whyte, D. (2019a) Postfascism in Spain: The struggle for Catalonia, *Critical Sociology*, 46, 4–5: 761–776.

Bernat, I. and Whyte D. (2019b) Catalonia, postfascism and popular sovereignty. In: Bernat, I. and Whyte, D. (eds.) *Building a New Catalonia: Self-determination and Emancipation.* Barcelona and Edinburgh: Pol-len Edicions and Bella Caledonia, 23–70.

Bernat, I. and Whyte, D. (2020) Spain must be defended: Explaining the criminalization of political dissent in Catalonia, *State Crime,* 9(1) 100–117.

Brandariz, J.A. (2007) *Política Criminal de la Exclusión.* Granada: Comares.

Brown, M. (2014) *Penal Power and Colonial Rule,* London: Routledge.

Christie, N. (1986) Suitable enemy. In: Bianchi, H. and van Swaaningen, R. (eds.) *Abolitionism: Towards a Non-Repressive Approach to Crime.* Amsterdam: Free University Press.

Ciocchini, M. and Khoury, S. (2018) A gramscian approach to studying the judicial decision-making process, *Critical Criminology,* 26, 75–90.

Cohen, S. (1985) *Visions of Social Control,* Cambridge: Polity.

Cohen, S. (2002) *Folk Devils and Moral Panics,* London: Routledge.

Corriera, D. and Wall, T. (2018) *Police: a field guide,* London: Verso.

Dadusc, D. (2020) Criminalizing activist spaces: privatisation, public order, and moral order. In: Turner, B., Wolf, H., Fitzi, G. and Mackert, J. (eds.) *Urban Change and Citizenship in Times of Crisis: Figurations of Conflict and Resistance.* London: Routledge.

Emsley, C. (2001) The origins and development of the police, In: McLaughlin, E. and Muncie, J. (eds.) *Controlling Crime,* London: Sage.

Hall, S., Critcher, C., Jefferson, T., Clarke, J., and Roberts, B. (1978) *Policing the Crisis: mugging the state and law and order,* London: MacMillan.

Harcourt, B. (2011) *The Illusion of Free Markets: Punishment and the Myth of Natural Order,* Cambridge Mass.: Harvard University Press.

Human Rights Watch (2017) Spain: Police Used Excessive Force in Catalonia.

Jiménez, F.D. (2019) *Market-State-Prison: Under Neo-Liberalism.* London: EG Press and OSPDH.

Linebaugh, P. (2003) *The London Hanged: Crime and Civil Society in the Eighteenth Century,* London: Verso.

Melossi, D. (2008) *Controlling Crime, Controlling Society: thinking about crime in Europe and America,* Cambridge: Polity Press.

Neocleous, M. (2000) *The Fabrication of Social Order: A Critical Theory of Police Power,* London: Pluto.

Oliver, P., Martín, O., Maroto, M. and Domínguez, A. (2015) Ciudades de Excepción: Burorrepresión e infrapenalidad en el estado de seguridad. In: García, S. and Ávila, D. (eds.) *Enclaves de Riesgo: Gobierno neoliberal, desigualdad y Control Social.* Madrid: Traficantes de Sueños, 229–250.

Reuters Staff (2019) *Spain told by U.N. body to free jailed Catalan separatists,* May 29, https://www.reuters.com/article/uk-spain-un-catalonia-idUKKCN1SZ1Z1

Rusche, G. and Kirchheimer, O. (2003) *Punishment and Social Structure,* New Brunswick: Transaction.

Scraton, P. (1987) *The State of the Police,* London: Pluto.

Sharpe, J.A. (1982) The history of crime in late medieval and early modern England: A review of the field, *Social History,* 7, 2.

Sim, J., Scraton, K. and Gordon, M. (1987) Introduction: Crime, the state and critical analysis, In: Scraton, K. (ed.) *Law, Order and the Authoritarian State,* Milton Keynes: Open University Press.

Smart, C. (1989) *Feminism and the Power of Law,* London: Routledge.

Taibo, C. (2014) *Sobre el nacionalismo español.* Madrid: Catarata.

Vegh Weis, V. (2017) *Marxism and Criminology: A History of Criminal Selectivity.* Chicago: Haymarket.

Vitale, A. (2017) *The End of Policing,* London: Verso.

13

NOTES FROM THE FIELD I

State denial to harass the messengers: The case of OSPDH/SIRECOVI

Alejandro Forero-Cuéllar and Daniel Jiménez-Franco

Negacionismo de estado que persigue al mensajero

El caso del OSPDH/SIRECOVI

Alejandro Forero-Cuéllar & Daniel Jiménez-Franco

In his book *States of Denial*, Stanley Cohen distinguished three ways to deny barbarism or atrocity. *Literal* denial rejects the fact itself. *Interpretive* denial does not reject what happened but formulates a reinterpretation of the fact. *Implicative* denial does not reject the fact or its interpretation, but its effects. Denial is a relevant sociological phenomenon that justifies impunity, amnesia and forgetfulness, but its implications depend on whether the responsibility lies with an individual, a group, or the state.

"There is no torture in Spain"; "What happened can't be depicted as torture but as regulatory use of the minimum indispensable force"; "Interventions have been undertaken principles of consistency, appropriateness and proportionality"; "There is no torture in Spain and, if anything, isolated cases are being investigated to the very end". This is precisely the way that state authorities usually *deny* the evidence of torture and ill-treatment according to Cohen's three categories: this *state of denial* shields the state powers from the existence of that state crime. *State* denial is therefore more serious than that of private individuals, because the first is performative: it creates (negative) reality through a grievous exercise of symbolic violence that reinforces institutional violence.

We keep on being told that "there is no torture within the Spanish state", but that same state has already been condemned up to ten times by the European Court of Human Rights (ECHR). In one of its last rulings (*Portu Juanenea and Sarasola Yarzabal v. Spain, 2018*), the ECHR goes further than in the eight previous judgments, not only stating that the Kingdom of Spain had violated its Article 3 (*prohibition of*

DOI: 10.4324/9781003144229-18

inhuman or degrading treatment) in procedural terms (that is, *insufficient investigation of a complaint of torture*), but also that Spain may have materially violated this article, which means that such mistreatment *could have happened*. The judge of the *Audiencia Nacional* [National High Court], who had not investigated these complaints of torture for which Spain was finally sentenced, is Fernando Grande-Marlaska, current Minister of Home Affairs, and this is not the only case: five of those ten ECHR rulings point to the current head of the security forces and bodies, intelligence services, migration detention centers and all state prisons (except those in Catalonia).

When we are told "any eventual case of malpractice is investigated to the very end", they might be referring to gubernatorial *pardons*. Most of the few sentences for torture or ill-treatment imposed by the Spanish courts have been resolved through pardons. All successive governments of PP and PSOE have shamelessly applied this "solution" to half of 62 sentences imposed on police officers. They also pardoned the senior officials who were found liable for GAL's[1] state terrorism in the 1980s, and General Armada—one of the ideologues of the 23-F (1981) attempted putsch[2]. Another landmark in this kingdom of oblivion is the fact that so many of those individuals convicted for mistreatment have ended up being awarded and decorated by the state authorities.

The Kingdom of Spain is shocked when we talk about torture. However, a report by the Basque Government (2017) compiled a list of 4,113 cases of torture and ill-treatment committed between 1960 and 2014[3]. Likewise, the 50 entities and Human Rights groups comprising the State Coordinator for the Prevention and Reporting of Torture recorded over 9,000 people affected by attacks, torture and ill-treatment[4] in its 14 years of existence. Although these horrific figures are well-known (and far lower than the real numbers), *states of denial* encourage and legitimize these actions. Too many politicians, judges, prosecutors and security officials keep taking our reports—thus, our work and our mere existence as human rights defenders—as an unlawful attack on their honor and reputation.

It is within this context that our colleague and teacher, Iñaki Rivera, director of the Observatory of the Penal System and Human Rights [OSPDH] of the University of Barcelona, faced criminal charges in 2018 after speaking about the existence of torture and ill-treatment deals in prisons in a program on Catalan public television. He faced complaints lodged by some unions of prison workers referring to an alleged crime of libel and slander against a whole professional body.

These attacks are longstanding. Everything started in 2004, when the OSPDH brought to light the beatings of numerous inmates by dozens of prison guards after a riot in *Quatre Camins* Catalan prison. Some civil servants' unions launched a criminalization campaign against Iñaki and the OSPDH. In addition, the General Directorate of Prisons banned the OSPDH from visiting its penitentiary facilities, but a judicial process would end up condemning, in 2013, several officials and the medical deputy director, who also beat the injured prisoners as they entered the prison infirmary—this medical deputy director belongs to *Comisiones Obreras* (*CCOO*), the same union that would retake and lead the persecution against Iñaki five years later.

Since the events of 2004, the entry ban on OSPDH members and the harassment campaign by some union leaders lasted over ten years. The turning point came in March 2015, when Iñaki tried to visit a prisoner who was very ill after a long hunger strike. Following his request, a warning signal in the system showed that he was personally banned from entering prison, and this gave rise to a report by the *Síndic de Greuges* [Catalan Ombudsman] that denounced this veto before the Catalan Parliament.

As a result of these events, the OSPDH decided to work on a new strategy to register cases of institutional violence, a rapid reaction system that could receive and share any information with national/international institutions and entities, so the victims could be given a more effective protection. This is how the *SIRECOVI* project (System for the Registration and Communication of Institutional Violence[5]) started operating in December 2016, with the endorsement of the then UN Special Rapporteur against Torture. It was also helpful to count on the goodwill and change of criteria by the General Secretary of Penal Measures, Rehabilitation and Attention to Victims, since it gave us permission to visit all prisoners who may request it. This has been essential for our work, although our return to the prisons has not gone unnoticed by the most reactionary sectors of the prison unions—who not only direct their attacks on us but also against the secretary general and the Catalan Justice Office.

The last stage in this long and grim story starts with the criminal complaints initiated by CCOO union's prison officers' section. This decision, which can only be understood within fierce union competition among prison workers, entailed many internal problems of external de-legitimization and disaffiliation for the union. This new attack on Iñaki as a gesture to "defend their honor" was made in the midst of an electoral process, and this union battle to prove "who is tougher" is evident from a statement released by CSIF union on 12 September 2019: "We were the first to take the step and we will reach the very end. We are pleased to see that other union forces undertake similar actions"[6]. "The very end"! Again! Doesn't it sound too familiar? After CCOO's denouncement (which finally withdrew its accusation) came a complaint from the ACAIP association of prison officers, but the Provincial Court of Barcelona ordered the dismissal of the criminal case opened against Rivera in July 2020, after 20 months of persecution.

When everything seemed to be over, a fourth complaint signed by over 100 officers under the cover of *Marea Blava* ["Blue Tide"][7] arrived, in October 2020. Despite certain formal problems due to the lack of correct identification of the officials, the lawsuit was declared admissible. A court will soon (*again*) decide whether to definitively file it or start a judicial proceeding.

We are very aware that all the serious personal and economic harm caused by this judicial (let us not forget: *criminal*) persecution does not come from a general feeling among prison workers, but rather from a sector of union leaders who entrench themselves in a sort of "heavy corporatism" caused by internal struggles for union representation quotas and low cultural levels concerning the defense of fundamental rights. Through systematic denial of violence, this perverse corporatism does nothing but perpetuate institutional violence.

We should also note that this stubborn criminalization was quickly responded to by a wave of solidarity from many Catalan, Spanish and international colleagues and organizations, with permanent statements in support of Iñaki's and OSPDH's activity. In December 2018, the World Organization Against Torture (OMCT) addressed a letter to the Spanish state administration expressing concern over this harassment campaign. The letter was quickly echoed by the European Group for the Study of Deviance and Social Control, which expressed their collective support together with a list of individual support letters from all over the world.

Hence, some more threats from other unions and the number of penal processes would be responded to by a huge campaign during the summer of 2019. A press conference was held on 30 September by several representatives of national and international entities and institutions, such as the World Organization Against Torture, Irídia, the Catalan Institute of Human Rights, Families of Prisoners in Catalonia, the Commission of Defence of Barcelona Bar Association, Catalan Association for Human Rights, Intersindical-CSC union, or Barcelona City Council, who came together in support of Iñaki and the OSPDH team. It was the end of a campaign of support launched through the urgent call by the World Organization Against Torture and the International Federation for Human Rights and signed by more than 60 organizations and 130 academic researchers and human rights activists from all around the world.

All these expressions of solidarity and support came to be fundamental in obtaining a number of popular votes for a candidacy promoted by various associations of prisoners' families through which Iñaki was given the National Human Rights Award by the Spanish Pro Human Rights Association (APDHE) in November 2020.

We must remain vigilant. This whole process is part of a widespread strategy of denial, and we are not the only ones attacked in this regard. Far from it: Nor are we the ones who receive the harshest attacks at all. We must stay attentive to accusations made by the apparatuses of a criminal exceptionalism that was not dismantled after the disappearance of ETA, since its attacks have been transferred to the repression of free speech and any kind of street protest. In Catalonia, CDRs[8], political parties, youth organizations such as *Arran* or the *Sindicat d'Estudiants dels Països Catalans* [Catalan Students Union], independence supporters, and many other protesters have had to face harsh charges and sentences. Among the aftermath of the demonstrations against the judgment of pro-independence leaders in October 2019, the police forces stated that both the groups responsible for the riots and those that denounced police abuse were using the *Kale Borroka*[9] strategy. It is no coincidence that judge Manuel García Castellón and the National Court prosecutors planned to include any event occurred in Catalonia since October 2019 in a macro-case for terrorism.[10]

We know that this will not be the last attack we will receive for doing our work. We also know very well that this is not just an attack on us, but on every human rights organization and anyone who denounces torture and promotes the fundamental rights of those who live under institutional abduction. But this same conviction is the reason why we will keep on, together with all these other colleagues, friends and comrades, surely with much more strength and determination than ever.

Notes

1 *Grupos Antiterroristas de Liberación* [Spanish for "Antiterrorist Liberation Groups"], death squad established by officials of the Spanish government to fight ETA [*Euskadi Ta Askatasuna*—Basque for "Basque Homeland and Freedom"]. Their activity took place from 1983 until 1987, under Spanish PSOE-led governments.
2 Speech by EH Bildu party MP Mertxe Aizpurua in the Spanish Congress on 17/09/2019.
3 https://canales.diariovasco.com/documentos/Conclusiones-Investigacion-tortura-malostratos-2017.pdf
4 https://ala.org.es/informe-2018-sobre-la-tortura-en-el-estado-espanol-por-la-cpdt/
5 https://sirecovi.ub.edu/
6 CSIF files a suit against Iñaki Rivera https://www.csif.es/contenido/cataluna/general/282549
7 This same organization had forced the resignation of *Brians 1* prison director in 2018, after an odd campaign of threats.
8 The *Comitès de Defensa de la República* [Catalan for "Committees for the Defence of the Republic"], previously named Committees for the Defense of the Referendum, are a grassroots network developed on a local, regional and national level in Catalonia, created with the aim of facilitating the Catalan independence referendum in 2017.
9 *Kale Borroka* was the name given to the street fight in the context of political violence in the Basque Country.
10 https://www.lavanguardia.com/politica/20191114/471596774024/audiencia-nacional-investigar-terrorismo-disturbios-cataluna.html:"The National Court wants to investigate the latest riots in Catalonia as acts of terrorism".

Bibliography

Cohen, S. (2005[2001]). Estados de Negación, Buenos Aires: Facultad de Derecho UBA.

Forero, A. (2019). Estados de negación, corporativismo y criminalización de la denuncia contra la violencia institucional. *Revista Critica Penal y Poder* n° 17. OSPDH: Universidad de Barcelona, pp. 10–16.

Forero, A., and Jiménez, D., (2020), "Court orders the dismissal of the cause against Iñaki Rivera", in *European Group for the Study of Deviance and Social Control Newsletter*, September, http://www.europeangroup.org/sites/default/files/EG%20September%202020%20NEWSLETTER.pdf

Current cases of over-criminalization of dissent in the Global South

14

SOCIAL PROTEST AND PUNITIVE TREATMENT IN ARGENTINA

An analysis from Latin American critical criminology

Gabriela L. Gusis and Rodrigo F. Videla

This chapter analyzes the enforcement of crime control against social organizations' demonstrations in Argentina. Relying upon the Latin American critical criminology framework (Aniyar de Castro 1987, Zaffaroni 2011), the chapter traces similarities among different historical periods to understand the link between the demands for better living conditions (land, health, work) raised through constitutionally admitted tools and the criminalization of those who tried to put those rights into practice.

Based on categories such as social protest and political dissidence, primary and secondary criminalization (Zaffaroni et al. 2002) and subterranean criminalization (Aniyar de Castro 1987), the chapter exposes the existence of different (punitive) tactics for social control including criminalization and "repressivization". The chapter includes a case study that deals with the events known as "Avellaneda Massacre". On 26 June 2002 in Buenos Aires, Argentina, two social activists, Darío Kosteki and Maximiliano Santillan, were killed by the police. The case is relevant because it shows the specific punitive tactics that operate in the global margins, with law enforcement agents using deadly force as part of their contention techniques. The study does not reflect on how disadvantaged social groups have resisted conditions they consider unjust, but rather on the link between those resistant strategies and the government tactics and techniques for the administration of pain (Christie 1984).

Neoliberalism, social protests and the ban on constitutional rights

Following the welfare state model of the 1980s, the 1990s political and economic neoliberalism gave rise to policies that "…were promoted worldwide by the International Monetary Fund (IMF), the World Bank (WB), the European Commission, and the European Central Bank. As a result of such policies, the European Union (EU) experienced increasing unemployment and a marked decrease in the workers' income, particularly in the countries of the Eurozone"

DOI: 10.4324/9781003144229-19

(Navarro 2009). This resulted in massive welfare cuts (Monedero 2009). As in other Latin American countries, the impact of the 1990s neoliberalism in Argentina produced welfare cuts, privatizations, labor flexibilization and less workers' rights. This process culminated in a great economic, social and political crisis in 2001, unprecedented in national history. The local neoliberal governments were guided by the idea that the private sector was more efficient and should assume former public services. As a result, the social gap as well as unemployment and poverty increased. As Castel (2006) states, the process of change that the capitalist model underwent progressively transformed the social view of life itself: in the welfare state, everyone could see "a better tomorrow" as part of the society of progress, but this was diluted by the progression towards a financial market model of capitalism. Legal protections grew seemingly less significant and lost their ability to challenge existing power dynamics. Moreover, the law sometimes deepened the existing social gaps.

In the year 2000, "democracies [were] highly conditioned by external and internal debt, the privatization of state enterprises, oligopolies economies and natural resources under corporate rule. The mass of unemployed and excluded people [was] growing" (Graciarena 1984, & 1988). The "regulated management of inequalities" previously mediated by collective spaces, as well as by socially oriented public policies, gradually diluted, generating greater individualism and a negative impact on the bonds of social cohesion among `workers´. Eventually, the state support was lost. Mbembe's states that

> there are no longer any workers as such: there are only labor nomads. If before the drama of the subject was to be exploited by capital, now the tragedy of the multitudes is not to be exploited at all. Their doom is to be postponed in a superfluous humanity that is abandoned and totally dispensable for the functioning of capital.
>
> (Mbembé 2016, 29)

Also Castel (2006), following Elias' doctrinal developments, maintains that "'the society of individuals' is one where the ability to conduct oneself as a social actor is increasingly required and valued, based on an idea of self-sufficiency. In this sense, social risks are an increased reality in various spheres, they even transcend the social sphere and advance on humanity, and even ethics. Social difference is also projected onto the urban plane where district lines are re-organized, making the working-class neighborhoods appear as sensitive, and risky by the privileged 30% of society, cataloging the remaining 70% of society as disposable and excluded other".

In this context, various social demands for economic and social rights proliferated in Argentina and the region. Indeed, the reclaiming of public space extensively reappeared towards the end of the dictatorship period (1976–1983) as a way of pursuing "solutions to conflicts through the intervention of the authorities. Protest is the way to draw the attention of the public and the authorities to the conflict or to the needs that are claimed to be met" (Zaffaroni, 2010, 3) and, except for isolated acts, it has been carried out without violence. What is then a social protest? This notion could be defined as:

> the visible events of contentious public action by a group, aimed at sustaining a demand which, in general, refers directly or indirectly to the state. This notion places special emphasis on the contentious and intentional nature, on the one hand, and on public visibility, on the other

And as "any action that alters the social order, breaking or temporarily interrupting the reproduction of the dominant social relations" (NPO 2000). In Argentina, the protests that acquired the most visibility were demonstrations and public meetings that involved roadblocks of main accesses to cities, or to central city streets. This type of protest was known as *"piquete"* and its organizers were called *"piqueteros"*. The *"piquetero* movement" emerged then as a political actor.

Repressivization as a technique to suppress the *piquetero* movement

Exerting a claim through non-institutional means is not a new phenomenon[1], "when the poor and working classes rebel it is not because they are inherently disruptive. They rebel because they have limited alternative means to express their opinions and to press for change" (Eckstein 2001). Moreover, there is a constitutional right to protest when fundamental rights are involved, which is regulated as part of the right to petition before the authorities and the freedom of expression (Gargarella 2005), which has been judicially recognized (Gargarella 2006). Zaffaroni (2010, 2) points out that "in Argentina, especially the constitutionalists and the non-governmental organizations that worked on the issue, conceived the social protest that is exercised through these means as a legal right, and its repression as the criminalization of social protest". Therefore, when the state, through the police or security agencies, frustrates a social protest, it is argued, there is a process of criminalization.

However, we propose that the concept of "criminalization" is insufficient to understand and explain the phenomenon in all its magnitude. Therefore, in our opinion, the category "repressivization" is more appropriate as it allows us to assess the repression of protest as a punitive technique aimed at specific purposes and as a part of the "subterranean penal system" (Aniyar de Castro 1984). We argue that "the [formal] criminal system refers to the group of agencies that exert the criminalization (primary and secondary criminalization) or participate in its production" (Zaffaroni et al. 2002, 18). These agencies manage social conflicts through a punitive decision-making model[2] composed by the parliament, police agencies and the judiciary. Besides these formal agencies, there is a "parallel criminal system" that consists of the "enormous part of punitive power, which is exercised by other agencies without specific punitive functions, but whose latent function of punitive social control is no different from that of the criminal system" (Zaffaroni et al. 2002, 37). Within this parallel system, we find asylums that "when they do not pursue an immediate therapeutic end, closely resemble imprisonment" or "welfare authorities that decide on the institutionalization of the elderly and children" (Zaffaroni et al. 2002, 25). Thus, although the parallel criminal system has its own particular functions, its latent functions of social control, as described, replicate the punitive model. Finally, there is something else: the "subterranean criminal system", a term coined by Lola Aniyar de Castro (1984) as part of the Latin American critical criminology. Indeed, Latin American critical criminology was a pioneer in revealing that, in addition to the mentioned criminal systems, there is this "subterranean penal system" that comprises all punitive power exercised outside the law, i.e., the *abusive* exercise of power (Aniyar de Castro 1987, 97). The categories of institutionalized violence and institutional violence, which are also characteristic of Latin American criminology, are also important to understand the concept of subterranean criminal system: when violence is systematically exercised by a legal authority, violence becomes institutional (Alagia & Codino 2019). For example, a law that discriminates against a certain section of the population is still violent but is institutionalized. Institutional violence, on the other hand, is identified with the illegal practices of agencies of the penal system including executions without trial, forced detention or forced disappearances (Zaffaroni 2003, 17). In summary, even beyond Latin-American countries[3], the subterranean penal system conceals the state's desire to address social conflict through institutionalized violence (Aniyar de Castro & Codino 2013, 299).

Within this framework, repression appears as a punitive tool that, though formal and informal paths, ensure social exclusion. It is well known that cultural patterns (Garland 1999) and economic models (Rusche & Kirchheimer 1984, Melossi & Pavarini 1980) tend to have a direct influence on what is defined as a crime, on the models of punishment, and on who will be the accused. Generally, those who do not agree with existing public policies and those who do not accept with resignation the violation of their rights will suffer a punitive approach (Christie 1984).

Therefore, we note not only an expansion of criminalization by the formal criminal system via the proliferation of new types of criminal offences (some of which are the consequence of pressure exercised by global economic powers[4]) and more law enforcement (Silva Sanchez 1999), but also an extension of "repressivization" by the underground criminal system, which exceeds the legally regulated limits for the use of violence. Thus, "repressivization" is the punitive tactic by which excessive violence is exercised outside the limits of the rule of law and the rational use of force (i.e., to take advantage of the benefits that illegality grants) on subjects who would not necessarily be labeled as deviant and, therefore, not necessarily formally criminalized.

As shown, repressivization as a criminological concept is more comprehensive in explaining the phenomenon that operates in subterranean or parallel penal systems. Criminalization is a phenomenon that articulates with the formal criminal justice system in a broad sense as legal agencies operating within the punitive system (executive, legislative, judicial agencies) but does not explain what happens in Latin America everyday life. There, most the punitive power is applied through the parallel and underground criminal justice systems. Table 14.1 clarifies the distinction.

TABLE 14.1 Formal and Subterranean Criminal System

Criminal System	Formal	Subterranean
Social control technique	Criminalization	Criminalization and/or repressivization
Violence	institutionalized	institutional

We argue that the specificity of "repressivization" allows for a more comprehensive analysis than that using "criminalization", even to describe the forced disappearances occurred during the last Argentine dictatorship[5]. These were punishments applied outside the scope of formal justice. Moreover, even when the existing legal framework legalized the death penalty via an executive decree, the military forces opted for illegality because of the "advantages it granted over the enemy" (Duhalde 1983). One of the heads of the unlawful government, Emilio Massera, declared that "this method [detention-disappearance] guarantees that for four generations there will be no more political activists" (quoted in Del Olmo 1990, 78). Even when forced disappearances are no longer the rule, the goal remains the same: the punitive administration of social dissidence through illegal means.

Notably, the formal punitive system does not only operate against those it "repressivises", but it also tries to dissuade and control the whole population. As Foucault pointed out (1975), this mechanism relies on a positive shaping power that is projected, through the legitimizing discourses of the mass media, as a true pedagogy of fear (Rodriguez Molas 1984, Malaguti Batista 2016). To this is added that repressivization is a process that selects people based not only on the same stereotypes that govern criminalization. It goes beyond. In those cases in which the ethical limit would not support applying the criminal label—e.g., a worker demanding a wage increase—there is only room for repressivization. Moreover, repressivization also has a gender dimension. For example, in the recent demonstrations in Chile and Argentina carried out by the "Ni Una Menos" movement (a collective that emerged in Argentina to confront violence against women), women did not only endure arrest but also suffered for excessive punitive tactics that inflicted gender-specific pain[6], including touching, forced nudity, blows to the vagina and breasts, sexual insults, threats of rape or beating pregnant women and forcing abortions.

Case study: The Avellaneda massacre, the killing of Kosteki and Santillan

In the historical context outlined in the section above, more than 50% of the population in Argentina was below the poverty line. On 26 June of 2002 groups of unemployed workers, together with '*piquetero*' organizations, carried out massive protests blocking all access to the City of Buenos Aires. They raised slogans and demands such as "increase in unemployment benefits", "social welfare", "food assistance", "dismissal of criminal cases against social activists", and "solidarity with the workers of the Zanon company", who were at risk of being evicted after having taken over the factory when the employers closed it.

To avoid the roadblocks in the main accesses, the national government deployed four security forces (Gendarmerie, the Navy, Federal Police and Buenos Aires Police). Specifically, at the access called *"Puente Pueryrredon"* (Pueyrredon Bridge), which links the city of Avellaneda (Buenos Aires province) with the City of Buenos Aires, the four forces set up a *"cordón"'* (police line) to prevent picketing. Once the activist groups arrived, the police forces started a strong repression that left 33 wounded people and two others killed by police gunfire. Dario Santillan and Maximiliano Kosteki, militants in the Movement for Workers and the Unemployed (MTD), which was part of the Coordinating Committee of Unemployed Workers Aníbal Verón (CTD), were the ones killed at the train station in the city of Avellaneda.

Days before, the executive branch had suggested that the organizations that were in the demonstration were part of a plot to overthrow the government. Such a rhetoric had no other objective than to legitimize the repression against the protesting groups. The mass media helped by referring to the massacre as a confrontation between groups of demonstrators, downplaying the responsibility of the security forces (Perelman 2010). Notably, these killings were part of a series of events in which law enforcement agencies suppressed social protest, including 30 people killed in the demonstrations held on 19& 20 December 2001. This was the event of that led to the resignation of President Fernando De la Rua. In a similar vein, the Avellaneda massacre forced the national government to call for presidential elections (Gayol & Kessler 2018).

The victims of the Avellaneda Massacre were not "criminalized". Instead, and as described, they were subjected to repressivization. The absence of a judicial process against the protesters might be due to two reasons: the lack of social legitimacy given the conflicting constitutional laws that guarantee the right to protest, or the practical use of fear as a product of the uncertainty produced by the shifting of the legal framework. Indeed, protesters are often seen as social deviants (Becker 2009), and repressivised to silence their claims, discipline the social group or movement to which they belong, and block any collective social cohesion, generating a social disruption aimed at breaking the bonds of solidarity. When institutionalized violence does not achieve its goal, institutional violence is used. That is, when criminalization does not achieve its goals, repressivization is used.

Thus, we are not simply analyzing crime control, i.e., the persecution of protesters as criminals—but something that has a distinct ideological content as it operates intentionally as an illegal punitive tool to preserve an exclusionary economic and social model that would otherwise be massively rejected by the vulnerable sectors. Likewise, the fact that both the government and the media tried to show that the killing of Kosteki and Santillan was the result of a confrontation between *piqueteros* reveals a main difference in relation to criminalization, that requires someone identified as a possible criminal as a clear divide between a "(criminal)them" and a "(law-abiding)us" (Zaffaroni 2011). In the events described, the only purpose of the repression was to make the general population fear the activists and not the state criminal response to the demonstrations.

Conclusions

No theory can properly explain and predict the full range of ways in which social groups will express their anger, or the effects that challenging the *status quo* will have. However, we can propose conceptual specificity to make the political virulence of the punitive practices visible. If we limit ourselves to describe what happened in cases like the Avellaneda Massacre as "criminalization", we are missing the perpetrator's intentionality, which is linked to a specific socio-economic order that requires the application of punishment even outside legal limits.

Furthermore, the distinction allows us to identify that when society raises the need to de-criminalize social protest, it refers to the absence of criminal proceedings against protestors, and to the absence of repression against protestors. Additionally, unveiling the specific objectives of a practice allows for a historical awareness of our reality[7], which will lead to specific modes of resistance. Resistance against criminalization can entail the elimination of certain criminal offenses targeting protest. But addressing the pains that the illegal repression causes is a much more difficult road to take.

As the Mothers of the Plaza de Mayo taught us in relation to the forced disappearances, repressivization did not strengthen our acceptance and obedience, but it had the opposite effect. Meanwhile, the kidnapping of their child work as a catalyzer that urged the mothers to act, we believe that by revealing the functioning of the repressivization practices will achieve precisely the opposite to what the perpetrators desired: it will make social activists aware rather than prevent them from protesting against social injustices. Hopefully, this conceptualization will allow us to generate a repressive counter-pressure to defend the rule of law.

Notes

1 Perelman (2017, 10) explains that "around 1880, the first modern processes of social protests linked to the emergence and development of the working class appeared along with the building of the national state and a capitalist economy linked to the production of primary commodities for export. During the first decades of the 20th century and until 1930s, labour conflicts—between capital and labor—defined the central aspects of social protest. In the following decades, social protest was organized in close relation to the role of the state and by virtue of the processes of social and political integration of workers during the rise of Peronism. The military coup against the government of Juan Domingo Perón initiated a cycle of political instability and polarization which culminated in the mid-1970s' military dictatorship".

2 Thus, we can define this model as one that sorts out conflicts through "a coercion that deprives of rights or inflicts a pain (penalty) without pursuing a restorative end or neutralizing an ongoing damage or imminent danger" (Zaffaroni et al. 2002, 37).

3 The magnitude and modes of the subterranean criminal system depend on the characteristics of each society and each criminal system, on the strength of the judicial agencies, on the balance of power between the agencies and on the actual controls among the different powers (Zaffaroni et al. 2002, 26).

4 Such is the case with `Terrorism´ required by the FATF (Vegh Weis 2019).

5 This was an important tool for the dictatorship. Notably, "the most concentrated sector of the financial, industrial and agricultural sectors, in alliance with the multinational corporations, were the ones in charge of the national economic policies. The project was relatively simple: it involved a new international division of labor, which condemned Argentina [and the countries in the region] to the schemes prevailing in the 19th century: a country that exported commodities and imported processed products. This required a policy of 'disciplining' society that would allow the partial reduction and definitive submission of the wage-earning sector" (Garcia Méndez 1987, 269).

6 https://latfem.org/pacos-abusadores-violencia-politica-sexual-en-chile/ and https://www.bbc.com/mundo/noticias-america-latina-50354968

7 Where market totalitarianism—in its current financial phase—is based on the double idolatry of the market and punitive power. (Zaffaroni 2019)

References

Alagia, A. and Codino, R. (2019) *La descolonización de la criminología en America*, Buenos Aires: Ediar.

Aniyar de Castro, L. (1984), Derechos humanos, modelo integral de la ciencia penal y sistema penal subterráneo, en Zaffaroni, R. (coord.), Sistemas penales y derechos humanos en América Latina, Primer Informe, Buenos Aires: Depalma.

Aniyar de Castro, L. (1987) *Cirminología de la Liberación*, Maracibo: Ediluz.

Aniyar de Castro, L, Codino, R. (2013), *Manual de Criminología Sociopolítica*, Buenos Aires: Ediar.

Becker, H. (2009) *Outsiders - hacia una sociología de la desviación and Howard Becker*. Buenos Aires, México: Siglo XXI.

Castel, R. (2006) *La inseguridad social, qué es estar protegido*, Buenos Aires: Editorial Manantial.

Christie, N. (1984) *Los límites del dolor*, México: Fondo de cultura económica.

Del Olmo, R. (1990) *Segunda uptura Criminológica*, Caracas: Universidad Central de Venezuela.

Duhalde, L. (1983), *El estado terrorista Argentino*, Barcelona: Editorial Argos.

Eckstein, S. (2001), *Poder y protesta popular en America Latina, en Poder y protesta popular, movimientos sociales latinoamericanos*. México: Siglo Veintiuno.

Foucault, M. (1975), *Vigilar y Castigar. Nacimiento de la prisión. Madrid*: Siglo XXI 1992.

Garcia Méndez, E. (1987) *Autoritarismo y control social: Argentina*, Uruguay, Chile, Buenos Aires: Editorial Hammurabi.

Gargarella, R. (2005), *El derecho de protesta: el primer derecho*, Buenos Aires: Ad-Hoc.

Gargarella, R. (2006) *Carta abierta sobre la intolerancia*. Buenos Aires: Siglo XXI.

Garland, D. (1999) *Castigo y Sociedad Moderna*, México: Siglo XXI.

Garland, D. (2010) *Castigo y Sociedad Moderna*. Madrid: Siglo XXI, 2da reimpresión.

Gayol, S. and Kessler, G. (2018) *Muertes que importan: Una mirada sociohistórica sobre los casos que marcaron la Argentina reciente*. Buenos Aires: Editorial siglo XXI.

Graciarena, J. (1984) "El Estado latinoamericano en perspectiva. Figura, crisis, prospectiva". *Revista Pensamiento Iberoamericano* 5: 39–74.

Graciarena, J. (1988) *Los dilemas de la equidad social en la Argentina finisecular*. Santiago de Chile: Documento de la Cepal.

Malaguti Batista, V. (2016) *El miedo en la ciudad de Rio de Janeiro*, Buenos Aires: UNSAM Edita.

Mbembé, A. (2016) *Crítica de la razón negra: Ensayo sobre el racismo contemporáneo*. Barcelona: NED Ediciones.

Melossi, D., Pavarini, M. (1980) *Cárcel y fábrica. Los orígenes del sistema penitenciario (siglos XVI – XIX)*, México DF: Siglo XXI ed.

Monedero, J.C. (2009) *Disfraces del Leviatán: el papel del estado en la globalización neoliberal.* Madrid: Akal.

Navarro, V. (2009) El conflicto de clases a nivel internacional, en El viejo topo www.elviejo-topo.com N° 263.

NPO 2000 Deberia ser: OSAL, 2000 citado en: AA.VV., "*Transformaciones de la protesta social en Argentina 1989-2003*", Instituto de Investigaciones Gino Germani, Buenos Aires, 2006. Disponible en http://biblioteca.clacso.edu.ar/Argentina/iigg-uba/20100720094530/dt48.pdf

Perelman, M. (2010) *Narrativas en disputa sobre violencia y protesta. De 'el movimiento piquetero amenaza desestabilizar el gobierno de Duhalde' a 'el anterior gobierno tuvo que adelantar las elecciones por la muerte de piqueteros en el Puente Pueyrredón'.* Buenos Aires: Laboratorio.

Perelman, M Coord. (2017) *El derecho a la protesta social en la Argentina.* 1a ed. Ciudad Autónoma de Buenos Aires: Centro de Estudios Legales y Sociales CELS.

Rodriguez Molas, R. (1984) *Historia de la tortura y el orden represivo en la argentina,* Buenos Aires: Eudeba.

Rusche, G., Kirchheimer, O. (1984) *Pena y estructura social,* Bogotá: Temis

Silva Sanchez, J.M. (1999) *La expansión del derecho penal. Aspectos de la política criminal en las sociedades postindustriales,* Madrid: Civitas.

Vegh Weis, V. (2019) "Towards a Critical Green Southern Criminology: An Analysis of Criminal Selectivity, Indigenous Peoples and Green Harms in Argentina", available online in https://www.crimejusticejournal.com/article/view/12

Zaffaroni, R. (2003) *Criminología, aproximación desde un margen,* Bogotá: Temis.

Zaffaroni, R. (2010) Derecho penal y protesta social, in Bertoni, E. (eds.), *Es legítima la criminalización de la protesta social? Derecho penal y libertad de expresión en América Latina.* Buenos Aires: Universidad de Palermo.

Zaffaroni, R. (2011) *La palabra de los muertos: Conferencias de criminología cautelar,* CABA: Ediar.

Zaffaroni, R. (2019) *La nueva crítica criminológica.* Buenos Aires: Ediar.

Zaffaroni, R., Alagia, A. and Slokar, A. (2002) *Tratado de Derecho Penal, Parte general,* Buenos Aires: Ediar.

15

COLOMBIA'S MURDEROUS DEMOCRACY PRE- AND POST-COVID-19

The assassination of social leaders and the criminalization of protest

Natalia Ruiz Morato

This chapter focuses on the case of Colombia which is a breeding ground for a panoply of social protests of the 21st century, from class struggle and Indigenous revindications to human rights, peace, LGBT and environmental movements, and issues resulting from internal and regional migration. This case study is particularly relevant because, even though the country is historically considered a democracy untainted by dictatorships, it has suffered from one of the armed conflicts of the 20th century, which served as a buffer preventing social reform. Section 1 exposes this history of criminalization of social protest. Section 2 explores how, following the successful negotiation of the 2016 Peace Agreement, there has been an increase in social protests, killings of social leaders and police violence—all of which have been worsened by the Covid-19 pandemic. Section 3 evaluates the implications and difficulties of the Supreme Court's ruling STC7641 of 22 September 2020 that protects the right to protest in times of pandemic.

Colombia's murderous democracy and the Criminal Law of the Enemy. The socio-legal impossibility of the right to protest (1919–2016)

It is a tradition in the speeches of Colombian presidents at international events (Uribe Velez 2016) to say that Colombia is one of the few stable democracies of Latin America. This is a problematic statement given that the right to protest is a constitutional and axiological ground of democracy and Colombia has been criminalizing social protest during most of the 20th century (Peñas Felizzola 2019, Valencia Villa, 1987).

The first law that dealt with the suppression of social protest was the Act, 78 of 1919, which regarded as illegal strikes by union leaders, students, peasants, or communists who criticized the government and penalized these actions with fines and

DOI: 10.4324/9781003144229-20

prison time (Peñas Felizzola 2019).This kind of law allowed for events like the mas-sacre in the banana plantations in 1928, when over 1,000 people were killed by the army for striking against state repression.This event was immortalized by the novel-ist Gabriel García Márquez in his book "One HundredYears of Solitude".Although the constitutional reform of 1936 recognized the right to strike with limitations, it did not achieve any institutional change. The repeated declaration of states of emergency throughout the 20th century allowed for the uninterrupted control of social movements, the preservation of the traditional social order preferred by the economic, political and religious elites, and the justification of state violence for social control (ValenciaVilla 1987, PNUD 2003, Peñas Felizzola 2019).

A socio-legal and ideological element that has evolved since 1930 and continues to hold sway today is clear in the historical archives of the military intelligence that allowed the Colombian state to construct the figure of the "enemy of the state" (Ugarriza & Pabon 2017). Military intelligence found that manuals of various guer-rilla groups, including the FARC *(Fuerzas Armadas Revolucionarias de Colombia,* or *Armed Revolutionary Forces of Colombia)*, actively encouraged social protest as part of their strategy of social subversion, with the aim of provoking the public forces to react despotically and thus proving the contradictions of the capitalist system (Ugarriza & Pabon 2017). Consequently, in this ideological war, the Colombian Armed Forces assumed the role of social protesters as communist-terrorist elements.

Since the 1970s, Colombia avoided being yet another repressive military dicta-torship by contextualizing the repression of protest as part of the internal armed conflict and terrorism.The security statute of the Turbay government of 1978 was the Statute of Repression: all rioting, insubordinate movement, or illegal assembly related to the crime of terrorism (Uprimny & Sanchez, 2010 56). Protesting citizens were prosecuted for crimes of assault, violation of freedom to work, disruption of transportation and vandalism.The treatment of protesters was regarded as an anti-social behavior (Morizot & Kazemian 2015) or as a crime of terrorism. Later, the Political Constitution of 1991 made fundamental changes in Colombia's judicial and social system by enshrining the right to protest, the right to political freedom and expression, and the right to strike as fundamental human rights. However, the armed conflict has impeded the normal application of the Constitution, while the incursion of the drug trade by the guerrillas has caused profound damage to social mobilization.

Closer in time, another historical legal milestone that criminalized the right to protest was Uribe's Democratic Security Policy (2002–2010), which received help from vague criminal definitions and prevented the emergence of a constitutional rationale for the protection of the right to protest as a fundamental right (Uprimny & Sanchez, 2010). During the Uribe administration, 7,134 selective detentions of peasants, Indigenous peoples and members of community boards, as presumed col-laborators of the guerrilla, took place without judicial orders. Human rights activists were also targeted by linking them to crimes associated with the armed conflict (Carvajal, 2008, Human Rights First, 2009). An especially striking case happened in 2008: despite the existence of a special Indigenous authority and the fact that they had legal control over their territory, three Indigenous leaders from the Minga community were prosecuted for kidnapping and personal injury in 2008, which happened in the context of a community trial in the Indigenous territories and under Indigenous Law (Human Rights First 2009, *Corte Suprema de Justicia* 2017). Uribe's democratic security policy has been revived by the Duque administration, in power since 2018.

Despite the extension of the "criminal law of the enemy" and the securitization paradigm under terrorism claims, social protest did not vanish completely. Between 1975 and 2015, Colombia saw as many as 7,000 rural and urban social protests (Archila Neira et al. 2019) by peasants, victims of the armed conflict, the mothers of "false positives"[1], workers, students, ethnic groups, LGBT+ groups, prisoners, independent workers and environmentalists. The cases have also been diverse, ranging from environmental and land issues, labor and housing, to public services, physical infrastructure, social services, public policies and government failures. It is worth noting that social movements have used different forms of expression and showed great organizational capacity to demand rights, such as national strikes, roadblocks, marches, sit-ins, riots and hunger strikes, and employed a diversity of legal resources, including international lobbying and media (Archila Neira et al. 2019).

Moreover, social movements have been the most dynamic force of Colombian constitutionalist doctrine, pointing to the neglect of human rights by the state. This explains the particularity of the Colombian constitutional law (Preuss 1995) known as bottom-up constitutionalism (De Sousa Santos 2010). However, the constitutional decisions in Colombia have symbolic efficacy but little material efficacy, because it has been difficult for the Executive to comply due to insufficient budget or political will. Besides physical and legal resistance, social movements have also related to the government through negotiations, turning Colombia into a coexistence between democracy and violence (Archila Neira 2019, 142).

The 2016 Peace Agreement and the martyr leaders (2016–2019)

The "Agreement to End the Armed Conflict and Build a Stable and Lasting Peace", commonly referred to as the 2016 Peace Agreement, stood for a new starting point, especially for social movements, because it involved multiple structural reforms addressing political, social and economic issues. Furthermore, this agreement had a particular focus on peacebuilding, implying the involvement of local communities and efforts to reconcile this society. One of the expected effects of the agreement was the de-criminalization of social protest through the inclusion of the guerrilla and the victims in the political process.

However, peacebuilding is fragile in Colombia, and "stable and lasting peace" seems a cynical phrase. Criminal gangs, paramilitary groups and guerrilla movements such as the ELN continue to be active. To this is added that the 2016 referendum and the election of President Duque in 2018 defined a political agenda that wants to change the conditions of the agreement and return to Uribe's democratic security policy. As many experts in Colombia have pointed out, the 2018 elections in Colombia proved the conservative tradition of a closed society that does not accept neither the entry of socially marginalized actors into politics nor the introduction of a progressive rural social agenda, misleadingly labeled "*castro-chavismo*"[2], or the implementation of the Peace Special Jurisdiction.

This has unleashed a political polarization over the future of the Peace Agreement that has been a catalyst for social protest in Colombia, but also a vicious circle of criminalization and repression, with the most devastating feature being the assassinations of social leaders in the rural areas of the country. A social leader is understood to be anyone who develops a social cause, such as community mothers, youth leaders, environmental leaders or individuals who campaign against powerful legal or illegal vested interests, for land restitution, victims' rights, ethnic autonomy or the environment—"all policies reaffirmed in the 2016 agreement. [...] Therefore, these targeted killings often have the effect of silencing a community and ensuring its submission" (International Crisis Group 2020, 2). The current government's response to the deaths is that they are homicides committed by illegal groups linked to drug trafficking due to the increase of coca cultivation in the country. This creates a cycle of re-victimization as poor families must give press statements defending those killed so that they are nor regarded as involved in criminal groups or criminal activities.

The years 2017 and 2018 saw new mass social movements in the big cities, such as the National University Strike of 2018 that protested the financial crisis in the educational sector and state repression of student movements, reaching an agreement with the government to increase the budget for higher education. Although it was a peaceful movement, denunciations of police violence (Las Dos Orillas 2018) were made by the militarized police group ESMAD *(Escuadrón Móvil Antidisturbios,* or *Mobile Anti-Disturbances Squadron).* This led up to 2019 as the year of urban democracy and police repression. The growing number of social movements converged in November 2019 in the creation of the National Strike Committee, which gave a massive voice to a range of citizen complaints protesting the economic, social and environmental policies of the government of President Duque, the noncompliance with the Peace Agreement, and with the agreements with the student movement of 2018. Fuel was added by feminist groups against gender violence, anger at police violence and the homicides of social leaders, accompanied by calls for reform of the ESMAD. Spontaneous demonstrations like the night of the *cacerolazo* on 21 November ranging from the poorest neighborhoods to groups from upper-middle income brackets also took place in the big cities (El Tiempo 2019).

The Duque government responded saying that protesting is a right that should not be exercised in a violent manner, while some other members of the executive stigmatized the protest. The Ministry of Defense and the mayors of the most important cities approached the issue as a problem of public order. The acts of vandalism presented in the protests justified their labeling as a terror campaign orchestrated by criminal groups (Cifras y Conceptos & Cancino 2019). In this context, ESMAD killed three young people, including a college student. Bogotá council member Diego Cancino presented a report showing that between 21 November and 19

December 2019, the Police made 872 arrests of which only 25 were taken to court: the rest were illegal or arbitrary. There were 62 cases of cruel and inhuman treatment. The NGO *Temblores* set out that, since the creation of the ESMAD it has been involved in 34 homicides of students, peasants and Indigenous people who were exercising their constitutional right to protest.

These events triggered two antagonistic responses. The first was the passing of a bill in December 2019, issued by the governing Democratic Centre Party, in defense of public order to control individuals considered antisocial and unpatriotic. Since then, protestors must buy insurance policies, authorizing the ESMAD to use of electroshock weapons and controlling the clothing and accessories used by the protesters. The second response came from international organizations, NGOs and council members, defending the right to protest and denouncing human rights violations by ESMAD forces. In January 2020, the victims of the police violence in the National Strike in 2019 and the social movements, University professors and Human Rights organizations who took part in the Strike, brought the *"Accion de Tutela"* or legal action to protect fundamental rights, to defend the right to protest, for freedom of expression, press freedom, citizen participation, personal integrity, due process and not to be subjected to forced disappearance. They claimed the Colombian government violates these rights through: *"(i) systematic, violent and arbitrary intervention by the public forces in demonstrations and protests, (ii) "stigmatization" of those who, without violence, take to the streets to question, refute and criticize the work of the government, (iii) disproportionate use of force, lethal weapons and chemicals, (iv) illegal and abusive detentions, inhumane, cruel and degrading treatment, and (v) attacks against freedom of expression and press"* (*Corte Suprema de Justicia* 2020, 3).

Although the Duque government started a strategy of "National Dialogue" to manage the demands of the social movements that took part in the 2019 protests, this process was inconclusive due to the Covid-19 pandemic, and the declaration of a state of economic, social and ecological emergency on 17 March 2020 that has been kept throughout 2020. This led to 156 days of lockdown, the so-called "mandatory preventive isolation", and became one of the longest in the world.

The Supreme Court's ruling STC7641 of 22 September 2020, The constitutional rights of the misfits

An exceptional feature of this decision is the context of the Covid-19 Pandemic. Various specialists and NGOs have reported the abuse of the state of emergency by the Colombian Government, calling it the "Corona Dictatorship" (Marquardt 2020) and accusing the President of using the lockdown to concentrate power in the hands of the executive and restrict fundamental rights. Transparencia Internacional (2020) launched an alert on the loss of balance of power in Colombia, because the President appointed new directors for the entities of control, such as Ombudsman's Office and attorney general's office and Comptroller General of the Nation, thus reducing their independence. Furthermore, the Duque government issued 115 legislative decrees (Uprimny 2020) on issues that exceed the discretion granted to overcome the health and economic emergency (Transparencia Internacional 2020).

In 2020, despite the Covid-19 pandemic, the assassination of social leaders did not stop: 291 were killed in 74 massacres as of November 2020 (Indepaz 2020). Colombia also has a "George Floyd". Javier Ordóñez, who was murdered by agents of the National Police on 9 September, triggering a series of protests across the country. The 2020 demonstrations against police violence were initially peaceful, but some led to violence and the destruction of 75 police stations. Overall, 261 police officers and 260 civilians were injured, nine of whom died as a result (Redacción Bogotá 2020).

In reaction to these occurrences, the institutional arguments for 2019 were repeated, with the difference that the new mayor of Bogotá, Claudia Lopez, denounced police violence and problems in the chain of command, and demanded that the National Police not use lethal weapons. The Ministry of Defense presented a report in which the protests were described as having been infiltrated by dissidents of the FARC and ELN aiming to attack the state. The Inter-American Commission on Human Rights and the EU, however, condemned the acts of violence by Colombia's National Police and called for the need to protect the right to protest. At the climax of the citizen protests and police violence, the Supreme Court concluded in its decision STC7641 of 22 September 2020 that taking part in peaceful and non-destructive protest is a fundamental right protected by Article 37 of the National Constitution and by international human rights law ratified by Colombia:

> The democratic function of social protest is to draw the attention of the authorities and public opinion to a specific problem and to the needs of certain sectors, generally minorities, so that they may be taken into account by the authorities.
>
> (Redacción Bogotá 2020, 89)

The jurisprudence of the Constitutional Court has decided that the right to protest and to prove in public implies an affectation of public space and a tension with the maintenance of public order. However, the conception of public order by the jurisprudence of the Constitutional Court is "the set of conditions of security, tranquility and health that allow general prosperity and the enjoyment of human rights" (Redacción Bogotá 2020, 53). The maintenance of public order "cannot be done by suppressing public freedoms because it is not compatible with the democratic ideal" (Redacción Bogotá 2020, 54). Moreover, when dealing with the regulation of the right to protest, "the legislator cannot go beyond the principles of reasonableness and proportionality by establishing restrictions whose vagueness leads to the prevention of such a right" (Redacción Bogotá 2020, 45) and the police power must keep public order but in the interest of the enjoyment of those rights.

The Supreme Court reviewed the evidence and proved a systematic violation of fundamental rights, saying that the ESMAD forces are not capable of guaranteeing order without violating the freedoms and rights of citizens. What is more, the methods of these forces are protesters' harassment, directly provoking a violent turn of events and leading to illegal detentions of citizens. Training courses for the use of weapons by ESMAD were considered inadequate. The Court further ruled that the Colombian state is not meeting its international human rights obligations in the areas of protest, freedom of expression and the press as fundamental elements of a participatory democracy.

The Court issued 14 orders, two of which were specifically for the executive branch with the aim of moral reparation. The first demanded the Minister of Defense present an apology for the excessive use of force by police officials, especially the ESMAD Mobile Anti-Riot Squad. The second called on the government to issue an administrative act ordering the members of the executive branch to maintain neutrality when non-violent demonstrations occur, even if they questioned their own policies. More substantially, the executive was ordered to guarantee the right to protest, the exercise of the fundamental rights to expression, assembly, peaceful protest and freedom of the press, even during events of (i) foreign war, (ii) internal unrest, or (iii) a state of emergency. The rest of the orders called for a regulation of the use of force by the police, and to set up a working group to restructure the guidelines according to international human rights law and constitutional law on the use of force in demonstrations and protests within 60 days. The Supreme Court also ordered the entities of the Public Ministry to design plans and programs to go with the public protests, and the Ombudsman's Office must control all actions of the police force in the demonstrations. It set up three types of guidelines with the aim at restoring order, not at the deprivation of life or unjustified aggression. The Supreme Court ordered the suspension of the use of the 12-gauge shotguns for intervention in protests.

The Supreme Court's decision protecting the right to protest has been called into question by sensationalist headlines such as "Court ruling divides the country" (Portafolio 2020). Even two of the Court's magistrates expressed in their abstentions that it is an emotional ruling, which exceeds the functions because there were other defense mechanisms available[3]. Duque's government said it would "appeal"[4] the ruling, the Minister of Defense did not offer proper apologies, and an administrative act by the President of the Republic ordering the neutrality of the executive branch has not been officially published.

The Supreme Court's decision is consistent with binding constitutional precedents and with a high evidentiary burden. It is typical of the neo-constitutionalist trend in Latin America (Gargarella 2005) that constitutional judges give public policy orders[5] to guarantee real and effective protection of fundamental rights, especially when the executive branch continuously fails or the legislative branch acts by omission by not regulating properly. It is a new legal culture that breaks with a traditional civil interpretation of the law, which criticizes any progressive decision. As of the date of writing, there has not been a social protest to evaluate if the police will follow the ruling and whether social movements can enjoy their right to protest.

Conclusions: overcoming the criminalization of protest through the implementation of the right to protest

This socio-legal study has proved that a determining factor in the criminalization and stigmatization of protest in Colombia was the Internal Armed Conflict and the ambivalent content of the 20th century norms for the control of public order, which allowed the legal interpretation and actions of the state authorities to criminalize social protest as a subversive action supported by guerrillas. Although the Constitution of 1991 guaranteed the right to protest, a constitutional modernization of the police force as a civilian entity has not been achieved, and the police continue to have wide discretion in their handling of disruptions of public order, construing them as counter-terrorist actions.

The Supreme Court's decision in 2020 on the right to protest constitutes a pedagogical and cultural agenda that allows citizens to check the actions of the police. It also sets the constitutional limits to the regulation of the right to protest, to avoid criminalization and misleading terrorist accusations. Furthermore, this jurisprudential precedent set up that the right to protest cannot be limited as a result of the declaration of emergency because the right to protest is at the core of participatory democracy and the last bulwark preventing the emergence of dictatorship. The urban social movements, which have managed to unite diverse agendas and be multitudinous, must have a long-term agenda for action and cannot take the Supreme Court ruling for granted. However, the situation is tougher in rural Colombia, where the direct killing of social leaders is the strategy of repression of social change. This *modus operandi* of the state since 1919 means that profound cultural, social, political and economic changes are necessary.

Colombian institutions will face a new wave of social demands, protest and frustration in the aftermath of Covid-19 due to the increase in poverty, the increase in inequality and the crisis of the economy. The murderous social governance based on an old idea from the last century that protesters "are young people indoctrinated by the ELN and FARC" (Judicial 2020) who want to overthrow the state, is, at least, inadequate. Will the post-Covid-19 social movements be able to impose new forms of rural and urban social governance to overcome the logic of the enemy and the transformation of the bloody conflict that has done so much damage to Colombia? More specifically, the post-Covid-19 period imposes a concrete agenda on civil society and the military-police power in Colombia, which calls for an independent role in its relations with the executive branch. That institution has been thoroughly discredited and faces the very real possibility of being prosecuted at the national and international human rights courts, for taking on the dirty work of resolving with violence what an investment social policy should do.

Notes

1 The "false positives" were the victims of illegal killings by military forces under the Uribe administration, in which innocent young men from the poor neighborhoods were assassinated and then disguised as enemy combatants.

2 Castrochavismo, is a term used by the right-wing political parties in Colombia advocating the failure of Venezuela for its socialism with the aim of blocking progressive social agendas.

3 What is interesting about the case is that the Supreme Court's Civil Chamber, not the Constitutional Court, resolved the "*Tutela*" action protecting fundamental rights. By design of the constitutional jurisdiction all judges of the republic resolve the "*tutela*" action. The Constitutional Court only operates for revision.

4 President Duque erroneously suggested that the sentence could be appealed: the only recourse would be to request a revision before the Constitutional Court.
5 The issue of giving public policy orders is broad, as it has been for the attention of ethnic populations, Decision T-025 of 2004, protection of the right to health Decision T-760 of 2008, protection of the deforestation of Chocó Decision T-622 of 2016 and Amazonia Decision STC 4360 of 2018.

References

Archila Neira, M. (2019) ´Control de las protestas: Una cara de la relación Estado y movimientos sociales, 1975–2015´ in Archila Neira, M, García Velandia, M.C., Parra Rojas, L., Restrepo Rodríguez, A. M. (ed.) *Cuando la copa se rebosa: Luchas sociales en Colombia, 1975 – 2015*. Bogotá: Fundación Centro de Investigación y Educación Popular – Programa por la Paz CINEP-PPP, 95–156.
Archila Neira, M., García Velandia, M.C., Parra Rojas, L., Restrepo Rodríguez, A.M. (2019) *Cuando la copa se rebosa: luchas sociales en Colombia, 1975 – 2015*. Bogotá: Fundación Centro de Investigación y Educación Popular – Programa por la Paz CINEP-PPP.
Carvajal, J. (2008) *El Estado de Seguridad dentro del Estado de Garantías. La seguridad democrática y el caso de las privaciones de la libertad en Colombia durante el período 2002-2006*. Bogotá: ILSA.
Cifras y Conceptos, Cancino, D. (2019) *Persiguiendo fantasmas* [Online]. Available at: https://cifrasyconceptos.com (Accessed: 30 October 2020)
Clavijo, S. (2001) *Fallas y fallos de la Corte Constitucional*. Bogotá: Alfaomega-Cambio.
Corte Suprema de Justicia, Sala de Casación Penal (28 de junio, 2017). Sentencia Tutela. [M.P. Eugenio Fernandez Carlier.
Corte Suprema de Justicia, Sala de Casación Civil (16 de septiembre, 2020). Sentencia Tutela. [M.P. Luis Armando Tolosa Villabona].
De Sousa Santos, B. (2010) *Refundación del Estado en América Latina. Perspectivas desde la epistemología del Sur*. La Paz: Plural Editores.
El Tiempo (2019) ´Asi fue la jornada de cacerolazos y protestas del 23 de noviembre´ *El Tiempo*, 24, November.
Gargarella, R. (2005) 'The constitution of inequality. Constitutionalism in the Americas, 1776–1860' *International Journal of Constitutional Law*, 3, (1), 1–23.
Human Rights First (2009). *Baseless Prosecutions of Human Rights Defenders in Colombia. In the dock and under the gun*. Washington: Human Rights First.
Indepaz (2020) *Informe de masacres en Colombia durante el 2020, website*.
International Crisis Group. (2020) Leaders under Fire: Defending Colombia's Front Line of Peace. Latin America Report N°82.
Judicial (2020). 'Investigación de la Dijín revela que disidencias adoctrinan jóvenes en Bogotá' RCN radio.com, 23September [online] https://www.rcnradio.com/judicial/investigacion-de-la-dijin-revela-que-disidencias-adoctrinan-jovenes-en-bogota
Justicia. (2020a) 'Duras críticas de magistrados que se apartaron del fallo de protestas', *El Tiempo*, 24, September.
Justicia. (2020b) 'Tutelantes estudian interponer desacato por disculpas del mindefensa' *El Tiempo*, 25, September.
Las Dos Orillas (2018) 'Los abusos del Esmad contra los estudiantes no paran', 6 December.
Marquardt, B. (2020) 'Coronas Políticas y Corona Derecho: Un viaje comparativo al mundo del 2020 en estado de excepción, constitucionalismo y anticonstitucionalismo en una crisis inesperada' in Marquardt, B. (ed.) *Corona Democracia o Corona Dictadura? Reflexiones del mundo confinado del 2020. Anuario IX del Grupo de Investigación Constitucionalismo Científico*. Bogotá: Grupo Editorial Ibanez.

Morizot, J., Kazemian, L. (2015) *The Development of Criminal and Antisocial Behaviour.* Switzerland: Springer International Publishing.

Peñas Felizzola, A. (2019) 'Criminalización de la protesta social en Colombia (1919–1936) in Marquardt, M., Llinas, D., Perez, C. (ed.) *Querétaro 1917 and Weimar 1919: El centenario del constitucionalismo de la democracia social, Anuario VIII del Grupo de Investigación CC-Constitucionalismo Comparado.* Bogotá: Grupo Editorial Ibañez, 339–390.

PNUD (2003) *El conflicto, callejón sin salida. Informe Nacional de Desarrollo Humano para Colombia 2003, website.*

Portafolio (2020) 'Fallo de la Corte Suprema sobre manejo de protestas divide al país' *Portafolio*, 24 September

Preuss, U. (1995) *Constitutional Revolution: The link between constitutionalism and Progress.* New Yersey: Humanities Press.

Redacción Bogotá (2020) 'Nuevos detalles de lo que pasó en los días de protesta', *El Tiempo*, 18, Septiembre. [online] https://www.eltiempo.com/bogota/protestas-en-bogota-que-paso-el-9-y-10-de-septiembre-538693

Transparencia Internacional (2020) *Alarmante concentración del poder en el ejecutivo en Colombia, website.*

Ugarriza, J., Pabon, N. (2017) *Militares y Guerrillas. La memoria histórica del conflicto armado en Colombia desde los archivos militares (1958–2016).* Bogotá: Editorial Universidad del Rosario.

Uprimny, R. (2020) 'Un Duque que quiere reinar', *El Espectador*, 6 September.

Uprimny, R., Sanchez, L. (2010) 'Derecho penal y protesta social' in Bertoni, E. (ed.) *Es legítima la criminalización de la protesta social? derecho penal y libertad de expresión en América Latina.* Buenos Aires: Universidad de Palermo.

Valencia Villa, H (1987) *Cartas de batalla: una crítica del constitucionalismo colombi. a*Bogotá: Universidad Nacional de Colombia y CEREC.

16

VIOLENCE AND VIOLATIONS OF RIGHTS AGAINST LEADERSHIPS IN THE BRAZILIAN AMAZON

Paula Lacerda and Igor Rolemberg

In Brazil, the Amazon region extends over nine federative units in Brazil, covering an area of 5,217,423 km², which corresponds to about 61% of the Brazilian territory. Historically, the state has implemented projects that aim to "develop" the region. Such projects involve the execution of large infrastructural constructions (opening of highways, construction of dams and hydroelectric plants, implementation of mining, agrarian and stockbreeding enterprises, among others), which are associated to projects of land distribution that resulted in land concentration (Velho 1972). Although there is no single cause for the violence taking place in the Amazon, the territorial conflicts that resulted from these state projects are, in great measure, responsible for the violence and violations of the populations' rights in the region. This includes violence towards leaderships involved in the defense of social and human rights, which we aim to discuss in this piece.

In this chapter, we depart from an analysis of situations classified by our interlocutors as "violence" to understand the scenario of threat to life, freedom and dignity faced by leaderships and members of social movements who acted or act in the Brazilian Amazon throughout the last democratic period (1988–2020). The research demonstrates how different types of violence, criminalization and human rights violations are directly related to state actions, from dismantling institutions dedicated to supervising and preserving the environment, or lenience by the police and the justice system, to statements by the executive power that signal to different groups that practices are tolerated or, on the contrary, disavowed. As such, we describe and analyze practices conducted by state institutions, activities by social groups with an interest in the degradation of the environment for the expansion of their economic activities, as well as actions and reactions led by leaderships and members of social movements. Despite political actions lead by leaderships, social movements, as well as international and local entities that defend human rights, situations of violence are recurrent, and have clearly intensified since 2017.

DOI: 10.4324/9781003144229-21

The chapter is organized in three parts. The first presents the conflicts that characterize the region from the perspective of our interlocutors, leaderships and members of social movements in the Amazon. The second describes practices that target a specific dimension of our interlocutors' lives: their reputation, which in turn affects their legitimacy as leaders to carry out political action. These tactics frequently accompany, and at times makes acceptable, other acts of violence and criminalization discussed in the previous topic. Finally, the conclusion provides a consideration on the ruptures and continuities of violence and criminalization, as well as signals possible future tendencies.

The descriptions and the development of our analysis are based on materials produced by social movements, press materials, in addition to interviews and fieldwork conducted over the last ten years with leaders of social movements in the Brazilian Amazon. Among the materials produced by social movements, this research pays close attention to public statements and reports, types of documents that materialize the denouncements produced. In such documents, activists describe in detail the situations of violence, under and over criminalization as defined by Vegh Weis (2019), experienced by themselves or their partners, and sometimes use instruments for quantifying information, such as statistical data. The research defines social movements as collectives formed by various processes of association and communication with the objective of elaborating causes and public issues. We agree with Goodwin and Jasper (2015) regarding their analytical proposal to understand social movements as a group of actions and actors that do not necessarily depart from institutions with some degree of formal organization, and that can assume the ephemeral form of protests. However, to pursue the questions that frame this chapter, the collectives to which these leaderships belong are an important dimension of the research. Institutions such as NGOs, unions and confessional organizations are targeted by the agents responsible for the violation of rights, and they are eventually referred to as "enemies" or as "dangerous", de-legitimizing them and setting the basis for further criminalization.

This chapter aims to deepen knowledge of state practices and policies that produce and reproduce dynamics of violence in the Brazilian Amazon but can also shed light on other contexts where the state merges with corporations involved in predatory practices against the environment, harming the populations living in these territories. Indeed, the works of Tsing (2005) and Li (2014) on forest regions and regions of Indigenous and peasant communities, and the work of de Borrás et al. (2012) for Latin America and the Caribbean, describe similar scenarios. Hence, circumstances of land grabbing, deforesting for the commercialization of wood and the implementation of monocultures or pasture, the construction of large infrastructure projects and enslavement, can all be observed in other regions where borders are redesigned to include territories and populations involved in capitalist chains of production, distribution and global trade.

The polysemy of violence in the Amazon

Leaderships participating in processes of social mobilization against actions and projects that are considered to promote development and that are driven or vouched for by state institutions are victims of different types of violence, criminalization and violation of their rights. Our interlocutors presented many categories for classifying violence, and these did not always coincide with juridical-administrative categories. Despite occupying the fourth place in the ranking of countries with the most murders of leaderships defending environmental causes, Brazil does not have statistical data on conflicts that involve leaderships and members of social movements. Nevertheless, threatened leadership can plead for their inclusion in the Program for the Protection of Human Rights Defenders, a public policy that offers protection to leaderships and activists threatened of death. The process of inclusion in this program is not automatic and one must go through different stages in order to be approved. Therefore, the number of threatened leaderships is always larger than that which the program's numbers indicate. A fact that calls attention, however, is that most of the members benefiting from this policy work to defend the rights to land, territory and the environment—82.24% of them, in October 2017, — initiatives that correspond to those which our interlocutors are engaged in.

The most complete survey on violence and violations against leaderships and members of social movements is not conducted by any state agency but rather by a confessional organization, the Pastoral Land Commission (*Comissão Pastoral da Terra– CPT*) , which has statuary autonomy and an ecumenical profile. This is the most comprehensive quantitative study on "conflicts in the countryside" in Brazil, category which, in the annual reports published by this organization, involve "conflicts due to land", "conflicts due to water" (mostly related to the constructions of dams and hydroelectric plants) and "labor conflicts" (cases of forced labor) "Conflicts due to land" include (i) direct actions for the occupation of land and organized camping by social movements, and the (ii) "occurrences of conflict", also called "violence against possession and occupation", which involve situations such as illegal expulsions, judicial evictions, threats of eviction and expulsion, as well as the destruction of houses, goods and farms. In all the categories under "conflict in the countryside", "violence against individual subjects" is also considered, which includes murders, attempted murders, threats to death, torture, imprisonments and aggressions.

Therefore, we can see a detailed process of documenting these cases, and the range of meanings and situations that the terms "violence", "criminalization" and "violation" can evoke, all of which are part of the experience of our interlocutors. Due to their activities, leaderships feel vulnerable to various types of violence, criminalization and violations of their rights. Leaderships understand that opposing development projects (opening of highways, construction of dams, implantation of mining projects, etc.) means opposing the interests of an economic and political elite that are frequently associated with criminal practices, such as illegal possession of weapons, land grabbing, etc. This indicates the fragility, even after re-democratization, of the objective conditions for the exercise of civil and political rights, such as freedom of manifestation, meeting and protest in the country and, specially, in the Amazon, which concentrates the most cases of murder and attempted murder against leadership and members of social movements.

The situations and their corresponding forms of classification presented in the CPT reports conform the repertoire of our interlocutors, regarding the terminology for naming, and their perception of, violence and violations of which they are victims. That said, and departing from the arguments of Vegh Weis (2019), we argue that situations of violence and violation of rights involving leaderships include mechanisms of under-criminalization, which corresponds to a selective treatment and impunity by the police and judicial institutions of the executors of these violations and, most importantly, the people mandating such violent actions against activists and over-criminalization, which is the instrumental use of legal means to criminalize leaderships and their conducts, in addition to illegal actions such as murder attempts, death threats, imprisonments and aggressions. Thus, we give special emphasis to the situations that involve lawfare—or the instrumental use of judiciary means to produce the criminal conviction of certain target groups, such as leaderships of social movements, therefore disrespecting the legal due process, on the one hand, and homicide and massacres, on the other, for this dual mechanism reflects the circulation of illegal activities from private actors to those in charge of the application of the law. It reveals the mutual implication of over-criminalization and under-criminalization in our scenario: cases of the first one imply that those who caused the need for social mobilization in the first place go unpunished.

In Brazil, there is no longitudinal research nor studies on the workflow of the criminal justice system to measure the arbitrary selectivity, laxness and impunity of crimes against leaderships, which would allow for us to provide detailed considerations on the mechanisms of under-criminalization in our field of research. Taking into consideration, however, the existing records on this theme in CPT's database[1], the estimate is that in the 1,496 cases of homicide in the context of "conflicts in the countryside" that took place between 1985 and 2019, of which there are 1,973 victims, only 120 of the cases were judged, and resulted in the conviction of 35 conspirators and 106 executors (Cabral 2020). Nevertheless, this does not mean that the sentences were carried out, especially in the cases that involve a conspirator, who has the financial means to pay for the judicial costs and attorney services needed to explore possibilities within the law and cases of jurisprudence in their favor so as to remain in freedom until the judicial case is settled or the penal action is enjoined. In the case of the massacre in Eldorado dos Carajás, in 1996, of which more than 100 people were victims, the judgment of the officials that mandated the massacre only took place in 2002. Once condemned, the defendants remained in freedom until the last possible appeal, at which point their preventive apprehension was declared, in 2012, 18 years after the fact (Afonso 2014).

Contrastingly, the actions that we consider to be classified as extrajudicial executions were particularly frequent in 2017. During this year, the largest number of homicides against leaderships and members of social movement was recorded (a total of 71 cases), within the period of a decade from 2010 to 2019. This was due to the fact that there were, in 2017, five massacres[2], out of which four happened in the Amazon. One of these massacres, which took place in the city of Pau d'Arco, is revealing of the ways in which the repression and criminalization of conducts by leaderships and members of social movements operates. Those involved in the massacre were all civil and military police officers from the south of Pará, who went in search of participants of a land occupation to apply a court order that mandated the detention of the members of the occupation under the justification that they had disobeyed the previous judicial decision for reintegration of the land and that they were involved in the death of one of the private guards of the farm. The operation had a legal basis, but it was executed as an armed siege. Although some of the police officers claimed that there was a confrontation, the reports from the later investigation showed that the executions of all ten fatal victims were arbitrary, while ten other victims managed to live, some of which became witnesses in the prosecution. Regarding the crimes committed by the police officers, the investigation process was concluded, but there still is no date defined for their judgment. Although there are strong indications that this programmed execution of leaderships was organized in partnership with other actors, the investigations have not extended, up until this moment, to a consideration of those involved in the authorship of the crimes, or its conspirators. The countless police reports and inquiries for the investigation of crimes such as arson (of property and goods), homicide and threats to death against leaderships have not proceeded. Such omissions make up the acts of under-criminalization, as we mentioned previously.

The administrative act that originated this massacre consists of a repossession order for a farm of which the property title had not been verified with the appropriate federal agency. There were suspicions that this farm was public land, illegally occupied with a falsified title. Furthermore, the local military police[3] was summoned to execute this eviction, going against the recommendations by the state's judiciary branch that evictions should be made by a division of police officers from the state's capital. Such recommendation reveals that these state agencies assume that local police can be partial and act under the influence of municipal elites. In face of these details, we consider that the massacre of Pau D'Arco demonstrates blurred borders between the legal and illegal, especially when public security officers, in addition to being in line with the interests of local elites, possess a working relationship with private security companies, which offers services to protect properties where mining, woodcutting, agrarian and stockbreeding farming enterprises and land grabbing, happen.

The forms of violence and violation of leaderships' rights in the Brazilian Amazon also involve biased penal persecution, when not entirely illegal, which begin with arbitrary detainments and are achieved in the instrumentalization of legal means both via law production—to turn some conducts into crime—as well as through the administrative and judicial interpretation and application of the law. This is the phenomenon of lawfare and leaderships' criminalization, one of the elements of over-criminalization we are analyzing. The case involving Father José Amaro is exemplary in this sense. The priest has acted in the region of Anapu since the 1990s, with the missionary Dorothy Stang (murdered in 2005), to defend the rights of small farmers and in favor of agrarian reform. Due to his activism, he had denounced farmers and loggers many times for irregularly possessing lands and promoting illegal deforestation. The denunciations elaborated over the years were documented, as well as the death threats he received, which were registered in local police stations.

In March 2018, Amaro was pre-emptively detained due to an investigation conducted by the civil police in Anapu, under the accusation of commanding a criminal organization that invaded lands in the municipality, of extorting and laundering money, and of committing sexual assault. The investigation was prompted by a report filed by a farmer claiming to own land that was supposedly being threatened to be invaded by squatters led by Amaro. However, there is a judicial sentence that affirms that the area where this farm was claimed to be located does not belong to any private owner, rather it is federal public land and, therefore, should be destinated to agrarian reform. This fact should automatically classify the farmer's conduct as a crime for the illegal occupation of public land—*grilagem*, in vernacular terms—but there is no known investigation or punishment of the farmer due to this crime. Once again, we see a case in which under-criminalization and over-criminalization occur simultaneously.

Amaro's conviction involves a series of violations: in 2016 and 2017 when shooters set fire to the camping site located on the land, which was being considered for agrarian reform, according to CPT's records (Bellini & Muniz 2019). By the end of 2019, one of the leaderships who acted with Amaro and who was a witness for the defense in the penal case against the priest was murdered. In a public note, a group of lawyers working for CPT and who act in the defense of Amaro, raised legal weaknesses in the accusation's case. Amaro was detained for 92 days, until he got the right to *Habeas Corpus* issued by a justice of the Supreme Court (*Superior Tribunal de Justiça*) who, in his decision, pointed to evidence of criminalization and lawfare, and therefore, to the arbitrariness of the detainment. Not only are there no material or forensic proof of the crimes attributed to Amaro, but there are also irregularities in the proceedings, once the defendant was being accused, on his own, of the crime of criminal association. In 2020, Amaro is still answering this legal proceeding, but in freedom. Finally, it is worth noting that the crime of sexual assault was excluded from the case from the beginning due to lack of evidence. It is probable that this crime was initially reported in order to morally de-legitimize Father Amaro. Such tactics have been employed against leaderships, as we will discuss in the next section, and compose the scenario of forms of violence and violations against leaderships and members of social movements.

Tactics for morally de-legitimizing leaderships

Up to this point, we have discussed situations characterized by our interlocutors as violence, such as homicides, attempted homicide, death threats, arbitrary detainments and biased or illegal penal persecutions, and framed here as an interrelation between under- and over-criminalization. How are these processes carried out without causing social outrage? By a prior de-legitimization of the attacked environmental activists. In the context of the Brazilian Amazon, development projects and large infrastructure construction projects that favor the association between economic elites and public authorities results in a climate of insecurity that is unfavorable to leaderships that confront the meaning of development associated to such projects. This climate of insecurity and hostility is verified, for example, in rumors about "how much a leadership's head is worth". In other words, how much would a conspirator be willing to pay to execute someone who is in the way of their projects. The conspirator, in general, has an unknown identity, though one could suppose the names of a few people who would be interested in that leadership's death. Such information circulates through rumors and is successful due to the effect of producing terror (Das 2006).

As a result of acting socially and politically in the Amazon region for over 20 or 30 years, and of being in dialog with specialists in universities in Brazil and abroad, leaderships and members of social movements, in general, criticize the development model applied in the Amazon, which is characterized by the absence of dialog and the disrespect of forms of life that depend on natural resources. Because of this, however, leaderships began to be referred to as "enemies of progress and development", and are associated with retrograde and inadequate values, or are even accused of "profiting" from the "economic stagnation" of that region. We will return to this issue later.

Gender is a productive component of tactics for the moral de-legitimization of leaderships. When looking at women in these roles, their leadership is referred to in an ironic tone, it is minimized. Women tend to be more easily associated with a "tradition" that would hinder the "development" of the city. In Altamira, when faced with the implementation of the Hydroelectric Plant of Belo Monte, which took place in the decade of 2010, women leaders were pejoratively called "long skirt women" (*mulheres do saião*), an expression that re-inscribes these women in their gender roles and associates them with what is considered an old-fashioned way of dressing and thinking. The expression also triggers markers of sexuality, once it suggests that these women, almost all of them beyond the age of 60, were considered to be beyond the age of exercising their sexuality. In these situations, moral de-legitimization uses local grammars of gender and power in an attempt to silence or minimize the position of these leaders.

A gendered grammar also falls upon men, as they are feminized in their leadership roles because of their association with public actions that are almost always pacific and dissociation from common signs of hegemonic masculinity in these spaces, such as big cars, guns, chainsaws, etc. The criminalization of Father Amaro, as discussed above, points to the use of gender for the effect of moral de-legitimization in another sense. For, being a priest, the most serious moral accusation would not be his femininization, but rather the supposed act of sexual assault. It is no accident that the titles of the news reports that circulated at the time of his detainment presented this accusation with great prominence. Other leaderships defended Father Amaro, especially religious ones, and were judged negatively by public opinion that accepted the accusation of sexual assault without question, one that not long after was revealed to be unfounded. Moral violence, however, was nevertheless produced.

The institutions in which these leaderships acts are referred to as unproductive or are said to have suspicious intents that are contrary to what would be in the "true" interest of the people. Strategically using the language of "development", which is productively associated to valued elements, such as a "job" or "enrichment", elites in Amazon cities construct the image of leaderships and their respective institutions as being distant from reality and the collective interest. The fact that they receive resources from international institutions for environmental protection activities is a preferential target of suspicion and accusations against the moral of our interlocutors.

The US missionary Dorothy Stang, before being murdered by six close-range gunshot wounds, was a target of intense defamatory campaigns that combined elements of gender and suspicion of her commitment to the causes of environmental protection and defense of agrarian reform. The Stang case presents yet another factor that is frequent in the strategies for de-legitimizing moral leaderships in the Amazon, which is the xenophobic content that adheres to accusations of the supposed international interest in the "stagnation" of the region. The xenophobic argument insinuates that the leaderships are infiltrators that should return to their own countries instead of "remaining in the way of development" in Brazil. Sometimes, in protests or manifestations over social media, the idea of the "Amazon for Brazilians" is, paradoxically, not directed at foreign companies that explore natural resources, but at leaderships such as Stang. The fact that this missionary, as well as of other leadership's that act in Amazon, belongs to an ecclesiastic institution is used by her antagonists to indicate her "deviance" from her position as a religious figure, for she would be infringing on the inexistent separation between politics and religion.

Ruptures and continuities in violence

The overall phenomenon of over- and under-criminalization after the de-legitimization of those resisting environmental harms is framed within a process of ruptures and continuities of state and corporate violence. The history of public interventions under the guise of projects that aim to develop the region created the opportunity for forms of violence that are related to a conflict of view over the concept of development and uses of natural resources. In this chapter, therefore, we used the notion of cases or episodes and, at the same time, of process. In this final section we analyze ruptures and continuities in the violence in the Brazilian Amazon, hoping to explain, specifically, why diverse forms of violence occurring within a historical continuity are more acute during specific moments of time. We argue that there are a group of causes that involve direct actions and "symbolic actions" (Fearnside, 1987) by public administration, at the local and federal level.

First, it is important to say that in Brazilian legislation, since the 1960s, "conflict for land" is the very condition of possibility to access policies for agrarian reform, once the "critical zones" or "zones of social tension" are considered priority in the lengthy process of settlement. Therefore, instead of appeasing conflicts, the legislation becomes the element that accelerates disputes (Alston 2000). This is, in great measure, due to the fragility of local institutions—that would be responsible for the identification of areas of "tension'—and, as we demonstrated, due to an involvement of these agencies" staff with the interests or with enterprises of local elites. Therefore, violence is an aspect that becomes naturalized as constitutive of social relations between antagonist groups in the Amazon, a region where much of the land belongs to the state. The social and economic fragility of a group, contrasted with the capacity for hiring private guards by the other, combined with the criminal justice system's bias (Vegh Weis 2019), unequally distributes violence, putting leaderships and members of social movements at a disadvantage.

In the 1990s, after the massacre of Eldorado dos Carajás, new headquarters for local administrative institution responsible for land regularization and agrarian reform were inaugurated, as well as institutions of justice focused, specifically, in investigating and preventing agrarian conflicts. In parallel, there was a significant increase in the number of settlements created in the region set for agrarian reform. The period immediately after an event of violence—particularly one of great repercussion, such as is the case of Eldorado dos Carajás—is marked by measures that break with the scale of violence. Sadly, this rupture is temporary and is directly related to violent events that culminate in the murder of leaderships, which reinforces the argument presented in the previous paragraph: that conflicts are incorporated into the flow of legal and administrative work that should instead aim to avoiding them.

Since 2017, we can see an expressive increase in violence against leaderships and members of social movements in the Brazilian Amazon, especially in the cases of murder of Indigenous people, maroons (*quilombolas*) and rural workers. This period corresponds to both activities that aim to make agencies responsible for the surveillance and protection of the environment more fragile (as for example, the dismissal and transfer of staff, closing of administrative headquarters and budget cuts), as well as judicial changes that aim to legalize conducts that were previously considered criminal, especially in the field of land regularization, rewarding land grabbing (Menezes 2015, Sparovek et al. 2019). This group of actions refers to what Fearnside (1987) considered to be "symbolic actions", or, in other words, public gestures that are confused with concrete measures, that produce effects on existing practices.

Over the last few years, concrete measures for the fragilization of environmental institutions have been combined with symbolic actions, such as declarations contrary to Indigenous rights and to environmental preservation, in addition to the announcement of new measures that are later not made concrete but that inform, signal and communicate. This scenario allows for us to affirm that beyond the combination of forms of violence (threats, aggressions, homicides, attempted homicides and property damaging crimes), farmers, loggers and miners, among other agents that integrate the elites in the Brazilian Amazon, can not only count on the arbitrary selectivity, slowness and impunity of the criminal justice system, but also benefit from the creation of new legal measures in their favor. This became possible based on Brazil's new political juncture, in which perspectives against the environment and social movement are formally represented by elected officials serving at all levels of the federation.

Conclusions

The main result of our analysis is the mutual reinforcement of over- and undercriminalization in Brazilian Amazon. In fact, the present research shows that violence and violations are accompanied by a high rate of impunity or under-criminalization (arbitrary selectivity and slowness in the criminal justice system) of its perpetrators. More recently, under-criminalization of environmental crimes and misappropriation of public lands has occurred not only because of the arbitrary selectivity and slowness of the judiciary, but also because of initiatives by the legislative branch at the federal level, which provide amnesty, without a counterpart, to several illegal actions committed by local rural elites. This results in the informal legalization of land grabbing and *grilagem*.

The over-criminalization of activists that are mobilized against large colonial projects called "development" in the Amazon is part of an extensive chain of illegal initiatives that take place through illicit alliances between public and private actors. This is clear in the two cases described and analyzed in the chapter: the massacre of Pau d'Arco and the lawfare promoted against Father Amaro. Illegal expulsions of small farmers from their lands have been committed by shooters, sometimes formally employed by private security companies, in association with military and civilian police, indicating the existence of rural militias, an organization which recently began to appear in investigations by the Public Prosecutor. This series of phenomena happens due to the weakening of public agencies responsible for inspecting, preventing and fighting agrarian and environmental crimes, especially after the rise of an extreme right-wing politician in the federal executive power. If our analysis of the mutual reinforcement of over and under criminalization in the Brazilian Amazon is correct, one would see that the occurrence of violence, criminalization and violations against leaderships tends to remain at high rates for many years. Unfortunately, this is precisely what the statistical data we shared indicates.

Notes

1 CPT's database is made up of forms with information taken from primary sources (declarations, records and reports sent by agents at the front working for the pastoral teams spread all over the country, and reports of events that involved conflict sent by allies from the social movements) and secondary sources (different newspaper reports, official documents).
2 CPT defines "massacre" as a violent event that ends up in the death of three or more people.
3 As Brazil is a federative republic, there are public security forces for each entity of the federation. The "Federal Police" (*Polícia Federal*) has an investigative role and belongs to the federal government, while every state has its own "Civil Police" (*Polícia Civil*), responsible for the investigation of crimes, and the "Military Police" (*Polícia Militar*), responsible for ostensible policing.

References

Afonso, J. (2014) 'A difícil luta para punir os responsáveis pelos crimes no campo', in Comissão Pastoral da Terra (ed.), *Conflitos no Campo Brasil 2013*, Goiânia: CPT Nacional, 113–117.

Alston, L. (2000) 'Land reform policies, the sources for violent conflict, and implications for deforestation in Brazilian Amazon', *Journal of Environmental Economics and Management*, 39, 162–188.

Bellini, J.A. and Muniz, M. (2019) 'Anapu, barril de pólvora', in Comissão Pastoral da Terra (ed.), *Conflitos no Campo Brasil 2018*, Goiânia: CPT Nacional, 121–130.

de Borrás, S.M. (2012) Land grabbing in Latin America and the Caribbean, *The Journal of Peasant Studies*, 29 (3–4), 845–872.

Cabral, D. (2020) 'Não sejamos cúmplices! Violência e impunidade no campo em 2019', in Comissão Pastoral da Terra (ed.), *Conflitos no Campo Brasil 2018'* Goiânia: CPT Nacional, 172–179.

Das, V. (2006) *Life and Words: violence and the descent into the ordinary*. Berkeley, Los Angeles and London: University of California Press.

Fearnside, M. (1987) 'Deforestation and international economic development projects in Brazilian Amazonia'. *Conservation Biology*, 1(3), 214–221.

Goodwin, J. and Jasper, J. (Eds.) (2015) *The Social Movements Reader: Cases and Concepts*. 3rd ed. Oxford: Wiley Blackwell.

Li, T. (2014) *Land's End: Capitalist Relations on a Indigenous Frontier*. Durham and London: Duke University Press.

Menezes, T. (2015) 'A regularização fundiária e as novas formas de expropriação rural na Amazônia. *Estudos Sociedade e Agricultura*, 23 (1), 110–130.

Sparovek, G. et al. (2019) 'Who won Brazilian lands?', *Land Use Policy*, 87, 104602.

Tsing, A. (2005) *Friction: An Ethnography of Global Connection*, Princeton and Oxford: Princeton University Press.

Vegh Weis, V. (2019) 'Towards a Critical Green Southern Criminology: An analysis of criminal selectivity, indigenous peoples and green harms in Argentina'. *International Journal for Crime, Justice and Social Democracy* 8(3), 38–55.

Velho, O. (1972) *Frentes de Expansão e Estrutura Agrária*. Rio de Janeiro: Zahar.

17

AN ANALYSIS OF THE CRIMINALISATION OF SOCIO-ENVIRONMENTAL ACTIVISM AND RESISTANCE IN CONTEMPORARY LATIN AMERICA

Israel Celi Toledo, Roxana Pessoa Cavalcanti, and Grace Iara Souza

The recent extensive fires in the Amazon and Pantanal regions have alerted the global community to an unparalleled loss of biodiversity alongside irreparable damage to forest areas that are crucial to the world's climate regulation. Amid this ecological crisis lie the loss of human lives and new forms of political authoritarianism, state and corporate harms that go under-criminalized. According to Global Witness' latest report (2020), 212 land and environmental defenders were murdered in 2019, making it the deadliest year of killings on record. Over half of these reported killings occurred in Colombia (64), the Philippines (43) and Brazil (24) (2020, 9). Despite scientific and political recognition of the important role played by environmental defenders for global sustainability, they face high rates of criminalization and victimization, including physical violence and assassinations).

The concept of over-criminalization enables an understanding of the social relations in which Indigenous communities in Latin America exist[1]. As Vegh Weis (2018, 20–21) explains, the creation of some laws and the selective implementation of them is a process demonstrably linked to biases, stigmatizing processes and inequalities relating to class, gender and "race". Over-criminalization is the process of subjecting ordinary activities, strategies of survival and minor misdemeanors to legislation and targeting through law enforcement. This chapter works chiefly with over-criminalization (e.g., the sanction of antiterrorist laws and new penal codes). Historically, as the examples here show, these intertwined processes have operated to dispossess, subjugate and eliminate Indigenous communities as well as green activists and environmental defenders. The production of criminality and dispossessed peoples via selective enforcement and legislation is a process that is intertwined with struggles over the expropriation of natural resources and territories where resistance to open racism and the dismantling of "rights" and socio-environmental policies takes place.

DOI: 10.4324/9781003144229-22

Indigenous peoples and rainforest dwellers are in many ways a heterogeneous social group, but they tend to perceive trees, rivers and every natural living being as part of their territory. Embedded in the reproduction of costumes, traditions, patterns of land use and cultural inheritance, they understand that nature and society belong to each other). Under this background, Latin American Indigenous people have been fighting for their land and rights since the first European invasion, although their struggle might not have always gained widespread attention. Instead, the over-criminalization of socio-environmental movements and the marginalization, direct, symbolic and structural violence against Indigenous peoples have seen a resurgence since the return of the far-right governments (de Carvalho et al. 2020). Indigenous peoples and allies have also been re-adapting their forms of resistance.

This chapter reflects on contemporary disputes over Indigenous territories and extractive practices, shedding light on the ways in which the legal system is used by states to criminalize activists resisting dispossession. In our comparative analysis of Brazil and Ecuador, we complement cross-national and subnational data with case-specific research strategies. Ten interviews were conducted in Ecuador with a range of socio-environmental activists and relevant actors in government and academia. We also considered journalistic articles published in the international and national media. We present a multilevel analysis to place Brazil and Ecuador in a global context. A range of highly different cases helps illustrate broader comparative trends and accompanying theoretical debates. Two of the authors of this chapter participated in green activism among Indigenous people in Ecuador (Celi) and Brazil (Souza). This insider view is complemented with official documents, reports, media and interviews. The argument is then that those colonial dynamics—visible through dispossession, racism and direct violence—are continuously reproduced in the politics of backlash that have become globally prevalent.

This chapter is divided into three parts. First, we consider a brief but broader history of criminalization in Latin America, reflecting on its linkages to capitalism and colonialism. Second, we reflect on contemporary uses of criminalization as a tool to control dissent, focusing on how socio-environmental activists and Indigenous peoples in Brazil have been marginalized and the ways they have resisted the current predicament. Third, we develop comparisons with the Ecuadorian case, highlighting the importance of localized and contextual understandings of each of these cases.

On the history of criminalization in Latin America

The history of criminalization cannot be separated from the history of capitalist development and the formation of a racial-patriarchal order. Federici (2014) persuasively unpacks the links between the transition from feudalism to a capitalist world order, which developed in tandem with colonialization and the persecution of peasant and proletarian women. She traces this transition to a period of population decline caused by the Black Death, and later by other diseases brought to the Americas by European colonizers, precisely at a time labor power was in high demand (Federici 2014, 86). The privatization of land and the demise of communal ways of living at this time were all elements and strategies that assisted the transition to a capitalist economy. This shift entailed a transformation of domestic relations, the construction of power differences between men and women, and "the concealment of women's unpaid labor under the cover of natural inferiority" (Federici 2014, 115). In turn, these processes enabled the capitalist system to expand the unpaid part of the working day and accumulate women's labor, as well as produce inequalities and hierarchies that "alienated workers from each other" (Federici 2014, 115).

In Latin America, the church and the Jesuits played a key role in controlling women's reproduction during this period, promoting the removal of Indigenous women's autonomy and creating new laws to construct married women as men's property and thereby discipline them. In this way, the law was used to control dissent and facilitate capitalist exploitation. For instance, "to ensure that Indigenous women reproduced the workers recruited to do *mita* work in the mines, the Spanish authorities legislated that no one could separate husband from wife, which meant that women were forced to follow their husbands" (Federici 2014, 110).

As well as using the law to enforce prohibitions that generated gendered inequalities and hierarchies among Indigenous populations, the construction of racial hierarchies was central in the strategy of "dividing and ruling" to separate Indigenous and mixed-heritage populations from the White population in the transmission of wealth and property. Such strategies sought to avoid resistance and alliances between oppressed groups. In other words, without the subjugation of women (e.g., through the erosion of women's rights and over-criminalization of their control over reproduction), colonization and the "blood and sweat that for two centuries flowed to Europe from the plantations", a global capitalist economy "may not have taken off" (Federici 2014, 103). This history reveals that in every phase of capitalist development, in every major crisis, strategies are used to cheapen the cost of labor and obscure exploitation, along with the over-criminalization of resistance against this process[2].

The criminalization of dissent in Brazil

The legal system has long been used as a means of controlling resisting subjects, activists and those considered marginalized. What is new is the intensifying use of the law in controlling dissent. The growing global convergence and political spread of far-right ideologies, fascism and authoritarianism has emboldened governments (e.g., often through the police) and non-government actors (e.g., militias and private security operators) to use new technologies and forms of coercion. It is important to note that some of these techniques were already in development under the governance of left-wing parties in Latin America. For instance, the label "eco-terrorists" was used during Correa's government in Ecuador to classify, criminalize and punish dissent. However, leftist and right-wing governments in Latin America should not be conflated (see de Carvalho et al. 2020 for a wider discussion). In the Brazilian case, a conversation[3] with a Latin American environmental activist (2 March 2020), reveals the intensification of the persecution of activists during far-right governments:

The criminalisation of activists is not new in Brazil. But new ways to criminalise are emerging, and new names for old practices. During the dictatorship we were already [labeled] 'terrorists'. We are constantly responding to lawsuits, but it is the first time our own president [Bolsonaro] goes on TV to call us '*vagabundos* (vagrants) getting on the way of progress'. Did you hear about the 'day of the fire' in Pará? Farmers decided via a WhatsApp group to set fire to the area. By 3pm the smoke had arrived in São Paulo making the city look dark like the night. Who ended up in jail? Four activists who were putting out the fire. The mechanisms of justice are being used against us (our translation).

The experience of activists in Brazil suggests that the criminalization of social and human rights movements is growing, alongside anti-environment narratives and anti-human rights sentiments. The discourses of leaders like the current president Jair Bolsonaro give *carte blanche* to law enforcement and civilians to kill and threaten activists. It is then that Indigenous people receive death threats and accusations of disturbing order when they form groups that intend to collectively protect the forest, their livelihoods and their spiritual relationship with nature. Authoritarian and far-right narratives are used to justify violence and the uses of tools of the law, even anti-terror laws against anyone who takes direct action. Examples include cases of imprisonment of activists from the landless movement MST (*Movimento Sem Terra*) based on anti-terrorist laws[4], and unfounded accusations of "extortion and improper collection of rent" as in the cases of former president Inacio Lula da Silva or the supporter and activist for the *Movement for Housing for All* Preta Ferreira (Fox 2019). Preta Ferreira was the leader of the successful occupation of Hotel Cambridge, a case that became widely known[5] through the documentary *The Cambridge Squatter* (Caffé 2017). These are not homogenous movements, they have different histories and dynamics, but they all share a territorial connection, a collective ethos and experiences of criminalization.

Moreover, many activists have been murdered for denouncing deforestation. Threats and intimidation form part of necro politics (Mbembe 2003), a concept developed to define forms of power and control that legally remove the autonomy and discriminate against people who are portrayed as less deserving: the, the Indigenous peoples, the marginalized and the poor. Necro power relates to a form of terror associated with the "sovereign capacity to define who matters and who does not, who is disposable and who is not" (Mbembe 2003, 27). The process of colonization and expropriation is continually re-enacted through dispossession, racist discourses and practices of criminalization. This can be seen in Bolsonaro' discourses:

You, criminals from the MST [Landless Workers' Movement] and the MTST [Homeless Workers' Movement], your actions are going to be labeled as terrorism. Either fall in line and submit to Brazilian laws, or you are going to end up like that drunk [Lula] in Curitiba (7 October 2018).

Such discourses provide the foundations, rationale and license for toxic conflicts. Often these conflicts engender methods of criminalization obscuring longstanding and time-honored rights over land use and ownership. In the Brazilian case, *cartórios* (registry offices) were historically run by families of oligarchs who "owned" the knowledge of the law and as a result utilized the law as an entry point for land grabbing (*grilagem*). According to activists, such colonial methods of appropriation have been "modernized" via state programs such as *Terra Legal* (Legal Land), launched in 2009, through law 11.952/2009 (Imazon 2013), so that "tenders can go to companies that register a claim to the land title remotely, online, pay a tax and acquire Indigenous land they had never set foot on" (conversation with Latin American environmental activist, 02/03/2020). New projects to make laws more flexible and facilitate exploitation, or authorize mining and extraction within Indigenous territories, have emerged during Bolsonaro's government. Such projects illustrate the convergence of at least two types of violence (Mbembe 2006: 309) the violence of the market, including struggles over access to resources and the social violence of structures belonging to society and state.

In September 2020, despite international and national pressure to tackle the high levels of deforestation in the Brazilian Amazon and the fires in the Pantanal's wetlands, Bolsonaro did not intervene to prevent the devastation of biodiversity rich biomes in Brazil or to ensure the rights of the Indigenous peoples as stated in the Federal Constitution and the international treaties of which Brazil is signatory. Instead, Bolsonaro labeled environmental non-governmental organizations (NGOs) working in the area as a "cancer" and accused them of creating an international conspiracy against his government). Meanwhile, the Chief Minister of the Office of Institutional Security, General Augusto Heleno, published a message on social media accusing the Articulation of Indigenous Peoples of Brazil (APIB) of committing a crime of injury against the Brazilian nation. Additionally, he singled out an APIB coordinator, risking her personal security:

> The Articulation of Indigenous Peoples of Brazil is behind the website defundbolsonaro.org, whose objectives are to publish fake news against Brazil, imputing environmental crimes to the President of the Republic and supporting international campaigns in favour of a boycott against Brazilian products. The organisation is managed by Brazilians affiliated to left-wing parties. Emergency APIB is chaired by the Indigenous Sonia Guajajara, a member of PSOL and linked to the actor Leonardo DiCaprio, a staunch critic of our country. The APIB website is associated with several others, who also work 24 hours a day to tarnish our image abroad, in a crime against our country (General Heleno on Twitter).

As illustrated by this post, the far-right government has been incriminating green activists and the Indigenous movement without evidence, insinuating that Indigenous peoples are working with international partners against the interests of the country. This approach increases political polarization while distracting attention from the deforestation of the Amazon and incentivizing illegal farmers, loggers, cattle-ranchers and miners to clear the forest.

The criminalization of socio-environmental activists and Indigenous movements has increased substantially since the return of conservative and far-right governments to mainstream politics in Brazil, prompting a strong movement of resistance. Indigenous peoples—who have been fighting for their rights to exist, support their ancestral ties and connections with territories since colonization—have adopted new weapons of resistance over time. The occupation of spaces in the UN, Brazilian Congress, universities, as well as self-representation against the Brazilian government before the Brazilian Supreme Court, all demonstrate that Indigenous peoples in Brazil can speak for themselves. What remains to be seen is whether green activists and the Indigenous movement can be heard instead of criminalized).

The criminalization of activists defending collective rights in Ecuador

Latin American countries have experienced the impact of a recent wave of natural resource extraction, stimulated by rising international demand and the influence of international business investors (Appel, Mason & Watts 2015). This wave has significant impact on the lives of millions of people in the region. The increase in the demand and supply is intertwined with the criminalization of green activism across the region. The criminalization of Indigenous and green activists in Bolivia, Ecuador and Peru[6] is used to constrain activist's resistance against extractive projects. This shows that state violence[7] plays an economic and political role within peripheral extractive economies (Harvey 2004, Peluso & Watts 2001).

In the Ecuadorian case, such violence often occurs in the form of over-criminalization of activists (Vegh Weis 2018) to protect business interests. This is done using formal institutions to centralize and warrant unconstitutional powers to the executive branch (Conaghan 2015). For example, in December 2013, the Ministry for the Environment invoked Executive Decree 16 to close Fundación Pachamama, a civil society organization closely aligned with green activists. The decision came after a demonstration against the petroleum industry. The ministry's order states that the foundation "carried out actions that were not included in its statutory aims and objectives" (*Ministerio del Ambiente y Agua* 2013). Over-criminalization was also facilitated by the 2011 judicial reform and the approval of the 2014 new criminal code (CELS 2016, PADH 2014, 95–96).

Moreover, over-criminalization is also fostered through the introduction of the executive branch into judicial processes against green activists, promoting the selective and arbitrary applications of controversial criminal offences, such as the "paralyzation of public services", "attack or resistance" and "incitement to discord" (Angulo 2019). These forms of criminalization have become systematically used to protect mining investments and state interests:

> Judicial and administrative measures, including criminal charges, trials, and imprisonment, have been employed at times. Violent repression has been used

too, intimidation, physical and psychological attacks, and discriminatory and stigmatising invective.

(CEDHU and FIDH 2010, 20)

However, the over-criminalization of green activism has not eliminated the resistance of important parts of the population. Environmental concerns and evidence of the failure of oil development have given legitimacy to the environmental discourse in Ecuador, a country that in its 2008 Constitution recognized the rights of nature for the first time in history Larrea 2016). Through mobilization, activists gained popular support for the protection of the Yasuní National Park and the prohibition of metal mining in protected areas in the referendum of 2017 (EFE 2019, Brown 2019). Also, important demonstrations have been organized by the Indigenous movement and small green activist groups. On 13 August 2015, violent clashes between several demonstrators and members of the National Police took place in Quito. Manuela Picq, a French-Brazilian journalist, academic and green activist, was arrested when peacefully demonstrating with Carlos Guartambel, her partner and leader of the Confederation of Kichwas Populations of Ecuador. Picq was arbitrary deported in violation of legal proceedings (Vera 2015). The conflict between green activism and the Ecuadorian state became more acute as the effects of oil extraction and mining exploitation have generated greater environmental and social damage (Larrea 2016). Luisa Lozano, women's leader of the Confederation of Indigenous Nationalities of Ecuador (CONAIE), also suffered criminalization in 2015:

> This conflict could be deepened by generational changes within Indigenous and environmental movements in Ecuador, whose environmental and social demands were channelled through an explosive social revolt in October 2019 that was brutally criminalised by the state.
>
> (interview[8] in Lozano 2020)

The revolt of October 2019 was motivated by state repression, racism expressed by right-wing elites and the refusal of Lenin Moreno's government to negotiate with social movements the measures that affected the popular economy. Since then, the Indigenous movement and green activists reinforced their commitment against neoliberalism and extractive investments. In the words of Luisa Lozano "there is a clear commitment on the path we must follow: the defense of the collective rights that we have won through social struggle" (interview, Saraguro 2019).

Conclusions

Environmental defenders and Indigenous peoples stand against land expropriation, against the commercialization of nature and against the expansion of capitalism. Drawing on the work of Federici (2014), Vegh Weis (2018), Mbembe (2003, 2006) and Yashar (2018), this chapter reveals how diverse forms of violence—symbolic, direct violence, the violence of the market—and criminalization operate as part of the continuous process of colonialization to control or limit dissent by green activists and Indigenous peoples struggling over access to resources and legal rights.

There are differences in how the Brazilian and Ecuadorian states have tolerated and promoted the repression and criminalization of Indigenous and green activists. Ecuador has used the arbitrary application of the law to criminalize. While in Brazil, this issue has also been exacerbated by the de-funding of environmental protection agencies, persecution of environmental workers and the discourses of leaders like President Jair Bolsonaro, which encourage law enforcement and civilians to threaten, criminalize and kill activists. In Ecuador, limited monopoly of force by the state combined with the Indigenous movement's capacity of mobilization in favor of green demands has generated powerful protests and riots. It is important to observe the prominence, the increasing participation and significant role played by Indigenous and Black women in protests, activism and politics. Further research is necessary to delve deeper into the gendered dimensions of the criminalization process. The issues discussed in this chapter, as we have argued, have resulted in complex forms of resistance and fostered new tensions in a social fabric that is submerged in harms and violence by states and corporations in their quest for "capitalist development" at the expense of human beings and the environment. What these political conflicts reveal is the place and significance of criminalization as a process embedded in unequal power relations.

Notes

1 Both under and over-criminalization processes affect Indigenous communities. Under-criminalization describes the failure to legislate against certain harms, and to apply those laws which do exist. For instance, the heinous acts committed against Indigenous populations in Latin America during colonialism, military dictatorships and today including land grabbing, violence, destruction of customary rights, burning of common lands and extermination of native populations have been largely under-criminalized. It is beyond the scope of this chapter to expand the discussion of under-criminalization (see more in Vegh Weis 2018)

2 Such strategies have varied from the use of violence through to persecution, demonization and criminalization of dissidents. During colonization, direct forms of violence were applied for this purpose instead of the criminal justice (see Vegh Weis's 2018 work on "original criminal selectivity").

3 In conversation with Cavalcanti.

4 Brazil enacted Law 13, 260 on 16 March 2016 to regulate section XLIII of article 5 of the Constitution, on terrorism.

5 With an incredibly powerful voice, Preta Ferreira has also recorded a song and music video paying homage to Indigenous women's struggles (see "*Minha Carne*").

6 Alongside the most diverse ethnic populations in South America.

7 The homicides of green activists and Indigenous people in these countries does not match the brutality of violence against Indigenous and green activists in Guatemala, Colombia and other countries in Latin America, which are disproportionately more affected by illicit economies and inadequate public security provision (Yashar 2018).

8 Interviewed by Israel Celi.

References

Angulo, A. (2019) *Paralización de servicio público, un delito reiterado en el paro nacional.* (online) Available from: https://www.primicias.ec/noticias/politica/paralizacion-servicios-publi-cos-delito-paro/ [Accessed 1 October 2020]

Appel, H., Mason, A. and Watts, M. (2015) *Subterranean Estates: Life Worlds of Oil and Gas* Cornell University Press: Ithaca, London.

Brown, K. (2019) Indigenous Waorani win landmark legal case against Ecuador government. *Aljazeera,* 26 April 2019. (Online) Available at: https://www.aljazeera.com/news/2019/04/26/Indigenous-waorani-win-landmark-legal-case-against-ecuador-govt/ [Accessed 1 August 2020]

Caffé, E. (2017). *The Cambridge Squatter,* https://www.imdb.com/title/tt5067984/ (film)

CEDHU/FIDH (2010) *Large-scale mining in Ecuador and human rights abuses.* 1–37. [online]. Available from: https://www.fidh.org/IMG/pdf/Exec_Summary_Large-scale_Mining_Human_Righs_Ecuador-LD.pdf [Accessed 1 October 2020]

CELS (2016) *Latin American state responses to social protest.* 1–57. (online) Available from: https://www.cels.org.ar/protestasocial_AL/en.html [Accessed 1 October 2020]

Conaghan, C.M. (2015) Surveil and sanction: The return of the state and societal regulation in ecuador. *European Review of Latin American and Caribbean Studdies,* (98), 7–27. doi:10.18352/erlacs.9979

de Carvalho, S., Goyes, D. and Vegh Weis, V. (2020) Politics of indigenous victimization: The case of Brazil. *British Journal Of Criminology Criminology.* 1–21. Available from: https://doi.org/10.1093/bjc/azaa060.

EFE (2019) *Rechazan ampliación de explotación petrolera en Yasuní, decretada por More Vistazo* [online]. Available from: https://www.vistazo.com/seccion/pais/actualidad-nacional/rechazan-ampliacion-de-explotacion-petrolera-en-yasuni-decretada

Federici, S. (2014) *Caliban and the Witch: Women, the Body and Primitive Accumulation.* Autonomedia: New York.

Fox, M. (2019) Clampdown on housing rights activists in Bolsonaro's Brazil. *The Nation,* 27 August 2019. (Online) Available at: https://www.thenation.com/article/archive/brazil-bolsonaro-activists-housing-homeless-rights/ [Accessed 3 May 2020]

Global Witness (2020) *Defending Tomorrow: The climate crisis and threats against land and environmental defenders.* (Online) Available at: https://www.globalwitness.org/en/campaigns/environmental-activists/defending-tomorrow/ [Accessed 1 August 2020

Harvey, D. 2004. The new imperialism: Accumulation by dispossession. *Socialist Register* 40: 63–87.

Imazon (2013) *A regularização fundiária avançou na Amazônia? Os dois anos do programa Terra Legal. Executive summary.* (Online) https://imazon.org.br/a-regularizacao-fundiaria-avan-cou-na-amazonia-os-dois-anos-do-programa-terra-legal/ [Accessed 1 October 2020]

Larrea, C. (2016) Petróleo, pobreza y empleo en Ecuador: De la bonanza a la crisis. En. H. J. Burchardt, C. Larrea, R. Domínguez and S. Peters (Eds.) *Nada dura para siempre: Neo-extractivismo tras el boom de las materias primas.* Quito: Abya-Yala.

Lozano, Luisa (2020) Interview by Israel Celi Toledo, *Saraguro, Ecuador,* 12, October.

Mbembe, A. (2003) Necropolitics. *Public Culture,* 15 (1): 11–40.

Mbembe, A. (2006) On politics as a form of expenditure. In: J. Comaroff and J. Comaroff. *Law and Disorder in the Postcolony.* Chicago: University of Chicago Press. 299–336.

Ministerio del Ambiente y Agua (2013) *Se disuelve la Fundación Pachamama, tras comprobarse que la ONG violó el Reglamento de Organizaciones Sociales* (online) Available from: https://www.ambiente.gob.ec/se-disuelve-la-fundacion-pachamama-tras-comprobarse-que-la-ong-violo-el-reglamento-de-organizaciones-sociales/ [Accessed 7 August 2020]

PADH (2014) *Informe sobre Derechos Humanos, Ecuador 2009–2013*. Quito: Universidad Andina Simón Bolívar.

Peluso, N. and Watts, M. (2001) *Violent Environments*. Ithaca: Cornell University Press.

Vegh Weis, V. (2018) *Marxism and Criminology: A History of Criminal Selectivity*. Chicago: Haymarket books.

Vera, C. (2015) *Manuela Picq se ha ido (para no ser expulsada) del país de la Ciudadanía Universal*. GK. (online) Available from: https://gk.city/2015/08/24/manuela-picq-se-ha-ido-no-ser-expulsada-del-pais-la-ciudadania/ [Accessed 1 October 2020]

Yashar, D. (2018) *Homicidal Ecologies: Illicit Economies and Complicit States in Latin America*. New York: Cambridge University Press.

18

NOTES FROM THE FIELD II

The judicial persecution in the Amazonian Indigenous struggle—"El Baguazo" —Amazonas-Perú

Saúl Puerta Peña-Pueblo Awajun

After many years of resistance in the defense of the collective rights of the Indigenous peoples of Peru, in 2009, the native communities faced a racist and discriminatory government. A regime that did not respect the norms and international treaties and abused its power to issue Legislative Decrees that affected the rights of the communities.

In this difficult and impossible approach with the State, the Amazonian leaders were forced into dialog and consultation with the communities and to report the harmful and unconstitutional decrees that the Government of Alan García Pérez had issued to promote private investment in ancestral territories without respecting the prior consultation established in Article 6 of Convention 169 of the International Labor Organization (ILO).

The Amazonian leaders proposed a work plan to discuss with the Government and aim to establish agreements to modify these harmful and dangerous articles, incorporated in the Legislative Decrees. However, the Government's response was negative, neither the Congress of the Republic nor the executive branch had the will to hold any dialog.

In 2008, the first Amazonian mobilization took place, which lasted 14 days, and two Legislative Decrees (1015 and 1073) were repealed. However, the mobilization was suspended because the government declared a state of emergency in the jungle, where the Amazonian social mobilization was taking place in the following regions of Peru—Amazonas, Loreto, Cusco and Ucayali.

The Amazonian leaders were charged with bringing the voice of the Indigenous peoples into dialog with the Government. Unfortunately, the intransigence of the latter meant that representatives were not heard, and the Government did not offer any appointment to propose the changes or modifications that had to be made to other Legislative decrees that threatened the life and existence of native peoples. An agreement could not be reached.

DOI: 10.4324/9781003144229-24

In 2009, the Indigenous peoples resumed the new Amazon mobilization to demand a repeal of the decrees that violated the rights of native communities. The Amazonian strike lasted 56 days in the area called the "Devil's Curve", a marginal jungle road in Amazonas.

On 5 June 2009 at 5am, the police began the violent eviction against the Indigenous brothers, leaving a balance of 15 people killed by firearms, including five Indigenous people, five peasants and ten policemen. Simultaneously, at station No. 6 of the Peruvian pipeline, 13 policemen were kidnapped and killed by unknown groups, and one police officer disappeared; a total of 28 Peruvians dead and one missing.

Some media strongly opposed the Indigenous people, calling them savages, manipulated, terrorists, and invented the "law of the jungle" noting that the Indigenous are violent groups; a discourse that was also reproduced by the Legislative and Executive Power.

With their majority, Aprista, from the government of Alan García, turned their backs on the people. The Public Ministry began a judicial persecution against the main leaders (including myself) with an international arrest warrant for the alleged crimes of sedition, mutiny, instigator, kidnapping and perpetration. As well as myself, 53 leaders were also denounced. The investigation process lasted more than six years and acquittal was achieved by the Bagua-Amazonas Transitory Criminal Chamber and Settlement, on 22 September 2016.

However, despite this acquittal, the Procurator of the Interior Ministry and the Mixed Superior Prosecutor's Office of Bagua, filed an appeal for annulment for the Supreme Court to rule in the final instance. The Supreme Court confirmed the judgment in the first instance, a situation that ended a story of abuse and suffering of the Indigenous brothers, declaring them innocent to all the denounced, and definitively filed the process.

The asylum

Finally, I faced an unjust arrest warrant against myself., Since my life was in danger, I applied for political asylum at the Nicaraguan Embassy. The government at that time granted me political asylum, and I was deported, against my will, to the city Managua-Nicaragua, and returned when the Judge varied the arrest warrant for a restricted appearance.

Returning to Lima, I continued my fight in defense of the Indigenous peoples, where I received threats from unknown persons, and restrictions on leaving the country. Since then, the judge ordered rules to enable my constitutional rights; just for having defended the rights of a people forgotten and marginalized by the state.

The worst thing about the government was that it ordered the dissolution of the highest Indigenous organization of Peru, the "Inter-ethnic Association for the Development of the Peruvian Jungle" (AIDESEP), in which I was a leader, occupying the position of national secretary. This was another government attack against Indigenous institutions. Said proposal did not prosper, because it was considered as a political revenge and hatred for the peoples, and, in an act of communion, the strategic allies of the Indigenous movement expressed solidarity, rendering the aforementioned attack without effect.

Not content with that, the government formed parallel organizations to weaken the forces and divide the unity of the peoples. Thanks to the trust and unity of the native communities, they did not achieve their objective, remaining with hatred. The government branded the Indigenous people as "Hortelano dogs" and as "second-rate people", clearly offending a people who only sought respect for their rights to be recognized in the Political Constitution of Peru, and in international treaties.

Justice acted abusively, apparently with orders from those who governed at that time, since it never began any investigation process against the government itself, or against those who were in charge of the violent eviction operations. Quite the contrary, the Amazonian leaders opened an investigation process into them; they even imprisoned two Indigenous brothers, one for five years and another for three years, without any order from the judge or evidence of a crime, but just because they had Indigenous features. In addition, violating their rights to defense and due process, or of not respecting the interpreter's rights.

It was total abuse. This is a regrettable story that should not be repeated. It should be prevented, and strategic alliances sought to enter dialog with native communities, since we seek respect for the right to prior consultation and respect for our ancestral territories.

State policy against native peoples is a weapon to make them disappear. However, the Indigenous peoples will always be united towards facing any attack against their rights and to reporting to international organizations.

Finally, we must not forget that 28 people died, and one disappeared, because of violent eviction and government persecution, and we are not free yet. We are attentive to any ruler who tries to destroy our territories and forests. In case this happens, we will gladly go to the front line in defense of our rights and of our peoples.

PART V

Challenges for a critical agenda on the over-criminalization of dissent

19

ARTIFICIAL INTELLIGENCE AND THE CRIMINALISATION OF ACTIVISM

Mark Cowling

What is artificial intelligence? The Oxford Dictionary definition of artificial intelligence is as follows: theory and development of computer systems able to perform tasks normally requiring human intelligence, such as visual perception, speech recognition, decision-making and translation between languages[1]. This chapter notes some of the likely developments of artificial intelligence over the next few years. A particularly important development is that a wide range of jobs are likely to disappear, being replaced by robots and algorithms. Also, there is likely to be increased class polarization, with the owners of the tech giants enjoying a massive accumulation of wealth, whilst those displaced by artificial intelligence end up with low paid and insecure employment. There is thus the basis of considerable social unrest to be followed by criminalization.

The situation is, although, more complex. On the one hand, the new media fostered by artificial intelligence facilitate the organization of activism. Thus, for example, another name for the Arab Spring was the Facebook Revolution. The UK riots of 2011, following the police shooting of Mark Duggan, were in part a protest facilitated by the use of Blackberry mobile phones. Some of the organization of the Black Lives Matter demonstrations, following the police murder of George Floyd, has been facilitated by the new media. On the other hand, artificial intelligence can be a method of repression. Facial recognition technology can be used to identify demonstrators. Its most extreme used to date is probably that in China, where the state is aspiring to control the lives of citizens using artificial intelligence. But it is also used by, for example, US and British police forces. Whilst some of this use is a legitimate way of attempting to catch criminals, it can also involve the labeling of individuals as dangerous, meaning that they are likely to be stopped aggressively, which in turn may lead them to resist, thus proving that they are violent. In particular, Black peoples' locales experience unwarranted levels of stop and search and unduly aggressive tactics when making arrests. Artificial intelligence opens the

DOI: 10.4324/9781003144229-25

possibility of intimidating peaceful demonstrators. If the data is bad, individuals will be wrongfully targeted. Criminalization and repression take place initially informally in the construction of algorithms but can lead on to more formal criminalization, mainly through use of all the existing laws. Building on this reasoning, this chapter will explore the paradox role of artificial intelligence which can lead to polarization and insecurity and thence to activism, while at the same time can also facilitate its repression via "intelligent criminalization".

Artificial intelligence and data gathering

Artificial intelligence works by gathering huge quantities of data and then analyzing it. According to Smith & Browne, (2019), we are ending this decade with about 25 times as much data as at the beginning of the decade, mostly held by corporations with the "consent" of the users. One Viennese citizen eventually prized out of Facebook a CD-ROM containing 1,200 pages of data (Smith & Browne 2019). He had "consented" to this by using Facebook. Something similar happens when people use websites. These invariably want to place a cookie on your computer. You have "consented" to this by allowing websites to place cookies on your computer. This allows them to harvest some of your data. Prior to 2016 this would also involve "consenting" to other third-party providers harvesting your data. A calculation in 2008 suggested that it would take 76 full days a year to read through all the agreements. This will have grown considerably since that time (Zuboff 2019). A team of researchers found, in 2015, that a visitor to the 100 most popular websites would accumulate no less than 6,000 cookies, 83% of them unrelated to the initial website visited (Zuboff 2019). This led the EU to develop its General Data Protection Regulation (GDPR) in 2016.

In turn, US citizens do not enjoy this protection. In June 2013, the *Guardian* newspaper revealed that nine major US companies that handle data, including Apple and Microsoft, had signed up for a program called PRISM, which allowed the NSA (the US National Security Agency) to spy at will on anyone who made use of programs provided by these companies (Smith & Browne 2019, 250). The *Guardian* knew about this thanks to Edward Snowden, who absconded from an NSA center bearing about a million documents, which kept journalists busy for the next year or so. Intrusion by the NSA was *prima facie* a violation of the 4th Amendment, which guarantees US citizens security from unwarranted searches and seizures, and, obviously, there are similar expectations in other Western democracies (Smith & Browne 2019, 328). This presented technology companies with a major dilemma: how could they protect their customers from unwarranted state intrusion, while cooperating with legitimate concerns of the NSA? (Smith & Browne 2019, 507). Indeed, Microsoft received in one year 50,000 search warrants from the governments of 70 countries (Smith & Browne 2019, 624). Potentially this is extremely serious: the technology companies are in danger of colluding in major instances of state crime.

Confronting this scenario, Zuboff describes the current era as one of "surveillance capitalism", meaning "a rogue mutation of capitalism, involving concentrations of wealth, knowledge and power unprecedented in human history, the foundational framework of a surveillance economy … A threat to human nature" (2019). For example, the basis of Google's massive accumulation of wealth is its unprecedented intrusion into personal life. With the ability to probe what people are doing online, using cheap cameras to photograph geographic locations and cheap storage, "your whole life will be searchable", as Larry Page, one of the founders of Google, remarked in 2001. Another intrusion fostered by Google is the ability to track one's location via one's smart phone, all for the benefit of advertisers—thousands of locations can be tracked each day (Zuboff 2019). To keep on accumulating, corporations such as Google and Facebook lobby vigorously to oppose any restrictions on their right to intrude. Indeed, Google spent around $18 million each year on lobbying in Washington, and it is also the largest individual lobbyist in the EU (Zuboff 2019).

Artificial intelligence and employment

Besides threatening individual privacy, artificial intelligence is also changing the labor market. Earlier technological developments have led to a change in employment patterns, which can be extremely unpleasant for the individuals concerned. In the 19th century many people were forced off the land and ended up in noisy, unsafe factories, working long hours and living in harsh conditions, as charted so brilliantly in *Capital*.

A major disruption is extremely likely thanks to artificial intelligence. The current degree of automation enables very large quantities of products to be the work of relatively few people. For example, all the many Heinz products made in Britain, including 3 million cans of baked beans, in a factory which works round the clock and seven days a week, require a workforce of about 1,500. This explains why, although the UK remains the seventh-largest country for manufacturing in the world, the manufacturing workforce is much smaller than it used to be. Between the early 1980s and 2018 the manufacturing workforce shrank by 3 million, representing a fall from 21% of the UK workforce to 8%. Despite this, from 1970 to the present day, the country has ranked somewhere between 6th and 8th in the world, with China now top, the USA 2nd, Japan 3rd, Germany 4th, South Korea 5th, and then France, Britain, Italy and various other countries moving in and out of 6th to 9th place. Bastani points to similar effects of artificial intelligence and the use of robots in US industry, of greatly increased production with a much smaller workforce (2019). Moreover, Kessler charts how, since around 2002, the bulk of the growth in the US employment market is in the form of self-employment. People are increasingly independent contractors, and therefore do not get the fringe benefits (holiday pay, sick pay, medical cover, pensions, etc.) enjoyed by employees (2019, 9, Srnicek & Williams 2016). Highly skilled professionals such as higher-level programmers and website designers can do very well, these are a tiny portion of the workforce. Conditions for very many self-employed people are insecure and poorly paid. This certainly applies to US citizens, many of whom are desperately insecure. In 2015, a report by the Federal Reserve found that 47% of US citizens could not cover an unexpected expense of $400 from their savings or their credit card (Kessler 2019, 189). They are likely to have inadequate medical insurance, so such an emergency is only too possible.

The increasing application of artificial intelligence is likely to result in even increasingly automated operations. In other words, in the foreseeable future an extensive disruption can be foreseen as very large numbers of workers are displaced by artificial intelligence. Warehouses will be increasingly automated, as will distribution involving either self-driving transport or drones. Factories will be increasingly staffed by robots, shelves will be stacked and clothes folded by robots (Russell 2019, 74), drivers will be replaced by self-driving vehicles—according to Russell, cars in cities will largely be replaced by free self-driving buses (2019, 67),—perhaps the hundred thousand or so people currently employed by Facebook to watch a daily diet of extreme pornography in order to decide if it needs to be censored, will be replaced by computer programs, low-level legal work will also be computerized—computers did better than law professors at analyzing non-disclosure agreements,—insurance underwriting will soon largely be done by computer, as will at least some medical diagnoses, as will telemarketing, credit checking, tax accountancy, operating checkouts and baking (see, amongst others, Dyer-Witherford 2015, Bastani 2019, Russell 2019, 118-9, Tegmark 2018, 101, 122). Even call centers are likely to require far fewer staff, as voice recognition software improves, and enquiries can be dealt with by computer programs (Smith & Browne 2019).

The result of this process is that, in contrast to the accumulation of poverty at the bottom end of society, there is a massive accumulation of wealth at the top. Russell reproduces an alarming graph produced originally by the US Bureau of Labor which shows from around 1970 onwards productivity doubling by 2005 while the rewards going to workers in the sector which produces goods remained static (Russell 2019, 118, Fuchs (2019) points to something similar in Germany). As Susskind points out, Amazon, Google and Facebook have an accumulation of wealth roughly equivalent to the GDP of Canada (2018, 319). There are structural reasons why this is so: these firms have an oligopoly of data, making them hard to displace, and they have relatively few employees, meaning that the number of people who benefit from their position is rather small (Susskind 2018, 321). As factories become automated, work previously taken offshore to, for example, China, will increasingly be done by robots in, for example, Germany (Fuchs 2019). Plainly, extremely dramatic disruptions are in prospect. At least some of the people whose lives are disrupted will turn to crime, and doubtless their crimes will be detected using artificial intelligence.

Protest, criminalization and repression

The background described above of widespread insecurity and increasing polarization provides a great deal to protest about. Some forms of protest and solidarity occur within the new social media, driven on by algorithms. Thus, there are organizations devoted to launching petitions, for example 38 Degrees, Sum of Us, Change.org and Avaaz, while others use petitions as part of their work, for example Amnesty International, Greenpeace, Compassion in World Farming and Reprieve. Petitions can be backed up by the organized writing of emails to MPs, government ministers, heads of corporations, etc. Legal actions can be crowdfunded. Recent examples of such legal actions launched in Britain are attempts to prosecute Dominic Cummings, attempts to force the Crown Prosecution Service to prosecute more cases of rape and sexual assault, and a legal action associated with dismally poor government advice to care homes during the Covid-19 crisis. These actions are legal, and may indeed be facilitated by legislation, so they are not generally repressed. It is difficult to tell how effective petitions are: they can certainly raise public awareness, for example shaming the UK government into continuing to provide school lunches for impoverished children during the summer of 2020. Other petitions appear to be pushing on an open door, for example the petition that Captain Tom Moore, who raised over £30 million for the NHS should be given a knighthood. And petitions are likely to be accompanied by the lobbying of politicians and comments in the media, so there is no precise way of getting to grips with cause and effect.

The Chinese state is towards the other end of the scale. Under President Xi it is aspiring to increasingly rigid control of Chinese citizens. There has been control since the founding of the state through local and workplace committees under the leadership of the Communist Party, which aimed, for example, to enforce the "one child" policy. However, although the "one child" policy has now been relaxed, control has tightened considerably under Xi, and is now reinforced by the use of facial recognition technology. Jaywalking pedestrians can be instantly shamed, with their picture getting flashed up on an electronic billboard and a fine levied before they have got to the pavement on the other side of the road. This is accompanying increasingly tight control of dissidents who can be intimidated through imprisonment. There is very vigorous repression of the Muslim Uyghur population of East Turkistan (Xinjiang), with allegations of over one million out of a population of about 11 million being held in "re-education", or "vocational training" camps, but in such poor conditions that an appropriate name would be "concentration camps", half a million children held in state-run orphanages because their parents are being re-educated and the Uyghur language prohibited in schools. This whole very sad situation appears to have been triggered by the riots of 2009, in which groups of Uyghurs attacked and killed numerous Han Chinese. The Chinese authorities responded by summarily executing numerous Uyghurs, became very worried about a significant source of dissent, and adopted the measures described here. In addition to what has already been described, artificial intelligence is used for facial recognition, with cameras installed ubiquitously, including at the entrance of almost every household. There is an aspiration to build a database of Uyghur DNA. Mosques are being destroyed and the practicing of Islam repressed in a manner reminiscent of Cultural Revolution. The halal labeling of food has been prohibited, and Muslims encouraged to eat pork. Books in the Uyghur language are being prohibited. China has a relatively low rate of imprisonment, but 25% of Chinese prisoners are Uyghurs (this is apart from the re-education camps) although Uyghurs are about 1.5% of the

Chinese population. The Chinese government is engaging in this repression and criminalization partly to avoid Isis- and Al Qaeda-style terrorism, and also to secure some of the main routes through which the Belt and Road initiative passes. There is a great deal of everyday resistance, based on small groups, but there has also been some much more deadly violence such as the Kunming train station massacre of March 2014, in which knife-wielding Muslims killed 29 people and wounded some 140 others, and in May that year a bomb exploded at Urumqi in a vegetable market killing 31 people and wounding many more. This is obviously an extremely ugly situation for all concerned. The attempt of the Chinese Communist Party to bring Hong Kong increasingly under the control of the mainland, and the various forms of resistance to this have been widely documented.

Artificial intelligence is also involved in the over-criminalization (see Vegh Weis 2018), and repression of Black populations in the USA and in the UK, which has led to the Black Lives Matter demonstrations. The over-criminalization of Black populations in the USA and the UK doubtless has roots going back to the time of slavery: it does not *require* artificial intelligence for Black people to die in the hands of police without justification, for them to be found guilty of driving whilst Black, to be on the wrong end of far more stop-and-search than White people, for Black men, particularly, to be imprisoned out of proportion to their numbers, and for Black lives to continue to be blighted after imprisonment by the restrictions of life on probation, and, in the USA, to be excluded from voting (see, for example, Ferguson 2017, Tegmark 2018, 106, Srnicek & Williams 2016). An important reference point for the UK is the Macpherson report of 1999, which followed on from the killing by White racists of Stephen Lawrence and the subsequent thoroughly bungled police investigation and introduced the concept of the police being institutionally racist is one starting point. Unfortunately, although the UK police have undoubtedly improved, too many of the prejudices charted by Macpherson remain.

Artificial intelligence is very extensively used in policing in some parts of the USA, notably in Los Angeles by the LA Police Department. On arriving for their shift, LA police are provided with a digital map of their area, complete with data culled from 4,000 databases of likely trouble spots, and the history of gang activity. However, racist prejudices can easily be written into the algorithms which supply police with this picture (Ferguson 2017), making oppressive policing more effectively bad, complete with a scientific gloss. Data can be inaccurately entered and processed, which is obviously likely to exacerbate existing tensions. In Los Angeles, Black persons can be identified as Chronic Violent Offenders, making it likely that they will be stopped aggressively by police, to which they may well respond violently, thus demonstrating that they are chronically violent (Ferguson 2017, 2182)! Ferguson points out that there is a class dimension to this issue: young people of all classes get drunk, take drugs and engage in minor criminality, but members of the upper classes do not normally get their collars felt (2017). Indeed, if they are British, perhaps they are members of the Bullington Club, in which case they may well end up as members of the Cabinet. On the other hand, there is the possibility of using artificial intelligence to monitor police misconduct and analyze its roots (Ferguson 2017).

Racialized policing and the unjustified police killing of Black people is the main origin of the Black Lives Matter movement. The way in which this has become widespread following the police killing of George Floyd has very much involved artificial intelligence. The nine minutes during which a police officer suffocated him was filmed on smart phones. His slow murder and the pleas of an off-duty firefighter are thus documented rather than just an alleged by onlookers. The widespread outrage which erupted following this killing has been fueled by social media, notably the availability of the video of Floyd's death on YouTube, together with numerous related YouTube sequences. The spreading of protests not only in the USA but worldwide has partly been fueled by social media. However, as this seems to be a movement whose time has come, being based as it is upon many years of social exclusion and oppressive policing, in the UK at least the movement has very much gone mainstream. The main TV channels have featured programs on the killing, and also programs in which Black people talk of their experiences at the hands of the police. There have also been series about various aspects of Black history. When playing the West Indies this summer the England cricket team, who are mainly White, took the knee before games and had Black Lives Matter embroidered into their shirts. Part of what is going on is a feeling that, although there is a great deal wrong here, at least UK police generally do not shoot people and are better trained than many members of the police in the USA. Black people are also more integrated with a much higher degree of intermarriage. There has been public debate about the statues of men who made their money from slavery, following events in Bristol where the statue of Edward Colston was dumped in the harbor. Something of a consensus has emerged, on the lines that at least some statues should be removed to museums and others should include an explanation of the role that the prominent man played in the exploitation of slaves.

In contrast, in the USA, President Trump has poured petrol on the flames. He has organized the repression of reasonably peaceful demonstrations, including praising the actions of a White vigilante who shot and killed two demonstrators. He has also made this an election issue, presenting the issue as one of lawlessness which needs to be dealt with firmly. Artificial intelligence has featured strongly in his presidency, not only in his constant tweeting, but also in the extremely finely tailored algorithms which channeled particular advertisements and news items to potential voters at the time of his election. This was facilitated by the UK firm Cambridge Analytica. There are also allegations of intervention by the Russian state in favor of Trump, who has been relatively favorable towards Russia. Given that Hillary Clinton actually got more votes than Trump, who was elected thanks to role of the Electoral College, artificial intelligence may actually have got Trump elected in the first place. Watch out for the use of artificial intelligence in the 2020 election.

Let us turn finally to the #Me Too movement. The movement was started by Tamara Burke in 2006 on MySpace. She was concerned about sexual harassment, which she had experienced, particularly as it affected young and vulnerable women. The movement really took off in a big way with a posting on Twitter by Alyssa Milano in October 2017. She called attention to widespread sexual harassment, particularly by powerful men in the film industry, and invited other women to share their experience using the hashtag #Me Too. She pointed people towards her blog, which contained, in particular, allegations about the conduct of Harvey Weinstein. By the end of the day on which she proposed the hashtag it was repeated no less than 200,000 times. The way in which allegations against Weinstein multiplied, leading eventually to his trial and conviction should be well known. Milano had obviously drawn attention to something tremendously important and extremely widespread, going well beyond the film industry, and including music, academia, science, politics, churches (where widespread abuses in the Catholic Church has already been exposed in the Boston Globe), schools, finance, Silicon Valley, particularly focusing on Uber, sport, the military and the pornography industry. This tweet led to further social mobilization and the unearthing of a huge social problem. Indeed, the Washington Post conducted a survey of US women that found that 54% had experienced "unwarranted and inappropriate" sexual attention, and that in 96% of cases nothing whatsoever was done about it.

The movement rapidly spread internationally, to at least 85 countries, including Australia, Belgium, France, Germany, India, Israel, Italy, Japan (a country which has been particularly backward in dealing with allegations of rape), Nigeria, Norway, Pakistan, South Korea, Spain, Sweden and the UK. In the UK there were, notably, allegations about politicians in both the Labour Party and the Conservatives. Accusations made against the Minister of Defence, Michael Fallon, and the unofficial Deputy Prime Minister Damian Green, led to both resigning from Theresa May's cabinet.

Conclusions

This chapter has shown that artificial intelligence is extremely important both in causing major social disruption, leading to increased insecurity and impoverishment at one pole, and massive accumulations of wealth in a very few hands at the other. It moves on to discuss the massive accumulation of data in the hands of the tech companies, used primarily for commercial gain, but also exploited by the security services. In the final part, there is an illustration of the role of artificial intelligence in various forms of protest and in attempts to repress them. It is difficult to do justice to all the sections of the chapter, as they could all be enormously expanded. Students of protest movements ignore the role of artificial intelligence at their peril! It seems time for criminology to focus in an increasingly threatening phenomenon: "intelligent criminalization" is already here.

Note

1 There is a substantial and increasing volume of literature on artificial intelligence. Here is a sample: Adams & Kletter 2018, Ferguson 2017, Dyer-Witherford 2015, Dyer-Witherford, Kjosen & Steinhoff 2019, Fuchs 2019, Fuchs is a leading editor of and major contributor to the journal *tripleC: Communication, Capitalism and Critique*, which very frequently carries articles in this area, Srnicek & Williams 2016, Kessler 2019, Foer 2017, Schwab & Davis 2018, Smith & Browne 2019, Bastani 2019, Zuboff 2019, Susskind 2018. Books and articles on artificial intelligence and its implications are coming out all the time.

References

Adams, J. and Kletter, R. (2018) *Artificial Intelligence: Confronting the Revolution*, Endeavour Media.

Bastani, A. (2019) *Fully Automated Luxury Communism: A Manifesto*, London: Verso.

Dyer-Witherford, N. (2015) *Cyber-Proletariat: Global Labour in the Digital Vortex*, London: Pluto Press.

Dyer-Witherford, N., Kjosen, A. and Steinhoff, J. (2019) *Inhuman Power: Artificial Intelligence and the Future of Capitalism*, London: Pluto Press.

Ferguson, A.G. (2017) *The Rise of Big Data Policing: Surveillance, Race, and the Future of Law Enforcement*, New York: New York University Press.

Foer, F. (2017) *World without Mind: Why Google, Amazon, Facebook and Apple Threaten our Future*, London: Vintage Digital Publishing.

Fuchs, C. (2019) *Rereading Marx in the Age of Digital Capitalism*, London: Pluto Press.

Kessler, S. (2019) *Gigged: the Gig Economy, the End of the Job, and the Future of Work*, New York: Random House Business.

Russell, S. (2019) *Human Compatible: Artificial Intelligence and the Problem of Control*, Harmondsworth: Penguin.

Schwab, K. and Davis, N. (2018) *Shaping the Fourth Industrial Revolution*, World Economic Forum.

Smith, B.L. and Browne, C.A., *Tools and Weapons: the Promise and Perils of the Digital Age*, London: Hodder and Stoughton 2019.

Srnicek, N. and Williams, A. (2016) *Inventing the Future: Post-capitalism and a World without Work*, London: Verso.

Susskind, J. (2018) *Future Politics: Living Together in a World Transformed by Tech*, Oxford: Oxford University Press.

Tegmark, M. (2018) *Life 3.0: Being Human in the Age of Artificial Intelligence*, Harmondsworth: Penguin.

Vegh Weis, V. (2018) *Marxism and Criminology: A History of Criminal Selectivity*, London: Haymarket.

Zuboff, S. (2019) *The Age of Surveillance Capitalism: the Fight for a Human Future at the New Frontier of Power*, London: Profile Books.

20

COVID COPS

A recent history of pandemic policing during the coronavirus crisis

Greg Martin

Government responses to the Covid-19 pandemic varied across liberal democracies, authoritarian and semi-authoritarian societies. In China and Singapore, for instance, where citizen compliance with lockdown measures was generally high (McCurry et al. 2020), success in tackling the virus was attributed largely to the fact those countries had previously experienced SARS and MERS. By contrast, death rates in other autocratic states, such as Iran, were relatively high, with the Johns Hopkins University and Medicine Coronavirus Resource Centre (2020) recording Iranian deaths at 33.81 per 100,000 population as of 9 October 2020, compared with 0.34 for China and 0.48 for Singapore.

Variations were also evident across liberal democratic countries, though many of the highest mortality rates were found in Europe (Johns Hopkins University and Medicine Coronavirus Resource Centre 2020). In those countries, governments grappled with a fundamental dilemma that pitted state intervention against citizen rights, freedoms and responsibilities. Indeed, what the Covid-19 crisis highlighted, perhaps above all else, is the limits of neoliberalism and the neoliberal obsession with private sector "efficiency" (see Collington 2020), along with the continuing need for state intervention in key areas such as healthcare and employment, and that, ultimately, "[t] he government should act like a government, like its job is to provide these things" (Lowrey 2020). However, in places like the UK, where government action initially took the form of a "stay at home" order, then a "stay alert" message clearly designed to instill greater citizen responsibility, periodic recourse to local lockdowns and other restrictions, like so-called circuit breaker measures, piqued disquiet amongst politicians to such an extent that they sought an amendment to emergency coronavirus legislation to increase parliamentary oversight on any future Covid-19 restrictions limiting social freedoms (Murphy et al. 2020)

Not only politicians but also some sections of the public voiced opposition to government restrictions making illegal some of the most mundane, innocuous and

DOI: 10.4324/9781003144229-26

taken-for-granted rights and freedoms citizens of liberal democracies are habituated to exercising in the course of their everyday lives, e.g., social gathering, physical exercise, shopping. People not only expressed concern about the increased involvement of police in their daily lives but also worried about perceived violations of civil liberties, such as via the use of face-covering mandates, as well as curbs generally on protest rights during the pandemic, not just when protest was Covid-related but also when it focused on other grievances, though, most significantly, Black Lives Matter. While racial violence and anti-mask protests had precursors at the time of the Spanish flu pandemic in the early 20th century, many of the same issues also coalesced in the more recent coronavirus crisis. What follows is an exploration of some of the ways protest was subject to processes of criminalization during the Covid-19 crisis, beginning with a brief examination of policing and regulation of everyday life in the Australian state of Victoria, which is an important case study, not least because every day policing provided the foundation for the policing and regulation of protest during the pandemic.

Policing everyday life in Melbourne's "second wave" of coronavirus infection

Following a surge in cases resulting from breaches of the hotel quarantine system used for returning citizens and permanent residents, Victoria experienced a second wave of Covid-19 infection in mid-2020. On 4 July 2020, the state saw its second highest rise in new cases since the pandemic began in early 2020. Of the 108 new cases, 23 came from 12 households in housing estates located in metropolitan Melbourne (Russo 2020). Acting swiftly, on 5 July 2020, the state government imposed strict lockdown measures on nine public housing tower blocks in Melbourne, banning some 3,000 residents from leaving their homes for a minimum of five days (Russo 2020). While the "sudden move to a police-enforced ring-fencing of public housing towers" was criticized for happening without notice (Fowler & Booker 2020), and potentially instilling fear in marginalized residents already suspicious of police, the hard lockdown was supported by Australia's Acting Chief Medical Officer, Professor Paul Kelly, who compared the threat of coronavirus spreading within the tower blocks to that of "vertical cruise ships" (Fowler & Booker 2020).

For a time, then, Victoria effectively became a police state. And not long after the lockdown of the tower blocks, further measures were introduced, as the spread of the virus could not be suppressed as quickly as the state government wanted. The everyday policing of rules and restrictions included around social distancing and gatherings, the compulsory wearing of face coverings, night-time curfews and daily exercise limits (Victorian Government 2020). Additional restrictions were justified mostly on the basis that too many people continued to flout the rules. For instance, on 30 July 2020, of the 500 people testing positive for Covid-19 who were door-knocked by Australian Defense Force personnel and public health officials, one in four were not at home (Bolger 2020). Along with growing infection numbers, this was, among other things, what led the Victorian government to introduce new

"Stage 4" restrictions on metropolitan Melbourne effective 6 pm, 2 August 2020, including an 8 pm to 5 am curfew (Victorian Government 2020).

As with other jurisdictions, in Victoria fines became a key tool of Covid-19 policing (Victorian Government 2020). At the lower end of the spectrum, the fine for not wearing a face covering without lawful exemption was $200AUD. Higher on the spectrum, an on the spot fine of $1,652AUD applied for breach of stay-at-home orders, which could be extended through the Magistrates' Court for repeat offenders to a maximum of $10,000AUD. Higher still, an on the spot fine of $4,957AUD would be issued for breaching isolation orders for a second or subsequent time after testing positive for coronavirus, which could be extended through the Magistrates' Court for repeat offenders to a maximum of $20,000AUD.

As the literature on fines demonstrates, despite being porous sanctions, "levied impersonally, without ceremony and regardless of the intentions or desires of the payee" (O'Malley 2009: 77) and in order to "compel obedience" without any accompanying feeling of guilt or wrongdoing (O'Malley 2009, 73), there exists a hidden punitiveness to fines, including "enforceability against the indigent" (Quilter & Hogg 2018, 16). In this sense, fines constitute not only a form of "monetarized criminalization" but could also be thought of as a latter-day version of what Valeria Vegh Weis (2017, xv) terms, "criminal selectivity", which refers to the unfairness that is "a mandated feature of the criminal justice system", and which results in the over-criminalization of groups at society's margins, while social harms perpetrated by the powerful are under-criminalized.

Not surprisingly, given Victoria was the only state or territory in Australia to experience a second wave of coronavirus infection, it issued fines at almost triple the rate of other states or territories, and had the harshest fines (McGowan et al. 2020). However, location data released by Victoria police revealed of the almost 6,000 fines issued for breach of public health orders, "there had been little correlation between enforcement of the orders and the spread of Covid-19" (McGowan et al. 2020). In an instance of criminal selectivity as just discussed, up to 17 May 2020, only 82 fines were issued in Stonnington, an affluent inner east area of Melbourne, despite that area having the state's second highest number of cases. However, areas with higher migrant numbers and greater social housing stock had relatively few cases but more recorded fines, raising concerns those communities were targeted and over-policed (McGowan et al. 2020, see also Boseley 2020). Police data raised similar concerns in New South Wales where lower socio-economic areas with fewer cases of coronavirus recorded a disproportionately higher number of fines compared to affluent areas with higher coronavirus cases and relatively fewer fines (Lee 2020).

Naming and shaming has also been a strategy employed in some Australian jurisdictions for fine defaulters (Quilter & Hogg 2018, 26–27), which were numerous in Victoria during the pandemic when, at one point, only 845 of the more than 19,000 penalty notices issued had been paid (Pearson 2020). Naming and shaming were sometimes a tactic employed by the mainstream media during the coronavirus crisis too. On one occasion, two African women who tested positive for Covid-19 after returning to Brisbane from Melbourne via Sydney without declaring they had visited coronavirus hotspots, were named and shamed by the media in what was widely regarded as sexist and racist reporting (Southern 2020). Indeed, naming and shaming has been roundly condemned, not least because it can lead to a perception that compliance rates are lower than they are (Muller 2020, Southern 2020). However, media stories about some of the more "egregious violations" that occurred in Victoria, for instance, such as anti-maskers assaulting police or conspiracy theorists driving through police checkpoints, were thought to play a role in driving compliance, with Professor Liam Smith of Monash University's Behaviour Works Australia, saying:

> It gets us angry and fired up and we all become citizen cops [...] So it creates outrage in a positive sense because it promotes some vigilantism and community policing is a powerful deterrent leading to greater and greater compliance.
>
> (quoted in Graham 2020)

On the other hand, the Covid-19 pandemic heightened existing concerns about extensive police and state use of surveillance technologies. In England, for example, Derbyshire police used drones to shame people into not driving to the Peak District national park during lockdown (Pidd & Dodd 2020), which was a measure described by former Supreme Court judge, Lord Sumption, as "reminiscent of a *police* state" (Dodd & Bowcott 2020). In Melbourne, "pop-up police spy stations" were introduced to find people breaking Covid-19 rules in places like public parks (Sarre 2020). And, in Western Australia, people breaking quarantine were fitted with tracking devices (Shepherd 2020a, 2020b). Disquiet was also expressed at state involvement in the development of smartphone apps to aid "test, track and trace" responses to the spread of the virus, which, in turn, fed into conspiracy theories about 5G being the real cause of the Covid-19 pandemic, which, at its extreme, was regarded "a hoax, a cover-story for more evil plans, of which 5G is a crucial part" (Hill et al. 2020).

These developments helped spawn a growing movement of so-called "sovereign citizens", or people who believe laws and government rules do not apply to them, and who threaten and confront, sometimes violently, police and law enforcement. Among other things, sovereign citizens protest at measures like mandatory social distancing and the wearing of masks, which some link to anti-government ideologies or conspiracy theories. In this context, resistance can either be individual or collective. An example of an individual act of resistance was the case of a Melbourne woman "charged with significant offences" after she "smashed the head of the policewoman several times into a concrete area on the ground" when approached by police for not wearing a mask (Butler 2020).

The response of police to this individual act of resistance resulted in *formal criminalization*, that is, criminal charges being laid against the person. By contrast, the increased encroachment of police into the daily lives of citizens, including via the use of fines as penalties for breach of Covid-19 restrictions, could be described as a type of *informal criminalization* or, alternatively, an example of the "criminalization of everyday life". Here, the use of fines functions as a disciplinary technology in the regulation, rather than correction, of those who may not represent a criminal justice problem but still require social control (O'Malley 2009, 75).

To McQuade & Neocleous (2020), however, police colonization of daily life during the coronavirus pandemic represented a return to "medical policing". Historically, that has entailed police-medically disciplining both under-criminalization and over-criminalization (Vegh Weis 2017, 107–141) as well as the exercise of police power beyond criminal law enforcement. Accordingly, "social police" have used "soft power", such as "in the management of life and ways of living [and] the policing of the health of individuals" (McQuade & Neocleous 2020, 4). On the other hand, medical policing during the Covid-19 pandemic constituted a departure from the past insofar as "criminal selectivity" (Vegh Weis 2017), while still clearly evident, was leavened by the net-widening effects of enforcing public health orders. To some degree, this reflects the trajectory of modern surveillance systems, which have transformed hierarchies of observation to become rhizomatic in nature (Haggerty & Ericson 2000). That means the entire population is now subject to scrutiny and monitoring, although the poor and marginalized remain more likely to "come into regular contact with a variety of surveillance systems related to social assistance and criminal justice" (Martin 2019a, 196). Hence, while unfairness and unequal treatment continued to operate via the use of police discretionary powers, McQuade & Neocleous (2020, 5) argue that to the extent members of the White bourgeoisie experienced the same powers—though, they stress, not nearly to the same extent—"complaints against the powers [were] heard far and wide in the mainstream media".

Moreover, fines were not only applied in contexts of *individual* protest and resistance but also issued to activists at mass demonstrations during the pandemic. The policing of *collective* action over mask-wearing, lockdowns, and indeed non-Covid issues, falls more squarely within the ambit of "criminalizing dissent" as that term is conventionally understood (Martin 2017a). As will be shown, in those cases, "health security and medical police coincide" (McQuade & Neocleous 2020, 8), with police invoking public health legislation *and* criminal law to charge protestors.

Anti-maskers of the past and present

Globally, pandemic-related protests during the Covid-19 crisis ranged from generalized anti-lockdown demonstrations to more specific protests over the mandatory wearing of face coverings, though issues often converged in one event. As with other medical matters during the pandemic, scientific knowledge about facemasks shifted over time. And as the science changed, so did official responses. In the state of New York, for instance, Governor Andrew Cuomo ordered all New Yorkers wear facemasks in public, "when social distancing is not possible, including on public transport, in stores and on crowded sidewalks" (Ferré-Sadurní & Cramer 2020), despite that being a direction seemingly in conflict with the state's penal code that considers the "wearing of a disguise" on the street a form of loitering (Lawrence Kane 2020).

The issue of facemasks divided not only scientific opinion (Glasziou & Del Mar 2020, Leung et al. 2020), but also political opinion. In a case he subsequently dropped, Georgia's Republican Governor, Brian Kemp, sued Atlanta's Democratic Mayor, Keisha Lance Bottoms, over the mandatory wearing of face coverings in public (Bogel-Burroughs & Robertson 2020). Meanwhile, Republican leaders in Texas and Arizona who initially saw facemask mandates as "the ultimate government overreach" that could lead to "unjust tyranny" eventually reversed their blocks on cities and counties implementing pandemic-related restrictions as Covid-19 spread in those states at unacceptable rates in mid-June 2020 (Meyer & Madrigal 2020).

Interestingly, anti-maskers of the Covid-19 period had eerily familiar historical counterparts who expressed many of the same sentiments during the Spanish flu pandemic, 1918–1919. Partly because it is a port city that could not readily seal itself off from the world in the way remote locations in the USA could, San Francisco was hit particularly hard by the influenza pandemic. While the city initially did a good job of tackling infection partly through four weeks of mask use in October 1918, by the end of November 1918, masks were no longer mandatory (Lawrence Kane 2020). And, as the city reopened, a second wave of illness and death exploded, such that in January 1919 more than 600 flu cases per week were being recorded (Lawrence Kane 2020).

Amidst calls for "re-masking" from public health officials and some politicians, there formed the Anti-Mask League, which like anti-maskers during the Covid-19 pandemic, comprised "a loose alliance of constitutional conservatives and economic boosters" (Lawrence Kane 2020). As in the coronavirus crisis, members of the Anti-Mask League argued "an obligation to cover one's nose and mouth was an affront to the principles of a free society" (Lawrence Kane 2020). They also expressed distrust of government and of experts, questioning, like some did during the coronavirus pandemic, the science behind wearing masks as a preventive public health measure (Lawrence Kane 2020, see also Luckingham 1984, 196, 199). The requirement to wear masks in San Francisco was nevertheless reinstated on 17 January 1919, and just as with Covid-19 those not adhering to that public health ordinance were fined ($5 or $10) and sometimes sentenced to periods in prison (Lawrence Kane 2020).

The city of Tucson, Arizona followed the example of San Francisco in seeking to enforce the use of masks, which it did via a public health order on 17 November 1918 that stated, "masks should be worn in any place where people meet for the transaction of necessary business" (Luckingham 1984, 194). Violators would be fined a minimum of $10 and could be imprisoned for up to 30 days. With pressure mounting from business establishments voicing concern at losing money as a consequence of official action designed to curb the epidemic, such as quarantine measures and restrictions on public gatherings (Luckingham 1984: 192), members of the local health board "decided to lift the influenza quarantine, but retain the masking order" (Luckingham 1984, 195). Schools were exempt, partly because, as with the Covid-19 pandemic, teaching could be staggered or divided into morning and afternoon sessions so to avoid overcrowding, and because children were not believed to be susceptible to the disease (Luckingham 1984, 195). However, individuals in any other places where people congregated had to continue to wear masks, including in churches, where, it was suggested, police officers should be stationed each Sunday (Luckingham 1984, 196).

As with mandatory mask wearing during the Covid-19 pandemic, enforcement was "extremely difficult" (Luckingham 1984, 194), and when an amendment was made to Tucson's original public health order, requiring the universal and unconditional wearing of masks on the street, "special ununiformed policemen" were appointed to assist the proper enforcement of the order (Luckingham 1984, 194). Despite numerous arrests, the masking ordinance was continually disregarded. In contrast to San Francisco, however, resistance to mask wearing in Tucson was not a collective enterprise, but appeared more individualized, as epitomized by a court hearing on 17 December 1918 of eight persons found guilty of mask-wearing violations, each with different excuses, including wearing masks improperly, such as over the mouth but not over the nose, or over the chin (Luckingham 1984, 198). In another case, a man was arrested so many times on 18 December 1918, that he lost count (Luckingham 1984, 199).

In Tucson, then, people clinging to perceived individual and/or constitutional "rights" to not wear masks, combined with the unwillingness of a significant minority to cooperate with the public health order and its enforcement, gave rise to a situation reminiscent of the rule-breaking of so-called sovereign citizens during the coronavirus pandemic:

> The ordinance "was incapable of enforcement. No matter how many citizens the city authorities might have taken to the lock-up, nor how many fines they imposed, they never could have brought about the general observance of masking". As "soon as the police were out of sight, the mask was dropped below the nose or down on the chin and not adjusted until danger approached".
>
> (Luckingham 1984, 202)

Accordingly, as with other measures introduced during the coronavirus pandemic, mass resistance, albeit it often individualized resistance to mask wearing, raised the prospect of the impossibility of criminalization. That is why, for example, when the mandatory wearing of face masks in English shops came into force on 24 July 2020, police chiefs said they would need to work in partnership with retailers and shopkeepers, since they did not have sufficient resources to enforce the law widely and issue £100 fines for non-compliance (Wood & Syal 2020). Similarly, at around the same time in San Francisco, restaurateurs and small business owners, already struggling financially, were expected to enforce mask wearing themselves, even though chastising potential customers for failing to wear masks would likely create an unwelcoming atmosphere (Lawrence Kane 2020). In Victoria, Australia, a similar scenario confronted staff at a Bunnings hardware store when a "sovereign citizen" not wearing a mask, contrary to the store's policy, was escorted off the premises by police after she threatened to sue two members of staff for violating her human rights (Estcourt 2020).

Protest policing during the Covid-19 pandemic

Another uncanny historical parallel to events that took place during the Covid-19 pandemic was the Red Summer of 1919. Referring to a series of "race riots" that took place in numerous cities across the USA, where for the first-time Black USA resisted White oppression, the "red" in Red Summer derived from fears newly demobbed African Americans, awakened by military service overseas during World War I—including being treated as equals by the French—might rise up Bolshevik style against the government (McWhirter 2011, 56). Among other things, the events of Red Summer originated in post-war tensions exacerbated by a severe economic downturn and the Great Migration of African Americans from the rural south of the States to cities like Chicago in the north (McWhirter 2011, 16–17).

Fast forward a century to the first wave of Black Lives Matter protests, which was sparked by the acquittal in 2013 of George Zimmerman for the shooting death of an African-American teenager, Trayvon Martin, in Florida in 2012, and the police killings in 2014 of African American men, Michael Brown in Ferguson, Missouri and Eric Garner in New York City. As with many social movements (Taylor 1989), Black Lives Matter lay in abeyance for a period until reinvigorated on 25 May 2020 after the brutal death of George Floyd at the hands of Minneapolis police officers. The incident was filmed by passersby and subsequently posted on social media, leading to global protests. Although little apart from coincidence might explain why both the pandemic of Spanish flu (1919) and the Covid-19 pandemic (2020) were coterminous with racial violence and protest, in terms of thinking about the criminalization of resistance, events subsequent to George Floyd's murder illustrate clearly the ways enforcement of coronavirus rules, regulations and restrictions impacted protest rights during the Covid-19 crisis.

In Australia, for instance, limits placed on the right to protest (Martin 2017a 2017b) were largely contained in public health directives. In the state of New South Wales, orders were made by the health minister under Section 7 of the *Public Health Act 2010* (NSW). Relevantly, Public Health (Covid-19 Restrictions on Gathering and Movement) Order (No 4) 2020 prohibited outdoor public gatherings of more than 20 people (cl 18(1)). Under clause 3(1) of that Order, a *public gathering* was defined as "a meeting or assembly of persons for a common purpose, including an organized or planned event, in a public place (whether ticketed or not)". Failing to comply with Ministerial direction is an offence under Section 10 of the *Public Health Act 2010*, such that individuals may face a maximum penalty of imprisonment for six months or a fine of up to $11,000 (or both) plus a further $5,500 fine each day the offence continues.

Although these are offences under public health legislation, not formal criminal law, insofar as they pertained to the operation of a blanket ban on public assemblies of a certain size under Covid-19 restrictions, they effectively criminalized or at least outlawed social and political protest and other collective expressions of dissent (O'Sullivan 2020a). The ban on protest, as with other mass gatherings, was justified by authorities concerned, not unreasonably, that protests might become "super-spreader events" and a key source of community seeding of the novel coronavirus. Accordingly, community health and safety prevailed over protest rights. At other times, however, the presence of public health directions and emergency legislation provided a context in which police could apply extant criminal law (Boseley 2020), as occurred in the case of people charged with "incitement" under Section 321G of the *Crimes Act 1958* (Vic) ahead of a proposed "Day of Freedom" rally scheduled for 5 September 2020 in contravention of the Victorian Chief Health Officer's directions (McGowan 2020). In the context of Covid-19, this produced a complex and problematic situation whereby protest, not ordinarily a criminal offence, nor an offence subject to a fine under public health legislation, could become a serious crime—normally incitement is linked to crimes like murder or assault—should police have chosen to pre-empt protest using an "incitement to protest" charge (O'Sullivan 2020b).

As in other jurisdictions, protests in Australia proceed on the basis of a "negotiated management" model (Martin 2011,Vitale 2005), whereby police and protesters confer before a protest event takes place in order to determine such things as the nature and purpose of a protest, expected protestor numbers and protest route. In New South Wales specifically, lawful protests are held in accordance with Section 23 of the *Summary Offences Act 1988* (NSW), which provides that for a public assembly to be "authorized" several conditions must be met, including that written notice of intention to hold the public assembly be given to the Police Commissioner. During the Covid-19 pandemic, a number of public assemblies attracting litigation were proposed in New South Wales, including plans to protest over Aboriginal deaths in custody as part of the Black Lives Matter movement, as well as mobilization around refugees feared to be at heightened risk of contracting coronavirus while in detention (Henriques-Gomes & Visontay 2020).

In *Raul Bassi v Commissioner of Police (NSW)* [2020] NSWCA 109, the Supreme Court of New South Wales, Court of Appeal, allowed the appeal of the protest organizer, Raul Bassi, on the basis there had been a violation of Section 27(2) of the *Summary Offences Act 1988* (NSW), finding that "Mr Bassi gave a timely notice, that is to say, a notice of intention to hold a public assembly more than seven days prior to it taking place" (*Bassi v Commissioner of Police Police (NSW)* [2020] NSWCA 109 at [38]). Unlike the Appeal Court, which only needed to adjudicate on a narrow ground of appeal, the judge at first instance did regard,

> The exceptional circumstance of the present health crisis in New South Wales and generally in Australia and the rest of the world is the significant consideration that is to be weighed against the right of assembly and demonstration on this occasion.
>
> (*Commissioner of Police v Bassi* [2020] NSWSC 710 at [24])

Finding the measures intended to be implemented by the protest organizers (e.g., social distancing, facemasks, hand sanitizer) would not mitigate the risk of spreading Covid-19, at first instance Justice Fagan held the public health order prevailed over "the exercise of the fundamental right of assembly and of expression of political opinion by gathering in numbers", adding that is a right "not taken away by the current Public Health Order, it is deferred" (*Commissioner of Police v Bassi* [2020] NSWSC 710 at [31]). In *Commissioner of Police v Gray* [2020] NSWSC 867, the court also made orders permitting a protest calling for an end to Black deaths in custody in Australia as part of the Black Lives Matter movement in the city of Newcastle, noting as a significant factor that protest was not included on the list of specific exceptions to limits on gatherings in the Public Health (Covid-19 Restrictions on Gathering and Movement) Order (No 4) 2020.

However, in two other cases heard in New South Wales during the Covid-19 pandemic, the courts prohibited protests from proceeding. In *Commissioner of Police (NSW) v Supple* [2020] NSWSC 727, Justice Walton made an order prohibiting the holding of the public assembly intended to call on the Australian government to release refugees held in detention. The proposed assembly was prohibited pursuant to Section 25(1) of the *Summary Offences Act 1988* (NSW) on the basis the public health risks outweighed the rights to public assembly and freedom of speech. Among other things, Justice Walton considered what he believed to be a sometimes overlooked yet nonetheless significant factor when making decisions in relation to relevant health risks associated with public assemblies, namely the "significant risks for frontline workers such as police" (*Commissioner of Police (NSW) v Supple* [2020] NSWSC 727 at [40]). In respect of protest rights, he also made the following important observation about the case of *Commissioner of Police v Bassi* [2020] NSWSC 710, after which:

> Justice Fagan was criticised for referring to rights deferred rather than rights extinguished […] but it seems to me that the true conclusion is that the balance of these considerations will necessarily shift over time, having regard to the changing public health risks and will be affected as well by the nature and circumstances of any public assembly when viewed against public health restrictions and other factors bearing upon the risks associated with a particular public assembly.
>
> (*Commissioner of Police (NSW) v Supple* [2020] NSWSC 727, per Walton J at [42]).

In *Commissioner of Police (NSW) v Gibson* [2020] NSWSC 953, and the subsequent appeal (*Padraic Gibson (on behalf of the Dungay family) v Commissioner of Police (NSW Police Force)* [2020] NSWCA 160), courts similarly prohibited the holding of a public assembly *to protest against Aboriginal deaths in custody and demand justice for David Dungay Jnr, a* Dunghutti man who died in Sydney's Long Bay Gaol in 2015, aged 26, after prison staff held him face down until he stopped breathing, lost consciousness and died in a manner not dissimilar to George Floyd (Allam 2020). Outrage followed the coronial inquest that took three years, only to find none of the prison guards would face disciplinary action, let alone criminal prosecution (Scott Bray 2019). In deciding the case, Justice Ierace of the New South Wales Supreme Court held, the balancing of the competing concerns of the right to free speech and to demonstrate, as against the safety of the community at large, at this particular phase of the pandemic, necessitates the granting of the order prohibiting the holding of the public assembly (*Commissioner of Police (NSW) v Gibson* [2020] NSWSC 953 at [84]). The protest took place regardless, with six people arrested and fined (Zhou 2020).

The findings of courts in New South Wales indicate the jurisprudence there on the status of protest rights amidst the Covid-19 pandemic was unsettled. Not unlike governments, courts strove to balance, on the one hand, rights of free speech and public assembly and, on the other, the significant public health issues arising from the COVID-19 pandemic (including the need to enforce the public health measures that have been put in place to minimize the scope for community transmission of that virus) (O'Sullivan 2020a) Some justices were more persuaded by public health arguments, while others were conscious to uphold protest rights or indeed procedures set out in legislation as occurred in *Raul Bassi v Commissioner of Police (NSW)* [2020] NSWCA 109. But, in all cases, courts heard and took into account expert evidence adduced by public health officials, among others, regarding the status of risks posed to public health and safety at any given time. Thus, although there appeared to be a blanket ban on protest, courts sought to account for local conditions, which, they opined, "necessarily shift over time" (*Supple* o cit.), and according to the "particular phase of the pandemic" (*NSW v* Gibson 2020.).

Conclusions

The Australian state of Victoria was not alone in implementing harsh measures to combat a second wave of Covid-19 infection. Amidst rising infection rates, in mid-September 2020 the UK government introduced an emergency "carrot and stick" plan, imposing a legal duty on people "required by law to self-isolate if they test positive or are contacted by the test and trace system as having been in contact with an infected person" (Helm et al. 2020). For those refusing to self-isolate, fines of £1,000 applied, rising to £10,000 for egregious offences and serial offenders (Helm et al. 2020). Up to that point, policing the crisis in the UK had largely been by consent whereby the vast majority had been cajoled into adhering to the rules around social distancing, self-isolation and so forth. The UK government was yet again faced with the conundrum of balancing citizen rights and responsibilities with the need to stop the spread of Covid-19 through state intervention.

Given the balancing exercise governments confronted during the coronavirus crisis, it may be instructive in conclusion to compare the analogous situation nation-states found themselves in following the terror attacks of 11 September 2001. Here, governments faced the prospect of safeguarding national security at the expense of civil liberties. In the event, many liberal democratic states chose to undermine individual rights, freedoms and legal protections on the basis of the seriousness of the threat posed by terrorism, justifying the erosion of rights as applying only to the very few individuals guilty of wrongdoing. We now know counterterrorism measures introduced post-9/11 "seeped" into areas beyond terrorism (see Martin 2014, 504), and while introduced as emergency measures for exceptional times they often became permanent features of the legal landscape and of government policy (Martin 2010, Masferrer 2012).

Indeed, McQuade & Neocleous (2020, 7) have identified a parallel tendency in state responses to the coronavirus, which in the UK at least involved the use of the same model of "levels of threat" to that adopted in the assessment of terror threats, with the argument here being "terrorism is a virus and viruses are a kind of terrorism". Accordingly, just as the war on terror sought to combat the threat of terrorism, so a health war was waged against the coronavirus. Moreover, while *national security* was at stake in the war on terror, *health security* was at stake in the war against Covid-19. So, in terms of thinking about arguments to do with the resurgence of medical police, what we are confronted with is "the war power and the police power coagulating around the notion of health security" (McQuade & Neocleous 2020, 8).

Similar concerns were also raised regarding the relative permanence of emergency measures introduced during the Covid-19 pandemic as were raised post-9/11, including concerns over use of surveillance technologies by medical police in the "new normal", such as immunity passports, as well as the potential migration of things like China's Health Code, Hong Kong's use of tracking bracelets, South Korea's use of CCTV data and facial recognition cameras, and, in China, Italy and the United Arab Emirates, police wearing of "smart helmets" with capabilities for facial recognition and body temperature detection (McQuade & Neocleous 2020, 5–6). Issues regarding the potential implications of these developments for civil liberties is one of the reasons MPs in Britain sought to increase parliamentary scrutiny of coronavirus legislation (Murphy et al. 2020).

In the coronavirus crisis "health war" and in the post-9/11 "war on terror", the nature of the enemy has been at once similar yet different. Terrorists remain elusive until caught, as does the virus, which was variously described as an "invisible enemy" or "wicked enemy", that is "brilliant", "cunning", "tough and smart", and thus ascribed with human qualities to signal malevolent intent, much like a terrorist (Davey 2020, Porubanova & Guthrie 2020). In both the coronavirus and post-9/11 contexts, courts have played a crucial role as well. Judicial deference to the executive in British courts post-9/11 was justified on the basis government ministers are better informed than courts on matters of national security, although in terrorist control order cases involving closed hearings and secret evidence, courts did robustly uphold due process rights (Martin 2014, 531, Martin & Scott Bray 2013, Scott Bray & Martin 2012). As we have seen, courts in New South Wales at least have recognized the democratic significance of protest rights, only striking them down on the basis of expertise adduced by public health officials, and only then determining the prohibition a temporary suspension of the right to protest. Although this has not amounted to a wholesale ban on protest, when protest has been prohibited it has in a sense gone beyond the criminalization of protest by abrogating the right of protest itself.

However, when protest has occurred it has often been criminalized and subject to police intervention, which has, at times, been heavy-handed. Thus, seeming to demonstrate police unwillingness to learn anything from the murder of George Floyd, one newspaper headline reporting on events in the USA read, "Protests about police brutality are met with wave of police brutality" (Gabbatt 2020). In some cities of the USA, a militarized police response potentially led to further harm when mass arrests brought people into close quarters and protestors were forced to remove their masks after being sprayed with tear gas (Dewey 2021: 64–65), therefore highlighting the problem of states' using a criminal justice approach to address social and health crises (Dewey 2021, 65/68).

Critics in Australia also had cause for concern over pandemic policing given the general country-wide assault on protest rights, advocacy and speaking out (Martin 2017a, 2017b 2019b, 339). As a case in point, during a protest at the University of Sydney on 28 August 2020, police used Covid-19 public health provisions as a pretext to repress students (Wang 2020), issuing a move-on order—backed by force from over 70 riot and mounted police officers—even before the event began, targeting a specific list of activists, but also fining and apprehending students indiscriminately, with one officer being overheard to say, "Let's pick'em off one by one".

References

Allam, L. (2020) 'Black Lives Matter organisers say they'll call off Sydney's rally if premier seeks Dungay death investigation' *The Guardian*, 27 July, available at: http://www.black-lives-matter-organisers-say-theyll-call-off-sydney-rally-if-premier-seeks-dungay-death-investigation.

Bogel-Burroughs, N. and Robertson, C. (2020) 'While virus surges, Georgia Governor sues Atlanta Mayor to block mask rules' *The New York Times*, 17 July, available at: http://www.brian-kemp-georgia-keisha-lance-bottoms-atlanta.html

Bolger, R. (2020) '"Simply unacceptable": One in four Victorians with coronavirus not at home when door-knocked' *SBS News*, 31 July, available at: http://www.sbs.com.au

Boseley, M. (2020) '"Overreach and overzealous": Concerns over Victoria's proposed new police powers' *The Guardian*, 12 September, available at: http://www.theguardian.com

Butler, J. (2020) '"Disgraceful" attack on police after anti-mask argument, as "sovereign citizens" create trouble' *The New Daily*, 4 August, available at: http://thenewdaily.com

Collington, R. (2020) 'The myth of the "efficient" private sector has been busted by Covid' *The Guardian*, 24 October, available at: http://www.theguardian.com

Davey, M. (2020) '"A wicked enemy": why Australia's second wave of coronavirus will be tougher to fight' *The Guardian*, 18 July, available at http://www.a-wicked-enemy-why-australias-second-wave-of-coronavirus-will-be-tougher-to-fight.

Dewey, J. (2021) 'The solution is the problem: What a pandemic can reveal about policing' in M.J. Ryan (ed.) *COVID-19: Social Consequences and Cultural Adaptations*. London: Routledge, 61–71.

Dodd, V. and Bowcott, O. (2020) 'Derbyshire police chief defends force's reaction to lockdown' *The Guardian*, 1 April, available at http://www.theguardian.com

Estcourt, D. (2020) 'Do you have a right not to wear a mask?' *The Age*, 27 July, available at: http://www.theage.com.au/national

Ferré-Sadurní, L. and Cramer, M. (2020) 'New York Orders Residents to Wear Masks in Public' *The New York Times*, 15 April, available at: http://www.15/nyregion/coronavirus-face-masks-andrew-cuomo.html

Fowler, M. and Booker, C. (2020) 'Anger at hard lockdown for towers without confirmed virus cases' *The Age*, 5 July, available at: http://www.covid-public-housing-wrap-20200705-p5596z.html

Gabbatt, A. (2020) 'Protests about police brutality are met with wave of police brutality across US' *The Guardian*, 6 June, available at: http://www.theguardian.com/us-news

Glasziou, L. and Del Mar, C. (2020) 'Should everyone be wearing face masks? It's complicated' *The Conversation*, 8 April, available at: http://www.should-everyone-be-wearing-face-masks-its-complicated-135548.

Graham, B. (2020) 'Why Aussies can't stop breaking coronavirus rules', http://www.why-aussies-cant-stop-breaking-coronavirus-rules

Haggerty, K. and Ericson, R. (2000) 'The surveillant assemblage' *British Journal of Sociology* 51(4) 605–622.

Helm, T., Savage, M. and McKie, R. (2020) '£10,000 fines warning for failing to self-isolate as England Covid infections soar' *The Guardian*, 20 September, available at: http://www.10000-fines-warning-for-failing-to-self-isolate-as-covid-infections-soar.

Henriques-Gomes, L. and Visontay, E. (2020) 'Australian Black Lives Matter protests: tens of thousands demand end to Indigenous deaths in custody' *The Guardian*, 7 June, available at: http://www.australian-black-lives-matter-protests-tens-of-thousands-demand-end-to-indigenous-deaths-in-custody.

Hill, T., Canniford, R. and Murphy, S. (2020) 'Why 5G conspiracy theories prosper during the coronavirus pandemic' *The Conversation*, 9 April, available at: http://www.why-5g-conspiracy-theories-prosper-during-the-coronavirus-pandemic-136019.

Johns Hopkins University and Medicine Coronavirus Resource Centre (2020), available at: http://www.coronavirus.jhu.edu/data/mortality.

Lawrence Kane, (2020) 'The Anti-Mask League: lockdown protests draw parallels to 1918 pandemic' *The Guardian*, 29 April, available at: http://www.coronavirus-pandemic-1918-protests-california.

Lee, S. (2020) 'On the bench: COVID-19 and public health fines' *Community Legal Centres NSW*, 30 April, available at: http://www.bench-covid-19-and-public-health-fines.

Leung, N.H.L., Chu, D.K.W., Shiu, E.Y.C., Chan, K-H., McDevitt, J.J., Benien J., Hau, B.J., Yen, H-L., Li, Y., Ip, D.K.M., Malik Peiris, J.S., Seto, W-H., Leung, G.M., Milton, D.K. and Cowling, B.J. (2020) 'Respiratory virus shedding in exhaled breath and efficacy of face masks' *Nature Medicine*, 3 April.

Lowrey, A. (2020) 'The lessons Americans never learn' *The Atlantic*, 21 August, available at: http://www.gofundme-economy-was-never-going-work

Luckingham, B. (1984) 'To mask or not to mask: A note on the 1918 Spanish influenza epidemic in Tucson' *The Journal of Arizona History* 25(2), 191–204.

Martin, G. (2010) 'No worries? Yes worries! how new South Wales is creeping towards a police state' *Alternative Law Journal* 35(3), 163–167.

Martin, G. (2011) 'Showcasing security: The politics of policing space at the 2007 Sydney APEC meeting' *Policing and Society* 21(1), 27–48.

Martin, G. (2014) 'Outlaw motorcycle gangs and secret evidence: Reflections on the use of criminal intelligence in the control of serious organised crime in Australia' *Sydney Law Review* 36(3), 501–539.

Martin, G. (2017a) 'Criminalizing dissent: Social movements, public order policing and the erosion of protest rights' in L. Weber, E. Fishwick and M. Marmo (eds) *The Routledge International Handbook of Criminology and Human Rights*. Abingdon: Routledge, 280–290.

Martin, G. (2017b) 'Secrecy's corrupting influence on democratic principles and the rule of law' *International Journal for Crime, Justice and Social Democracy* 6(4), 100–115.

Martin, G. (2019a) *Crime, Media and Culture*. Abingdon: Routledge.

Martin, G. (2019b) 'Turn the detention centre inside out: Challenging state secrecy in Australia's offshore processing of asylum seekers' in Billings, L. (ed.) *Crimmigration in Australia: Law, Politics and Society*. Singapore: Springer, 327–352.

Martin, G. and Scott Bray, R. (2013) 'Discolouring democracy? Policing, sensitive evidence and contentious deaths in the United Kingdom' *Journal of Law and Society* 40(4), 624–656.

Masferrer, A. (ed) (2012) *Post 9 and 11 and the State of Permanent Legal Emergency: Security and Human Rights in Countering Terrorism*. New York, NY: Springer.

McCurry, J., Ratcliffe, R. and Davidson, H. (2020) 'Mass testing, alerts and big fines: The strategies used in Asia to slow coronavirus' *The Guardian*, 11 March, available at: http://www.mass-testing-alerts-and-big-fines-the-strategies-used-in-asia-to-slow-coronavirus.

McGowan, M. (2020) 'Two men charged with planning Melbourne anti-lockdown protest' *The Guardian*, 1 September, available at: http://www.two-men-charged-with-planning-melbourne-anti-lockdown-protest.

McGowan, M., Ball, A. and Taylor, J. (2020) 'Covid-19 lockdown: Victoria police data sparks fears disadvantaged unfairly targeted' *The Guardian*, 6 June, available at: http://www.covid-19-lockdown-victoria-police-data-sparks-fears-disadvantaged-unfairly-targeted.

McQuade, B. and Neocleous, M. (2020) 'Beware: Medical police' *Radical Philosophy* 2(8)

McWhirter, C. (2011) *Red Summer: The Summer of 1919 and the Awakening of Black America*. New York, NY: Henry Holt.

Meyer, R. and Madrigal, A.C. (2020) 'A devastating new stage of the pandemic' *The Atlantic*, 25 June, available at: http://www.science/archive/2020/06/second-coronavirus-surge-here/613522/

Muller, D. (2020) 'Naming and shaming two young women shows the only "enemies of the state" are the media' *The Conversation*, 31 July, available at: http://www.naming-and-shaming-two-young-women-shows-the-only-enemies-of-the-state-are-the-media-143685.

Murphy, S., Elgot, J. and Stewart, H. (2020) 'MPs move to require vote on future Covid restrictions' *The Guardian*, 25 September, available at: http://www.mps-move-to-require-vote-on-future-covid-restrictions.

O'Malley, K. (2009) 'Theorizing fines' *Punishment and Society* 11(1), 67–83.

O'Sullivan, M. (2020a) 'Protest in a pandemic – The special status of public spaces' *AUSPUBLAW*, 27 July, available at: https://auspublaw.org/2020/07/protest-in-a-pandemic-the-special-status-of-public-spaces/

O'Sullivan, M. (2020b) 'Protests have been criminalised under COVID. What is incitement? How is it being used in the pandemic?' *The Conversation*, 3 September, available at: http://www.protests-have-been-criminalised-under-covid-what-is-incitement-how-is-it-being-used-in-the-pandemic-145538.

Pearson, E. (2020) 'More than 19,000 COVID-19 fines issued but only 845 paid' *The Age*, 12 October, available at: http://www.more-than-19-000-covid-19-fines-issued-but-only-845-paid-20201012-p564cf.html.

Pidd, H. and Dodd, V. (2020) 'UK police use drones and roadblocks to enforce lockdown' *The Guardian*, 27 March, available at: http://www.uk-police-use-drones-and-roadblocks-to-enforce-lockdown.

Porubanova, M. and Guthrie, S. (2020) 'Humanizing the coronavirus as an invisible enemy is human nature' *The Conversation*, 22 May, available at: http://www.humanizing-the-coronavirus-as-an-invisible-enemy-is-human-nature-138497.

Quilter, J. and Hogg, R. (2018) 'The hidden punitiveness of fines' *International Journal for Crime, Justice and Social Democracy* 7(3) 9–40.

Russo, M. (2020) 'Nine Melbourne tower blocks put into "hard lockdown" – what does it mean, and will it work?' *The Conversation*, 5 July, available at: http://www.nine-melbourne-tower-blocks-put-into-hard-lockdown-what-does-it-mean-and-will-it-work-142033.

Sarre, R. (2020) 'Melbourne is using **pop-up** police spy stations to find people breaking COVID rules – what does the law say?' *The Conversation*, 11 September, available at: http://www.melbourne-is-using-pop-up-police-spy-stations-to-find-people-breaking-covid-rules-what-does-the-law-say-145684.

Scott Bray, R. (2019) 'Death justice: Navigating contested death in the digital age' in Hviid Jacobsen, M. and Walklate, S. (eds) *Emotions and Crime: Towards a Criminology of Emotions*. Abingdon: Routledge, 169–187.

Scott Bray, R. and Martin, G. (2012) 'Closing down open justice in the United Kingdom?' *Alternative Law Journal* 37(2) 126–127.

Shepherd, B. (2020a) 'WA man set to be first Australian fitted with tracking device for alleged COVID-19 breach' *ABC News*, 30 August, available at: http://www.wa-man-tracking-device-after-alleged-covid-breach/12610482.

Shepherd, B. (2020b) 'Woman becomes the first person in WA to be fitted with a monitoring bracelet for allegedly breaching quarantine' *ABC News*, 12 September, available at: http://www.33-year-old-woman-fitted-with-bracelet-after-quarantine-breach/12658370.

Southern, C. (2020) 'Queensland's coronavirus controversy: Past pandemics show us public shaming could harm public health' *The Conversation*, 31 July, available at: http://www.queenslands-coronavirus-controversy-past-pandemics-show-us-public-shaming-could-harm-public-health-143699.

Taylor, V. (1989) 'Social movement continuity: The women's movement in abeyance' *American Sociological Review* 54(5) 761–775.

Vegh Weis, V. (2017) *Marxism and Criminology: A History of Criminal Selectivity*. Leiden and Boston: Brill.

Victorian Government (2020), available at: http://www.vic.gov.au/coronavirus-covid-19-restrictions-victoria.

Vitale, A. S. (2005) 'From negotiated management to command and control: How the New York police department polices protest' *Policing and Society* 15(3) 283–304.

Wang, C. (2020) 'National Day of Action education rally shut down by police, several fines issued' *Honi Soit*, 28 August, available at: http://www.national-day-of-action-education-rally-shut-down-by-police-several-fines-issued/

Wood, Z. and Syal, R. (2020) 'Sainsbury's and Asda say they won't enforce English face mask laws' *The Guardian*, 24 July, available at: http://www.sainsburys-asda-face-mask-laws-england-police-coronavirus-risk.

Zhou, N. (2020) 'Six arrested at Sydney Black Lives Matter protest as Dungay family deliver petition to parliament' *The Guardian*, 28 July, available at: http://www.six-arrested-at-sydney-black-lives-matter-protest-as-dungay-family-deliver-petition-to-parliament

21

PUNITIVE FEMINISM (OR WHEN AND WHY DID WE START DIVIDING THE WORLD BETWEEN GOOD AND EVIL, RATHER THAN BETWEEN OPPRESSED AND OPPRESSORS?)

Punitive Feminism

Tamar Pitch

In this chapter I shall discuss about "punitive feminism" and the ways in which it is used by governments to launch securitarian policies affecting especially on already marginalized populations and to criminalize political dissent. There is an enormous literature about our criminal justice systems being "sexist, classist, racist". Innumerable research have shown how our systems routinely "choose" the majority of their clients among the more marginalized sectors of society, starting from which behaviors are defined as crimes, going on with police searching and investigating for illegalities more within this particular population, judges more inclined to sentencing and convicting and finally incarcerating these people.

Yet, of course, if we look at our prisons' populations it appears that it is mostly constituted by males. So, in what sense do we say that our criminal justice system is sexist? Feminists have argued that it is sexist as far as it does not (or did not) consider crimes many behaviors that harm women rather than men, that when it does, these crimes are more rarely prosecuted, their perpetrators more often get lenient sentences and, especially in cases of sexual abuse, victims are re-victimized during trials. There are women in prison, to be sure, and as with men they come from the more marginalized sectors of society.

Feminist criminologists have been at first (late 1960s, early 1970s) occupied with the matter of the invisibility not just of women, but of gender, in criminological studies, critical criminology included. Then they researched women's prisons, both in history and nowadays, showing how also the prison system is geared to host men rather than women, whose prisons get even fewer resources than men's. Some hypotheses as to why men are criminalized and incarcerated more than women have been advanced, such as women are controlled more by other means, their

DOI: 10.4324/9781003144229-27

deviance sexualized and/or pathologized, etc. Now, the variable of gender is being explored in the case of men, showing for example the impact on crime and crimi- nalization of masculinities.

In this chapter, however, I want to address a different question, that came to the fore more recently: that of the so called *carceral feminism* (in the Anglo-Saxon world) or *punitive feminism* (elsewhere). I define "punitive feminism" as encompassing those movements which, in the name of feminism and the defense of women, call for the introduction of new crimes in penal codes and/or for an increase of penalties for already existing crimes. In the 1970s and 1980s of the last century women's move- ments in many countries engaged in two fundamental issues: a new definition of the crime and changes in court proceedings such as to avoid the re-victimization of the offended person. Two issues which were reasonable and necessary. Quite soon, however more explicitly punitive demands came to the fore, plus the categorization of women as "victims". As I shall say, the figure of the victim has assumed a central role in the social and political context of later years, together with other significant shifts in the definition and politics of the criminal question within the neoliberal rationality. Feminist mobilizations on violence *de facto* accompanied and sometimes supported these shifts, ending up by being used as justification for a punitive shift of which the politics and policies of security are an example (see also Simon, 2004)

Punitive feminism may be considered at least in part an inevitable consequence of the attempt on the part of women's movements to have harms women suffer from recognized as crimes, i.e., de-naturalized and de-privatized. Notable, among them, sexual violence and violence by partners or ex-partners, today mostly com- bined under the rubric of "gender violence", or even femicide. In time, the word "violence" has come to describe women's universal condition, and it has taken central stage both for militants and in international documents. I want to contend that this usage of violence is not innocent, deriving as it does from the "language" of criminal justice: not only it collapses together many different aspects concerning women's condition, and tends to unify their experiences (regardless of class, ethnic origin, citizenship, age) but it also contributes to the re-legitimation of the criminal justice system and to its contemporary centrality in the political scenario.

In this chapter, I shall describe the replacement of the notion of "oppression" by means of "violence" to later discuss two ongoing campaigns which I believe show the punitive turn taken by a part of feminists internationally as a response to "gender violence", i.e., the "abolitionist" movement regarding "prostitution" (or sex work), and the attempt at introducing a universal ban on surrogate motherhood.

"Gender violence" has also played and plays a role, however unintentionally, in many governments attempts at criminalizing entire groups of people, namely migrant minori- ties. One infamous example from Italy was the call to expel all Rumanians after one of them killed a woman in 2007. In Italy, more recently, as I shall say, gender violence was the excuse to introduce norms against political dissent, namely against those fighting against the construction of a fast train gallery between France and Piedmont. In general, the re-legitimation on the part of many feminists of the criminal justice system *de facto* supports governments' punitive turn, often directed to minorities and political dissidents.

Violence

How and why "gender violence", which is a fundamental feminist issue and a terribly serious question for all women, has been and is being used to legitimize and support security rhetoric and policies? I shall mainly use examples from Italy, but this is a widespread and by now well-known phenomenon in many other countries (indeed, within the powerful Argentinian movement NiUnaMenos, many warn against the rise of a "punitive feminism", for example, Nunez Rebolledo 2019, Daich & Varela 2020) and it is consistent with a hegemonic mode of government which has been called neoliberalism.

I believe that this use of "gender violence" has been facilitated by the collapse of all that concerns the asymmetric relationship between men and women into an issue called "violence". In turn, this collapse may be read as one of the results of the increasing hegemony of neoliberalism in these last 30 years. I shall even say at the outset that I do not like the term "gender violence", although this is the term used by international documents, as I think that male violence against women expresses much better the question we are discussing. Another term now in use is "femicide". All these ways of calling the problem have in common the fact that they are more and more used not only to indicate physical and psychological violence, but also, indiscriminately, inequality, exploitation, discrimination, etc. In a word, what once upon a time we called "oppression" is now called "violence".

Oppression was a term that much feminism of the second wave had acquired from the political vocabulary of the left. It indicated a condition which was pervasive and structural, a condition shared by all women because of their gender. At some point in time, most feminist movements started instead to use the word "violence". In the case of Italy, this happened in the late 1980s, during the long struggle to change rape laws. Since here the issue was rape, this use was legitimate and adequate to the problem tackled. But very soon the term "violence" became an umbrella term, covering all kinds of threats to women's freedom.

The adoption of the term "violence" had to do with the need of nominating the responsibility of single, concrete actors and at the same time to define one selves as political actors with voice. It was precisely the reconstruction of one selves as victims which led to the extension of the term violence (for a similar analysis in the USA context, see Bumiller, 2008, for a discussion on how the "politics of numbers" impacts on the interpretation of gender violence, see Trebisacce & Varela 2020). At the time, I thought the use of the term "violence" was due to the use of the symbolic potential of criminal justice and of its language, insofar as they allowed to neatly separate offenders and victims, so that victims were deemed innocent of the harms they suffered. I also thought that the self-assumption of victim status signaled the attempt at reintroducing "actors" on the political scene, whereas the term oppression evoked structures, systems, etc. But there were costs: the social and cultural context within which these harms took place was obscured, the complexity of the relationships within which the violent act occurred was simplified and criminal justice was re-legitimated (Pitch 1995).

The use of the symbolic potential of criminal justice was and is not, of course, limited to (a part of) the feminist movement. On the contrary, this use is so widespread that it appears that the only way to be recognized as political actors today is to adopt the status of victim. In this way, the criminal justice system has acquired a new centrality, consistent with the securitarian shift that has occurred in Europe and elsewhere in the last 30 years. We might ask then whether Nancy Fraser (2013a, 2013b) is right when she notes a collusion between some feminisms and the hegemonic neoliberal rationality. Fraser sees this collusion in the movement's fragmentation into plural identitarian requests which led feminism to be used within the neoliberal governance frame. Specifically, Fraser thinks that neoliberalism was nurtured by feminist critiques of the welfare state (its being patriarchal, oppressive and hierarchical) and by the feminist insistence on the value of individual freedom. I believe that the expansion of the self-assumption of victim status in order to claim voice belongs to the same frame: it is actually its reverse side. On the one hand, we observe the dominance of an idea of freedom as self-entrepreneurship and of personal responsibility as absolute independence, not only from all relationships, but, also, and especially, from state resources: from this stance comes the (moral) command to take all responsibility for the consequences of the risks we are incited to take. Those who cannot manage are the cast out, the marginalized and/or the new "dangerous classes". On the other side, we observe the proliferation of "victims".

The victim is precisely the other side of the neoliberal actor. This latter, I said, is constructed as somebody who must take risks on the labor market and shoulder himself (masculine intended) the consequences of his choices. This actor's freedom is an *a priori* freedom which does not depend on any specific social, economic, political context. Individualization and privatization of choices and their eventual costs mark a rupture with the political rationality of welfare states, where both were to be shared by the collectively through compensatory and protective measures, and where choices and costs were perceived as being tied to the context in which they took place.

In turn, the victim side of this neoliberal actor resides in the centrality of security policies and discourses as a tool to gain consensus. If we look at the criminal question, for example, we see how the centrality of security concerns works to separate and distinguish between good and bad citizens: the first are the (actual or potential) victims, i.e., all of us, the second are the (actual or potential) offenders. More in general, we observe a *privatization* and *moralization* of public discourse, where government's actions are justified in the name of "victims" (Garapon & Salas, 1996). The emergence of a "victims' society", therefore, testifies to a growing privatization of government and of a reduction of the social to the penal. And it is a penal with strong moralistic connotations: the neutralization of the bad is requested in the name of the good, but not just to protect the good from the actions of the bad, but also to compensate the suffering of those already hit by these actions. Private vengeance and collective vengeance converge. The retributive justification of punishment goes together with private retribution, often explicitly, as, for example, when alternatives to prison sentences are contested by particular "victims".

The term *violence* is strictly connected to criminal law: the one cannot but call for the intervention of the other. International documents on gender violence and feminist movements do insist on a more complex and nuanced comprehension of violence, taking into account inequalities of power and resources, cultural and institutional sexism, various kinds of discriminations: but what is acknowledged and, sometimes, converted into actual policies is usually just the penal and criminal side. This leads to an objective support of security politics.

First, there is a meaningful parallelism to be noted here, that between the legitimation of criminal justice actually given by gender violence and the justification of military interventions around the world in the name of "women's rights". Actually, it is fair to say that present wars, and many political conflicts, may be seen as wars against women, and/or over the control and possession of women. Argentinian anthropologist Rita Segato (2016) has written powerfully on this issue, especially in the context of the war on drugs in Latin America. Violence, and extreme violence, against women is indeed widespread and ferocious, though having a different impact and taking different meanings in different social and political contexts: actually, one of the problems is the undue universalization of the experience of violence, as if "women" were the same everywhere and shared everywhere the same condition (Iglesias Skulj 2017). Violence must be fought against, of course, and the criminal justice system is surely one of the tools to be employed in this fight. But not everything that today goes under the name of gender violence is "violence" in this extreme sense: as I tried to say, the conflation of everything into this umbrella term privileges law, and especially criminal law, to the detriment of politics. A rather extreme example of this conflation can be found in many works of Catharine MacKinnon (see, for example, 2006). For her, all is violence, legal abortion and heterosexuality included, not to talk of prostitution and surrogacy. Powerful as this usage may be from a rhetorical point of view, I think it is self-defeating from a political point of view, as it is outside of many women's lived experience, and *de facto* silencing those women which in this way are reduced to powerless and vulnerable victims.

Second, gender violence was also used to pass broader punitive reforms without connection to gender. In Italy, for example, measures to deal with gender violence were inserted into an omnibus piece of legislation named "security package" (2013), together with norms criminalizing political dissent, in particular the mobilization against the construction of a gallery between Piedmont and France for high-speed trains and other heterogeneous issues. In order to gain consensus, this legislation was presented as a law decree against femicide, which was urgent to approve in order to confront a phenomenon (femicide) described as "new" and increasing. Media approval was looked for and gained precisely in the name of something called "a femicide emergency", whereas the actual norms included in this law decree dealing with gender violence were not only a minimal part of the decree itself but were also merely declaratory.

Third, gender violence has also been used against male migrants, constructed as dangerous predators threatening "our" women (rapists are always "the others": indeed, the accusation of rape is what separates "us" from "them", as "we" marry, "they" rape). Migrants are constructed as those who pollute "our" culture, and in the dominant xenophobic and sexist discourse of many right-wing political forces, women are precisely seen as the repository of "our" culture, its traditions, and, of course, its future. Migrants, and all the Muslim world, are barbarians as it is shown by the way they behave with their own women.

Overall, what I call punitive feminism has here its origin, nowadays well exemplified by the campaigns to criminalize clients of sex workers and obtain a universal ban on surrogacy. These campaigns give voice to some, while silencing others, plus, of course, giving renewed support and legitimacy to the criminal justice system. And it should be forcefully noted here that the criminal justice system impacts, and always impacted, on the more vulnerable people in any given society: ethnic minorities, the poor and marginalized, migrants, racialized people. Giving support to, then, and re-legitimating it on the part of feminism may give voice to White, middle-class women to the detriment of poorer, racialized, women.

Surrogacy

A large part of European, and especially Italian, feminists greeted with jubilation the news that the Council of Europe had suspended and then approved with amendments Petra De Sutter's report on the rights of children born through surrogacy (Sept. 2016), after having rejected it at least twice. Sutter's report condemned commercial surrogacy, but was, though timidly, open to altruistic surrogacy, precisely the part that was amended.

In December 2015 the Italian feminist group *Se Non Ora Quando Libere* launched a campaign to request a universal ban on surrogacy, a practice already prohibited in Italy by the 2006 law on medically assisted procreation. In February 2016, a meeting in Paris launched the *No Maternity Traffic* initiative and the *Stop Surrogacy Now* campaign. All these initiatives were supported by feminists and different religious movements, plus right-wing political groups. The organizers also explicitly referred to the ongoing campaign to abolish prostitution (e.g., for the introduction of the so-called Nordic model everywhere). Their motivations and language were the same: to fight against "the reduction of female bodies to things", women's exploitation, women's slavery, etc. No question here, they maintained that freedom in these matters was always a neoliberal fiction, e.g., the freedom of selling one selves on the market.

Actually, feminists today employ many of the same arguments debated almost 30 years ago by Carmel Shalev (1989) and Carole Pateman (1988). According to Shalev, surrogacy contracts must be upheld as not to do so would imply denying women the rationality usually accorded to men on the basis of possessing a uterus. To extend the discipline of contract "all the way down", she says, means liberating women and recognizing them as fully responsible subjects. Shalev may be seen as adopting a notion of freedom similar to that of John Locke, i.e., as property of oneself and power to decide on the basis of reason and convenience. In turn, Pateman criticizes classic and contemporary contractualist doctrines precisely because they fail to recognize to women the property of themselves, which is what excludes them from participating in the social contract. However, she denies that contractualism liberates women, since it is precisely the female body that contractualism enslaves under the guise of sexual contracts, e.g., marriage. Here Pateman criticizes the modern subject of law and rights, who, while being posited as the abstract, neutral and universal subject, in fact reflects the historical experience of (White, adult, able, propertied) men. Besides, she says, using the Marxist critique of contract, that the contract hides inequalities and the relationship of subordination that it itself creates. To extend the contract all the way down, far from producing freedom, actually endorses a view of freedom as the *a priori* attribute of the rational subject: a disincarnated, abstract and individualistic view entirely consistent with the neoliberal rationality, which constructs freedom as freedom of choice, included that of selling and buying one self on the market. Surrogacy and prostitution are then seen, for Pateman, as modalities of women's subjugation and commodification.

It must be noted that the European Court of Human Rights (ECHR) has somewhat mitigated the prohibitions about surrogacy (this is how it is called in most documents I saw) practices existing in various European countries (Ronfani 2020). While it delegates to the single states the legal discipline of surrogacy, the ECHR has put limits to this discretion, by mandating that the superior interest of children and the protection of privacy should not be prejudiced by, for example, keeping children in an insecure filiation status, or by separating them from parents they have affective and care relations with, whether they are biological or intentional parents, or by denying them rights such as citizenship when national courts refuse to transcribe their birth certificates (Ouedraogo 2017).

Is there no alternative between the recognition of women's contractual capacity and the legal imposition of terms and limits to their self-determination, e.g., between the liberal and neoliberal views of freedom and the paternalistic intervention of the state? What are the conditions necessary for freedom, autonomy, self-determination? Many feminists have interrogated the validity of "autonomy" in contexts connoted by economic deprivation and social and cultural conditioning. Postcolonial and subaltern studies, for example, have argued that *agency*, if not "autonomy" may exist even in extreme conditions of deprivation and subjugation. On the other hand, feminists like Catherine MacKinnon, who is still very influential in radical feminism, think that patriarchy is so strong and pervasive as not to consent any significant freedom in decisions over one self. We may find here the old opposition between equality and freedom: while some contend that without equality freedom is impossible, others maintain that there may be perhaps not "freedom", but at least *agency*, even in conditions of inequality. From a legal point of view, the consequence of the first position is protective legislation, often accompanied by criminalization requests: "victims" here either have no autonomous voice, or they are denied voice because they are "not free". Even if criminalization is requested for purely symbolic reasons, once advanced it shifts the discussion on repression and control. The vocabulary of protection and that of repression get easily confused, so that campaigns for a universal ban on surrogacy and for the "abolition" of prostitution find themselves in bed with strange companions (O'Connell Davidson 2003).

But what were, and are, the objectives of these criminalization requests? Here I refer to the campaigns cited above, as in Italy surrogacy is already a crime. The three main objectives all criminalization requests pursue may be described as follows: the decrease of the problem thanks to the threat of a penal sanction and/or the incarceration of those causing it, the symbolic assumption of the problem as a universally recognized "evil", and the change in attitudes towards that problem. The two campaigns cited above pursue all three: protection of "victims" (surrogate mothers, prostitutes, children), punishment of intentional parents and of clients of prostitutes and education of citizens. Additionally, criminalization requests, especially when they achieve their goal, legitimize and promote the actors requesting them as influential representatives of those whom these actors define as victims. Criminalization, as I said, simplifies the problem, reducing it to a simple relationship between the author of the abuse and his and her victim, silences victims who do not recognize themselves as such and do not adopt the posture of the "good victim", plus, of course, legitimizes the criminal justice system. Also, criminalization may have very different consequences, often contrary to those intended by its promoters: for example, procreative tourism and the weakening of safeguards not only for those looking for surrogacy, but also, and especially, for surrogate mothers. Not to mention the children born this way, who risk being separated from intentional parents and put into some care home.

In Italy, influential feminist legal scholars (Niccolai & Olivito 2017) argue that we should stand by the Roman law maxim *mater semper certa est*, which is actually the criterion guiding most European laws on filiation. Mothers, then, should be considered only those who give birth. However, the problem is that this old maxim is no longer true: birth mothers and genetic mothers may nowadays be two different persons. On the basis of which logic can we say that only the first must be considered "real" mothers? In Italy this argument is particularly paradoxical. Surrogacy is prohibited but, according to our laws, a woman giving birth has the right to not recognize the baby (and remain anonymous) the baby may then be entrusted to its biological father, a type of "surrogacy" which clearly discriminates between women who are fertile but cannot carry the baby and women who are not fertile but can carry the baby. Plus favoring biological fathers.

On this very controversial and complex issue, many Italian feminists appear today to share the following position: no penal prohibitions, which in Italy already exist but may be seen to produce perverse consequences, such as procreative tourism and uncertainty in registering the birth, but instead a law which recognizes the "prevalent right" of birth mothers. Such a right, inscribed in law, would make birth mothers less vulnerable and less blackmailable. It would also make visible and would symbolically and legally legitimize a natural asymmetry: women, if fertile, need only a drop of sperm to reproduce themselves, whereas men need a commercial or affective relationship with one or more women. Surrogacy does not have necessarily to do with medically assisted procreation: it has existed for ages and in many different contexts. What is new is the possibility of separating genetic and gestational motherhood: this separation multiplies the figures implicated in reproduction and facilitates the creation and development of a market, but it does not decrease women's centrality.

Is there an alternative, then, to a universal ban on the one hand and contracts on the other? Two bills have been presented to our Parliament which try a different route: both of them try to protect birth mothers in various ways, the main one being leaving "the last word" to them, e.g., giving them some time after birth to eventually change their mind. This would certainly not solve all problems and would leave open the question of genetic motherhood: the natural asymmetry between men and women in relation to procreation is not limited to gestation, since to get ova is far more difficult and onerous than getting sperm. Yet it could be used as a guiding principle to legislate on surrogacy. If what we aim for is women's freedom, surrogacy cannot be prohibited, since it makes possible to have children also for women who, though fertile, cannot carry a child (something which in Italy, as I said, is already possible for men). But it must be regulated, in order to protect those women, who accept to carry children for others, whose freedom is as important and precious as that of the women needing this practice. The cardinal principle of this regulation, I believe, is women's centrality in the reproductive process.

"Prostitution"

"Prostitution" has always been a contentious and divisive question for feminists: is it slavery or sex work? Women selling sexual services must always be considered "victims" of gender violence?

Within this ongoing debate, a relevant role is played by the construction of (heterosexual) sex as always potentially dangerous (Pitch, 1995, Bernstein 2012). Indeed, sexual activity enjoyed "good press" for only a short period of time: the period between the introduction of the contraceptive pill and the Aids scare. Then it went from being "immoral" to being dangerous, and the feminists' campaigns against sexual violence have contributed to this construction. The panic about sex has become a new moral panic (Lamas 2020), where women (and children) are always "victims".

I put prostitution into inverted commas, because one of the problems is that there is no shared and comprehensive definition of what it means (Agustin, 2004). Laws about prostitution, whether criminalizing it or not, do not define it, as if it were self-evident. But it is not, especially nowadays, when the sexual market is incredibly complex and varied, including many different practices, in many different locations. How should we define, for example, those who give sexual assistance to the disabled, a recent profession recognized as such in some countries? Also, prostitution is debated about as if "prostitute" were a status, whereas selling sex might be a practice some people engage into for some time, or while also holding a "legitimate" job. Sexual services may be offered online, (and they may also consist of virtual sex), or in clubs, or, in many cases, from home.

So, what is usually meant with prostitution is *street* prostitution, i.e., visible prostitution, which is nowadays practiced mostly by migrants, who are overwhelmingly, but not only, women. The "migrants traffic frame" (Bernstein 2012) appears to hegemonize most debates and policies about sex work. It is a frame, though, that is contested not only by sex worker activists, but by many feminists in the Global

South (Capraban Duarte 2020, Daich & Varela 2014). Migrant labor in general is not only "traffic": often, it is "trafficked" because there are no other legitimate ways to enter a country. Different migration regimes engender different consequences for migrants. Trafficking, plus gender violence, are the two defining terms of the crusade to "abolish" prostitution. Women, in this scenario, are always victims, and what they may say to the contrary does not count, since it is often put down to what we might call "false consciousness", or to their lack of freedom.

Of course, many migrant women *have* been trafficked in order to be put on the sex market. Many have been deceived, coerced, blackmailed, raped. *Deception, coercion, blackmail and rape, though, are already crimes.* It is also true that many women have "chosen" this trade for lack of other alternatives, which calls for a struggle for social and economic justice, more efficient anti-discrimination measures, less strict migration regimes. We know women are paid less than men for the same job, that more women than men have menial and precarious jobs or none at all, that single women with small children make up a good part of those below the poverty line. Many women emigrating from poorer to more affluent countries do so in order to provide for children and family members at home. In Italy, they end up by mainly having three choices: domestic and care work, temporary farm labor and sex work. This last, though stigmatized and arguably more dangerous than the other two, may be more profitable. Migrant trans people have only this last choice. All issues that criminal law can do very little about.

In Italy, as in other European countries, selling sexual services is not a crime, but a number of related activities (for example, owning or managing a brothel, pimping—which may consist in two women sharing an apartment) are. In general, we can observe three main prostitution regimes: legalization (as in Germany), criminalization, and a grey area where selling sex is not a crime (though related activities are), but neither is it a fully legal and recognized profession. Abuses, violence, harassment by police, deportation, even homicides, are inherent risks of this work, more or less frequent and severe depending not only on the existing legal discipline but also on social and cultural attitudes, the presence of sex worker collectives and that of NGOs.

It is precisely the issue of "migrants trafficking" and gender violence that has been crucial in feminist demands for the introduction of a specific option within the grey area, the so-called Nordic model in dealing with (street) prostitution. This model was first adopted in Sweden in 1999 and later in Norway, Iceland, Northern Ireland, Ireland, Canada, France, South Korea and Israel, and has been the object of various recommendations and proposals of the European Parliament and the Council of Europe. Also called neo-abolitionist, it calls for the criminalization of clients and the offer of help and assistance for those women who opt for leaving prostitution. Indeed, the Nordic model rests on the vision of the good victim, ready to accept the help offered in order to leave a trade which is heavily stigmatized, and, for this very reason, quite dangerous. The trafficking frame, as Bernstein (2007) aptly argues, appears almost a copy of the similar late 19th and early 20th century scare about White Trafficking, and has the same protagonists: White middle-class women of the so-called first world in alliance with religious organizations promoting traditional family values.

The main idea behind this approach is that prostitution must be *abolished*. Prostitution is never "freely chosen", and it always consists in extreme violence against those who practice it (actually, men and trans people in the trade are rarely, if ever, mentioned, so it is in fact women who are the object of this legislation). Indeed, the introduction of the Nordic model in Sweden was part of the Women's Peace Bill (Holmstrom & Skilbrei 2017). The central aims of the Sex Purchase Act may be summarized as follows: (1) the decrease of prostitution in the short run, (2) its decrease and eventually disappearance in the long run, thanks to the educational impact of the law, (3) the prevention of human trafficking (Holmstrom & Skilbrei 2017). According to the rationale behind this act, there are no prostitutes but only *prostituted people*, who are most of the time trafficked by transnational criminal organizations. Criminalizing clients is supposed not only to deter them from purchasing sex, but also, and especially, to educate the general public and produce a change in attitudes in the younger generations. The faith in the pedagogical and symbolic potential of criminal law is here evident.

The consequences of the Nordic approach, as it often happens, are different according to different researchers. Holmstrom and Skilbrei (2017) present a comprehensive review and analysis of researches on the consequences of the Sex Purchase Act in Sweden, and a rich bibliography. Trying to assess the success or failure of the act's three main objectives, they find that while it is likely that street prostitution has decreased, this is not true of the indoor market, which, on the contrary, appears to have increased, also thanks to the internet. The proposed change in attitudes towards buying sex seems to have happened, as shown by the higher number of people (especially women, but also men), favoring its criminalization. However, the number of people in favor of the criminalization of the *sale* of sex has also increased, which may be interpreted as an unintentional consequence of the law: women selling sex are not seen as victims, but as active and willing partners of a "crime".

Moreover, criminalization of sex buyers appears to have had another negative effect on sex sellers, such as reinforcing the stigma linked to prostitution (something which interestingly the Swedish government's evaluation of the law's effects considers in fact a *positive* outcome, as the final aim is to eliminate prostitution altogether, Holmstrom & Skilbrei 2017, 97). In their encounters with social services and the police, sex sellers "experience distrust, discrimination and stigmatization" (Holmstrom & Skilbrei 2017, 97), especially when they try to report rape or robbery. A finding that resonates with the experiences of sex workers as related by the English Prostitutes Collective (2020) and those related in the report *Underserving Victims*, by ICRSE (http://www.sexworkeurope.org/news/news-region/undeserving-victims). Lack of trust in social workers and fear of losing custody of children are also often expressed in sex workers' online chats, as it appears they feel being judged by them: "One informant explains: 'They make you a victim, and if you don't comply on being a victim, it's like they make you a criminal'" (Holmstrom & Skilbrei 2017, 98). While some of the researches reviewed by Holmstrom & Skilbrei (2017, 98) find that sex workers' encounters with authorities and social services are sometimes judged by sex workers themselves to have been instead positive, the authors conclude that "people who sell sex still bear the burden of being considered the problem in the realm of prostitution".

It appears then that the criminalization of clients to "abolish prostitution", while decreasing the *visibility*, and probably the number, of sex workers on the street, has often perverse consequences, because of this very same fact. Sex workers look for more secluded places, which are more dangerous in terms of their physical safety and much less reachable by health and harm reducing activists. They are also less able to negotiate safe sex (i.e., the use of condoms), more at the mercy of clients, less able to call for help the police or other authorities, more at risk, if migrants, of deportation. Calling for the criminalization of clients, then, besides making more precarious and insecure the life of sex workers, again legitimizes the criminal justice system, where racist and classist aspects are either not seen, or intentionally ignored: which is something at the very least contradictory for movements fighting for women's freedom. The revolutionary core of second wave feminism is thus undermined and feminism itself reduced to a mere request of inclusion within the dominant male world. It is mainly institutional feminism which gains in terms of political recognition, at the cost of a "paternalism" denying voice and subjectivity to those it pretends to represent, reduced to victims. Since, as I said, "victim" is the other side of the neoliberal subject, in this way feminist demands are being captured by the neoliberal governmentality.

Conclusions

Does all of this mean that those who suffer from violence, coercion, abuse, etc., are not victims? Of course, they are, or, rather, *have been* victims, but only relatively to the crime they have suffered from. And, of course, these crimes must be criminally prosecuted: feminist critiques about the ways criminal justice fails women victims of violence are not only useful, but necessary. The belittling of offenses against women, their re-victimization during trials, the masculinist and sexist attitudes of many judges (women judges unfortunately included, see Boiano 2016), not only in criminal proceedings, but also in separation and divorce cases, are scandalous. Feminists *must* fight for a justice less hostile to women.

However, calling for the introduction of new crimes reduces politics to criminal politics and perpetuates a delusion which is today quite widespread, i.e., that criminal justice is the best solution for all kinds of problems. Actually, it is probable that these demands are advanced confiding in the symbolic potential of criminal justice. Such potential is certainly a "political" resource, widely used by traditional politics through the production of manifesto laws, promoted not to deal with a problem, but to gain consensus: producing as a result the call for more and harder prison sentences for almost everything by the general public.

One of the fundamental principles of liberal penal law is *nulla lex poenalis sine necessitate* (Ferrajoli, 1989). This means that, where possible, behaviors considered harmful, and offensive must be tackled with instruments different from criminal law. If we believe that surrogacy and "prostitution" are harmful practices, the first for birth mothers and eventually children, the second for sex workers, do we also think that penal prohibitions are the only way to contrast them? I contend, *vice versa*, that while penal prohibitions are being requested mainly for symbolic reasons, the empirical and symbolic consequences of these prohibitions are devastating, both for the people these prohibitions purport to protect, and for feminists who still adhere to feminism's revolutionary intent. Institutional feminism, on the other hand, composed mainly by White and middle-class women, is the one which in this way gains voice, visibility, recognition.

References

Agustin, L. (2004) *Trabajar en la industria del sexo y otros topicos migratorios*, Donostia, Gakoa

Bernstein, E. (2012) "Carceral Politics as Gender justice? The "Traffic in Women" and Neoliberal Circuits of Crime, Sex, Rights", *Theory and Society*, 41, 233–259.

Bernstein, E. (2007) "The Sexual Politics of the "New Abolitionism"", *Differences*, 18(3), 128–151.

Boiano, I. (2016) *Femminismo e processo penale*, Roma: Ediesse.

Bumiller, K. (2008) *In an Abusive State. How Neoliberalism Appropriated the Feminist Movement Against Sexual Violence*, London: Duke University Press.

Capraban Duarte, M. (2020) "De mujeres de la noche y madamas a proxenetas?", pp. 205–234, in Daich D., Varela C. (coordinadoras), *Los feminismos en la encrucijada del punitivismo*, Buenos Aires: Biblos.

Daich, D. and Varela C. (2014) "Entre el combato a la trata y la criminalizacion del trabajo sexual: las formas de gobierno de la prostitucion", *Delito y Sociedad*, 2, 38, pp. 63–86.

Daich, D. and Varela, C. (2020) *Los feminismos en la encrujada del punitivismo*, Buenos Aires: Biblos.

De Sutter, P. (2016) *Children's rights related tu surrogacy*, Council of Europe, 23 and 9.

English Prostitute Collective (2020) *No Nordic Model: Criminalising Clients Undermines Sex Workers Safety*, https://prostitutescollective.net/briefing-no-nordic-model/

Ferrajoli, L. (1989) *Diritto e ragione*, Roma-Bari: Laterza.

Fraser, N. (2013a) *Fortunes of Feminism*, London-New York: Verso.

Fraser, N. (2013b) "How Feminism Became Capitalism's Handmaiden", *The Guardian*, 14 Oct.

Garapon, D. and Salas, D. (1996) *La république pénalisée*, Paris: Hachette.

Holmstrom, C. and Skilbrei, M.S.S.-L. (2017) "The Swedish Sex Purchase Act: Where Does It stand?" *Oslo Law Review*, 4(2), 82–104.

Iglesias Skulj, A. (2017) "Como hacerse la sueca? Criminalizacion de la demanda de servicios sexuales: La gobernanza de la trata sexual en tiempo de feminismo punitivista", *Kula*, 17, 11–24.

Lamas, M. (2020) "El discurso hegemonico sobre el acoso sexual", 47–73, in Daich, D., Varela, C. (eds.), *Los feminismos en la encrucijada del punitivismo*, Buenos Aires: Biblos.

MacKinnon, C. (2006) *Are Women Human?*, Cambridge: Harvard University Press.

Niccolai, S. and Olivito, E. (2017) *Maternità filiazione genitorialità*, Napoli: Jovene.

Nunez Rebolledo, L. (2019) "El giro punitivo, neoliberalismo, feminismos y violencia de género", *Politica y Cultura*, 52, 55–81.

O'Connell Davidson, J. (2003) "Sleeping with the Enemy? Some Problems with Feminist Abolitionism Calls to Penalize Those Who Buy Commercial Sex", *Social Policy and Society*, 2, 1, 1–9.

Ouedraogo, R. (2017) "Saisir les enjeux de la maternité de substitution sous le prisme de la théorie générale du contrat, *Droit et Culture*, 73, 91–109.

Pateman, C. (1988) *The Sexual Contract*, London: Polity.

Pitch, T. (1995) *Limited Responsibilities*, London: Routledge.

Ronfani, L. (2020) "I nuovi scenari della filiazione e della genitorialità", in Ronfani, L., Maggioni G., "*Il diritto di fronte alle trasformazioni delle relazioni di filiazione e genitorialità*", in *Sociologia del diritto*, 1.

Segato, R. (2016) *La guerra contra las mujeres*, Madrid: Traficantes de suenos.

Shalev, C. (1989) *Birth Power*, New Haven: Yale University Press.

Simon, J. (2004) *Governing Through Crime*, Oxford: Oxford University Press.

Trebisacce, C. and Varela, C. (2020) "Los feminismos entre la politica de cifras y la experticia en violencia de género", in Daich D., Varela C. (coordinadoras), *Los feminismos en la encrucijada del punitivismo*, Buenos Aires: Biblos, 91–112.

22

GENOCIDAL ACTIVISM AND THE LANGUAGE OF CRIMINALITY

Reflections on the duality of the Nazi era and the avoidance of engagement with histories of social and political activism at the nuremberg trials

Wayne Morrison

In his 1966 Presidential Address to the Society for the Study of Social Problems, Howard Becker argued it was impossible to do research on deviance and crime 'uncontaminated by personal and political sympathies'. Even avoiding macro-level general theory, humanistic empirical skills allow us to see the framework the parties are located in and recognize the tragedy unfolding or bring out the imbalances between official morality and the lived values of the participants. How then could we be so-called 'value neutral' or detached and only interested in method? And what are we to report? We confront hierarchies of credibility and structures of interpretation that may reflect embedded hierarchical relationships of power that have already imprinted meanings on the lived worlds we move in and out of. Given all of that, the real question for Becker was simple: 'whose side are we on?' (Becker 1967, 239–247).

I recalled Becker's question when invited to contribute to this collection. The editor was clear: criminal justice and political and social activism have been systematically interrelated historically, and social elites have made significant 'use of criminal law, criminal justice agencies and the mass media in the modern period to define and prosecute political and social activism as "criminal"'. The editor sought diverse contributors, but specifically targeted 'activists from a diversity of struggles including feminist and LGBTQ, labor, migrant, prisoners and ecological movements', and 'those who have experienced criminalization themselves and are able to share their experiences through their personal narrative' (email to potential contributors).

There can be little doubt that the editor perceives political and social activism as a social good that elites have sought to denigrate and disparage or dissolve via criminalization. Asked as contributor to take a stance toward 'the criminalization of dissent', however, my contribution might be a salutary counter-narrative. It is not that I am opposed to social or political activism, far from it, our times and our global situation demands it. I certainly strive in my teaching to invoke a global

DOI: 10.4324/9781003144229-28

consciousness in which my students are encouraged to confront their emersion in global networks of production and consumption, not only of goods and services but also of domination and victimhood, of exploitation and pain delivery. The hope is that their future acts of dwelling in this world will be reflective and engaged.

My ambivalence flows from how I perceive the 'official' narrative that frames the subject area for my contribution, that is, genocide, more specifically the holocaust and the interaction of the holocaust with the acts of criminalization that founds the modern project of International Criminal Law. The holocaust has become the trope of pure evil in modernity, yet for all the masses of scholarly writing and media productions on it that exist, ignorance is rife, simple narratives abound. It is as if, borrowing the words of Nils Christie (1973), we accept criminological data as a mirror for society, but do not wish to look too closely in the mirror.

Let me situate myself: One course I teach is called *Law, Modernity and the Holocaust*. In it one confronts the perpetual cry of 'Never again, never again!' Each year, at least a considerable number of the class are clear; they undertake the course to learn more so that they can play their role in ensuring 'never again' is a reality. But to what do 'we' say 'never again'? This question is reflexive and almost never-ending: what was the Holocaust, what is genocide? And why do genocidal acts continue? My course is an elective, which means that students volunteer to take it; most have 'studied' the holocaust during A-level or equivalent history courses; several will have visited one or more concentration camps (the prime example is Auschwitz). My first class is purposively disorientating. I ask them to recall their prior learning as if a narrative with a plot and a set of characters and clashes, as if between good and bad peoples, and an ending: who won? This encourages them, as it does seem their earlier educational encounters have assumed a situation of 'them and us', and that the holocaust was caused by a 'them' who were different from 'us' and it occurred over there, i.e., in a place where we are not. Of course, some see though my ploys, usually the one or two Jewish students or those from Romania or Bulgaria who are aware of more existential ambiguity.

As to 'who won?' I admit it is a crude phrasing, deliberately so, and it tends to elicit the response that there were trials, people were prosecuted for the holocaust. 'Oops, ah… no' I say, not in the immediate post-war period. Some confusion ensures. Several students will be doing Public International Law or International Criminal Law. They respond that they have been told or have read in the introductory chapters to books that the Nuremberg Trials, (in particular, the International Military Tribunal), the UN Charter, the UN Universal Declaration on Human Rights and the UN Convention of Genocide are the four pillars upon which the edifice of modern Human Rights and International Criminal law is built. Moreover, they state, the prosecution of the leading Nazis for the holocaust is the glue that provides hope for future liability of powerful elites. So my course: this popular consciousness needs to be confronted with a more complex reality.

The trials came out of a compromise and addressed the various Allies needs' for some form of closure in dealing with Germany. A unique set of circumstances presented themselves, the Allies occupied the now defeated country; they were in possession of vast quantities of documents and film material; they held a considerable number prisoner including the remaining Nazi leaders and for a time had a political win to act. But act to do what? First to assure their home audiences who had either directly suffered, most grievously in the case of the Soviet Union, or made other sacrifices that retribution was being delivered. Second, or in the case of the USA, which had come late into the war, that their entry was necessary and correct. Third, to try and give meaning and perhaps justice to the veritable flood of images of atrocity now circulating. In the event, under US leadership given focus in the figure of Supreme Court Justice Robert H. Jackson, agreement was reached as to a Charter, the charges and the mode of trial. There was to be an International Military Tribunal (IMT) for a selection of the surviving Nazi leadership with Judges and prosecution from the four main victorious Allies but acting on behalf of the others who also participated, a United Nations of victory. It was to be predominately common law in procedure (i.e., adversarial), use the language of individualist criminality and make the major crime (the crime of crimes) that of waging aggressive war (or war against the peace of the world). The major victim was termed 'civilization itself' and the trial was cast as partly educative, to create a record of the evil that had threatened the whole world, and which had taken enormous resources and sacrifices to defeat.

It was to be path breaking and yet restrained. The decision to preserve the doctrine of state sovereignty meant it would only be events after the invasion of Poland in September 1939 that would be the subject matter of the trials and therefore the 'criminality' of the defendants. Given that Hitler, who would have been the main defendant and center of focus, was dead, how would the diverse defendants be bound together? The central charge was one of a grand or common conspiracy to wage aggressive war (war against the peace of the world), and thereafter evidence of war crimes and for a radically new charge, namely crimes against humanity, would be allowed. A range of subsequent trials by each of the victorious powers would also be held under the authority of the Charter (also called Nuremberg trials but before US, British and French military tribunals), and some different trials would be held in what had been German occupied countries, such as Poland, concerning events that had taken place therein.

Whether a fan or a critic, all agree the trials at Nuremberg was truly a revolutionary move. To make the criminological comparison, at Nuremberg we are in the stage of Classical Criminology. We are laying out the contours for a (transferred) rational criminal justice system, not on the terrain of the nation-state in the shadow of a Sovereign, but one searching for the basis of a world legal order, one that pieced the shield protecting National legal orders from International Law. Only it did not fully do that. For in preserving state sovereignty, one did not seek to go back into the recent history of Germany other than to tell a story of preparation for aggressive war. Earlier events, and thus earlier criminality, if demonstrated, were matters of concern for Germany. In effect, the events that were prosecuting and the persons who were charged were framed narrowly and the causation was implied rather than traced back to social and ideological roots. The result? One started at the end of the story and never read the beginning.

Jackson's Nuremberg, correctionalism at play

It would seem morally repugnant to have asked Jackson, Associate Judge of the US Supreme Court, a political insider to the Roosevelt administration, whose side he was on when he agreed to take on the task of organizing and leading the prosecution for a grand trial of the leading surviving Nazis. Nor would it have seemed appropriate to ask him to seek an appreciative stance towards the Nazis, in the face of the destruction experienced and the horrors being uncovered, it was a huge ethical task simply to ask that legal principles and due process be constituted and followed. Questions of 'understanding the Nazis as fellow humans' and trying to avoid a 'correctional' stance where all you were interested in was identifying their involvement in specific criminal activities and developing corresponding punishment would have seemed wholly inappropriate and inhumane to the victims. But one purpose of the trials was said to be education, narratives needed to be told, characters developed, lessons presented to the world.

Bloxham has observed that 'Nuremberg was the theatre in which to create the full sweep of the Nazi drama' (2001, 69). If, as Jackson stated, the future of civilization itself that was at stake, he was conscious that the appearance of the men in the dock was incongruous with the gravity of the crimes outlined in the indictment: 'twenty-odd broken men… their personal capacity for evil is forever past. It is hard now to perceive in these men [now our captives] the power by which as Nazi leaders they once dominated much of the world and terrified most of it'. However, tenderness towards them would be wrong: 'civilization can afford no compromise with the social forces which would gain renewed strength if we deal ambiguously or indecisively with the men in whom those forces now precariously survive'. If this put a huge burden on the defendants, the consequence, as defendant Albert Speer (1970: 513) related, was that the German people were freed of complicity: 'The trial began with the grand, devastating opening address by the chief US prosecutor, Justice Robert H. Jackson. But I took comfort from one sentence in it which accused the defendants of guilt for the regime's crimes, but not the German people'. Hitler's central role is evoked through acknowledging the *Fuhrerprinzip* (leadership principle or rule by commands of the Fuhrer as representative of the people), which Jackson derides and refuses to equate to a constitutional-legal principle, instead calling it 'a National Socialist despotism equaled only by the dynasties of the ancient East' (Trials 2: 99–100ff.).

After a few days, boredom ruled. Jackson's decision namely to rely upon German records and documentation and not to call many human witnesses meant proceedings lacked human interest. Additionally, the defendants looked increasingly at ease. Göring, in particular, cast as the 'leading Nazi' on trial, seemed to be almost enjoying the situation. Drama returned when on day eight the prosecution screened the hour-long film, Nazi Concentration Camps. This collection of scenes from when the US and British forces had entered various camps was introduced as representing 'in a brief and unforgettable form an explanation of what the words "concentration camp" imply' (Trials 2, 431–432). Some of the iconic imagery that we today associate with the result of the Nazi reign was presented. Shocking scenes that created a lens for viewing the Nazi regime (Hartouni 2012). Confronted with this incredible reality, how can one do justice? And what kind of people could be responsible for it?

The film cast an atmosphere of guilt and of boundaries transgressed; guilt must be assigned, those responsible must be identified and punished. But what kind of people could be responsible and in what conditions? It seemed that no society of legality could possibly be linked to the horrors; the scenes were of time and places interaction beyond the conceivable, only comparable (as it has been said by Primo Levi and George Stiner amongst others) to imaginative renditions of Hell brought into the world. None of the defendants could bear to watch for more than a few seconds. The screening was so powerful that the court immediately adjourned and there was no discussion of it the next day or thereafter. How it fitted into the overall charge of conspiracy or linked to any of the defendants personally was not a subject of argument.

Then, on 11 December, another film, The Nazi Plan, lasting nearly four hours, composed of Nazi newsreel and 'propaganda' films was shown, presented as evidence in the Nazis' own words and images of a grand conspiracy. There was no analysis of the film, the trial simply picked up from before the screening; it was simply assumed as successful. Looking back, preparing for the IMT, along with the subsequent subsidiary trials, provided a huge amount of documentary evidence available for practical use and later analysis for historical purposes, but they failed to engage the audiences either of the German people or of the so-called world community. While the 'persecution of the Jews of Europe' was a material subject, the treatment was fact asserting and descriptive and not analytic or explanatory. The passing use of the term genocide at the IMT and in the later Einsatzgruppen Trial does not detract from the fact that the genocide of the Jewish people was never on trial at Nuremberg. The innovations lay in the central charge of waging aggressive war and the added charge of crimes against humanity along with the more traditional war crimes charge (see Bloxham 2001). When Bloxham (2004, 414) rightly asserts that 'understanding perpetrator and perpetration is the essential element to understanding genocide', he does so in the context of acknowledging that 'understanding' has never really been the aim of any legal proceedings that have touched on genocide so far. In the case of Nuremberg, the approach set out by Jackson laid the foundation for a separation of Nazi elite and the people that has proved extremely difficult to shift. As Nathan Stoltzfus (2016, 10) put it: 'It is difficult to overstate the appeal of a two-dimensional portrait of Nazi power based entirely on brute force applied ruthlessly against the will of all people. This simplified version of the Reich is illustrated all around.'

What would appreciation - an alternative methodology - reveal?

The latent criminological approach taken by Jackson is control theory, a social disorder produced a chaos in which these criminals seized power and then destroyed all elements of a lawful state and used terror to coerce individuals who otherwise would not have acted or acquiesced into aiding and aiding in terrible events. Against the power and actions of the Nazi elite, the remedy, the solution, is clear: bring in law to rescue the situation.

This fails to explain the role of the others, and there were millions of others who contributed to the holocaust. The placement of Auschwitz as the iconic shorthand for the holocaust correctly draws attention to the factories of death. A powerful, disturbing and critical image, but one that makes the vast networks of mundane and every-day rational activities—such as lawyers in the Justice Ministry drafting the Nuremberg laws that solved the problem of who was a Jew by turning it into a legal category of race—pale in comparison. Consequently, Auschwitz becomes situated in a black hole of criminological (non)explanation. Let me be clear: if we were to undertake a visual jurisprudence of the Holocaust, we would not look to one event or one time but a whole geography of presences and absences over time. The iconic images are supported and given a foundation by masses of individuals who were simply ordinary, normal and rational who joined a movement or an organization and who later were involved in activities that would have shocked them once. We are now seventy years on from WWII. Nuremberg concentrated upon the idea of a culpable elite and presented forces of terror and coercion, conversely we now see seduction and co-operation and ideology operating not as a simple determinate force but as providing a general framework, sometimes constraining, at other times propelling, along with ideas of utopia, techniques of affiliation, coordination and order. Millions of people cannot be held together in diverse and often highly coordinated activities without order', without rules and expectations of predictable and responsible action, or, in other words, without law.

When Hitler was made Chancellor on 30 January 1933, a diverse group – later termed a criminal elite - gained control over the instruments of a modern, sophisticated, state system, but they were backed by a huge mass movement—the Nazi Party and its multifarious sub-organizations. What was the Nazi party? The NSDAP was perhaps the most successful social and political activist grouping in the 20th century. Originating in a scenery of diverse activist struggles in the post-World War I European arena and setting out its commitments in a 25-point program from 1920 through 1933 the Nazi Party was a core disruptive, militant social movement, similar to many described in the more contemporary social movement literature (Orlow 1969). In its early status, it always faced the threat of dissolvent but the (all-too-temporary) banning of the party and criminalization of its leadership after the failed November Putsch of 1923 and Hitler's subsequent imprisonment proved a watershed. Not only did the trial give Hitler the platform to address the nation but the luxurious conditions of imprisonment allowed a period of intense reflection and reorganization, that also allowed him to dictate and then publish his personal narrative: 'my struggle' or *Mein Kampf*. No other personal narrative of the struggles and ideas of a social activist has carried such power and achieved such mobilization of diverse people. In power, the party carried out its policies with commitment and ruthlessness with the dedication, cooperation and flexible and innovative assistance of millions of people not only in Germany but internationally. Its policies included the criminalization of other social and political movements to achieve a 'total' national movement, the sterilization and euthanasia of the handicapped to seek the eugenic utopia, the waging of war to gain lebensraum or 'living space', to 'solving' the 'Jewish question' ultimately through extermination.

Who are the masses of individuals wearing Brown shirts, depicted implicitly in the film *The Nazi Plan* as thugs that provided masses of street 'fighters for the NSDAP? Social activists. Consider Hermann Fuhrbach, born late 1907, in Muhlheim-Ruhr, the son of the building contractor his early memories bear the influence of the deaths of his older brother and two cousins in service in World War I. After the war, he is bullied by communist agitators and when he begins his building apprenticeship, he is pressurized to join a communist organization. He joins instead the defense league 'German Eagle' and in various wide cat strikes he is pitted against communist rivals. When France occupies the Ruhr, he participates in disruptive actions organized by 'German Eagle'. In late 1925, he takes part in a night march to Kettwig, and is fired as an apprentice. Later that day, he is in a group that displays 'the black, white, and red flag' and performs the stage play Tauroggen. 'Marxists and Communists on this occasion wanted to tear the uniforms off us. For two weeks we performed the play, and for two weeks we had to guard our uniforms, which, after all, we needed for our performance, day and night.' When Goebbels founds a local group of the NSDAP, he joins:

> 'From that point on, I fought untiringly against Communists, Marxists, Center Party people, and fellow travelers. On 4 July 1926, at the second Reich Party Rally, I took the oath on the flag before the Führer, the first man from Mühlheim to do so, a member of Storm Trooper Detachment 26. It was only then that I knew that Germany had a leader again. Our work never ended, even if it was only a matter of providing protection for meetings, or distributing leaflets, or other such things. We were persecuted day and night. We were called daydreamers, and the Center Party people insulted us with names like Nazi kids and pagans.'

In the September 1930 elections, he works 'day and night', distributing leaflets, hanging posters, providing security at meetings, sleeping on floors at Beer Halls. Then electoral breakthrough: 'our slogan, "Awaken, Germany!" had had its effect. One hundred and seven National Socialist deputies were elected to the Reichstag. Enthusiasm was high. The Jews were packing their bags, many were already running away, but they came back a short time later…'. So, he relates:

> we had to fight on, without flinching… The party organization was banned, and we had to take off our brown shirts. If we put on white ones instead, as we turned up to protect a meeting, the police beat us out of the hall with rubber truncheons. If we all wore blue caps, or black ties, we were subversive elements too. The Communists bludgeoned us down, the police put us in

prison, comrades were shot in the back. None of this could stop us, it could only strengthen us in our resolve to bring about the breakthrough of Adolf Hitler's idea among the German Volk. We were firm in our faith that one fine day we would have won our battle for the unity of the German Volk.

This account comes from a compilation of more than 700 accounts of 'ordinary' Germans who had joined the NSDAP before it assumed power (Abel 1938). We read stories of struggle, of resolve, of finding a case to strive for and fellowship of belonging, then jubilation when, on 30 January 1933, 'Adolf Hitler created a united German Volk'. Employment boomed and our subject here Fuhrbach returned to his full-time work, but remained committed to constructing 'the National Socialist state, until every German will understand the National Socialist ideology, faithful to our oath: For our Führer and his ideas we shall fight unto death'.

Many of the thousands who made up the early members shared feelings of being lost, of fearing for the future of Germany, of carrying, as an effect of World War I, a suspicion of betrayal, along with immense desire to do good for Germany. They read and internalized, to admittedly varying degrees, ideas on race, on Volk, on belonging, on equality (of kind), on strong leadership and of a future where things would be worked out, where the world cohered. When in the NSDAP, they used aggressive tactics and engaged in identity cultural politics, but the term "civil society activists" is wholly appropriate for these individuals and loose groupings. A political party and a radical social movement: we are dealing with something that is always more than a political party. Its feature as a social movement provides the foundations of the Nazis' growing effectivity for organization and propaganda, and later, when in power, institutions such as the police and the Gestapo could not function without an array of informers and considerable social support. Thousands and thousands of activists who linked and created organizational forms and grew to possess social expertise that were later utilized by the NSDAP as conduits to get feedback on the fears and needs of particular groups and to tailor new appeals to them, in other words to develop what we now term 'focus groups.'

And what of Hitler? We are usually looking backwards. Some are tempted to hold to the images of a crazed cartoon figure presented as if real in the Berlin bunker who committed suicide and tried to destroy Germany in his own death throes. We could more aptly refer to the figure of power in the scenes that come from the film Triumph of the Will of the 1934 Nazi party congress, and which were incorporated into the film The Nazi Plan shown at Nuremberg. Both images are a far distance from the minor army spy asked to infiltrate a far-right activist fringe organization, and who, on joining the minor party, found a future, a future in which he learnt the art of performance. An activist who deeply embedded in localities of struggle, constantly critically reassessed how he displayed his persona, who reviewed every mannerism and every speech act of his and refined them in the concrete 'battlefield' of social and political activism.

Serious scholars recognize the power of his life force on those he met and of his almost prophet like worldview (Weltanschauung). Ian Kershaw (2000, 2001) emphasizes the Weltanschauung as a program when he mediates the intentional-ist and functionalist interpretations of National Socialism and its path towards the holocaust. Even if one is simply interested in the 'German' arena, Hitler's vision is positively utopian, offering the creation of a unified 'people's community', it involves the rebuilding of national pride, grandeur and prosperity, and this occurs through purification. But purification means the destruction, not just defeat, of political opponents, the removal or elimination of those whose physical or mental weakness or disability were seen to threaten the health and strength of the population, the exclusion of Jews from public life and their physical removal from Germany.

Did Hitler command details? In Kershaw's now famous phraseology, 'working towards the Führer', Hitler was not a micro-managing Dictator, his Weltanschauung operated as a set of visionary aims rather than precise policy objectives. They pro-vided an integrative core around which the centrifugal forces of the Nazi Movement moved. Activists, and later, bureaucrats, lawyers and doctors, often pragmatic, oppor-tunistic and self-motivated, undertook actions and developed policy initiatives as interpretations of what was required to implement his expressed or implied will. Many have searched for the magical formula for why did the German civil service and institutions prove amenable to capture (co-ordination); why did the entire state structure not resist? Why instead, did its amenability provide Nazism after 1933 with an ability to reach everywhere and to find and exert a control that provided con-siderable domestic legitimacy? Partly, the answer is simple: its actions in power were an extension of the tactics adopted as a social activist movement. What had set them apart from other parties on the right from the very beginning was their openly aggressive tactics, their willingness to absorb the blows, insults and humiliations and now, in (partial) triumph, they could present themselves as the force that had his-tory on its side. If, they enticingly claimed, Weimar had allowed the emasculation of German identity, now a true German cultural identity was to the fore. And this true German identity mean a strong and pure racial Volk, with the 'removal' of the Jews a simple necessity.

Hitler's activism had always involved the Jews as the other (vermin or bacilli), given that the racial Volk replaced the nation-state, their status as parasite, or a germ, logically implied the excision to regain full health. Hitler's inherent early reflexiv-ity, illustrated in him going over and over his personal photographers photos of his body positions while speaking in order to be in total control of his image, partnered his obsessive drive for power with a superficial flexibility, a social movement would lose a range of seductive power if it appeared obsessively obsessed. The result is a semi-dialectical path, sometimes the party would push, other times activists seemed to demand measures against the Jews, on other times they needed a prod from the Fuhrer! But this is not some dialectical confrontation and cleansing and growth of ideas and understanding, the core remains and develops! For Kershaw, a path of radicalization became established in the 1930s: Hitler would either express a desire or others would presume his wishes. This gives a 'green light' to step up measures against Jews, such measures would then feed back to the 'elite' who would respond, either giving permission or ask that a route of legality be followed (the Nuremberg laws and so forth). The path may be winding but it keeps on and each stage is walked. For Koonz Hitler's public charisma, his art of seduction, was the practiced art of a reflexive social activist. From early on, he learnt to "begin by acquainting himself with his audience and studying their reactions to several topics. When he had identified their desires, he would explain confidently why only his Nazi movement could fulfil them. Listeners would say to themselves, 'Of course, that's just what I have always believed" (Koonz 2003, 18).

Conclusions: Whose side are we on? Unintended consequences, energies picked up and turned to other(s) uses

In 2015, the renowned historian Timothy Synder published *Black Earth*, a strangely unstable book. Black Earth refers to the lands of the Ukraine that were the spaces that Hitler believed held the fertile soil to feed his revitalized Germany—black earth, black in ash and mineral richness, and black in part from being seeped in blood. Synder provides incredibly detailed accounts of destruction of state power in the hands of the occupier (the Soviet Union and Nazi Germany) and destruction of the Jews (often with local aid). These accounts are sandwiched between a message on the crisis of climate change and our need to be social and politically active. The text's instability comes from the attempted demonstration of Hitler's message in terms of a distorted social ecology as a warning for us. In the first two chapters, 'Hitler's World' and 'Living Space', Synder reads *Mein Kampf* to reveal a global social ecology: "In Hitler's ecology, the planet was despoiled by the presence of Jews, who defied the laws of nature by introducing corrupting ideas" (2015, 28). We then transverse a collection of known, at least to the specialist, themes. Hitler brought down Christianized concepts of redemption, fulfilment, of being, and turned them into a natural struggle for existence in which race cast human identity, but he was also pragmatic. Success, for the average German, would mean achieving and surpassing the lifestyle of the American dream! Utopia brought down to everyday measurable indices! Precise linkages between the initial social activism and utopian vision and the actual process of killing are undeveloped, we are left with 'feel', but Synder's account certainly corrects those who continue to depict Hitler as psychologically unbalanced or intellectually superficial.

What of the warning? It is under-developed. Synder just assumes we recognize contemporary resonances in his argument that Hitler (rhetorically) returned humans to nature, to an accord with the earth. Certainly, arguments that for too long humans have followed ideas that presented them as separate, as different, as if the principles of life and the rhythms and laws that governed the ecological living world did not apply to us humans are a current staple of the current ecological movement. And we should ponder long on the fact that Hitler's utopia was thereinafter devastatingly clear: we must return the world to balance, which also entailed the salvation of Germany. 'The racial struggle for survival was also a German campaign for dignity, securing food, securing existence, clearing a purified space in which the pure German race could flex the strength of its blood, this meant conquest and purification.

My contribution herein is short, greater space would allow a tracing of individual careers, such as Hans Frank, or Otto Ohlendorf (see Ingrao 2013), both executed as Nazi criminals, to reveal times when they searched for answers, for a sight of utopia, and found it in Nazism, and devoted themselves to its cause. How those who out of fear of theoretical and existential anarchy, began as activists but ended becoming agents of extermination in practice involved twisted paths, but many trod them. We would do well to avoid stereotypes and simply correctional criminology when we seek, as we must, to take sides and commit our own energies.

References

Abel, T. (1938) *The Nazi Movement: Why Hitler Came to Power.* New York: Prentice-Hall.

Becker, H. (1967) Whose Side Are We On?, *Social Problems,* 14, 3.

Bloxham, D. (2001) *Genocide on Trial: War Crimes Trials and the Formation of Holocaust History and Memory,* Oxford: Oxford University Press.

Bloxham, D. (2004) 'The Holocaust and the Courtroom', in Dan Stone (Ed.) *The Historiography of the Holocaust.* Basingstoke: Palgrave Macmillian.

Christie, N. (1973) *Criminological Data as a Mirror for Society,* Oslo: Institutt for kriminologi og-strafferett, Universitetet i Oslo.

Hartouni, V. (2012) *Visualizing Atrocity: Arendt, Evil, and the Optics of Thoughtlessness,* New York: New York University Press.

Ingrao, C. (2013 and 2015) *Believe and Destroy: Intellectuals in the SS War Machine,* Cambridge: Polity.

Kershaw, I. (2000) *Hitler,* New York: Penguin.

Kershaw, I. (2001) *The Hitler Myth: Image and Reality in the Third Reich,* Oxford: Oxford University press.

Koonz, C. (2003) *The Nazi Conscience* (Cambridge: Belknap Press of Harvard University Press.

Orlow, D. (1969) *The History of the Nazi Party: 1919–1933.* Pittsburgh: University of Pittsburgh Press.

Speer, A. (1970) *Inside the Third Reich,* New York: Macmillan.

Stoltzfus, N. (2016) *Hitler's Compromises: Coercion and Consensus in Nazi Germany,* New Haven: Yale University Press.

Synder, T. (2015) *Black Earth: The Holocaust as History and Warning,* New York: Tim Duggan Books.

INDEX

accountability 4

activism xix, xxii, 1, 3–4, 7–11, 13–15, 19, 21–23, 25, 29, 31–34, 38–42, 46, 72, 75, 78, 131, 137–138, 184, 191–192, 196–198, 207–208, 246–247, 249, 251, 253–255

agency xxii, 66, 108, 182, 184, 208, 238

Amazonia 13, 178, 201–203

anti-apartheid 9–10, 71–72, 75–76

7 Aprile 10, 81–83, 85–89

Argentina xvii, xxii–xxv, 3, 6, 12, 161–163, 165, 167–168

artificial intelligence 5, 7, 13–14, 161, 207–214

assassination 12, 33, 170, 175

Australia xvii–xviii, xxi, 4, 9, 14, 71–75, 130, 214, 217–219, 222–226, 228

Austria xvii, 23

Belgium xvii, xxii–xxiii, 11, 130–131, 133–134, 136, 138, 214

Black Lives Matter 3, 5–7, 10–11, 14, 93–95, 98–99, 101, 103, 105, 107

Blacks xvii, 10, 93–96, 98–100

Brazil xvii, xix, xxi–xxiii, 6, 12–13, 180–198

capitalism 10, 33, 38, 51, 53, 55, 57–59, 105, 142–143, 162, 192, 197, 208, 214

castes 3, 9, 61–68

Catalonia xviii, 7, 12, 142, 144–145, 147, 149–151, 154, 156–167

citizen cops 219

civil organization 35

class xiv–xv, xxii, 2–3, 9, 15, 21, 23–25, 42, 46, 51, 53, 56, 59–62, 81, 83–84, 86, 93, 98, 101, 106, 111, 115, 120, 132, 135, 137–139, 141–142, 145, 150, 162–163, 167, 170, 180, 182–183, 185, 191, 193, 207, 212, 219, 232–235, 237, 241, 243–244, 247–248

climate xxiii, 11–12, 32, 34, 109, 130–140, 148, 185, 191, 255

Colombia xvii, xxiii, 5–6, 12, 170–179, 191, 198

constitution xix–xx, 1, 4–5, 9, 19, 25, 36, 65–66, 68, 83, 96, 105, 111, 138, 144–146, 149, 161, 163, 166, 170–172, 174–179, 195–198, 201–203, 221–222, 249

corporations 4, 13, 31, 37, 168, 181, 198, 208–209, 211

Covid-19 4, 12–14, 19, 44, 98, 144, 170, 174–175, 177, 211, 216–231

crime xv, 1, 22–23, 25, 30, 35, 38–46, 51, 56, 59, 67–68, 83, 88, 93–96, 103, 105, 107, 109, 111, 115, 120, 123, 131, 141, 143–145, 147, 153–154, 161, 164, 166, 171, 184–185, 195, 203, 208, 210, 224, 233, 239, 241–246, 248

criminality 15, 34, 44, 191, 212, 246–248, 251, 253, 255

criminalizing 4–5, 8, 10–11, 14, 19, 21, 23, 25, 27, 29, 35, 62, 72, 86, 101, 103, 116, 123, 125, 141, 147, 149, 170, 191, 220, 233, 236, 240, 242

criminal selectivity xxiv, 1, 59, 62, 138, 198, 218, 220

criminal trial 82
criminological xix, xxi, xxiii, 6, 8, 20,
    24, 30–31, 34, 37, 164, 232, 247–248,
    250–251
critical criminology xviii, xxi–xxii, 1, 12, 31,
    42, 142, 161, 164, 232

deadly force 6–7, 12, 161
defamation 6–7, 10, 34, 36, 44, 82, 86, 123
democracy xix–xx, 1, 5, 8, 10, 12, 20–22,
    24–26, 52, 56, 65, 82–83, 85, 93, 105,
    117, 119, 123, 144, 149, 170–173,
    175–177
denial 145, 153–156
discourse 6, 9, 22, 97, 116, 130–131, 144,
    197, 202, 235, 237
dissent 9, 150, 192–193

Ecuador xvii, xix, 6, 12–13, 192–193,
    196–198
El Baguazo 13, 196, 201
environment 4, 11, 32–33, 36, 38, 40–41,
    131, 134–137, 151, 173, 180–182, 188,
    194, 196, 198
environmental activism 11, 13, 32–34
equality 4, 8–9, 15, 61–63, 65, 68, 94–95,
    122, 238, 253
Europe xvii, 4–6, 8, 10–12, 15, 24, 26,
    51, 55–56, 58, 117–118, 123, 125, 130,
    141–142, 193, 216, 235, 237, 241, 250
European Union xx, 115, 161

feminism 14, 232–235, 237–239, 241,
    243–245
France xvii, 4, 19–21, 24, 56, 86–87, 209,
    214, 233, 236, 241, 252

gender xvii–xviii, xxi–xxii, 2, 7–8, 15, 24,
    29, 65, 97–98, 121, 141–142, 165, 173,
    186–187, 191, 232–234, 236, 240–241
genocide 247, 250
Germany xvii, xx, xxii, 3, 15, 20, 24, 32,
    130–131, 138, 209–210, 214, 241,
    247–248, 252–256
Global North 1, 4, 6, 10, 30, 32
Global South xvii, xxiv, 1, 3, 6, 8, 12, 15, 23,
    30–33, 35, 138

harms xxiii, 2, 4, 14, 31, 33–34, 38, 40–41,
    122, 131, 187, 191, 198, 218, 233–234
historical xviii, xxiii–xxiv, 1, 9–10, 12–13,
    15, 20, 23, 34, 43, 51, 59, 61, 72, 83, 88,
    96, 141, 161, 165, 167, 171, 187, 221,
    223, 238, 250

history xiv, xix, 3, 14, 20, 22, 29, 40–41,
    43, 55, 59, 61, 68, 75, 81, 95–96, 99,
    104, 117, 141, 147, 149, 162, 170, 187,
    192–193, 197, 209, 212–213, 216, 232,
    247–248, 254, 256
holocaust xxi, 9, 247, 251, 254, 256
human rights xix–xxv, 4–5, 13, 30, 33–37,
    119–125, 145–147, 153–154, 156,
    170–172, 174–177, 180, 182, 194,
    222, 238, 247; organizations 36, 174;
    violations xxi, xxiii, 121, 125,
    174, 180
Hungary xvii, xxi, 32

immigrants 5
India xvii, xix, 6, 9, 61, 63, 65–68, 214
Indigenous peoples xxiii, 3, 5, 40, 138, 171,
    192, 194–198, 201–203
inequality xix, 2, 8, 62, 68, 95, 142, 145,
    177–178, 234, 238
innovation 8–9, 42–43, 45–47, 52
Italy xiv, xvii, xxi, 4, 6–7, 9–11, 42–44,
    46–47, 53, 81–83, 87, 116, 120–121,
    124, 126–128, 209, 214, 227, 233–234,
    236–237, 239–241

judge, 54, 106, 110, 116, 120, 144, 147, 154,
    156, 176–177, 183, 186, 202–203, 219,
    224, 232, 242–243, 248–249

killing, 6, 40–41, 84–85, 104, 165–166, 177,
    212–213, 255

label 9, 14, 51, 54, 87, 165, 193
labelling 74
Latin America xvii, xix, xxii–xxiii, xxv, 4–5,
    7, 12–13, 35, 83, 87, 89, 119, 164, 170,
    176, 181, 191–193, 195, 197–198, 236
lawfare 11, 116, 119–120, 125–126,
    184–185, 189
laws 3–5, 19, 33, 53–56, 59, 65, 82, 85, 88,
    94, 99, 118–122, 125, 131, 142, 146, 148,
    151, 166, 191, 193–195, 198, 208, 219,
    234, 239–240, 243, 251, 255
left-wing 10, 71, 81–84, 86–89, 193, 195

machinery 9, 51, 56
Mahad Movement 9, 61, 63–64, 68
media xv, xxi, xxiii, 3, 7, 9, 11, 13–14,
    36, 44, 51, 95, 99–101, 105, 107–108,
    110–111, 116–117, 119–120, 123, 125,
    130–140, 148–149, 165–166, 172,
    187, 192, 195, 202, 207, 210–211, 213,
    218–220, 223, 236, 246–247

Mediterranean Sea 11, 115–116, 121, 125–127
migration xviii–xx, 11, 21, 115, 117, 120, 124, 126–128, 150–151, 154, 170, 223, 227, 241

Nazi 3, 15, 246, 248–257
The Netherlands xvii, 130
Nuremberg trials 15, 246–248

oppression 14, 56, 94, 223, 233–234
oppressor 14, 232
over-criminalization xvii, xxiv, 1–10, 12–14, 34, 51, 53, 55, 57–59, 61–62, 68, 82, 88, 100, 118, 120, 138, 183–185, 189, 191–193, 196–198, 212, 218, 220

Queensland xviii, 9–10, 71–76, 78–79

pandemic xxv, 4, 12–14, 19, 56, 98–99, 144, 170, 174–175, 216–230
Perú xvii, xxii, 6, 13, 201–203
policing xviii, xxii–xxiii, 4–7, 10–11, 13–14, 21–29, 43, 72, 103–105, 107–113, 117, 141–143, 151, 189, 212–213, 216–220, 223, 226, 228
politics of exception 5, 8, 19–27
poverty 93, 95, 162, 165, 177, 210, 241
primary criminalization 1–2, 4, 151
prison xiv–xv, 32, 44, 85–86, 96, 147–150, 154–155, 157, 171, 221, 225, 232, 235, 243, 253
protests xxiii, 1, 4–5, 7, 9–12, 14, 20–27, 32, 42–44, 72–73, 75–76, 78–79, 82–83, 86, 89, 97–100, 103–109, 112, 130–140, 143, 145–146, 148, 161, 163, 165, 167, 170, 172–176, 181, 187, 198, 213, 217, 220, 223–225, 228
punitive feminism 14, 232–233

race xviii, 2, 15, 62, 65, 94, 99–101, 108, 121, 125, 191, 223, 251, 253, 255–256
radicalization 254
repression xxv, 8–10, 14, 21, 26, 30, 51, 55, 81–86, 88–89, 96, 131, 138, 141, 147, 150, 156, 163–164, 166–167, 171, 173, 177, 183, 196–198, 207–208, 210–213, 238

repressivization 6, 12, 161, 163–167
right-wing 8, 13, 15, 20, 118, 177, 189, 193, 197, 237
rule of law 1, 6, 8, 20–22, 164, 167

secondary criminalization 1–2, 12, 161, 163
securitization 8, 21–25, 27, 119, 126, 172
social movement xvii, xxi, 35, 57, 61, 104, 149, 183, 188, 251, 253–254
social protest 1–2, 8, 161, 163, 165–167, 170–173, 175–177
socio-environment 13, 33–35, 37, 191–192, 196
solidarity 10–11, 43–44, 46, 81, 84, 86–87, 115–117, 121, 123, 125, 145, 156, 165–166, 202, 210
Spain xvii, xx, 4, 19, 43, 144–148, 150–154, 214
strategic litigation 123–125
strategy of power 12, 141–143, 145, 147, 149
suppression 5, 8, 59, 72, 170
Supreme Court 36, 144, 147, 149, 175–177, 185, 196, 202, 219, 224–225, 248–249
surveillance 5–6, 21, 74, 96, 103, 105, 109–111, 117–118, 188, 208, 219–220, 227
survive 10, 93, 249

torture 153–156, 182
truancy 134–135, 137
truth 52, 99

under-criminalization xxiv, 2, 4–7, 13, 51, 53, 55, 97–98, 183–185, 187–189, 198, 220
United Nations 36, 130, 248
United States 100

victim 67, 233, 235, 239, 241–243, 248
victimhood 247
victimization 14, 34, 98, 173, 191, 233, 243

West xix, 24, 213

youth xix, xxi–xxiii, 10–12, 55, 71, 87, 101, 130–131, 133–140, 156, 173

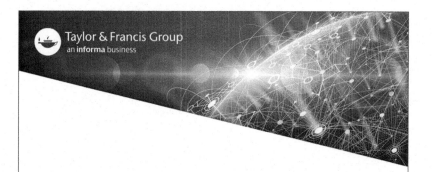